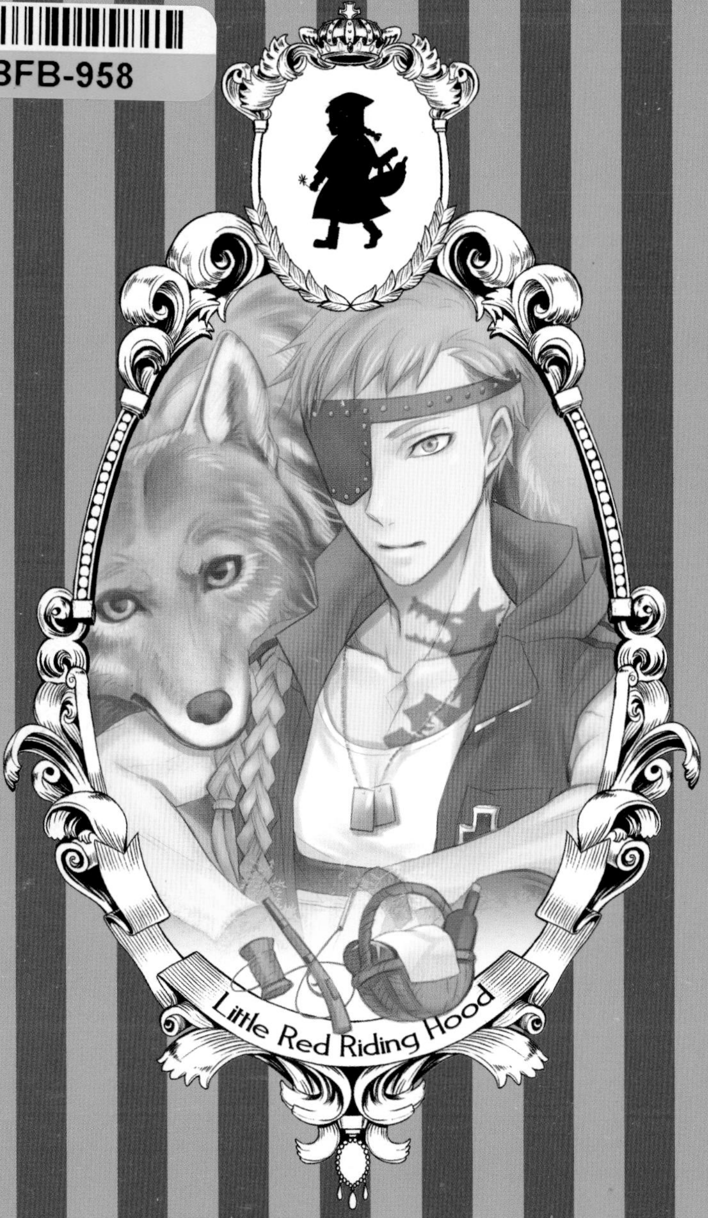
Little Red Riding Hood

# Dictatorial Grimoire

3

Ayumi Kanou

# Cast of Characters

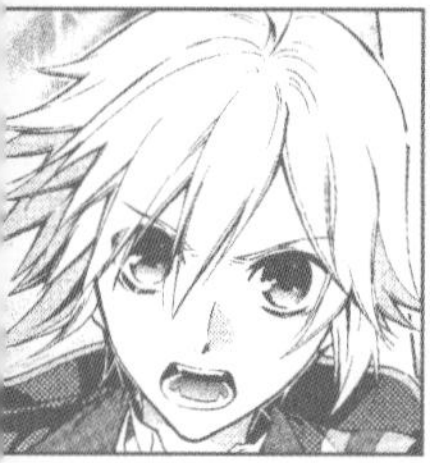

## Otogi Grimm

Our Hero. Eighth Grade student. His life is in danger because of an agreement made by his ancestors, the Brothers Grimm. A bit rude, but has a strong sense of justice.

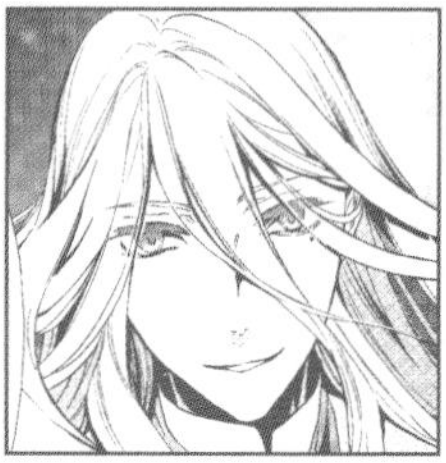

## Cinderella

Fairy tale demon (Märchen), and the basis for the Cinderella story. A devoted servant who loves to clean, good with a sword, and extremely masochistic.

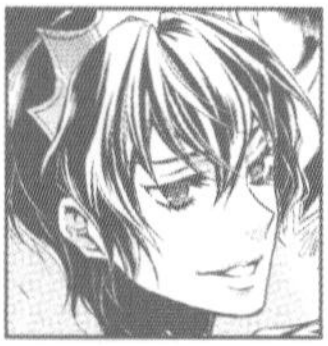

## Snow White

Märchen demon and the basis for the Snow White story. An expert in creating poisons and caring for venomous creatures. A complete narcissist.

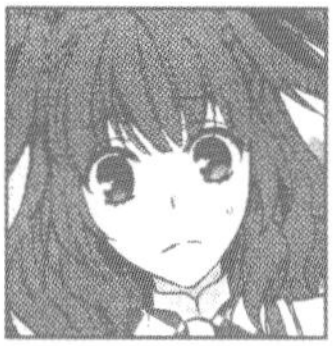

## Hatsushiba Hiyori

Grimm's classmate. Longs for friends, but her shyness and lack of self-confidence gets in the way. Unusually strong, and has a black belt in Judo.

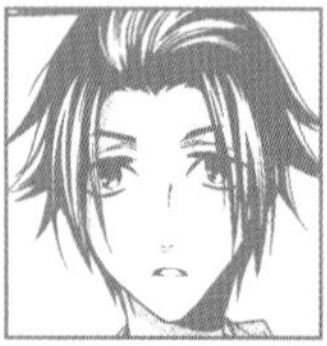

## Sorimachu Yuma

Grimm's classmate. Smart and very active in school, but seen as scary because of rumors from his past. His cheerful disposition masks a longing to be the hero.

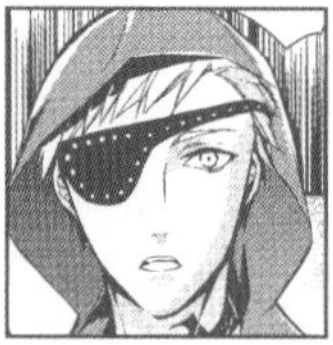

## Red Riding Hood

Märchen demon and the basis for the Little Red Riding Hood story. A quiet, mysterious figure who is currently part of Puss in Boots' Team Jäger.

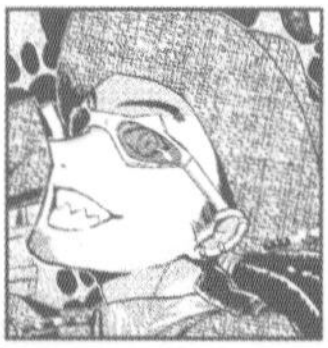

## Puss in Boots

Märchen demon and the basis for the Puss in Boots story. Called "Nekota," he works as an agent, turning ordinary people into stars—and bit players into heros.

# DICTATORIAL GRIMOIRE

## The Story So Far

Trapped by an agreement made by his famous ancestors, Otogi Grimm is forced to fight for his life against the fairy tale demons (Märchen). With the help of Cinderella, his classmates Hiyori and Sorimachi, and the recently won-over Snow White, Grimm is determined to hunt down his absent father so he can conquer his destiny.

Meanwhile, the conniving Puss in Boots has put together his own Team Jäger—a blade pointed right at Grimm and his friends!!

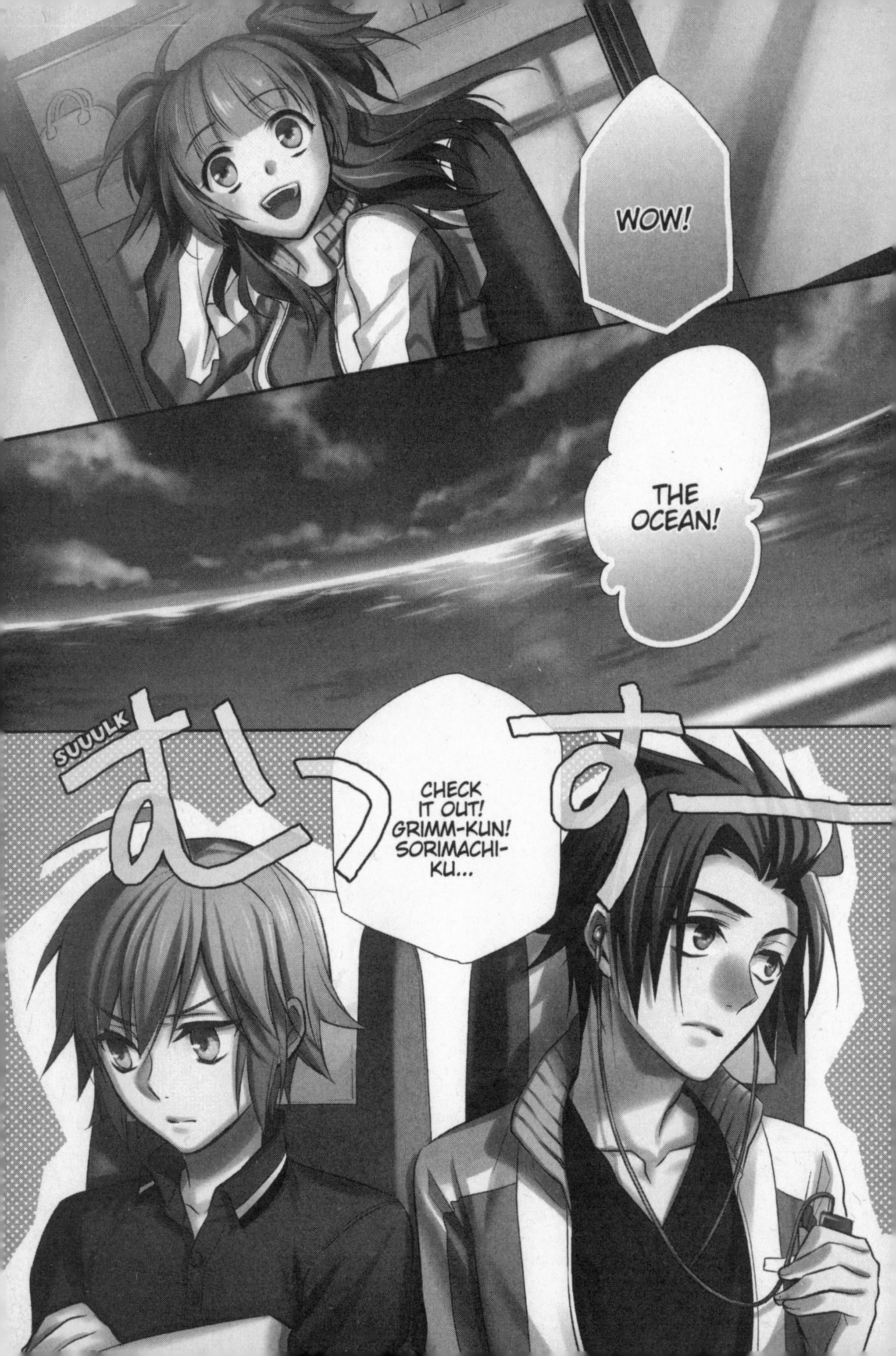
WOW!
THE OCEAN!
CHECK IT OUT! GRIMM-KUN! SORIMACHI-KU...
むっすー
SUUULK

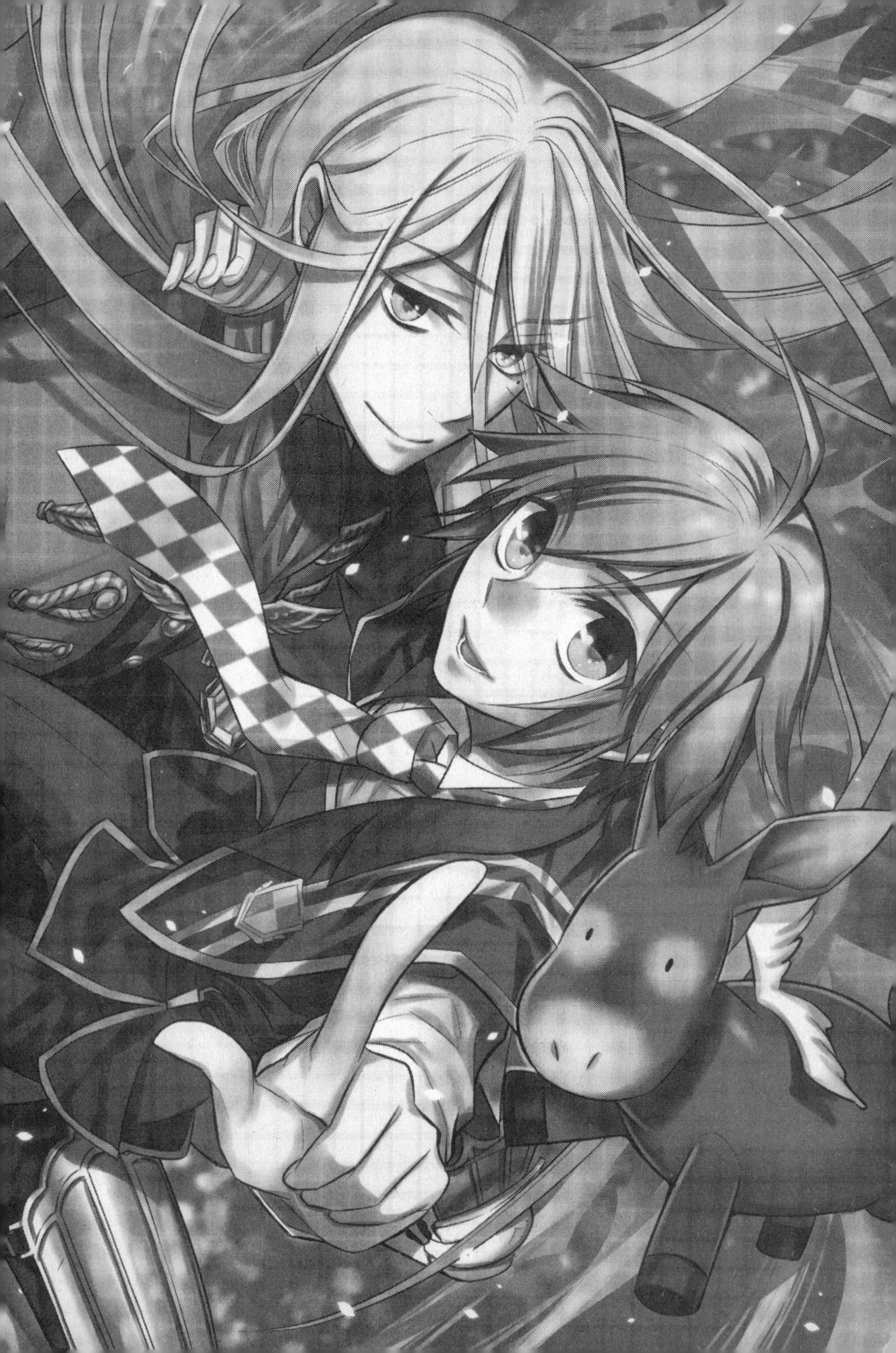

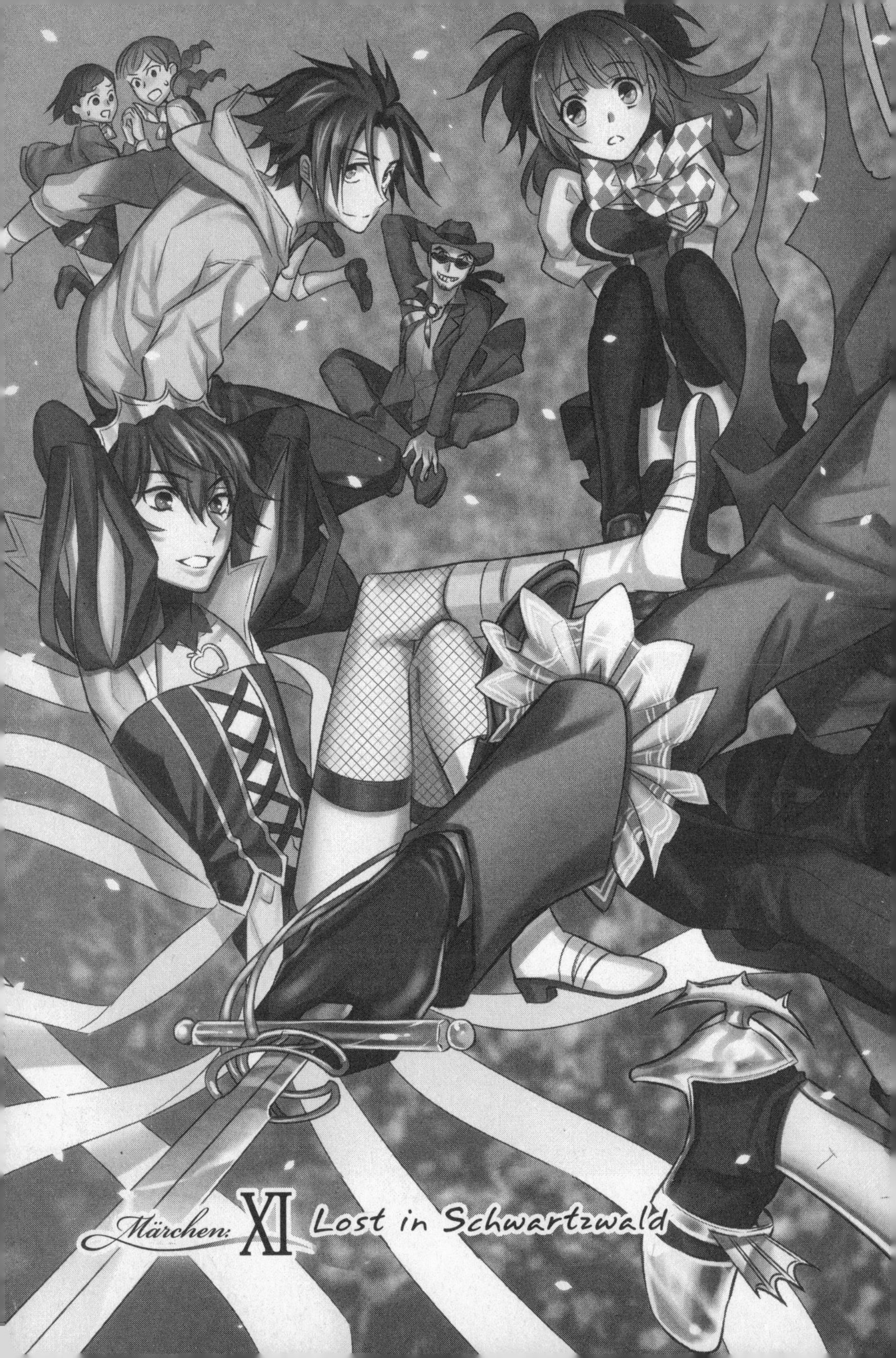
Märchen: XI Lost in Schwartzwald

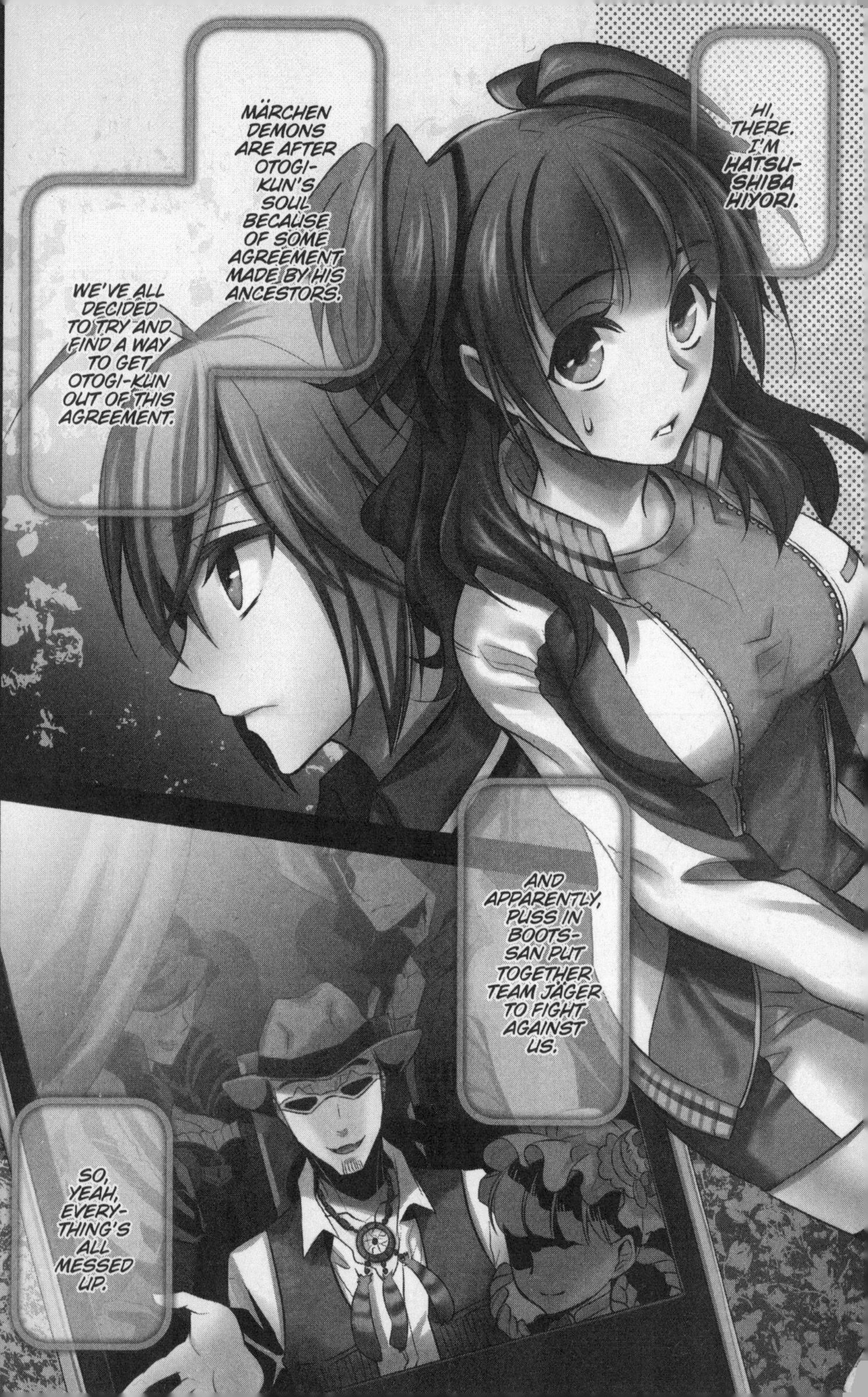
HI, THERE. I'M HATSU-SHIBA HIYORI.
MÄRCHEN DEMONS ARE AFTER OTOGI-KUN'S SOUL BECAUSE OF SOME AGREEMENT MADE BY HIS ANCESTORS.
WE'VE ALL DECIDED TO TRY AND FIND A WAY TO GET OTOGI-KUN OUT OF THIS AGREEMENT.
AND APPARENTLY, PUSS IN BOOTS-SAN PUT TOGETHER TEAM JÄGER TO FIGHT AGAINST US.
SO, YEAH, EVERY-THING'S ALL MESSED UP.

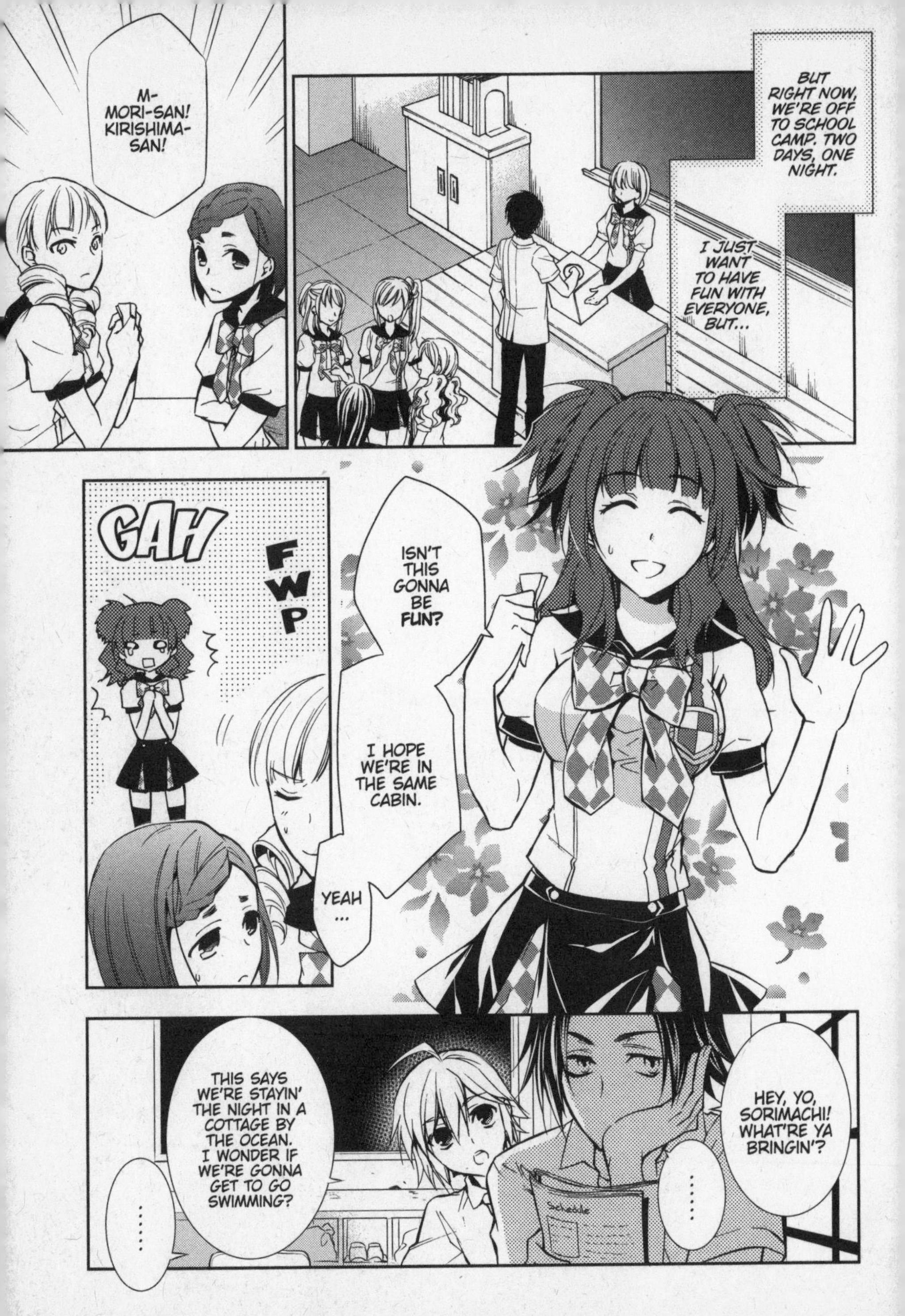

BUT RIGHT NOW, WE'RE OFF TO SCHOOL CAMP. TWO DAYS, ONE NIGHT.
I JUST WANT TO HAVE FUN WITH EVERYONE, BUT...
M-MORI-SAN! KIRISHIMA-SAN!
ISN'T THIS GONNA BE FUN?
I HOPE WE'RE IN THE SAME CABIN.
YEAH ...
GAH
FWP
HEY, YO, SORIMACHI! WHAT'RE YA BRINGIN'?
......
Schedule
THIS SAYS WE'RE STAYIN' THE NIGHT IN A COTTAGE BY THE OCEAN. I WONDER IF WE'RE GONNA GET TO GO SWIMMING?
......

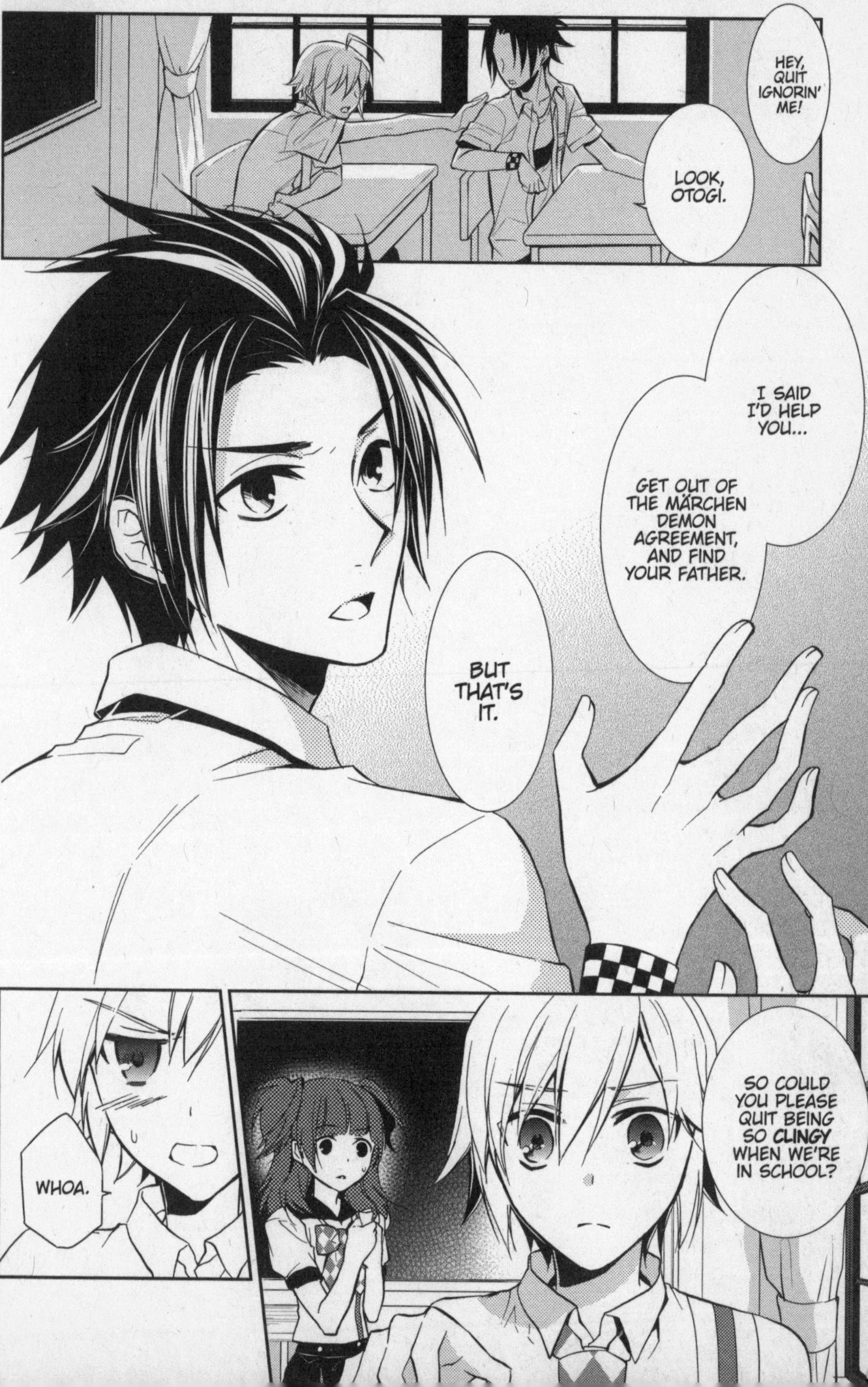
HEY, QUIT IGNORIN' ME!
LOOK, OTOGI.
I SAID I'D HELP YOU...
GET OUT OF THE MÄRCHEN DEMON AGREEMENT, AND FIND YOUR FATHER.
BUT THAT'S IT.
SO COULD YOU PLEASE QUIT BEING SO **CLINGY** WHEN WE'RE IN SCHOOL?
WHOA.

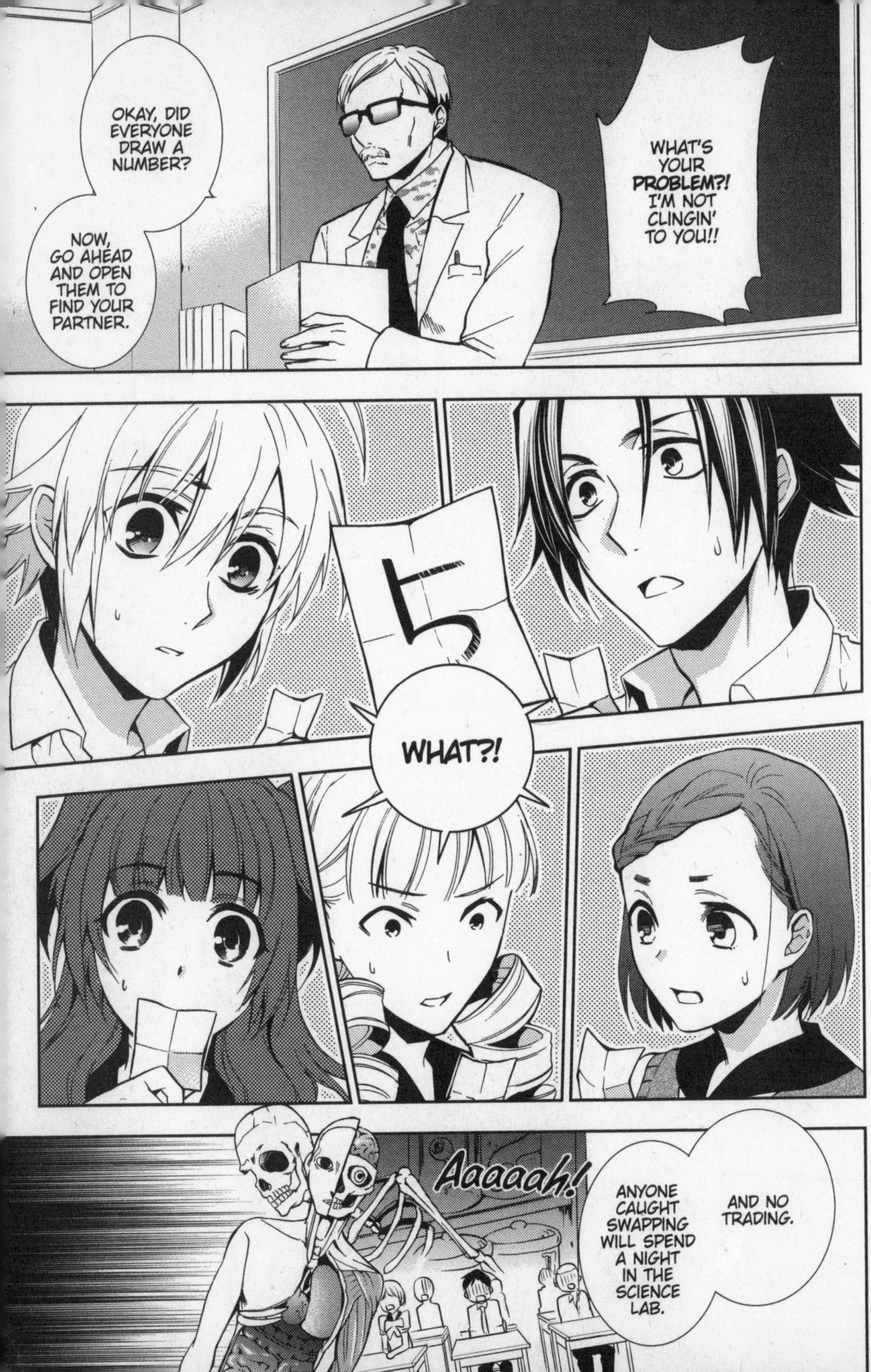
WHAT'S YOUR PROBLEM?! I'M NOT CLINGIN' TO YOU!!
OKAY, DID EVERYONE DRAW A NUMBER?
NOW, GO AHEAD AND OPEN THEM TO FIND YOUR PARTNER.
5
WHAT?!
AND NO TRADING.
ANYONE CAUGHT SWAPPING WILL SPEND A NIGHT IN THE SCIENCE LAB.
Aaaaah!

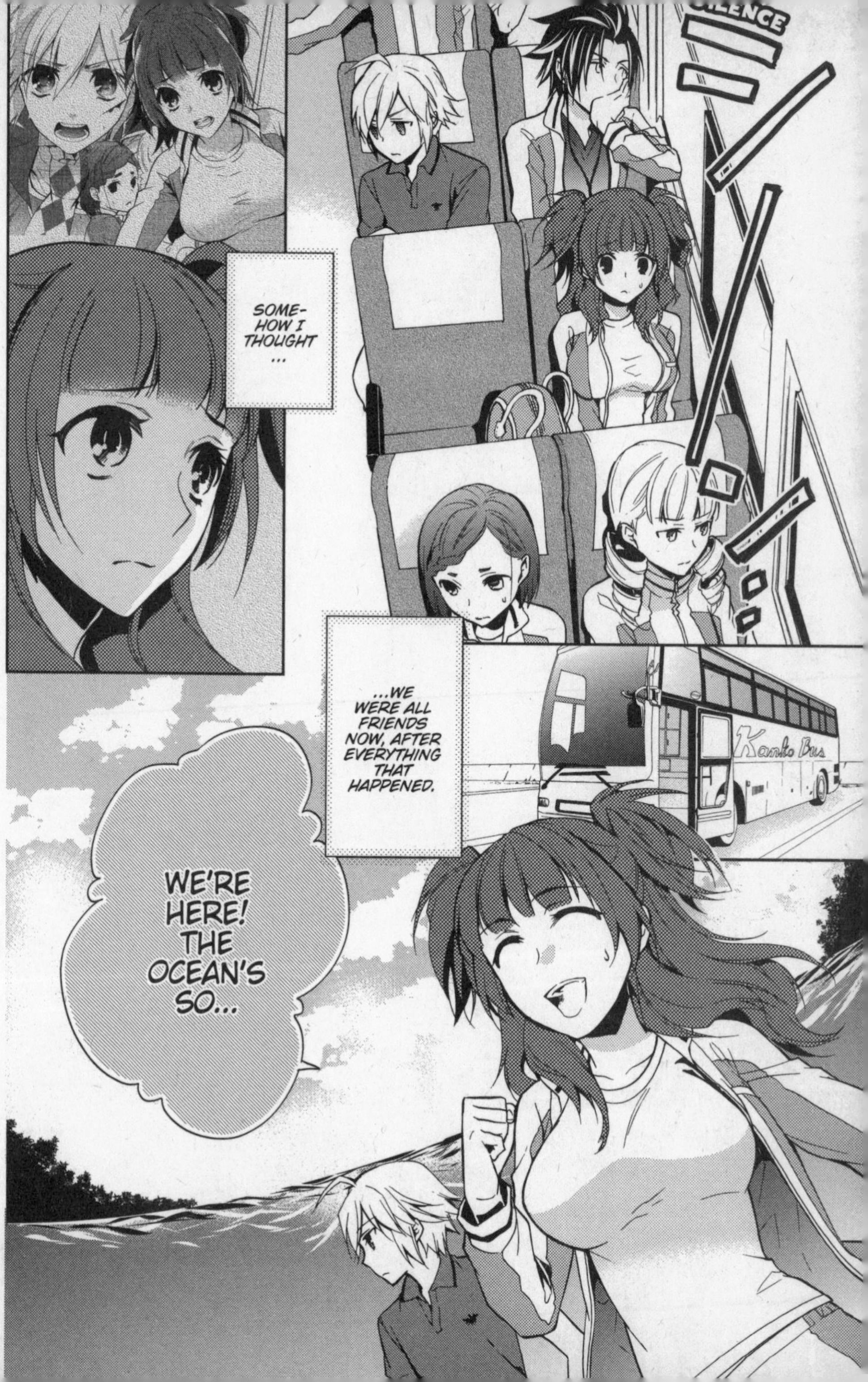
SILENCE
SOME-HOW I THOUGHT ...
...WE WERE ALL FRIENDS NOW, AFTER EVERYTHING THAT HAPPENED.
Kanko Bus
WE'RE HERE! THE OCEAN'S SO...

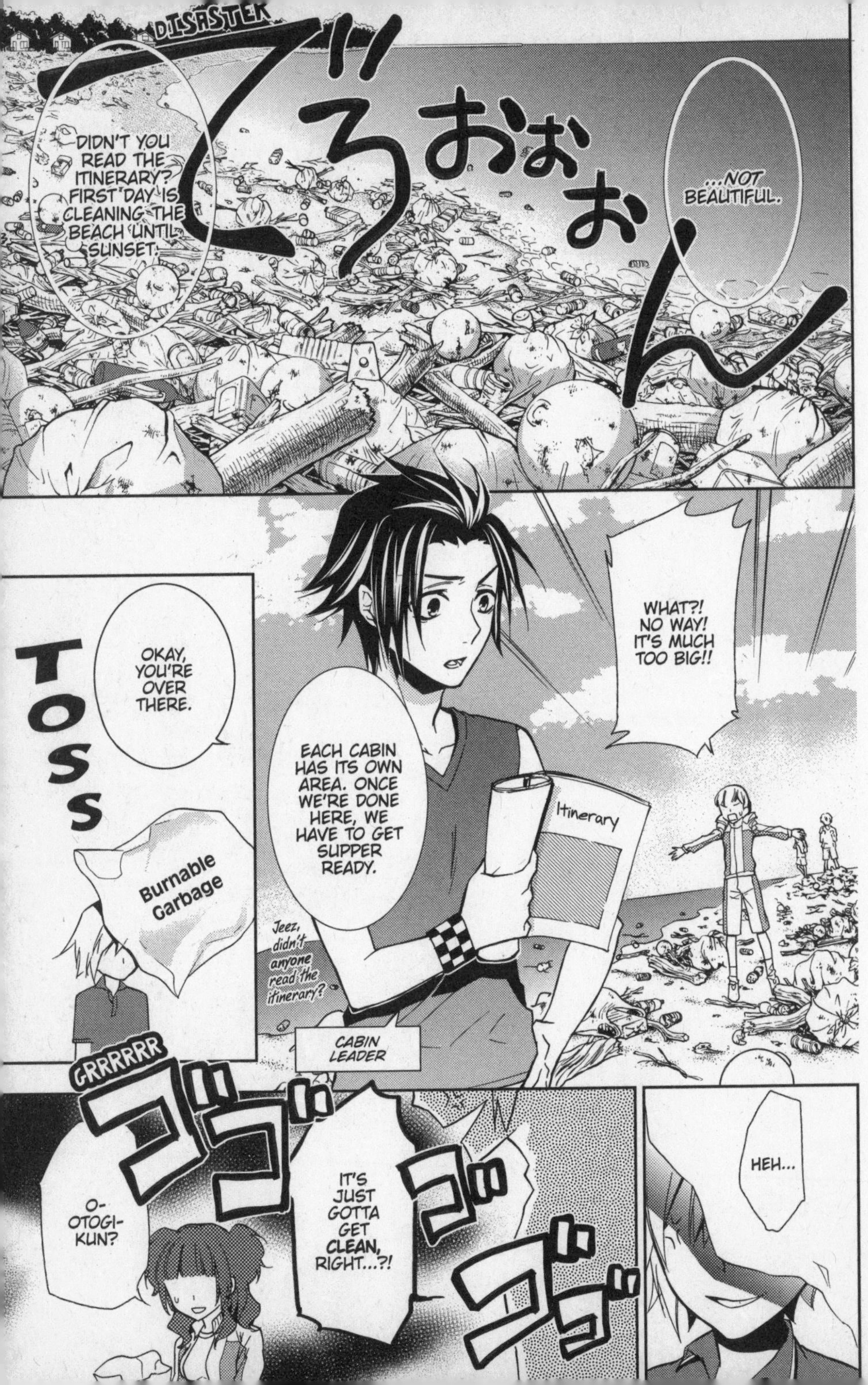
...NOT BEAUTIFUL.
DISASTER
ごろおぉおん
DIDN'T YOU READ THE ITINERARY? FIRST DAY IS CLEANING THE BEACH UNTIL SUNSET.
WHAT?! NO WAY! IT'S MUCH TOO BIG!!
EACH CABIN HAS ITS OWN AREA. ONCE WE'RE DONE HERE, WE HAVE TO GET SUPPER READY.
Itinerary
Jeez, didn't anyone read the itinerary?
CABIN LEADER
OKAY, YOU'RE OVER THERE.
TOSS
Burnable Garbage
HEH...
GRRRRRR
ゴゴゴゴ
IT'S JUST GOTTA GET CLEAN, RIGHT...?!
O-OTOGI-KUN?

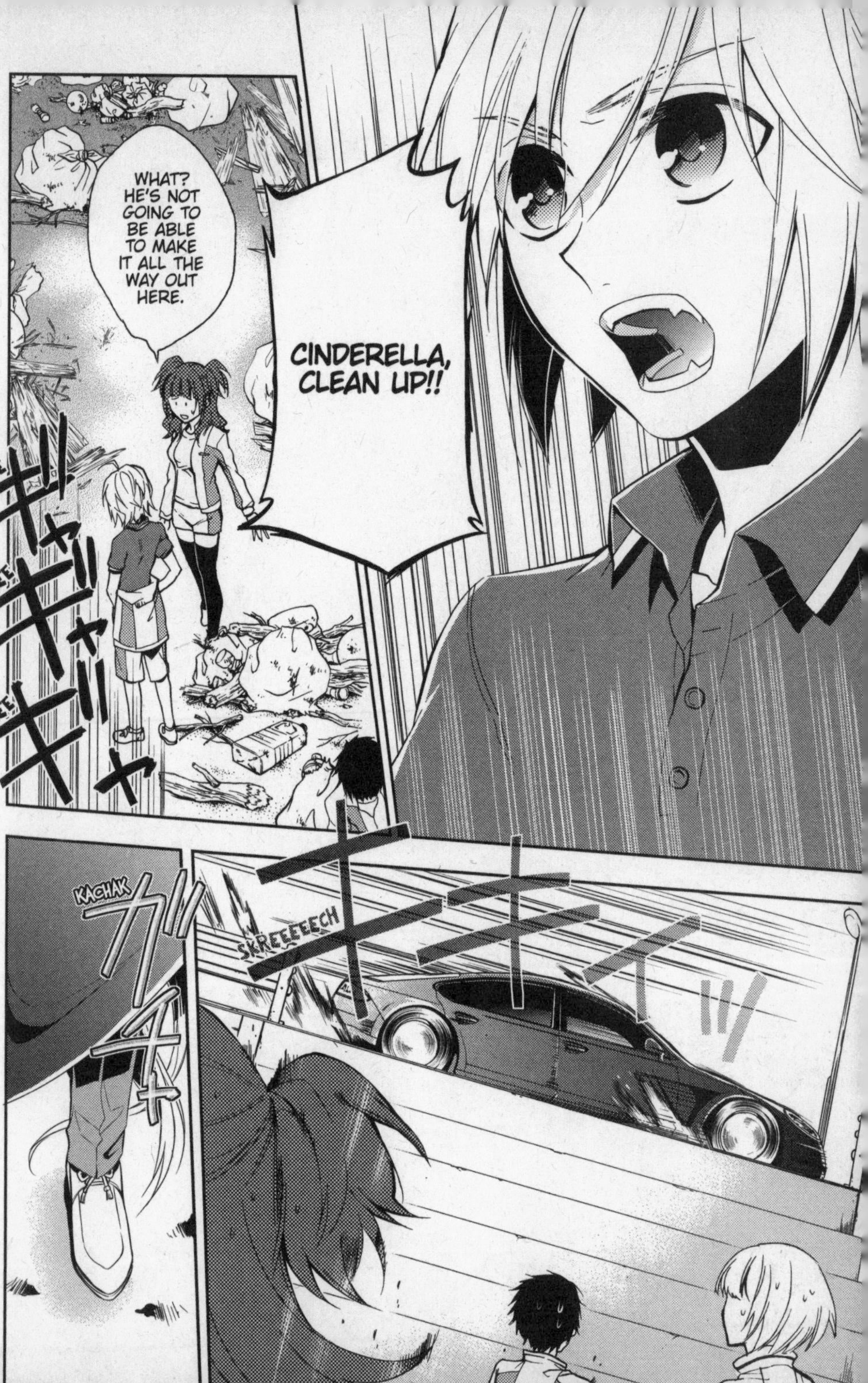

CINDERELLA, CLEAN UP!!
WHAT? HE'S NOT GOING TO BE ABLE TO MAKE IT ALL THE WAY OUT HERE.
SKREE
SKREE
SKREE
SKREEEEECH
KACHAK

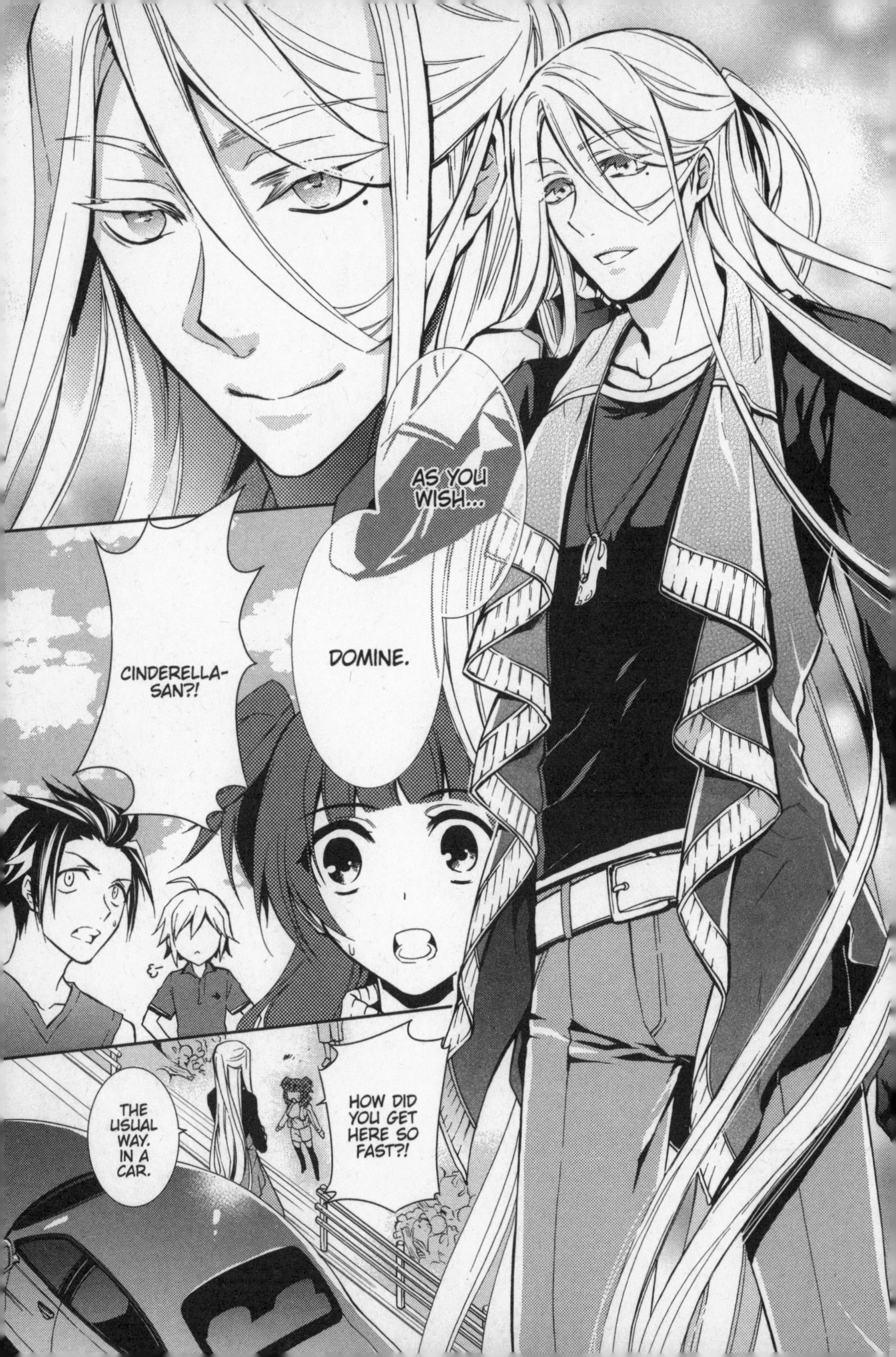
AS YOU WISH...
DOMINE.
CINDERELLA-SAN?!
HOW DID YOU GET HERE SO FAST?!
THE USUAL WAY. IN A CAR.

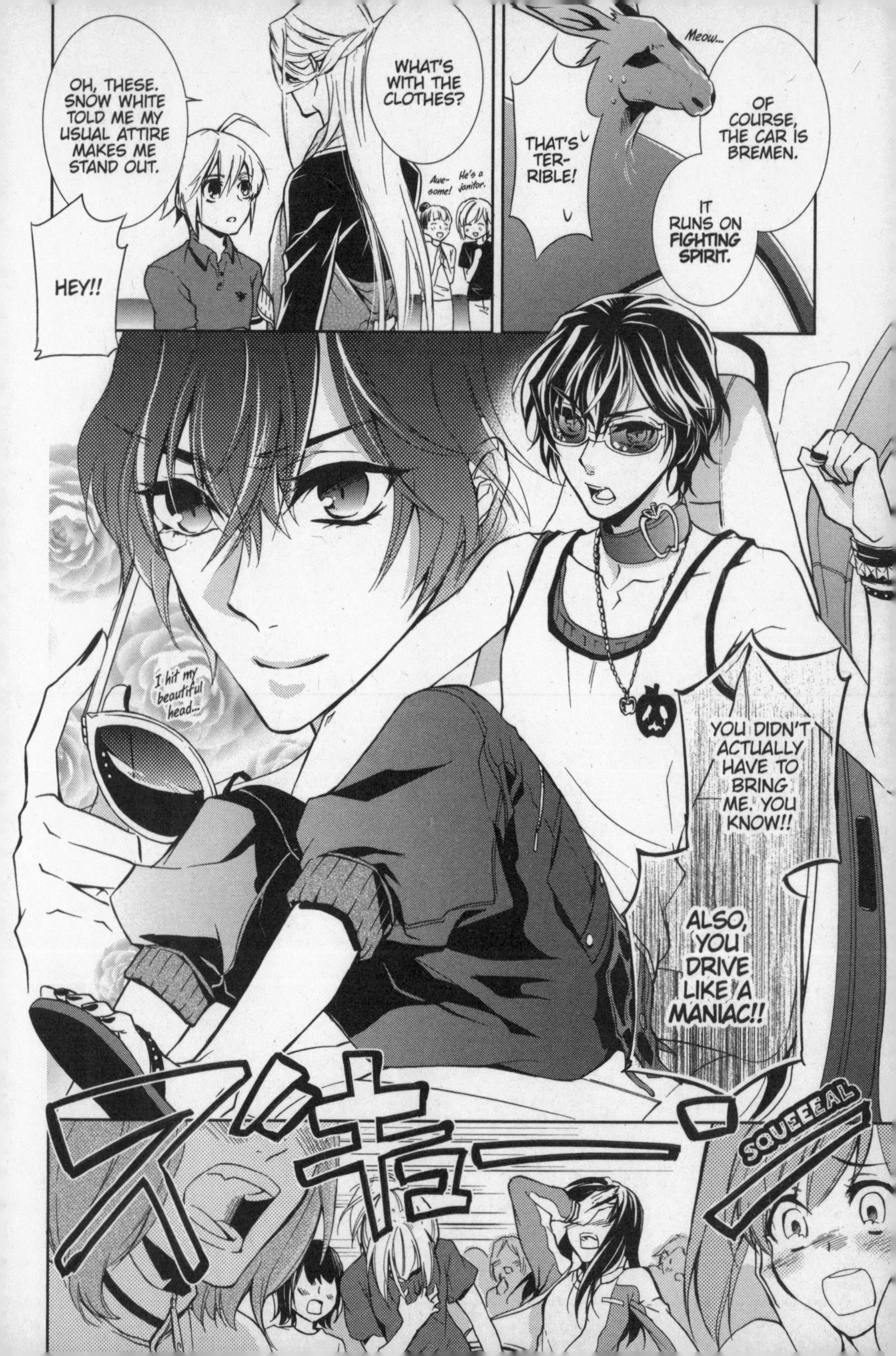
Meow...
OF COURSE, THE CAR IS BREMEN.
IT RUNS ON FIGHTING SPIRIT.
THAT'S TERRIBLE!
WHAT'S WITH THE CLOTHES?
He's a janitor.
Awe-some!
OH, THESE. SNOW WHITE TOLD ME MY USUAL ATTIRE MAKES ME STAND OUT.
HEY!!
YOU DIDN'T ACTUALLY HAVE TO BRING ME. YOU KNOW!!
ALSO, YOU DRIVE LIKE A MANIAC!!
I hit my beautiful head...
SQUEEEAL

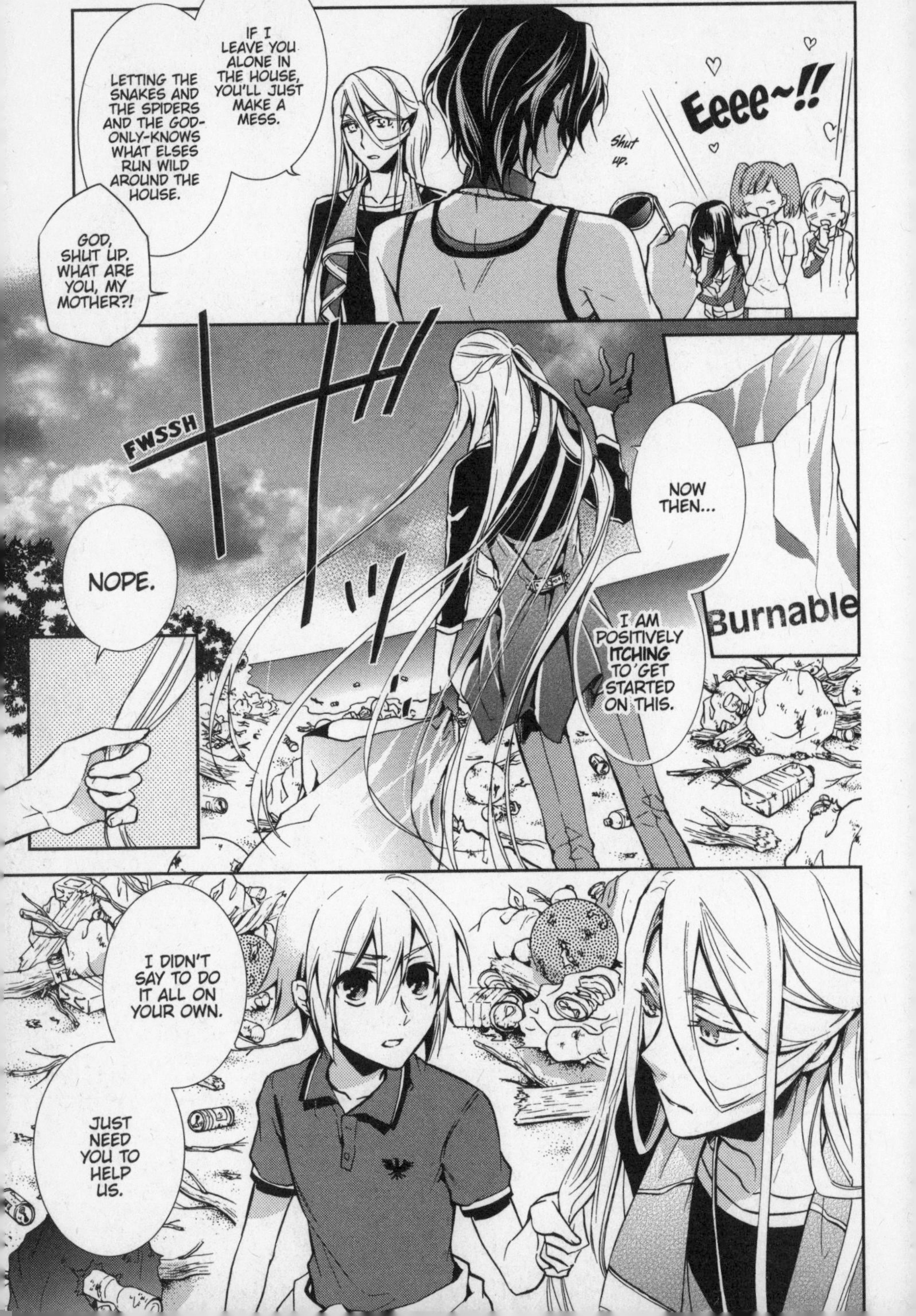
Eeee~!!
Shut up.
IF I LEAVE YOU ALONE IN THE HOUSE, YOU'LL JUST MAKE A MESS.
LETTING THE SNAKES AND THE SPIDERS AND THE GOD-ONLY-KNOWS WHAT ELSES RUN WILD AROUND THE HOUSE.
GOD, SHUT UP. WHAT ARE YOU, MY MOTHER?!
Burnable
NOW THEN...
I AM POSITIVELY ITCHING TO GET STARTED ON THIS.
FWSSH
NOPE.
I DIDN'T SAY TO DO IT ALL ON YOUR OWN.
JUST NEED YOU TO HELP US.

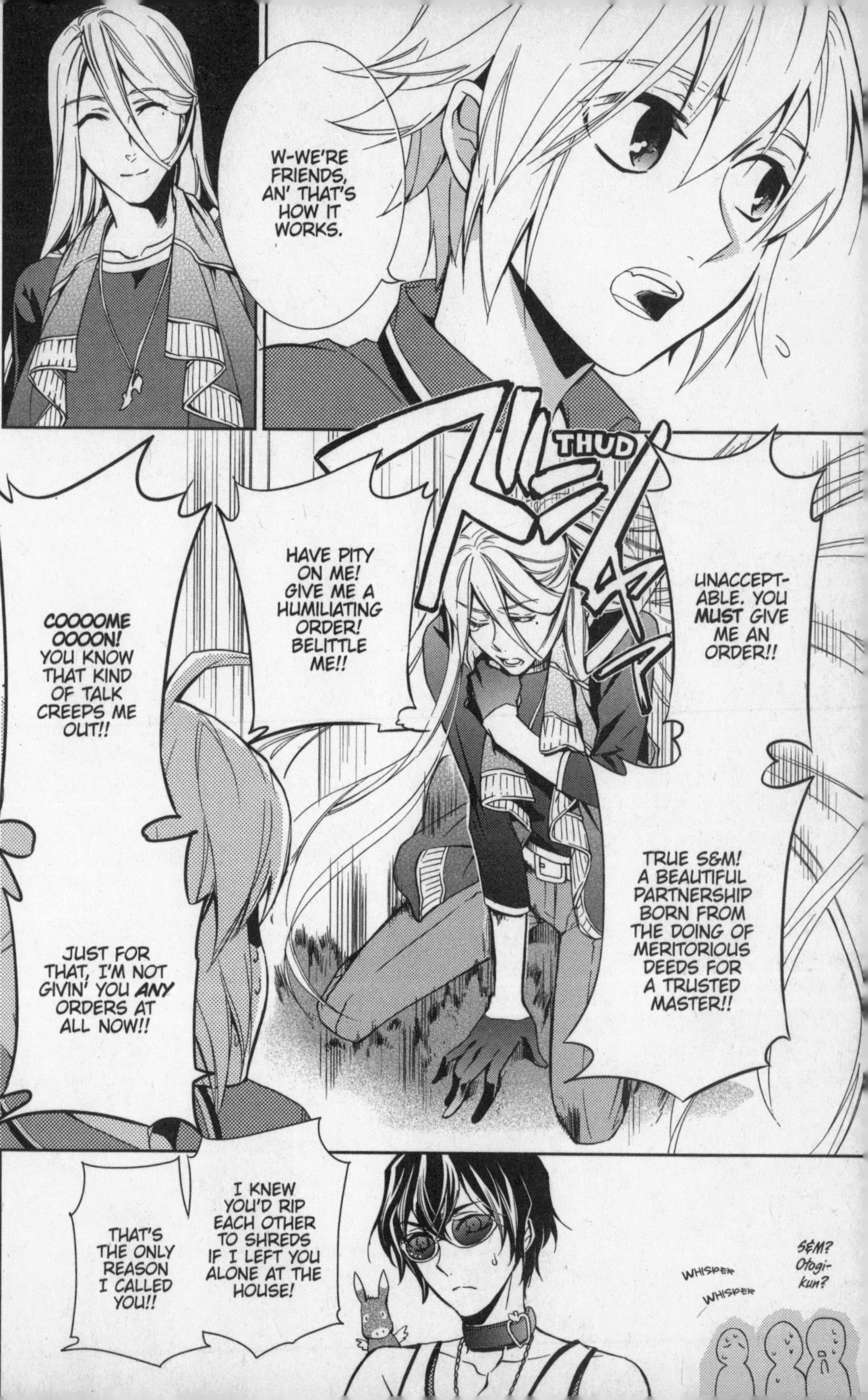
W-WE'RE FRIENDS, AN' THAT'S HOW IT WORKS.
THUD
UNACCEPTABLE. YOU MUST GIVE ME AN ORDER!!
TRUE S&M! A BEAUTIFUL PARTNERSHIP BORN FROM THE DOING OF MERITORIOUS DEEDS FOR A TRUSTED MASTER!!
HAVE PITY ON ME! GIVE ME A HUMILIATING ORDER! BELITTLE ME!!
COOOOME OOOON! YOU KNOW THAT KIND OF TALK CREEPS ME OUT!!
JUST FOR THAT, I'M NOT GIVIN' YOU ANY ORDERS AT ALL NOW!!
S&M? Otogi-kun?
WHISPER
WHISPER
I KNEW YOU'D RIP EACH OTHER TO SHREDS IF I LEFT YOU ALONE AT THE HOUSE!
THAT'S THE ONLY REASON I CALLED YOU!!

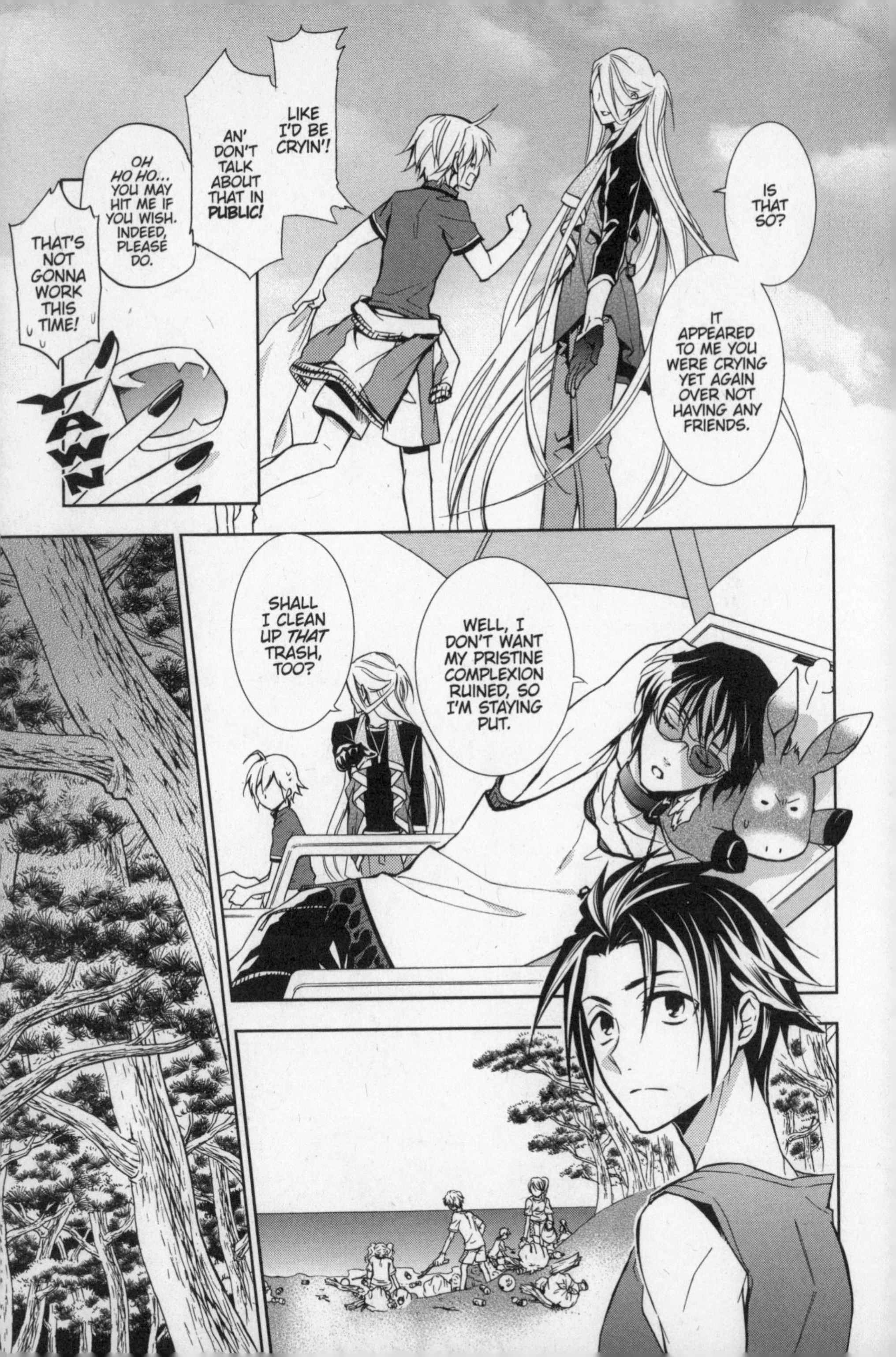
IS THAT SO?
IT APPEARED TO ME YOU WERE CRYING YET AGAIN OVER NOT HAVING ANY FRIENDS.
LIKE I'D BE CRYIN'!
AN' DON'T TALK ABOUT THAT IN PUBLIC!
OH HO HO... YOU MAY HIT ME IF YOU WISH. INDEED, PLEASE DO.
THAT'S NOT GONNA WORK THIS TIME!
YAWN
WELL, I DON'T WANT MY PRISTINE COMPLEXION RUINED, SO I'M STAYING PUT.
SHALL I CLEAN UP THAT TRASH, TOO?

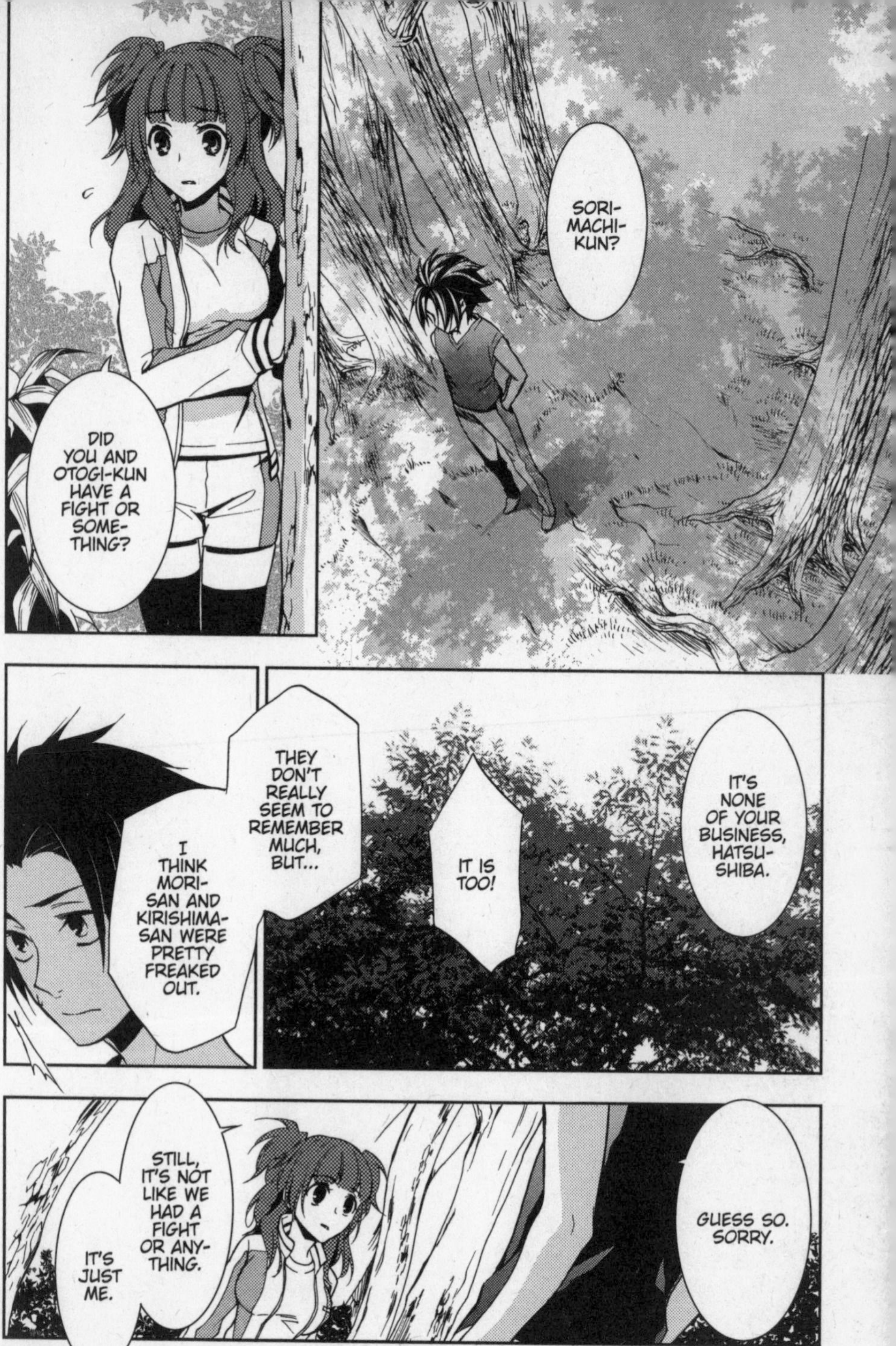
SORI-MACHI-KUN?
DID YOU AND OTOGI-KUN HAVE A FIGHT OR SOME-THING?
IT'S NONE OF YOUR BUSINESS, HATSU-SHIBA.
IT IS TOO!
THEY DON'T REALLY SEEM TO REMEMBER MUCH, BUT...
I THINK MORI-SAN AND KIRISHIMA-SAN WERE PRETTY FREAKED OUT.
GUESS SO. SORRY.
STILL, IT'S NOT LIKE WE HAD A FIGHT OR ANY-THING.
IT'S JUST ME.

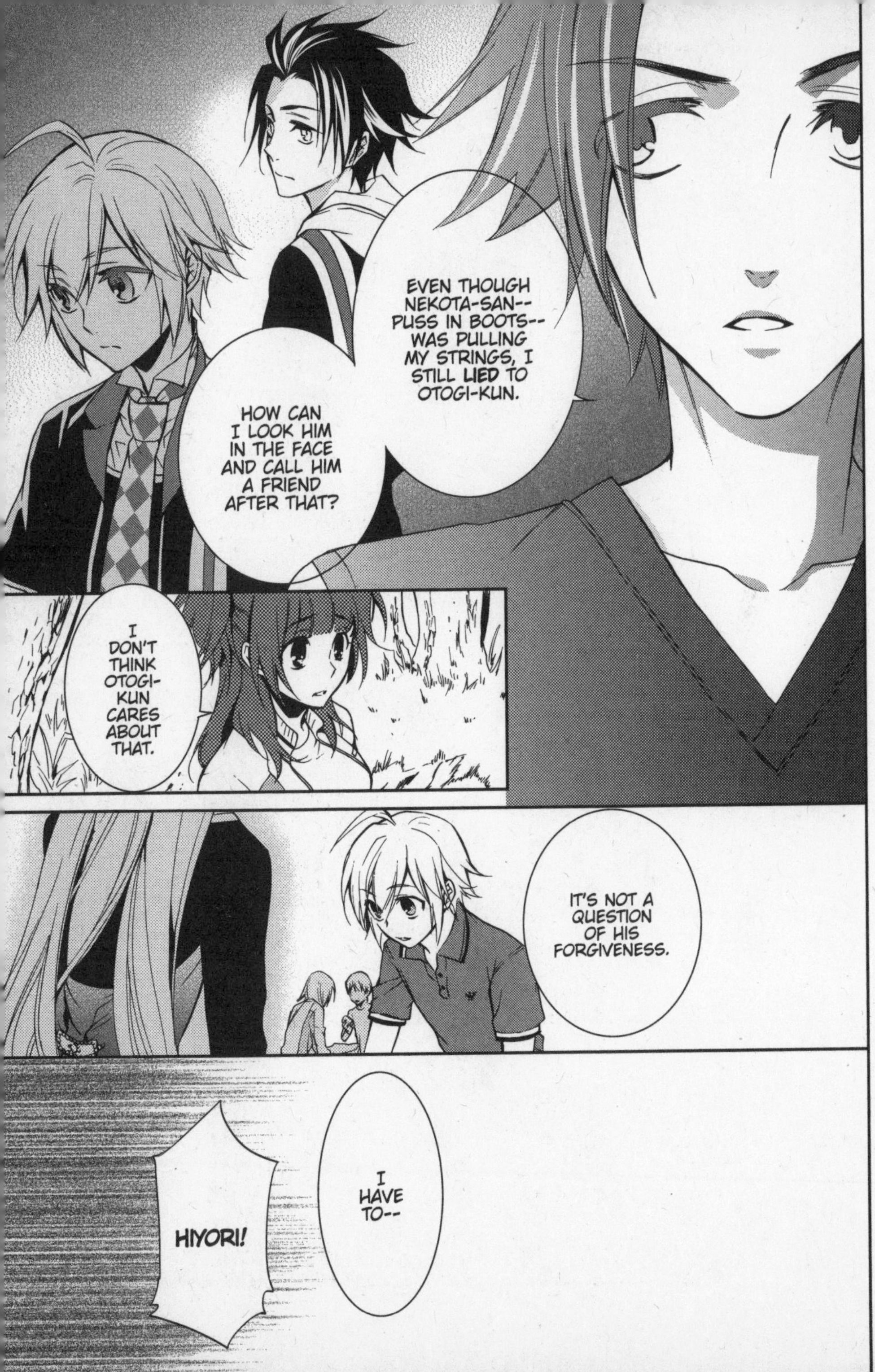
EVEN THOUGH NEKOTA-SAN-- PUSS IN BOOTS-- WAS PULLING MY STRINGS, I STILL LIED TO OTOGI-KUN.
HOW CAN I LOOK HIM IN THE FACE AND CALL HIM A FRIEND AFTER THAT?
I DON'T THINK OTOGI-KUN CARES ABOUT THAT.
IT'S NOT A QUESTION OF HIS FORGIVENESS.
I HAVE TO--
HIYORI!

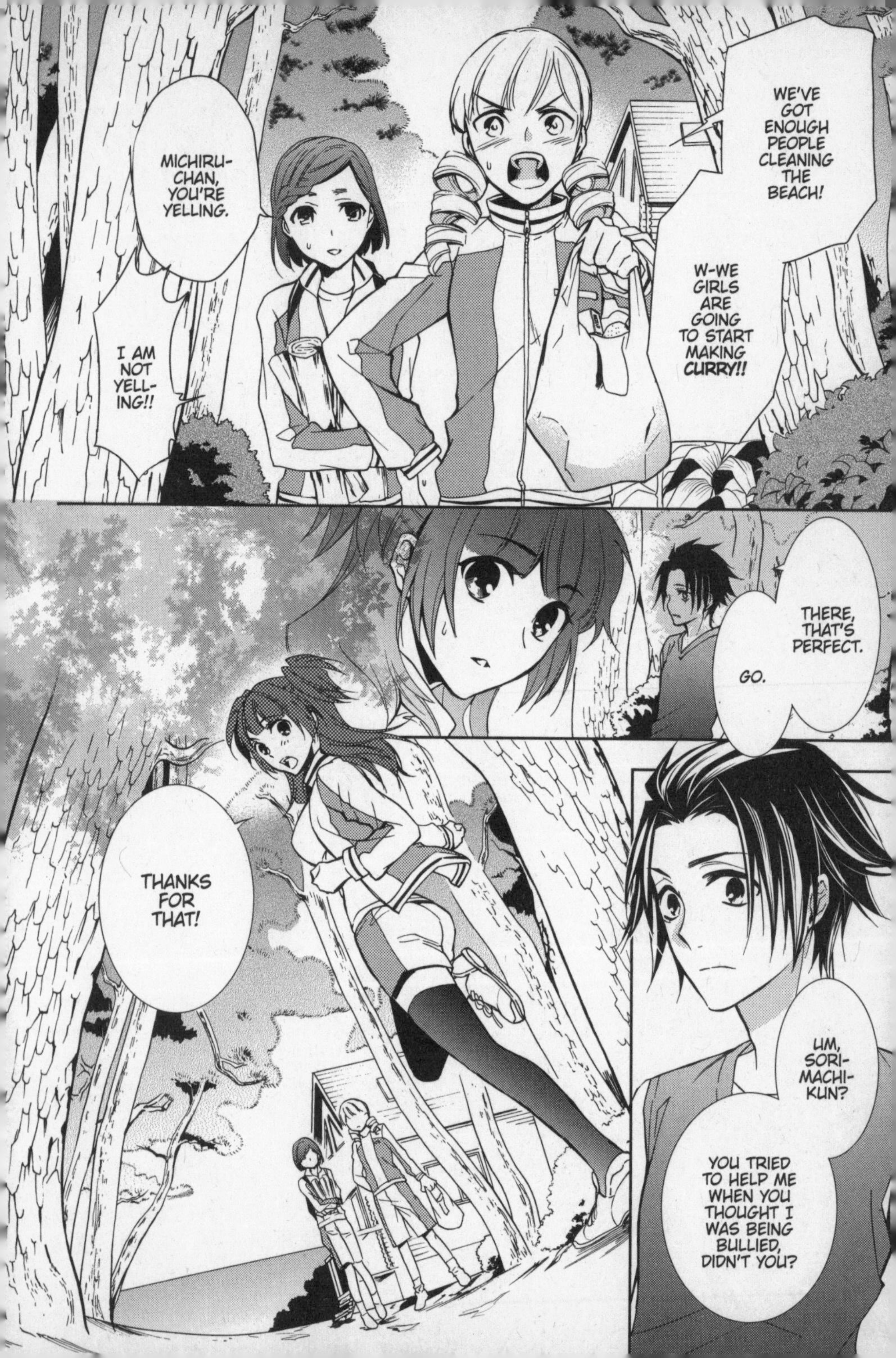
WE'VE GOT ENOUGH PEOPLE CLEANING THE BEACH!
W-WE GIRLS ARE GOING TO START MAKING **CURRY!!**
MICHIRU-CHAN, YOU'RE YELLING.
I AM NOT YELL-ING!!
THERE, THAT'S PERFECT.
GO.
UM, SORI-MACHI-KUN?
YOU TRIED TO HELP ME WHEN YOU THOUGHT I WAS BEING BULLIED, DIDN'T YOU?
THANKS FOR THAT!

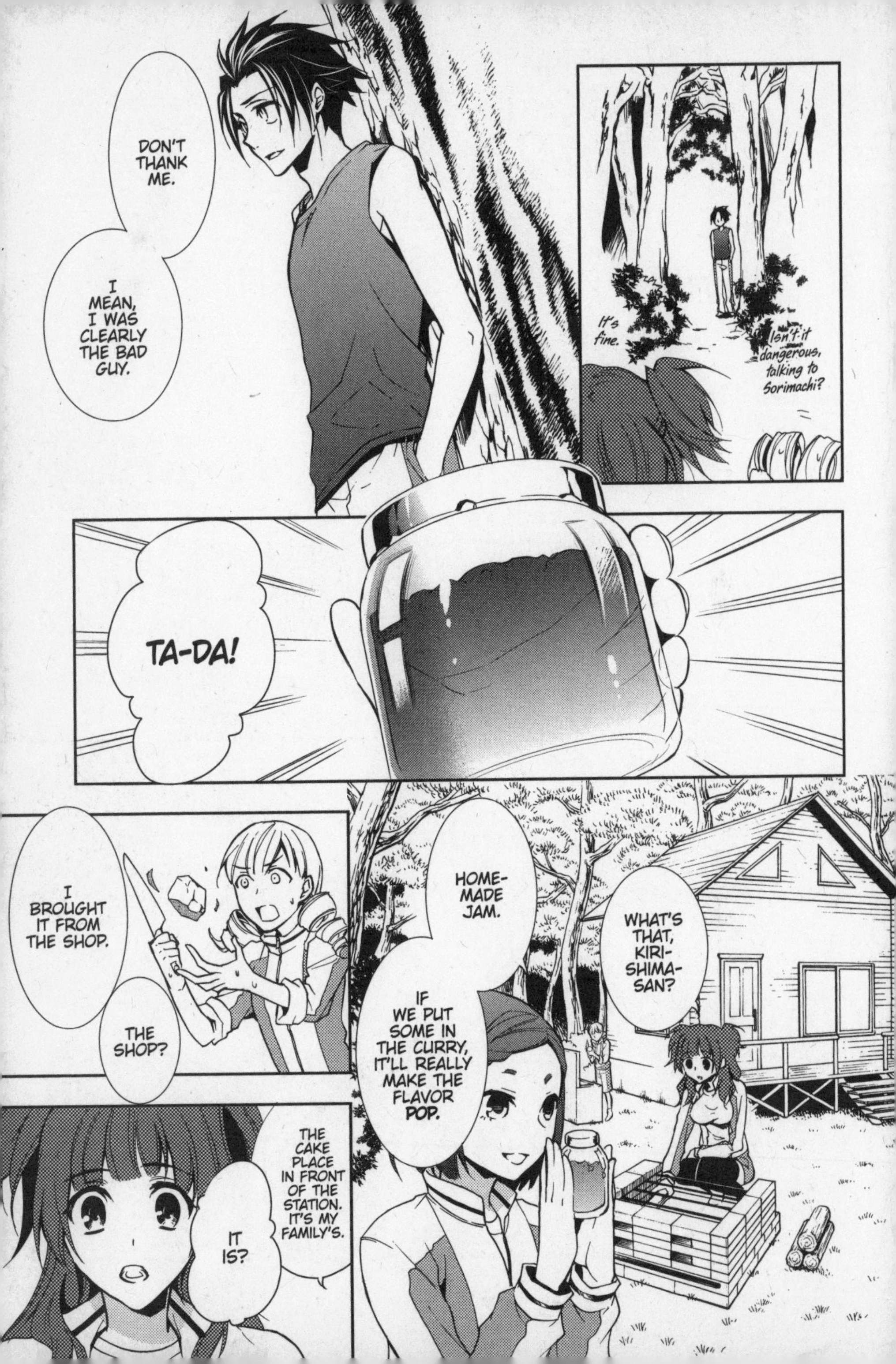
Isn't it dangerous, talking to Sorimachi?
It's fine.
DON'T THANK ME.
I MEAN, I WAS CLEARLY THE BAD GUY.
TA-DA!
WHAT'S THAT, KIRI-SHIMA-SAN?
HOME-MADE JAM.
IF WE PUT SOME IN THE CURRY, IT'LL REALLY MAKE THE FLAVOR POP.
I BROUGHT IT FROM THE SHOP.
THE SHOP?
THE CAKE PLACE IN FRONT OF THE STATION. IT'S MY FAMILY'S.
IT IS?

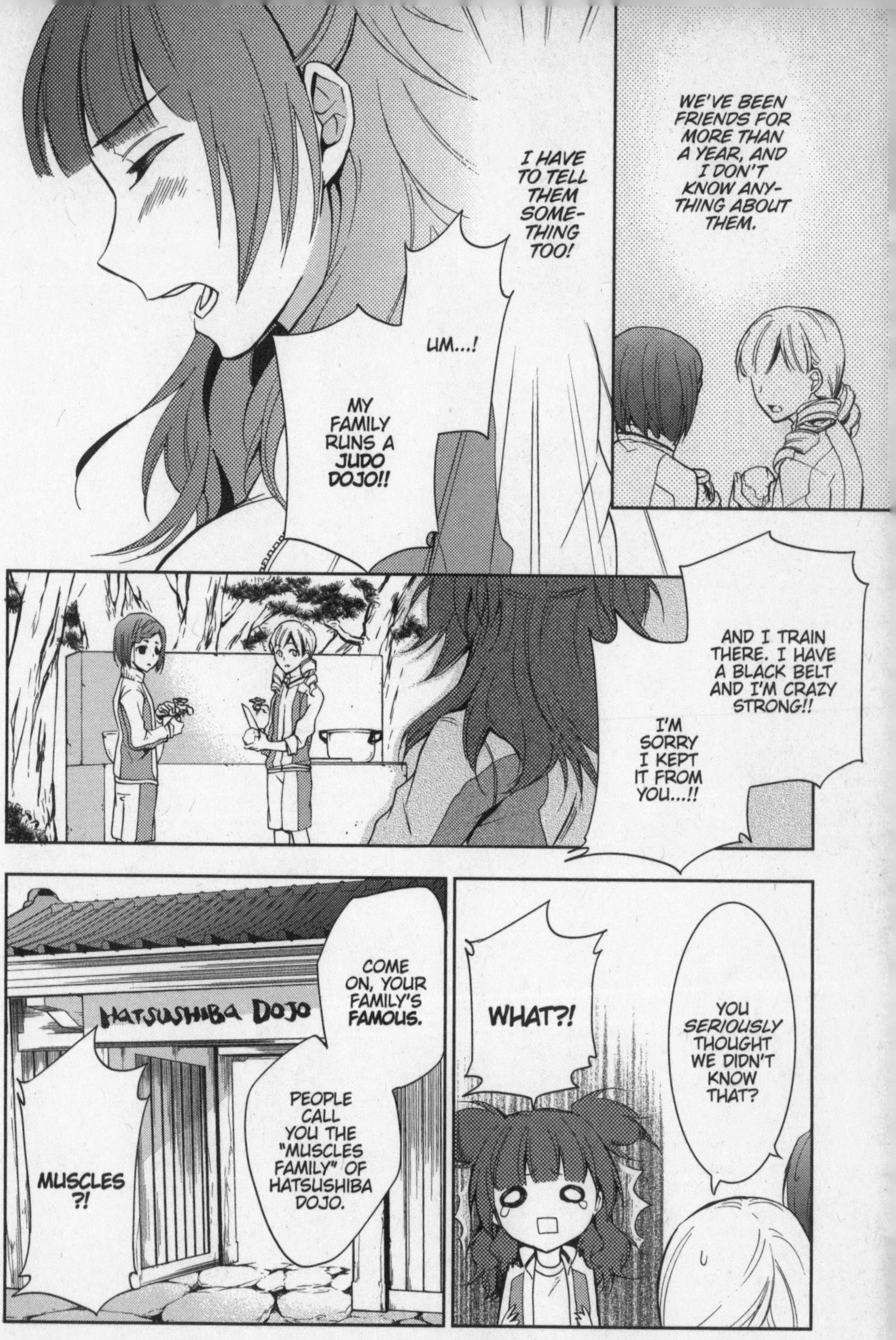
WE'VE BEEN FRIENDS FOR MORE THAN A YEAR, AND I DON'T KNOW ANYTHING ABOUT THEM.
I HAVE TO TELL THEM SOMETHING TOO!
UM...!
MY FAMILY RUNS A JUDO DOJO!!
AND I TRAIN THERE. I HAVE A BLACK BELT AND I'M CRAZY STRONG!!
I'M SORRY I KEPT IT FROM YOU...!!
YOU SERIOUSLY THOUGHT WE DIDN'T KNOW THAT?
WHAT?!
COME ON, YOUR FAMILY'S FAMOUS.
HATSUSHIBA DOJO
PEOPLE CALL YOU THE "MUSCLES FAMILY" OF HATSUSHIBA DOJO.
MUSCLES?!

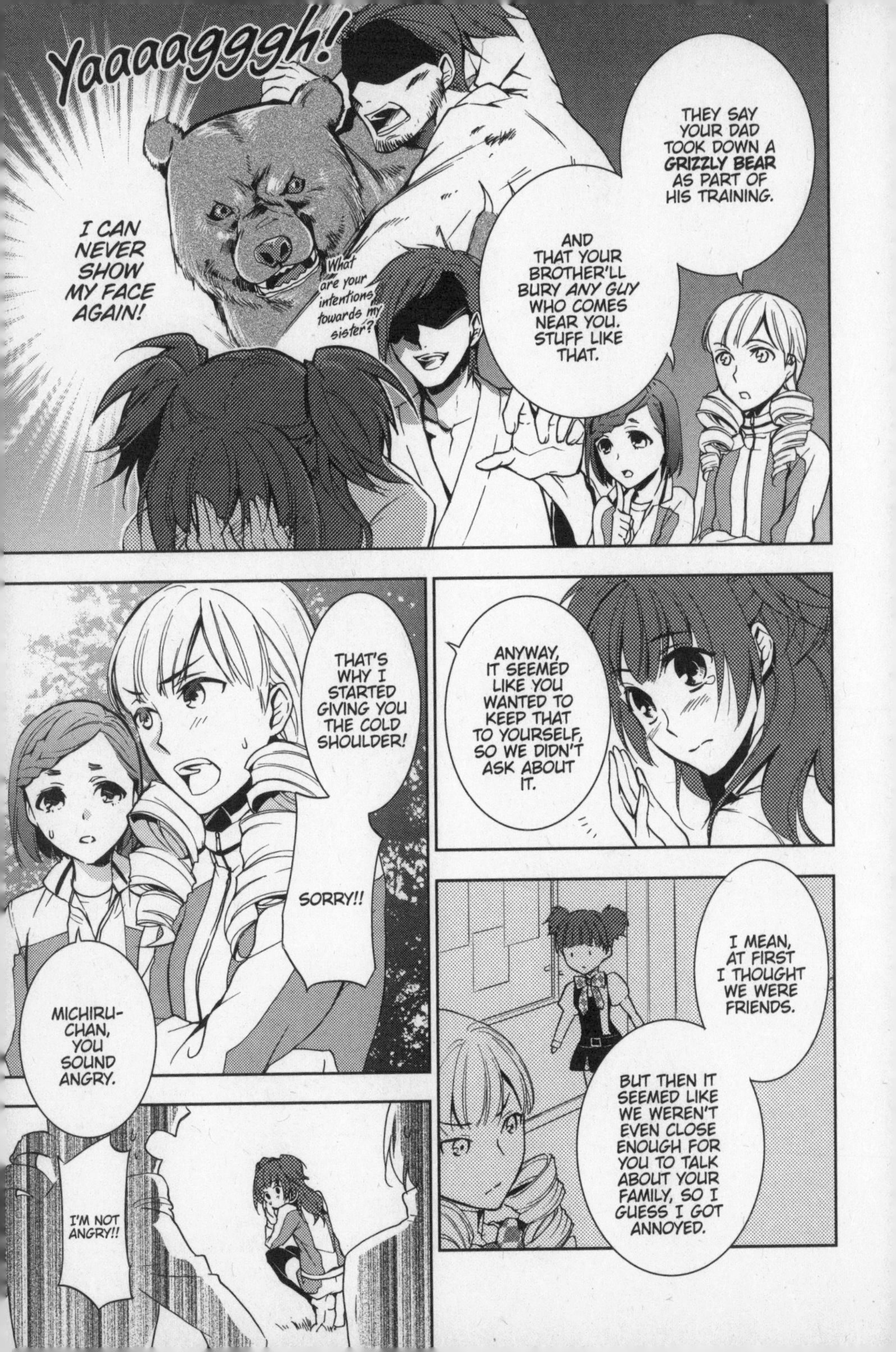
THEY SAY YOUR DAD TOOK DOWN A **GRIZZLY BEAR** AS PART OF HIS TRAINING.
AND THAT YOUR BROTHER'LL BURY *ANY GUY* WHO COMES NEAR YOU. STUFF LIKE THAT.
What are your intentions towards my sister?
Yaaaagggh!
I CAN NEVER SHOW MY FACE AGAIN!
ANYWAY, IT SEEMED LIKE YOU WANTED TO KEEP THAT TO YOURSELF, SO WE DIDN'T ASK ABOUT IT.
I MEAN, AT FIRST I THOUGHT WE WERE FRIENDS.
BUT THEN IT SEEMED LIKE WE WEREN'T EVEN CLOSE ENOUGH FOR YOU TO TALK ABOUT YOUR FAMILY, SO I GUESS I GOT ANNOYED.
THAT'S WHY I STARTED GIVING YOU THE COLD SHOULDER!
SORRY!!
MICHIRU-CHAN, YOU SOUND ANGRY.
I'M NOT ANGRY!!

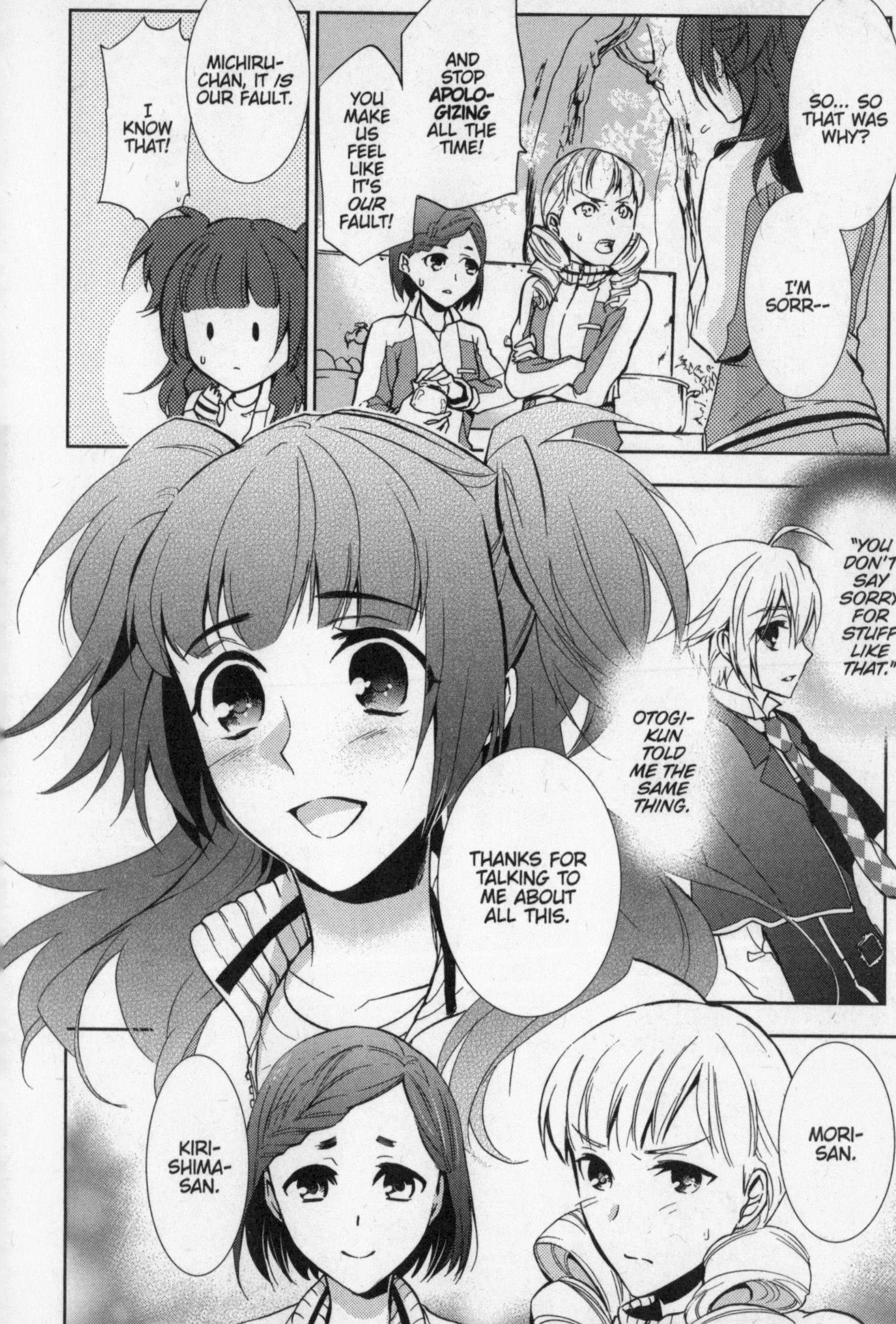
SO... SO THAT WAS WHY?
I'M SORR--
AND STOP APOLOGIZING ALL THE TIME!
YOU MAKE US FEEL LIKE IT'S OUR FAULT!
MICHIRU-CHAN, IT IS OUR FAULT.
I KNOW THAT!
"YOU DON'T SAY SORRY FOR STUFF LIKE THAT."
OTOGI-KUN TOLD ME THE SAME THING.
THANKS FOR TALKING TO ME ABOUT ALL THIS.
MORI-SAN.
KIRI-SHIMA-SAN.

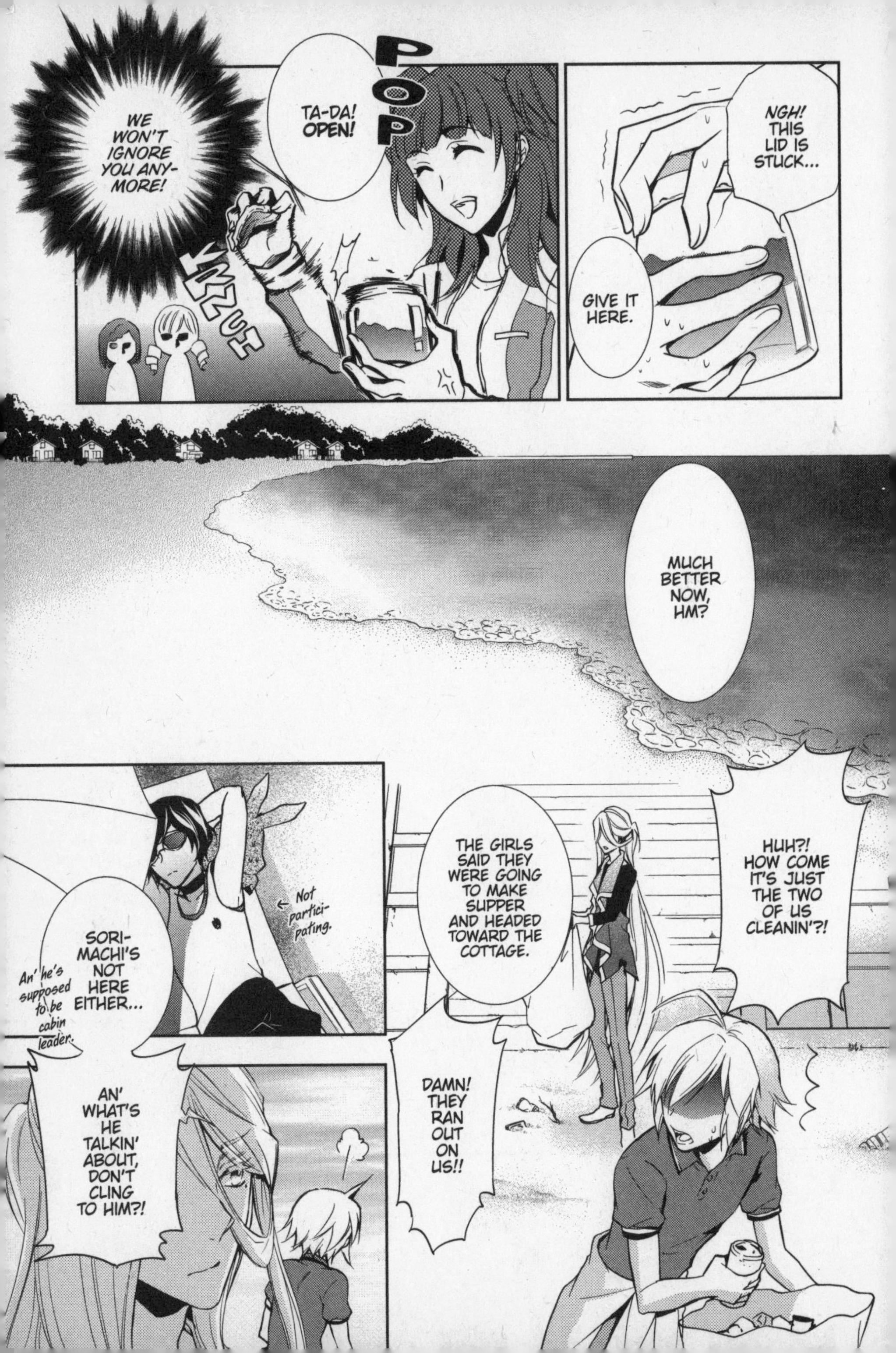
NGH! THIS LID IS STUCK...
GIVE IT HERE.
POP
TA-DA! OPEN!
WE WON'T IGNORE YOU ANYMORE!
MUCH BETTER NOW, HM?
HUH?! HOW COME IT'S JUST THE TWO OF US CLEANIN'?!
THE GIRLS SAID THEY WERE GOING TO MAKE SUPPER AND HEADED TOWARD THE COTTAGE.
DAMN! THEY RAN OUT ON US!!
SORI-MACHI'S NOT HERE EITHER...
← Not partici-pating.
An' he's supposed to be cabin leader.
AN' WHAT'S HE TALKIN' ABOUT, DON'T CLING TO HIM?!

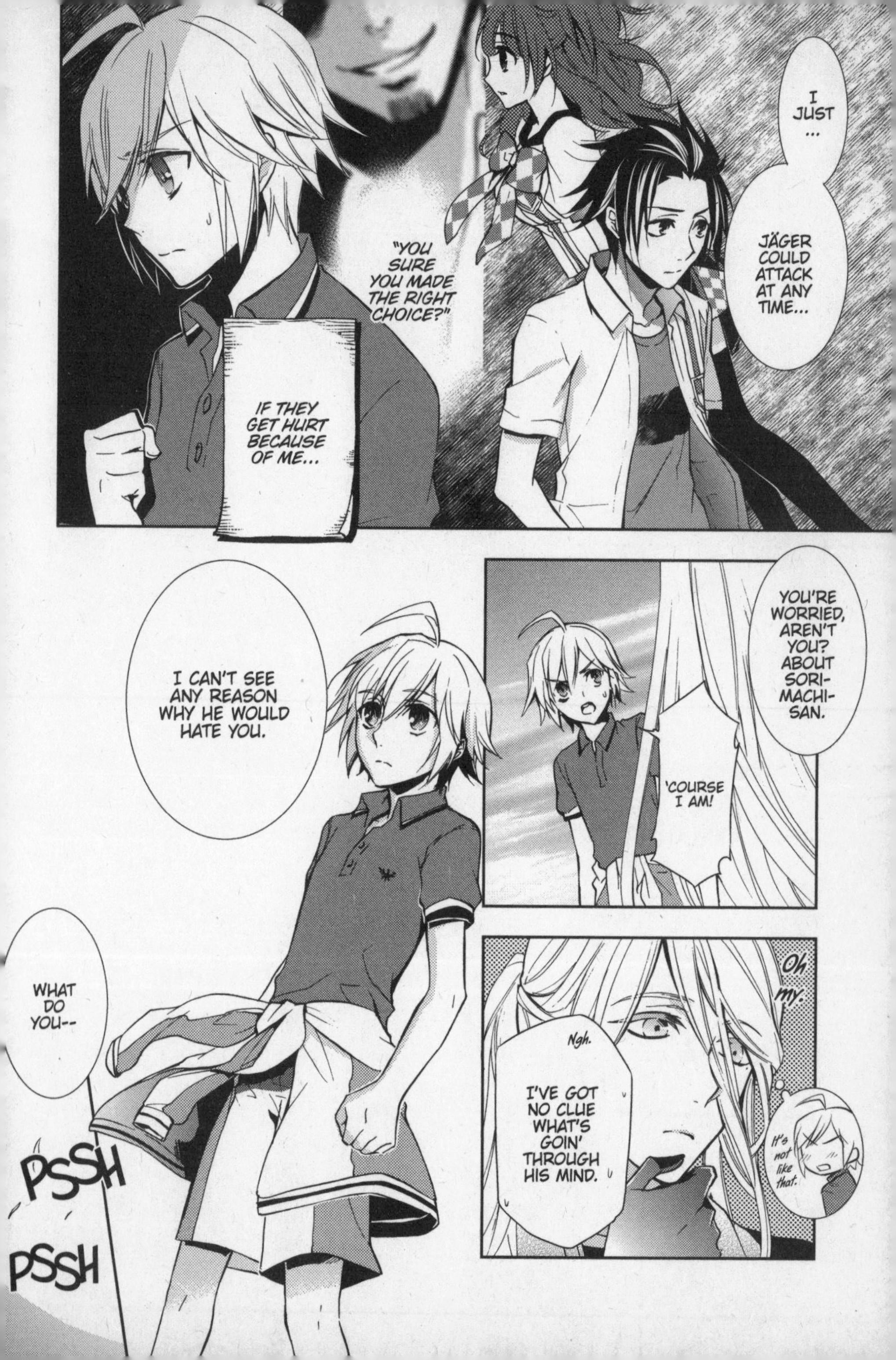
I JUST ...
JÄGER COULD ATTACK AT ANY TIME...
"YOU SURE YOU MADE THE RIGHT CHOICE?"
IF THEY GET HURT BECAUSE OF ME...
YOU'RE WORRIED, AREN'T YOU? ABOUT SORI-MACHI-SAN.
'COURSE I AM!
Oh my.
Ngh.
I'VE GOT NO CLUE WHAT'S GOIN' THROUGH HIS MIND.
It's not like that.
I CAN'T SEE ANY REASON WHY HE WOULD HATE YOU.
WHAT DO YOU--
PSSH
PSSH

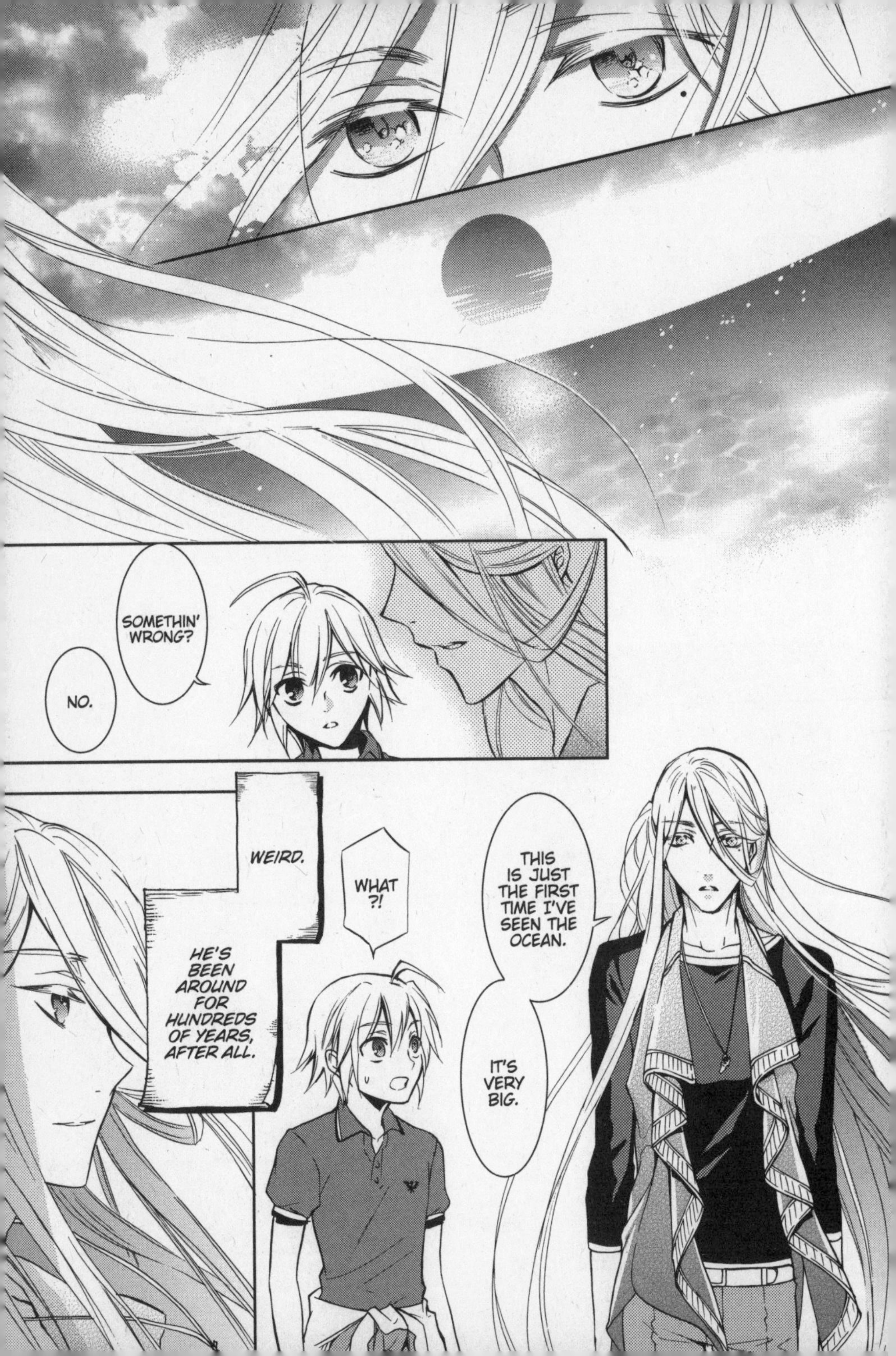
SOMETHIN' WRONG?
NO.
THIS IS JUST THE FIRST TIME I'VE SEEN THE OCEAN.
IT'S VERY BIG.
WHAT?!
WEIRD.
HE'S BEEN AROUND FOR HUNDREDS OF YEARS, AFTER ALL.

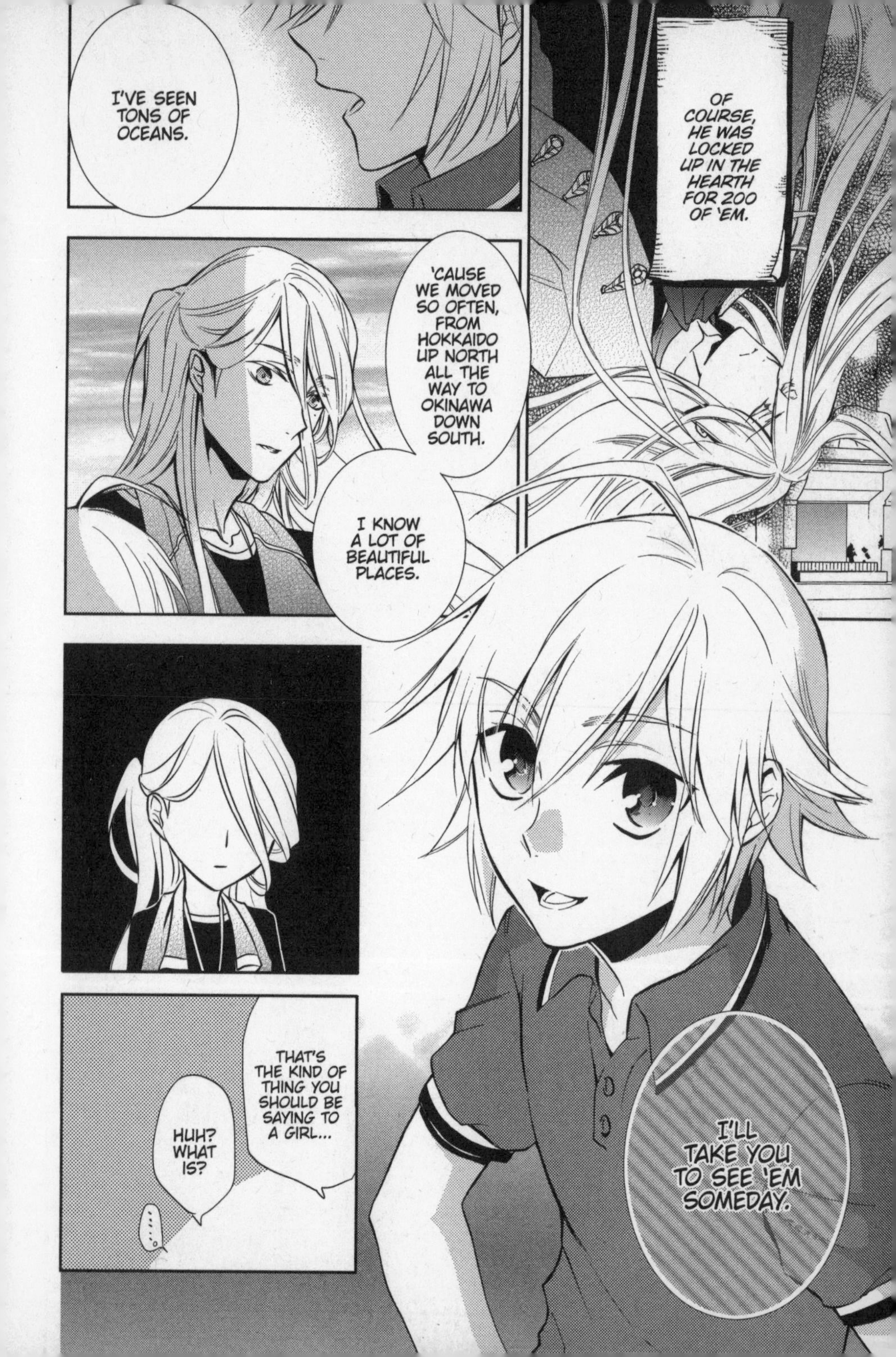

OF COURSE, HE WAS LOCKED UP IN THE HEARTH FOR 200 OF 'EM.
I'VE SEEN TONS OF OCEANS.
'CAUSE WE MOVED SO OFTEN, FROM HOKKAIDO UP NORTH ALL THE WAY TO OKINAWA DOWN SOUTH.
I KNOW A LOT OF BEAUTIFUL PLACES.
I'LL TAKE YOU TO SEE 'EM SOMEDAY.
THAT'S THE KIND OF THING YOU SHOULD BE SAYING TO A GIRL...
HUH? WHAT IS?
.....

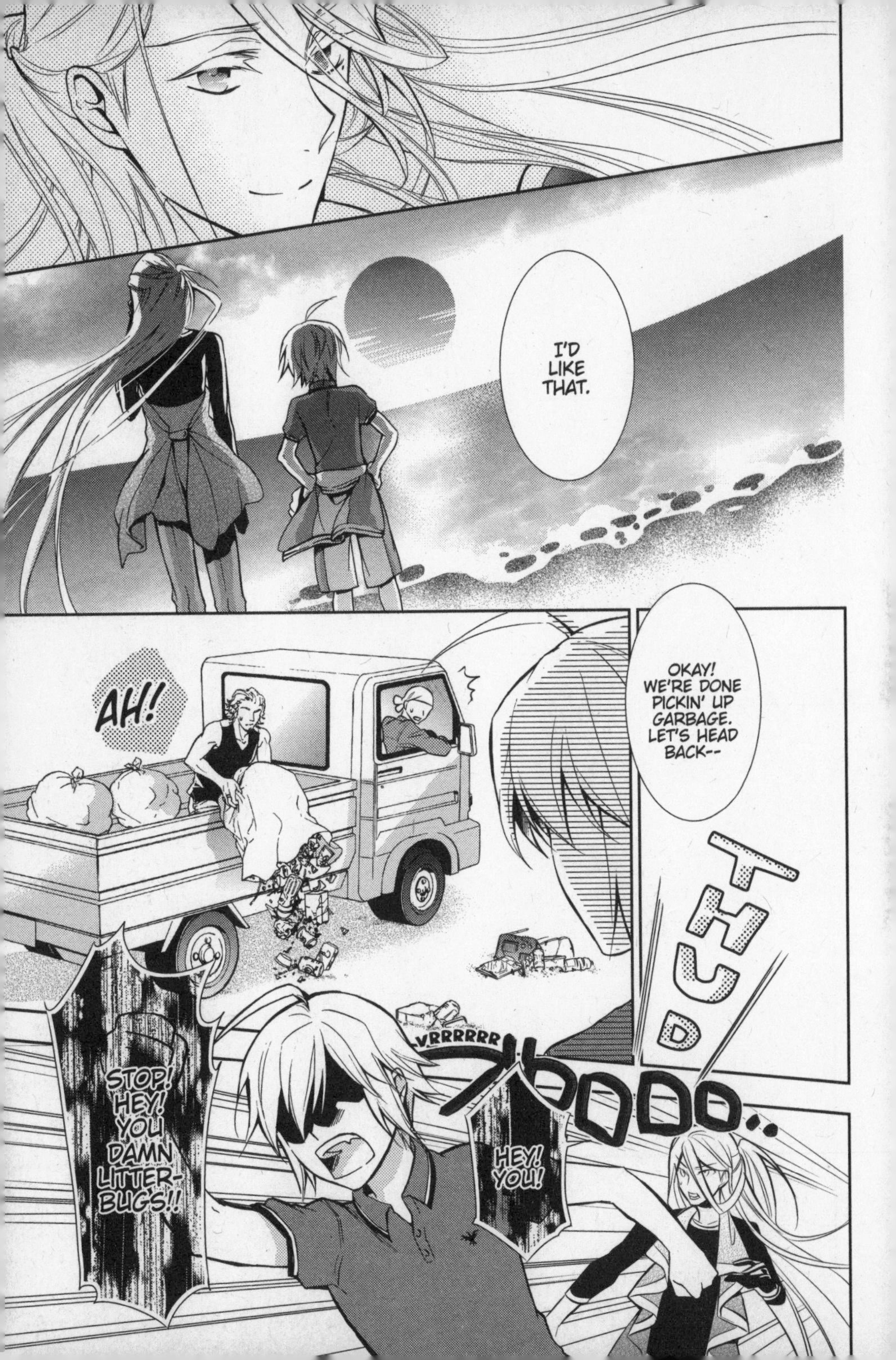
I'D LIKE THAT.
OKAY! WE'RE DONE PICKIN' UP GARBAGE. LET'S HEAD BACK--
THUD
AH!
-VRRRRRR
OOOO..
HEY! YOU!
STOP! HEY! YOU DAMN LITTER-BUGS!!

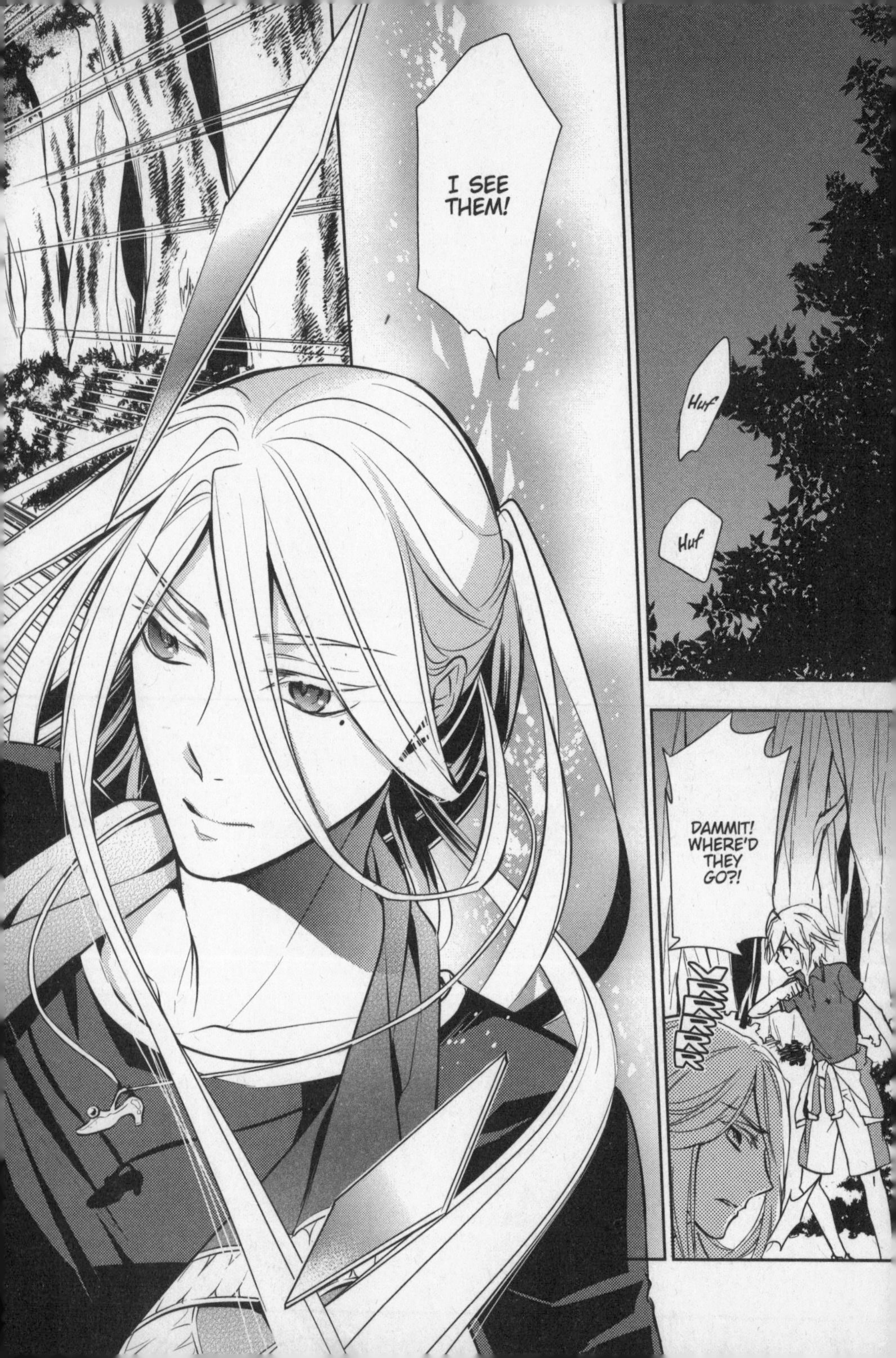
Huf
Huf
DAMMIT! WHERE'D THEY GO?!
I SEE THEM!

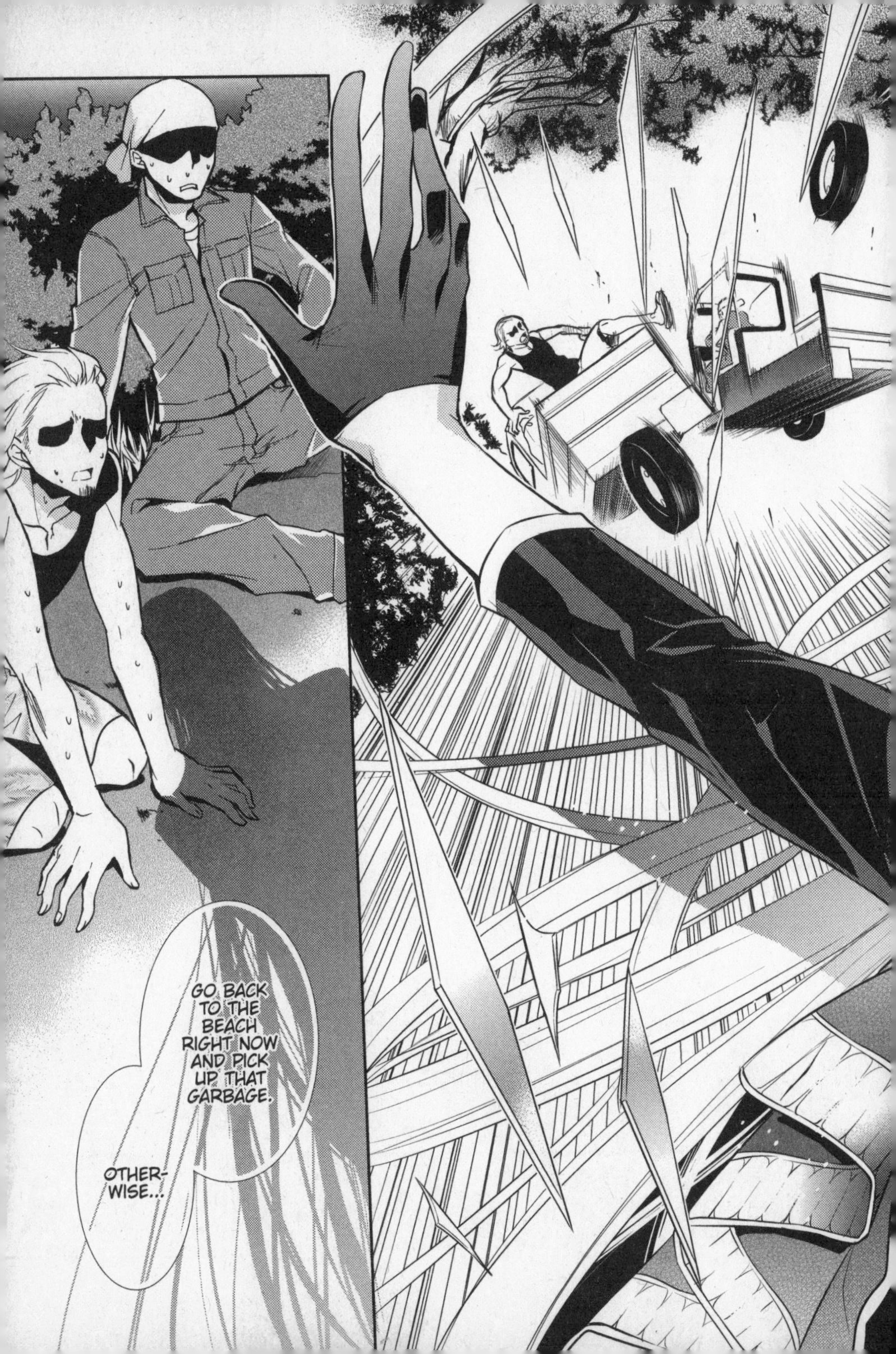
GO BACK TO THE BEACH RIGHT NOW AND PICK UP THAT GARBAGE.
OTHER-WISE...

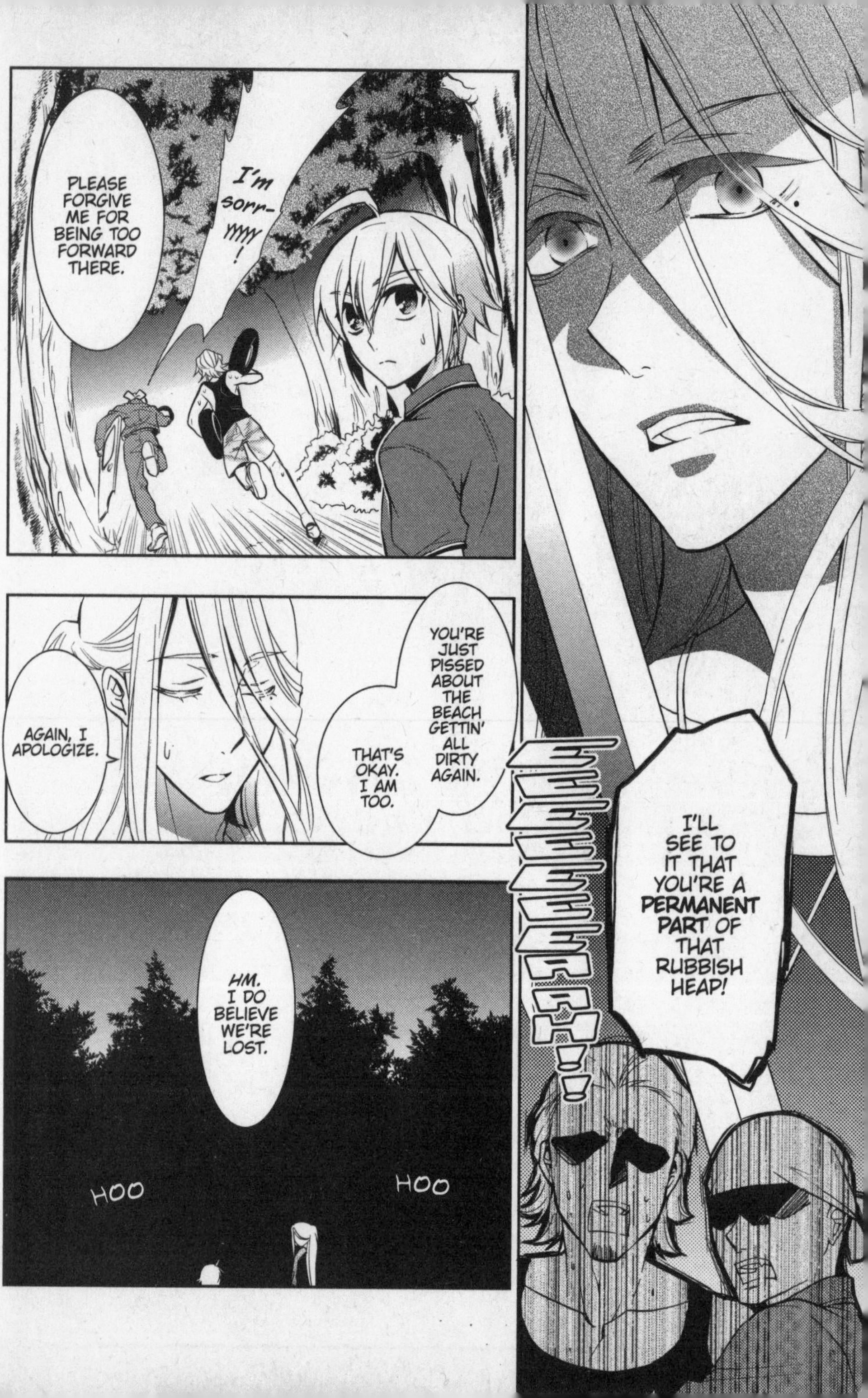
I'LL SEE TO IT THAT YOU'RE A **PERMANENT PART** OF THAT RUBBISH HEAP!
PLEASE FORGIVE ME FOR BEING TOO FORWARD THERE.
*I'm sorr-yyyy!*
YOU'RE JUST PISSED ABOUT THE BEACH GETTIN' ALL DIRTY AGAIN.
THAT'S OKAY. I AM TOO.
AGAIN, I APOLOGIZE.
HM. I DO BELIEVE WE'RE LOST.
HOO
HOO

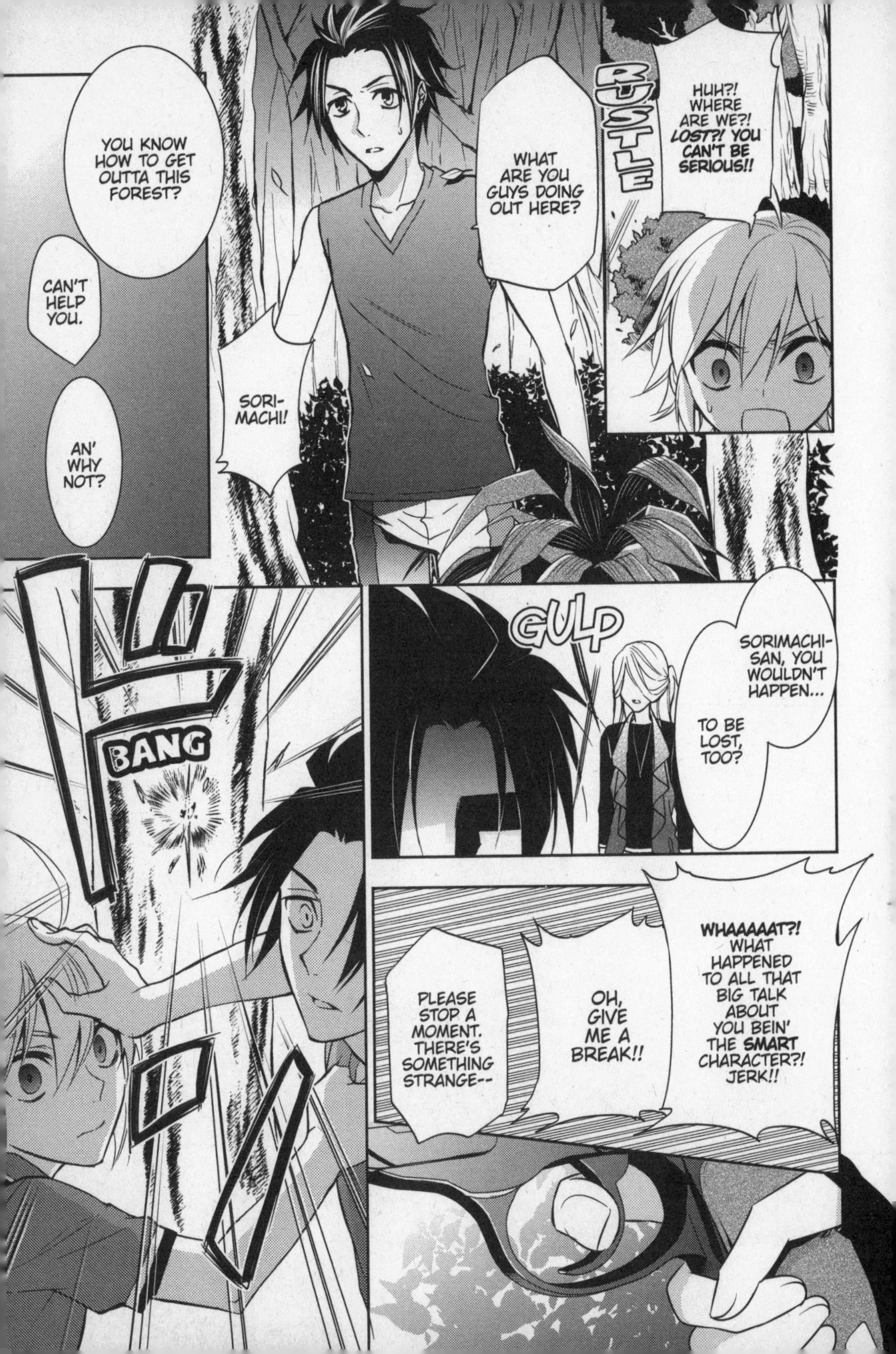

RUSTLE
HUH?! WHERE ARE WE?! LOST?! YOU CAN'T BE SERIOUS!!
WHAT ARE YOU GUYS DOING OUT HERE?
SORI-MACHI!
YOU KNOW HOW TO GET OUTTA THIS FOREST?
CAN'T HELP YOU.
AN' WHY NOT?
GULP
SORIMACHI-SAN, YOU WOULDN'T HAPPEN...
TO BE LOST, TOO?
WHAAAAAT?! WHAT HAPPENED TO ALL THAT BIG TALK ABOUT YOU BEIN' THE SMART CHARACTER?! JERK!!
OH, GIVE ME A BREAK!!
PLEASE STOP A MOMENT. THERE'S SOMETHING STRANGE--
BANG

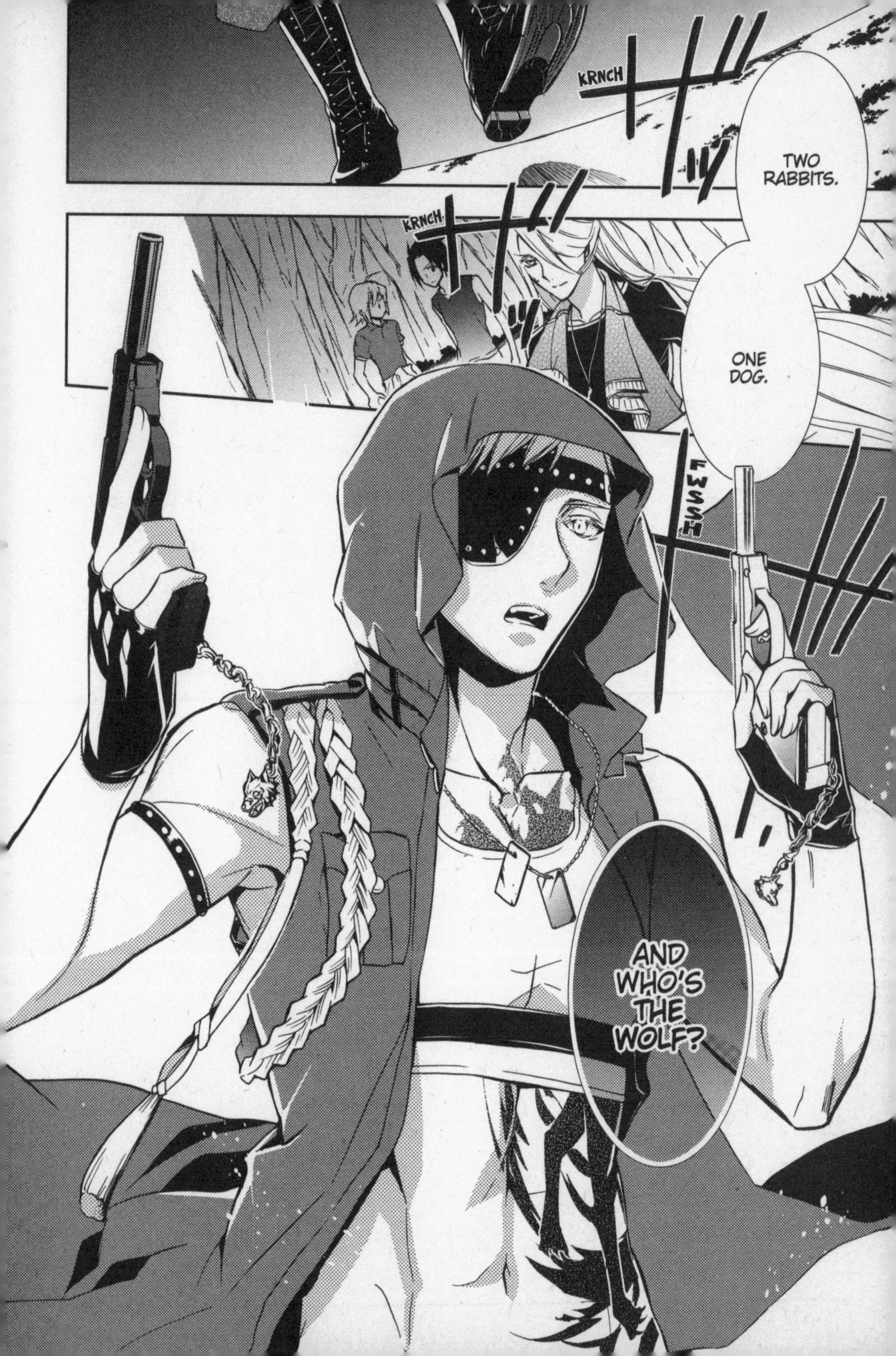
TWO RABBITS.
KRNCH
ONE DOG.
KRNCH
FWSSH
AND WHO'S THE WOLF?

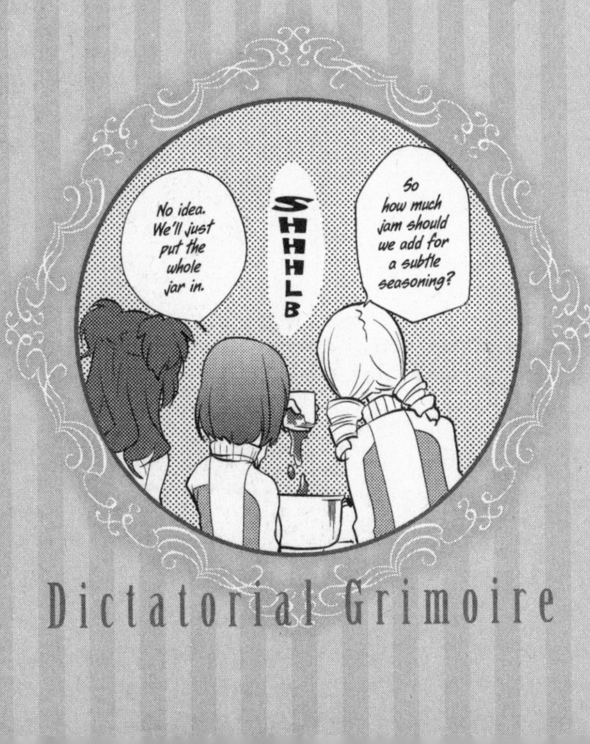
So how much jam should we add for a subtle seasoning?
SHHHLB
No idea. We'll just put the whole jar in.

Dictatorial Grimoire

独裁グリムワール
Dictatorial Grimoire

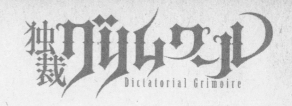

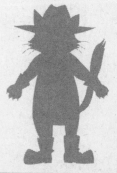

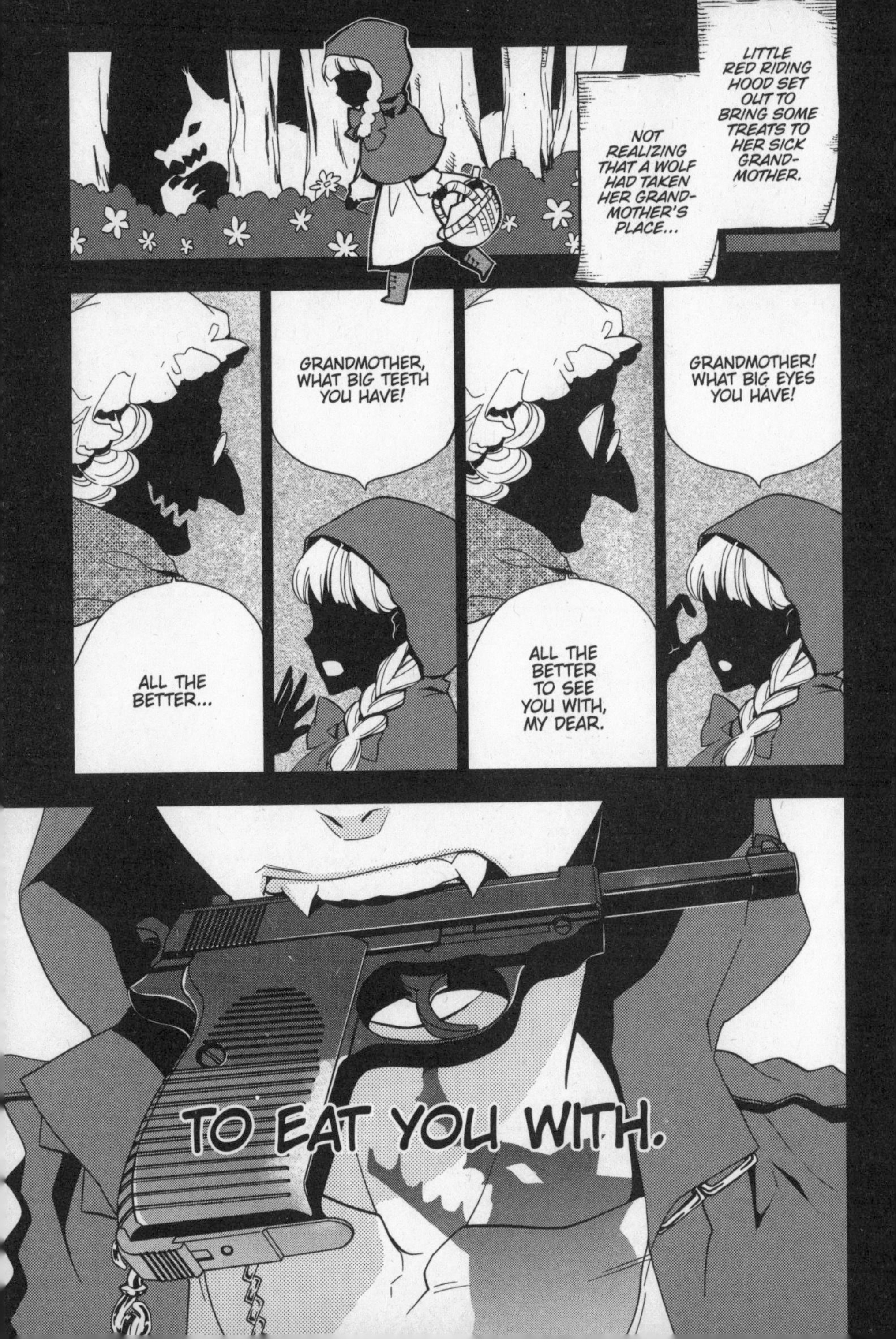
LITTLE RED RIDING HOOD SET OUT TO BRING SOME TREATS TO HER SICK GRAND-MOTHER.
NOT REALIZING THAT A WOLF HAD TAKEN HER GRAND-MOTHER'S PLACE...
GRANDMOTHER! WHAT BIG EYES YOU HAVE!
ALL THE BETTER TO SEE YOU WITH, MY DEAR.
GRANDMOTHER, WHAT BIG TEETH YOU HAVE!
ALL THE BETTER...
TO EAT YOU WITH.

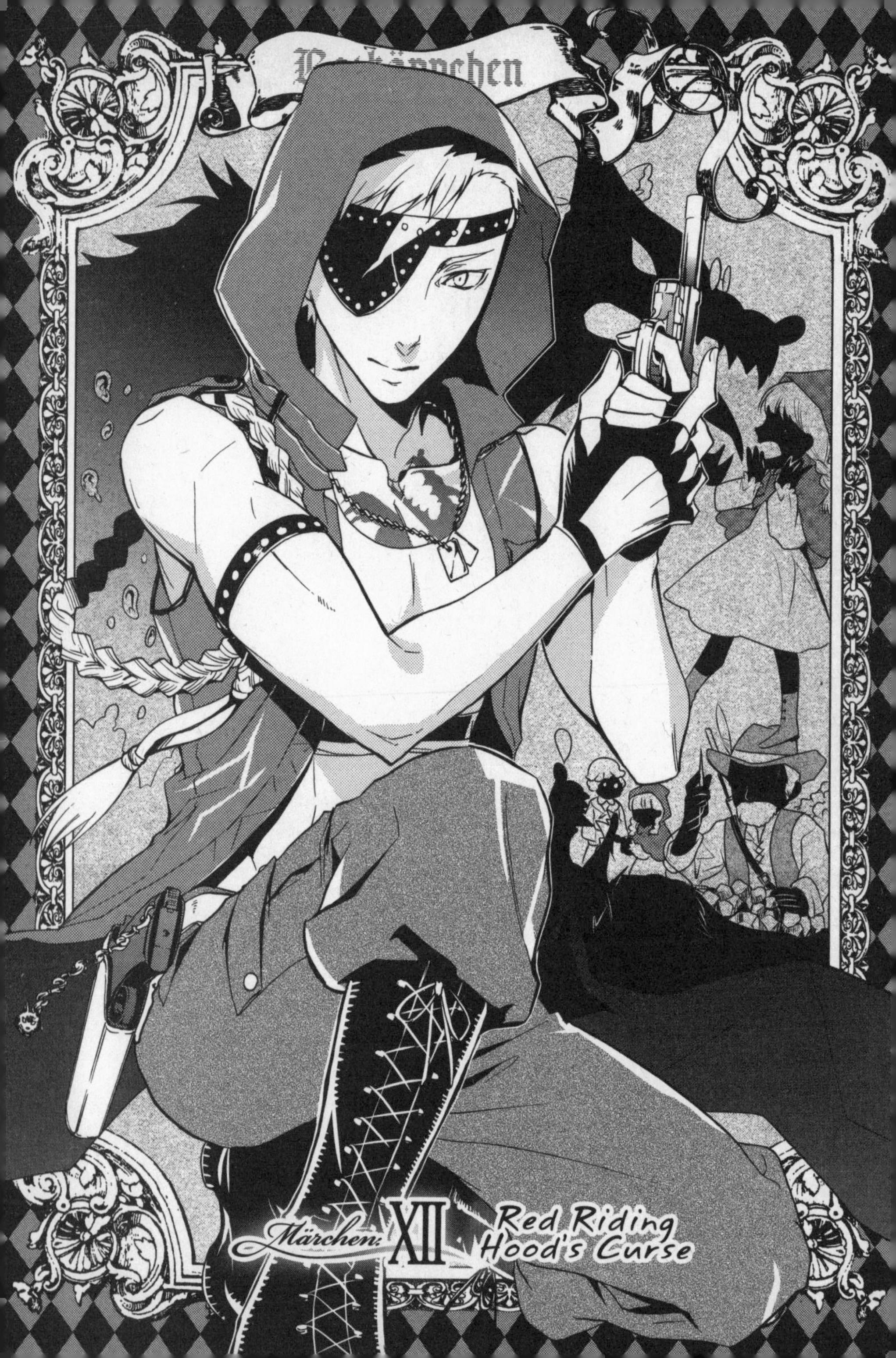
Märchen: XII
Red Riding Hood's Curse

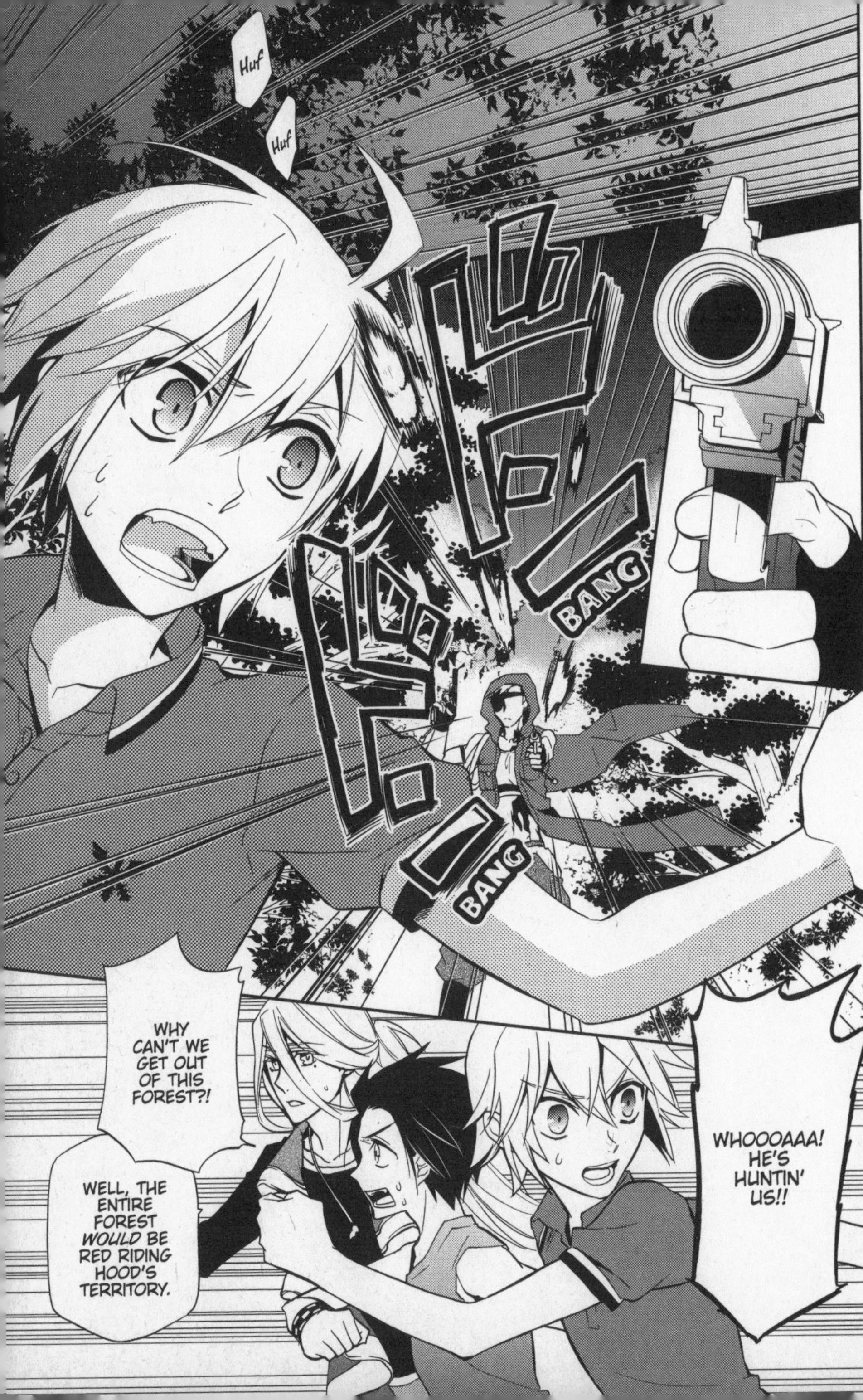
Huf
Huf
BANG
BANG
WHOOOAAA! HE'S HUNTIN' US!!
WHY CAN'T WE GET OUT OF THIS FOREST?!
WELL, THE ENTIRE FOREST *WOULD* BE RED RIDING HOOD'S TERRITORY.

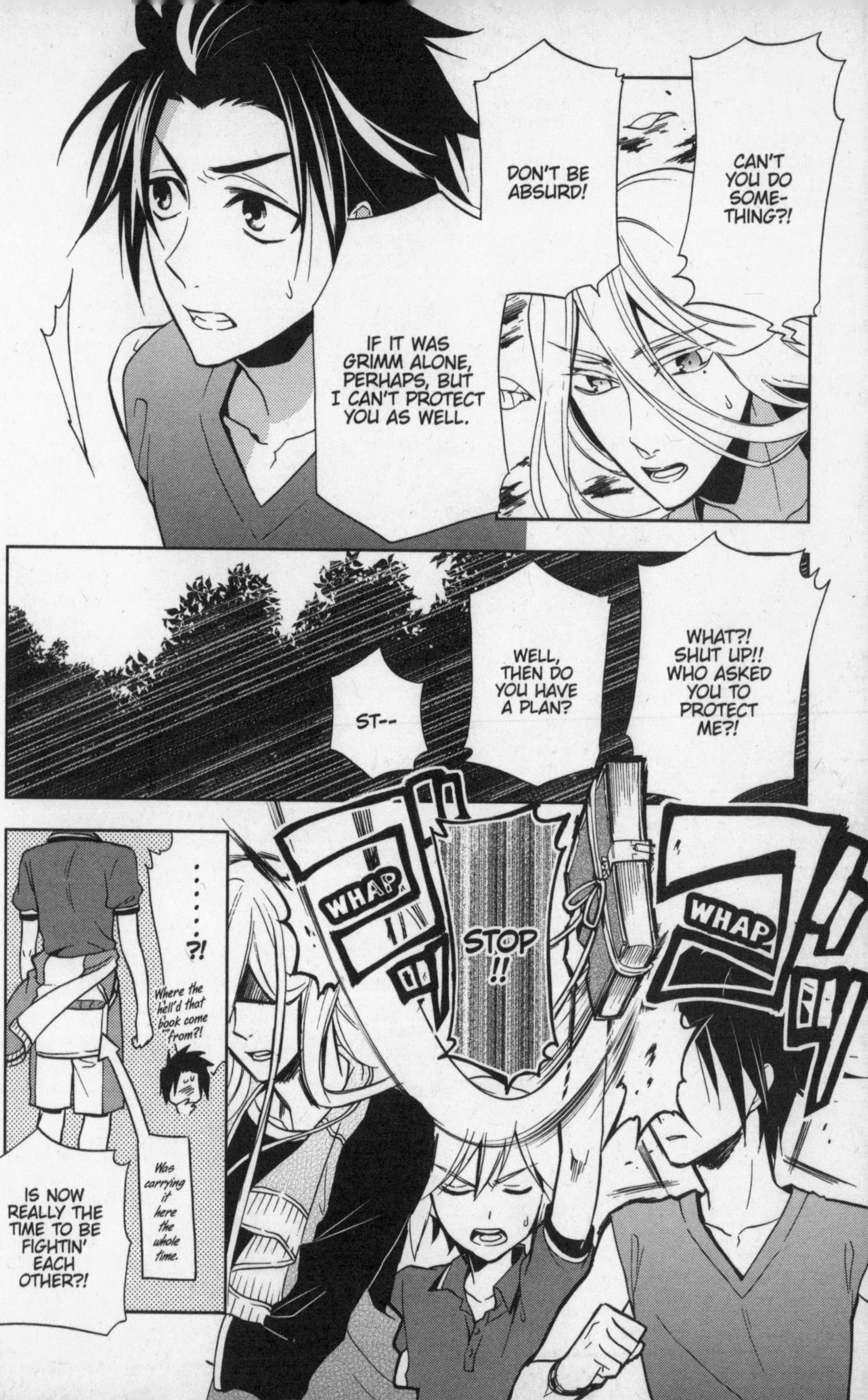

CAN'T YOU DO SOME-THING?!
DON'T BE ABSURD!
IF IT WAS GRIMM ALONE, PERHAPS, BUT I CAN'T PROTECT YOU AS WELL.
WHAT?! SHUT UP!! WHO ASKED YOU TO PROTECT ME?!
WELL, THEN DO YOU HAVE A PLAN?
ST--
WHAP
STOP!!
WHAP
......
?!
Where the hell'd that book come from?!
Was carrying it here the whole time.
IS NOW REALLY THE TIME TO BE FIGHTIN' EACH OTHER?!

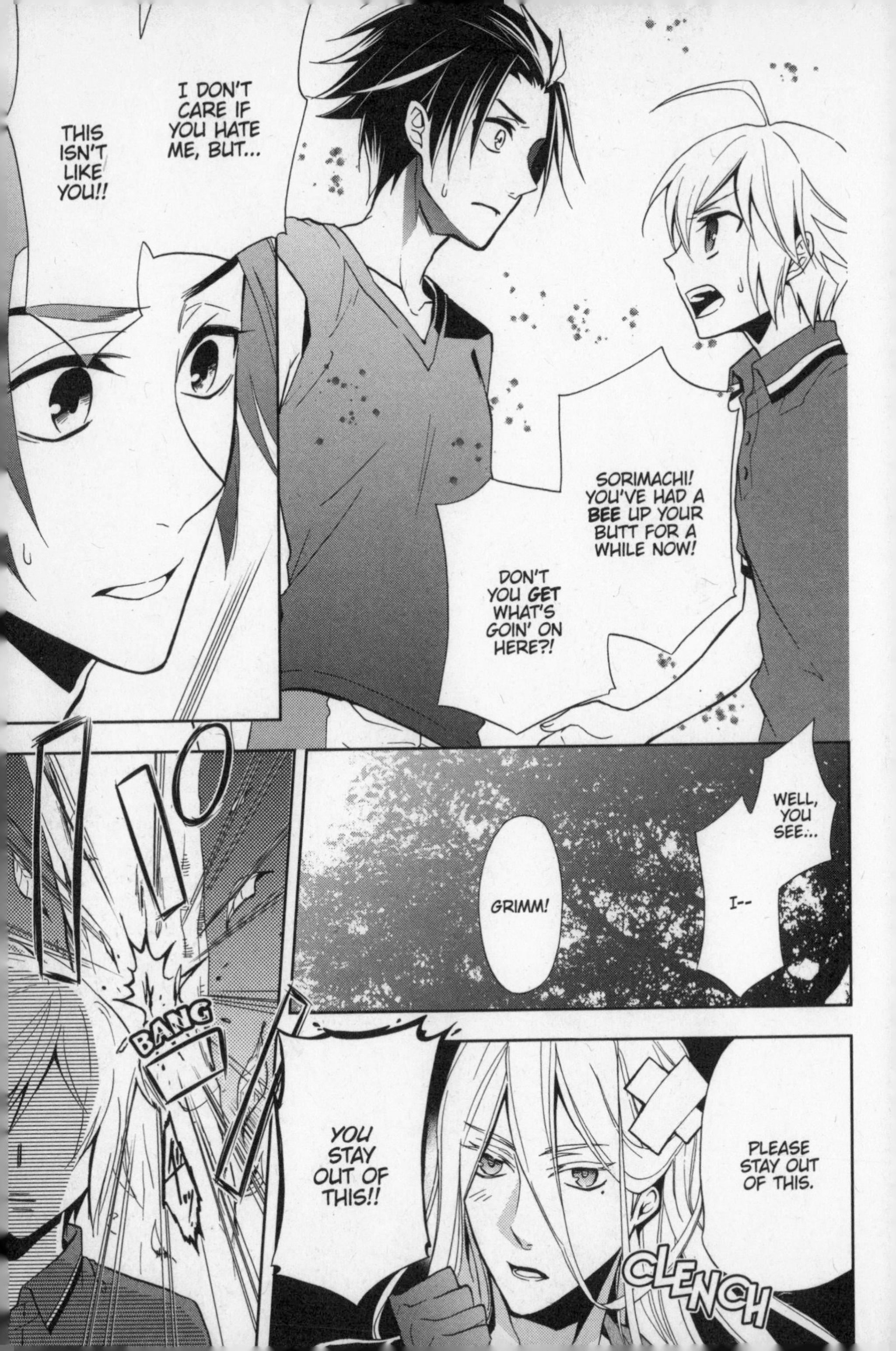
SORIMACHI! YOU'VE HAD A BEE UP YOUR BUTT FOR A WHILE NOW!
DON'T YOU GET WHAT'S GOIN' ON HERE?!
I DON'T CARE IF YOU HATE ME, BUT...
THIS ISN'T LIKE YOU!!
WELL, YOU SEE...
I--
GRIMM!
PLEASE STAY OUT OF THIS.
CLENCH
YOU STAY OUT OF THIS!!
BANG

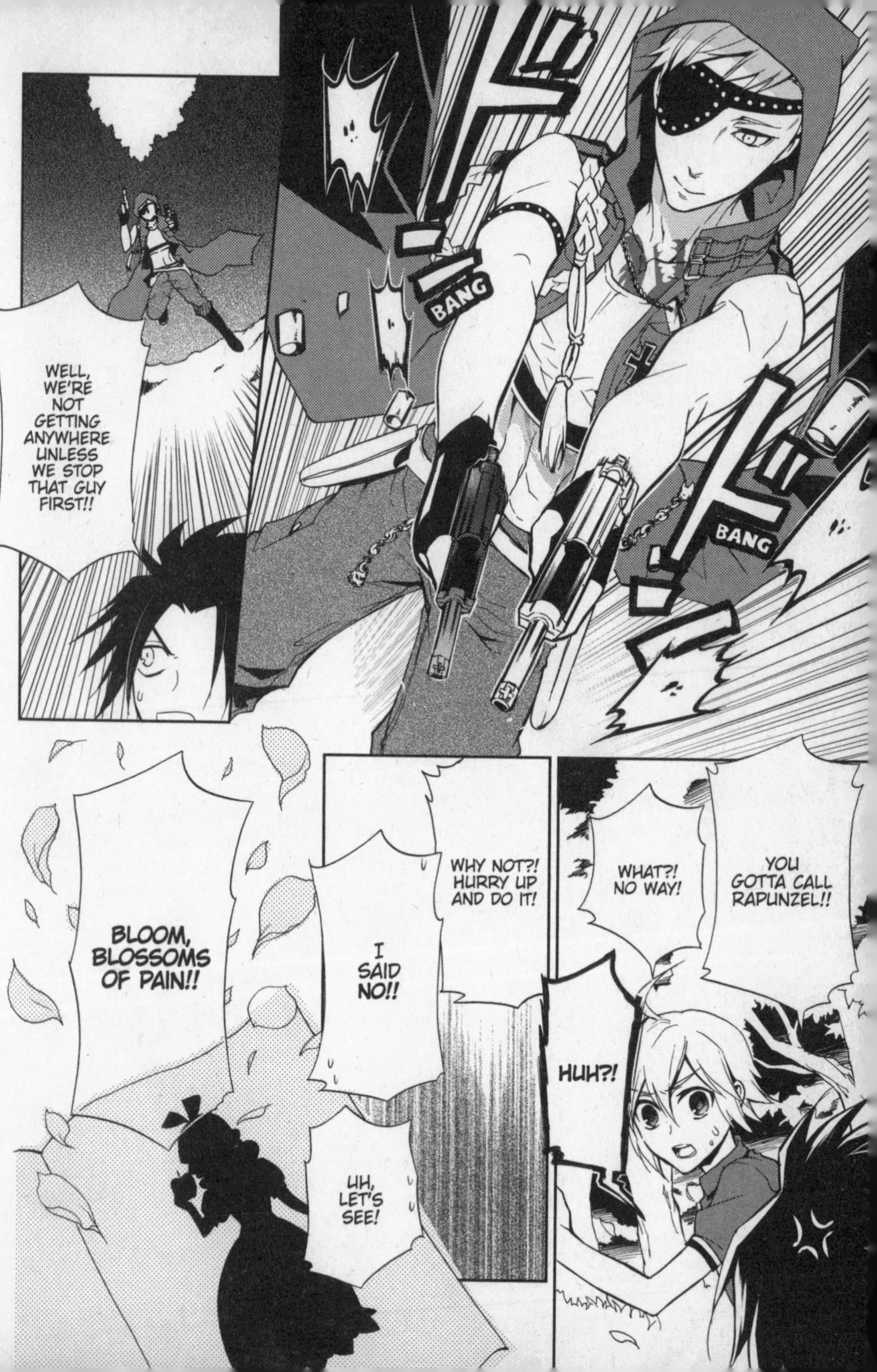
BANG
BANG
WELL, WE'RE NOT GETTING ANYWHERE UNLESS WE STOP THAT GUY FIRST!!
YOU GOTTA CALL RAPUNZEL!!
WHAT?! NO WAY!
HUH?!
WHY NOT?! HURRY UP AND DO IT!
I SAID NO!!
UH, LET'S SEE!
BLOOM, BLOSSOMS OF PAIN!!

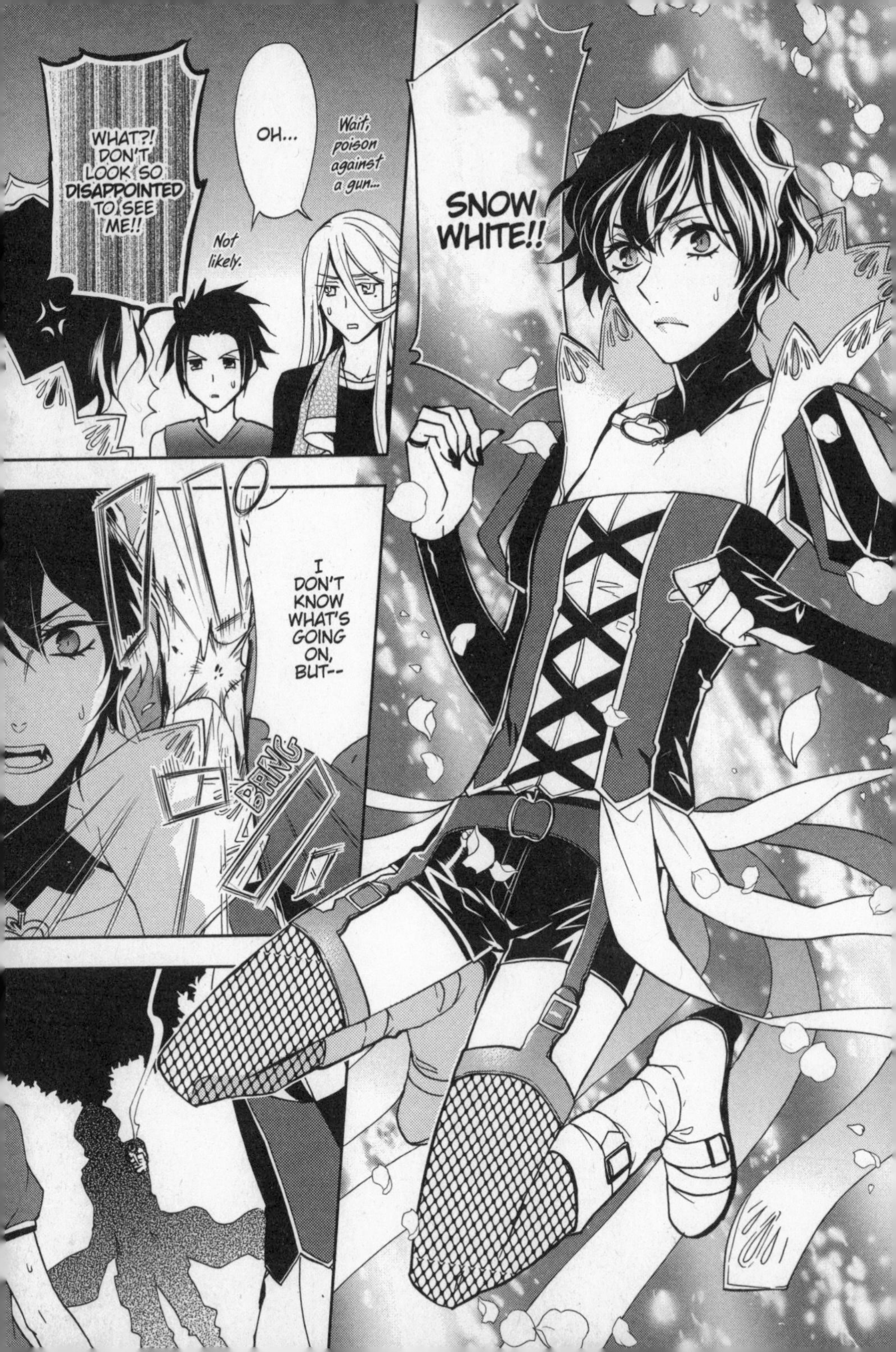
SNOW WHITE!!
Wait, poison against a gun...
OH...
Not likely.
WHAT?! DON'T LOOK SO DISAPPOINTED TO SEE ME!!
I DON'T KNOW WHAT'S GOING ON, BUT--
BANG

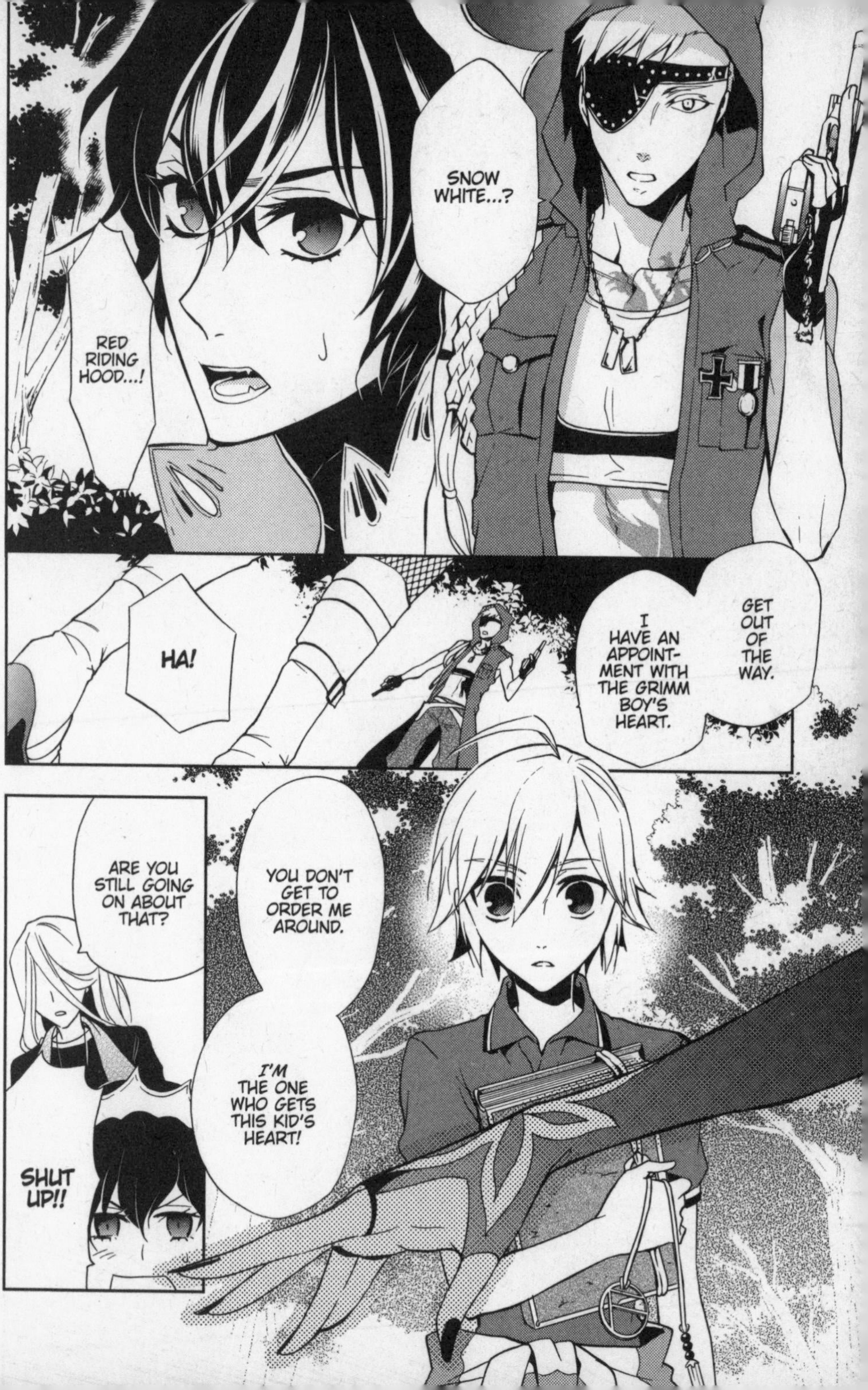
SNOW WHITE...?
RED RIDING HOOD...!
GET OUT OF THE WAY.
I HAVE AN APPOINTMENT WITH THE GRIMM BOY'S HEART.
HA!
YOU DON'T GET TO ORDER ME AROUND.
I'M THE ONE WHO GETS THIS KID'S HEART!
ARE YOU STILL GOING ON ABOUT THAT?
SHUT UP!!

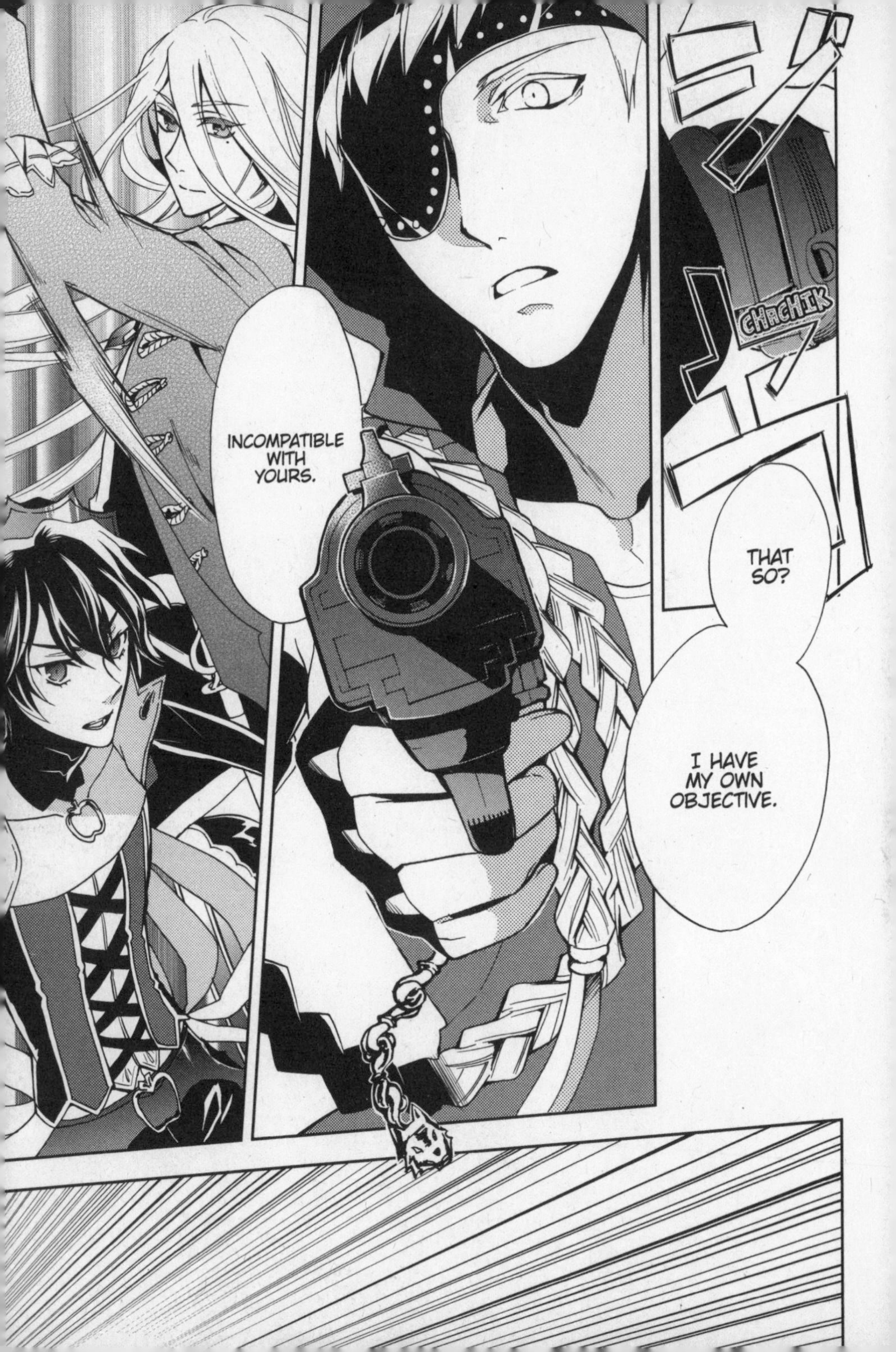
CHACHIK
THAT SO?
I HAVE MY OWN OBJECTIVE.
INCOMPATIBLE WITH YOURS.

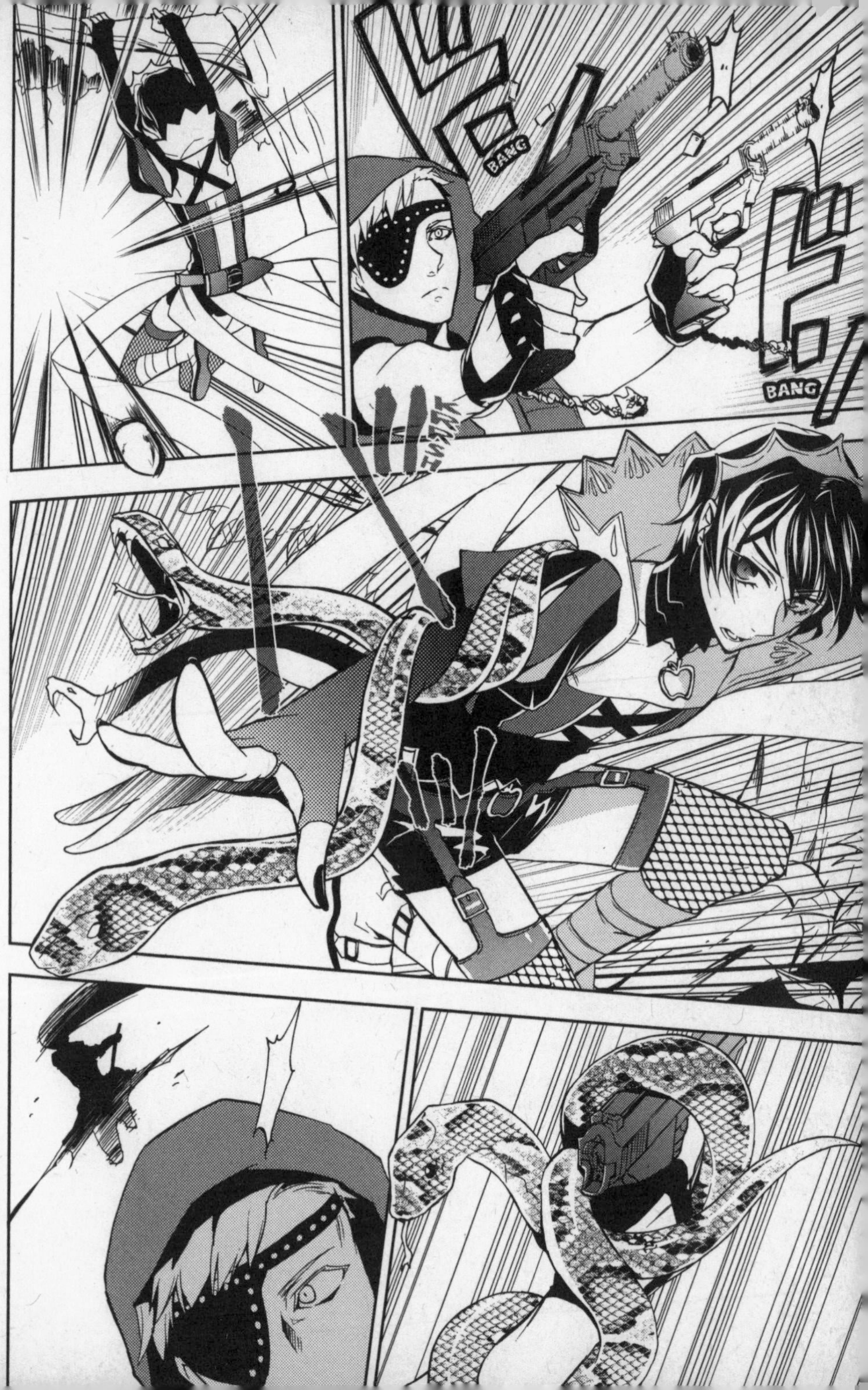
BANG
BANG

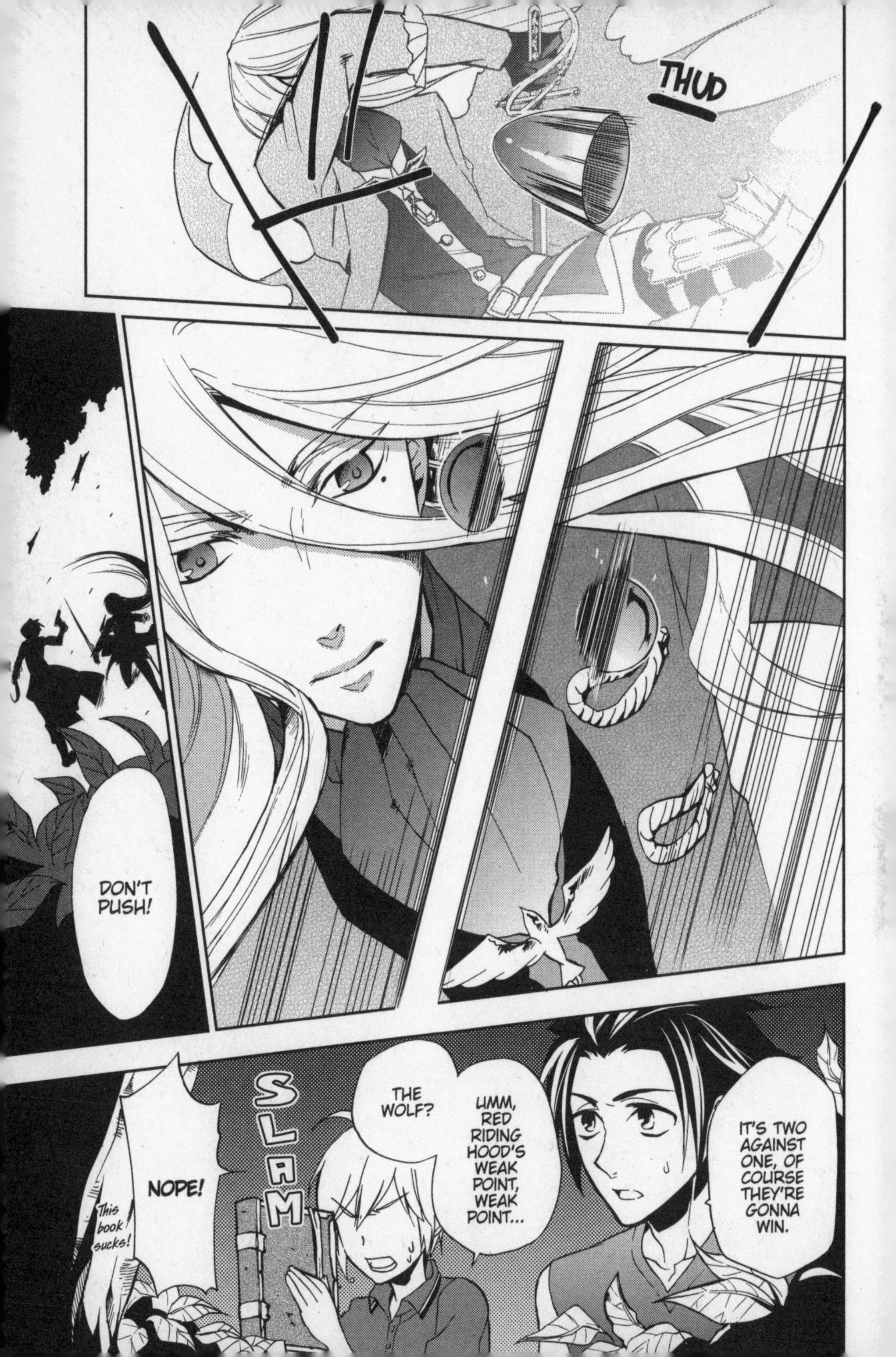
THUD
DON'T PUSH!
IT'S TWO AGAINST ONE, OF COURSE THEY'RE GONNA WIN.
UMM, RED RIDING HOOD'S WEAK POINT, WEAK POINT...
THE WOLF?
SLAM
NOPE!
This book sucks!

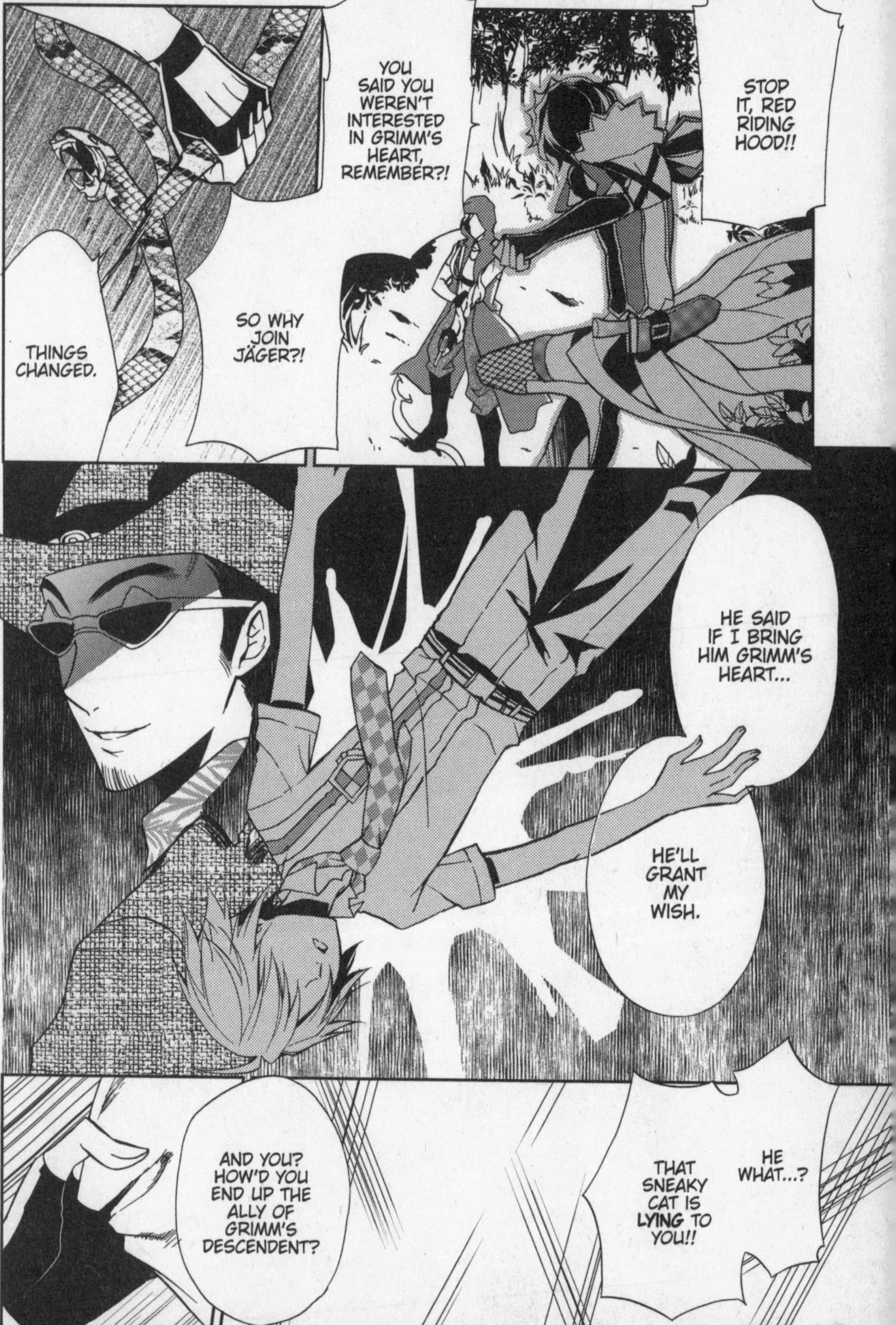
STOP IT, RED RIDING HOOD!!
YOU SAID YOU WEREN'T INTERESTED IN GRIMM'S HEART, REMEMBER?!
SO WHY JOIN JÄGER?!
THINGS CHANGED.
HE SAID IF I BRING HIM GRIMM'S HEART...
HE'LL GRANT MY WISH.
HE WHAT...?
THAT SNEAKY CAT IS **LYING** TO YOU!!
AND YOU? HOW'D YOU END UP THE ALLY OF GRIMM'S DESCENDENT?

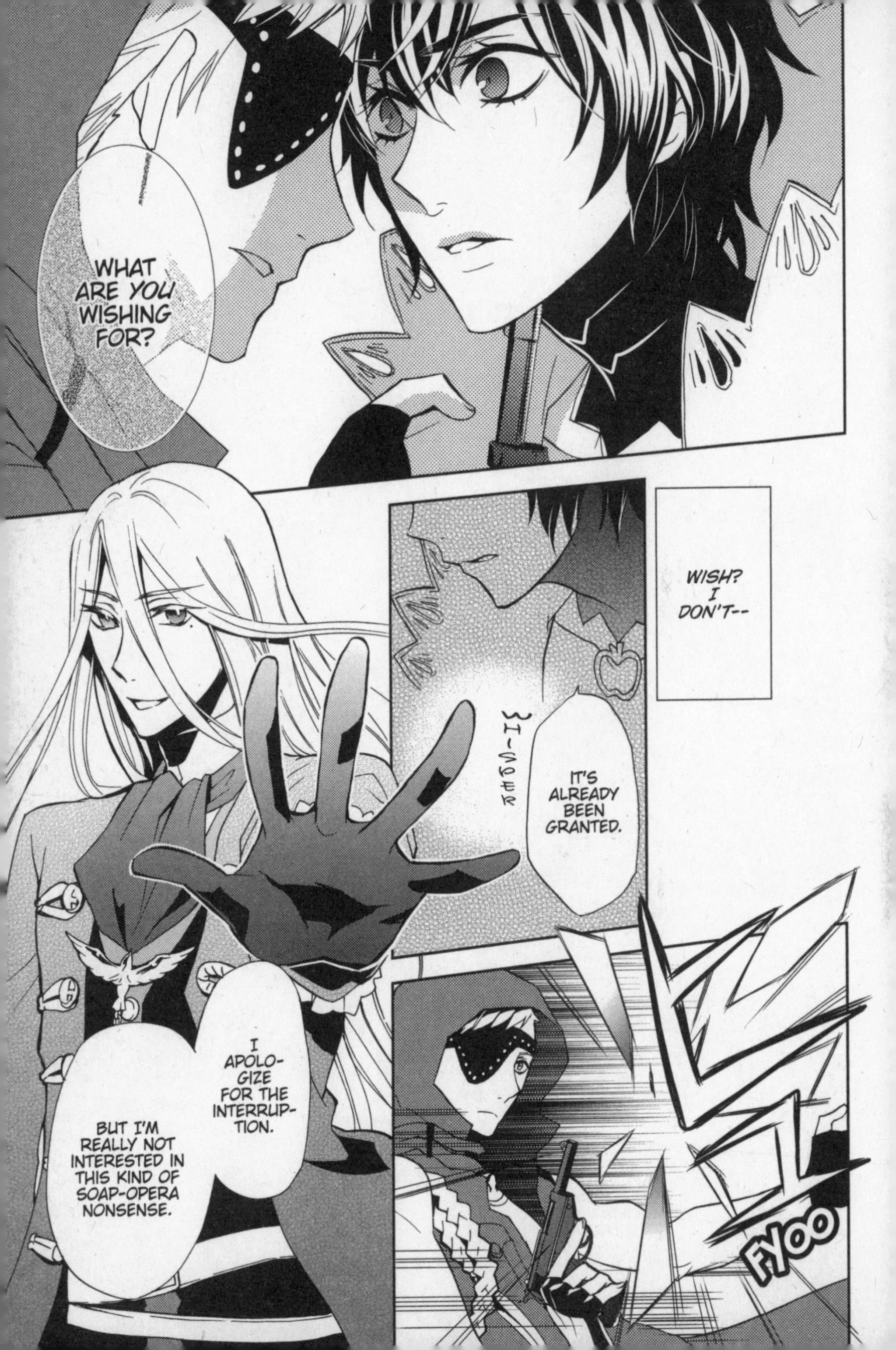
WHAT ARE YOU WISHING FOR?
WISH? I DON'T--
WHISPER
IT'S ALREADY BEEN GRANTED.
FYOO
I APOLOGIZE FOR THE INTERRUPTION.
BUT I'M REALLY NOT INTERESTED IN THIS KIND OF SOAP-OPERA NONSENSE.

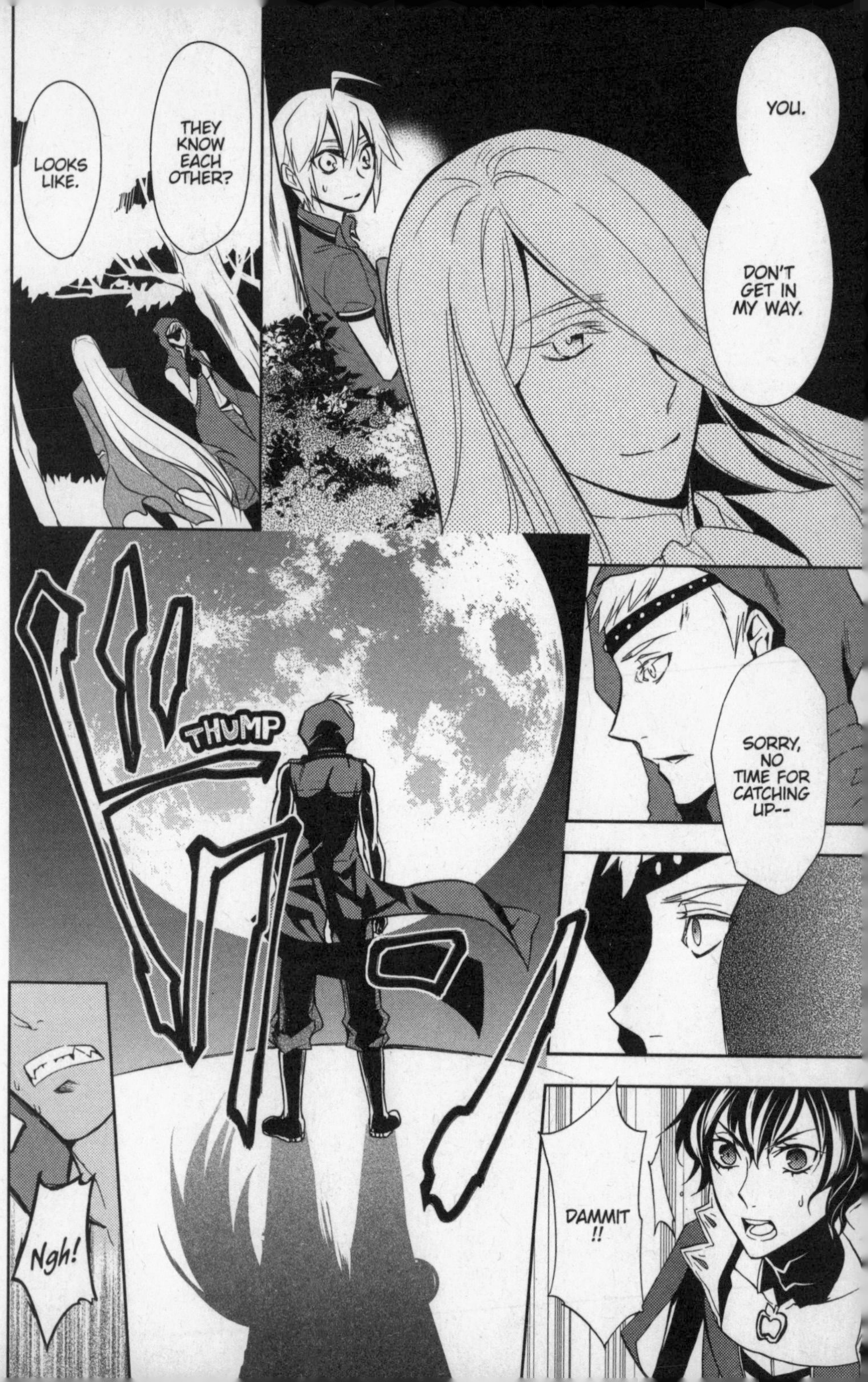
YOU.
DON'T GET IN MY WAY.
THEY KNOW EACH OTHER?
LOOKS LIKE.
SORRY, NO TIME FOR CATCHING UP--
THUMP
DAMMIT !!
Ngh!

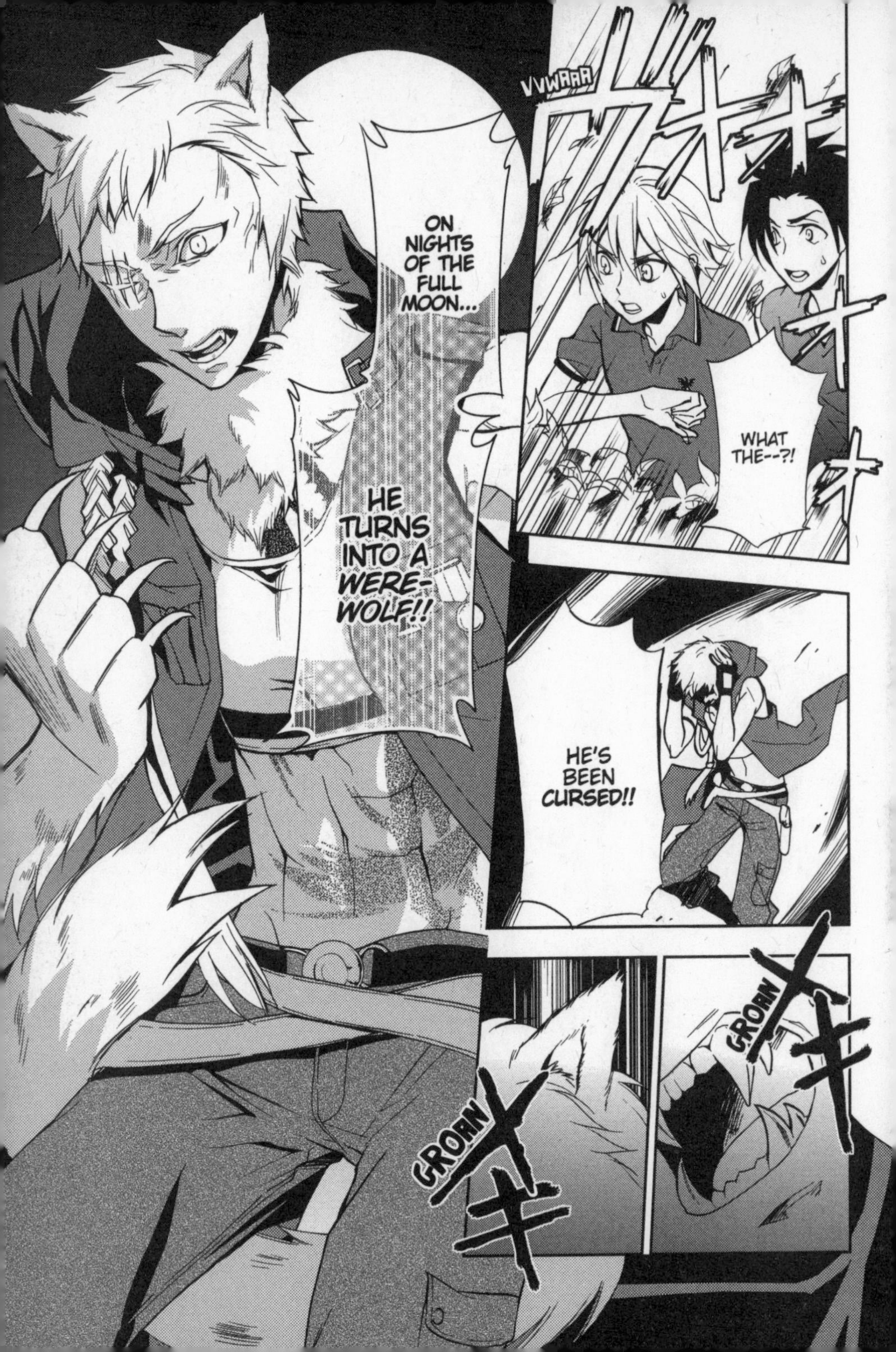
VVWAAA
WHAT THE--?!
HE'S BEEN CURSED!!
GROAN
GROAN
ON NIGHTS OF THE FULL MOON...
HE TURNS INTO A WERE-WOLF!!

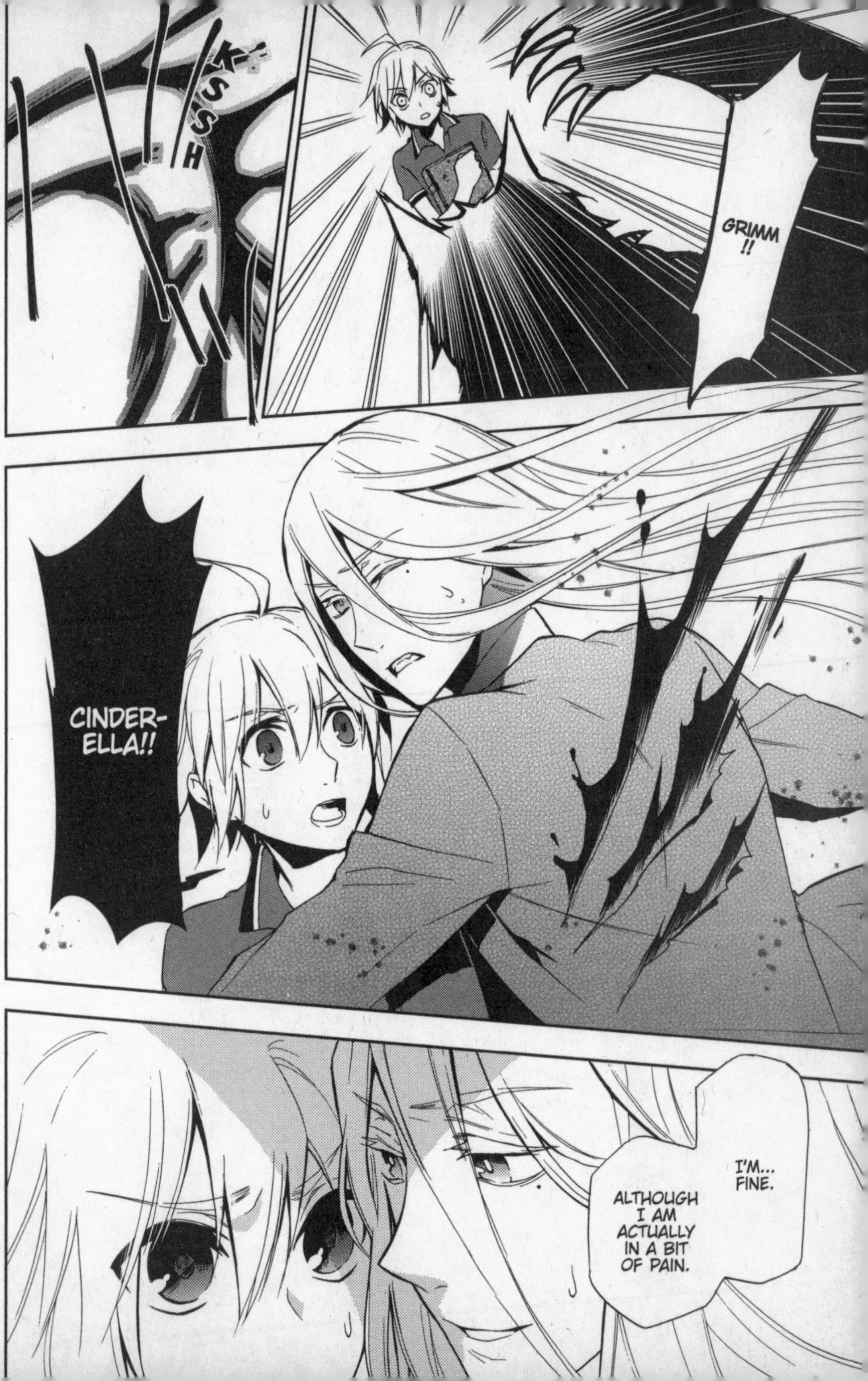
GRIMM!!
KSSH
CINDER-ELLA!!
I'M... FINE.
ALTHOUGH I AM ACTUALLY IN A BIT OF PAIN.

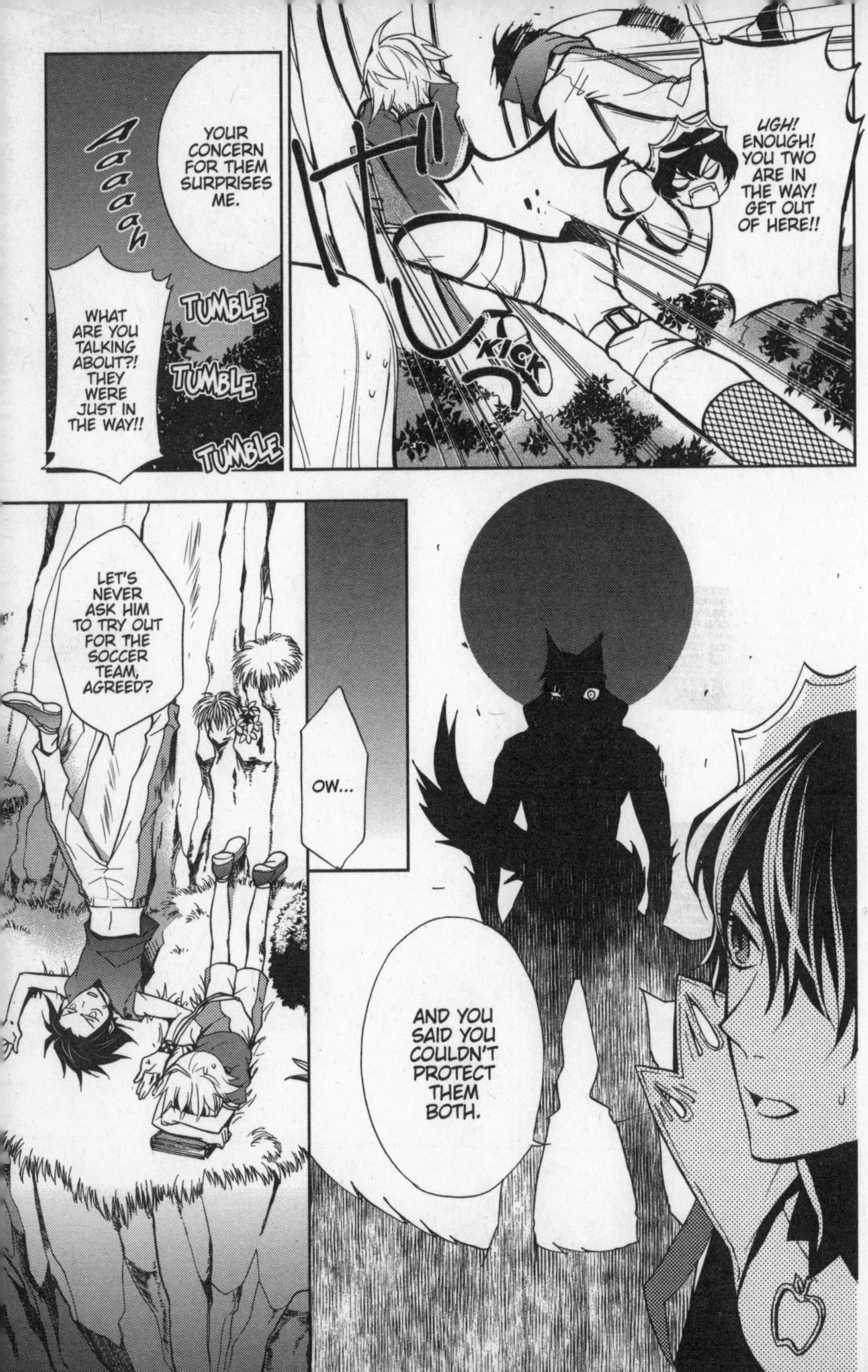
UGH! ENOUGH! YOU TWO ARE IN THE WAY! GET OUT OF HERE!!
KICK
YOUR CONCERN FOR THEM SURPRISES ME.
Aaaaaah
TUMBLE
TUMBLE
TUMBLE
WHAT ARE YOU TALKING ABOUT?! THEY WERE JUST IN THE WAY!!
AND YOU SAID YOU COULDN'T PROTECT THEM BOTH.
OW...
LET'S NEVER ASK HIM TO TRY OUT FOR THE SOCCER TEAM, AGREED?

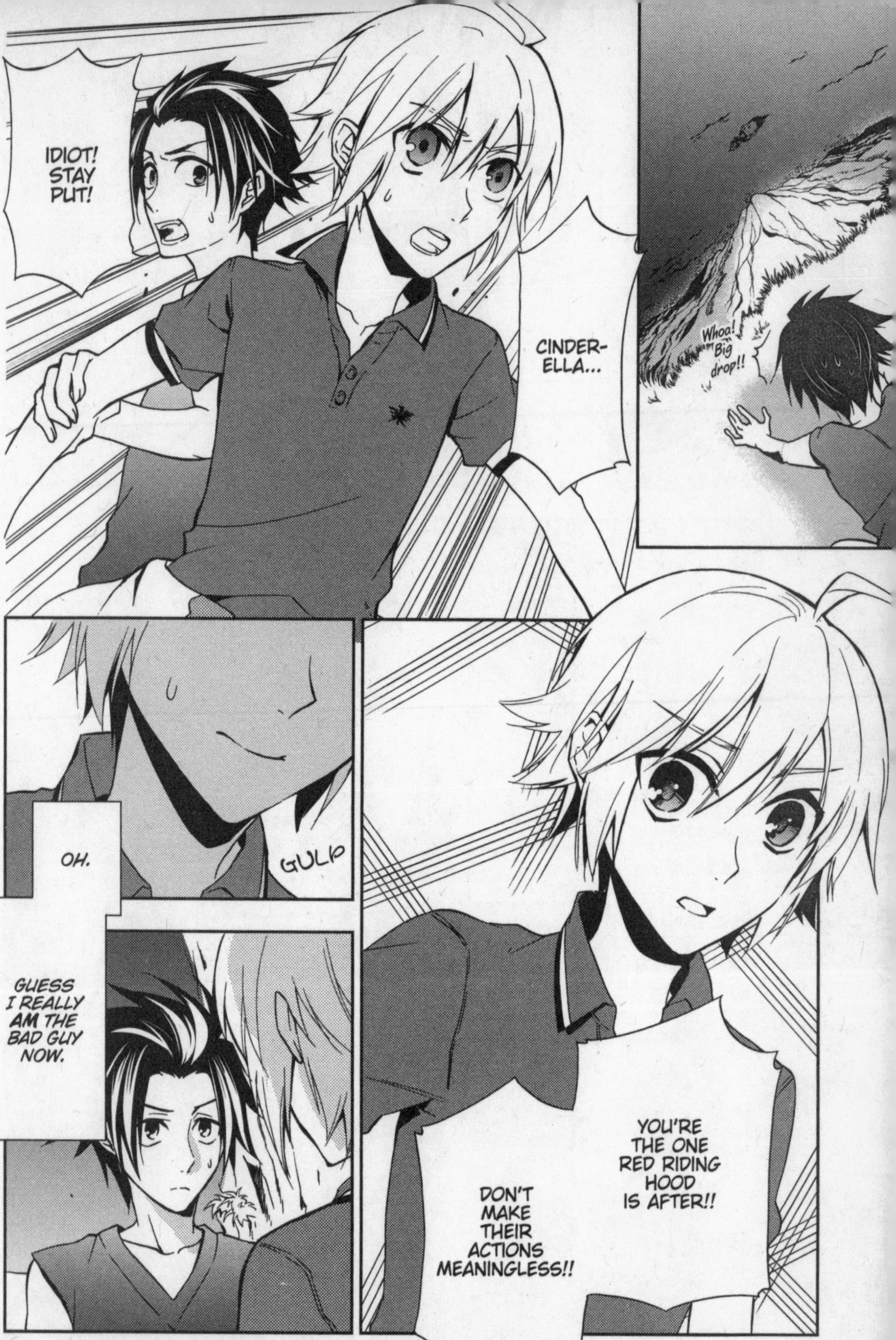
Whoa! Big drop!!
CINDER-ELLA...
IDIOT! STAY PUT!
YOU'RE THE ONE RED RIDING HOOD IS AFTER!!
DON'T MAKE THEIR ACTIONS MEANINGLESS!!
OH.
GULP
GUESS I REALLY **AM** THE BAD GUY NOW.

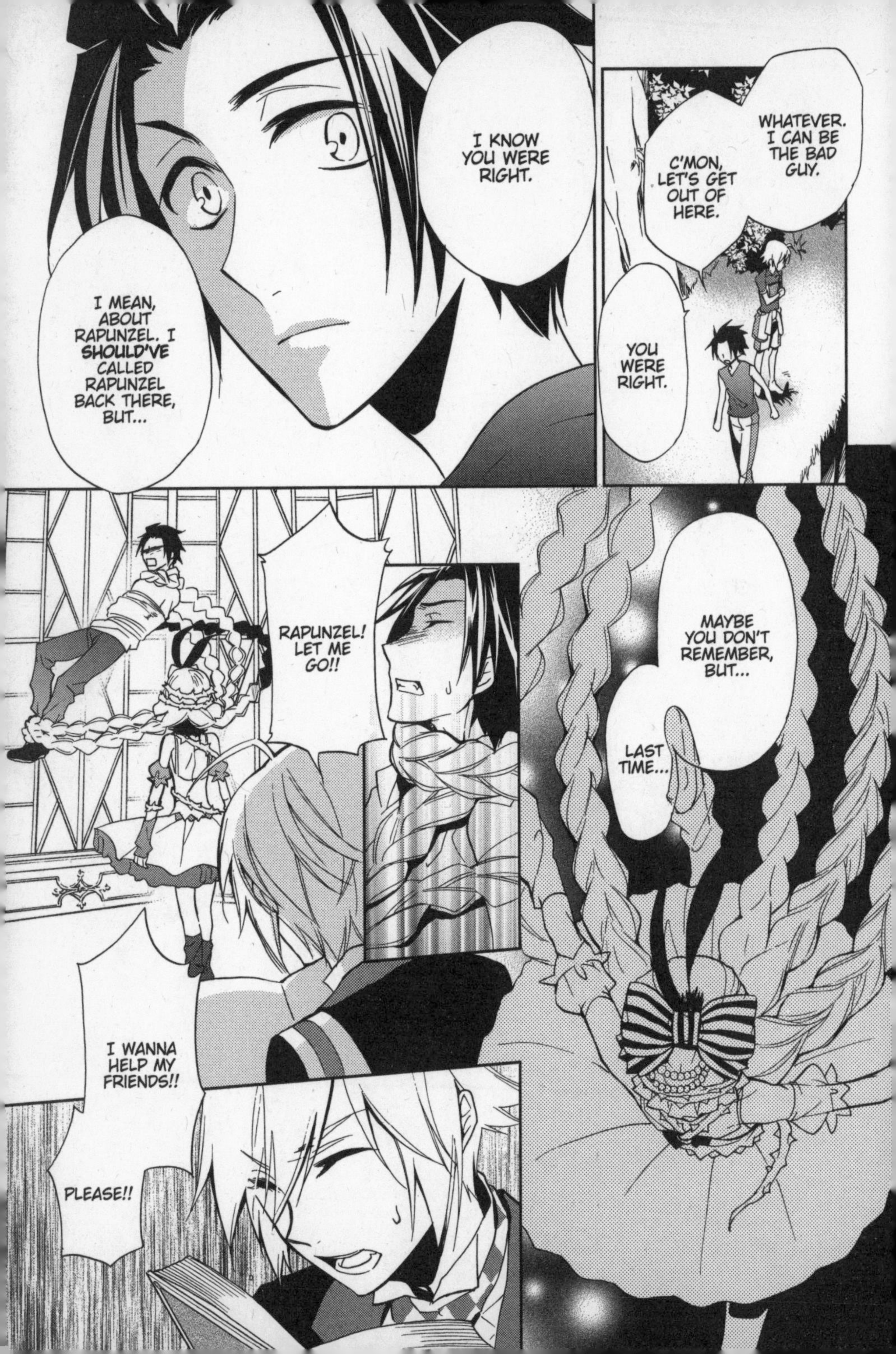
WHATEVER. I CAN BE THE BAD GUY.
C'MON, LET'S GET OUT OF HERE.
YOU WERE RIGHT.
I KNOW YOU WERE RIGHT.
I MEAN, ABOUT RAPUNZEL. I **SHOULD'VE** CALLED RAPUNZEL BACK THERE, BUT...
MAYBE YOU DON'T REMEMBER, BUT...
LAST TIME...
RAPUNZEL! LET ME GO!!
I WANNA HELP MY FRIENDS!!
PLEASE!!

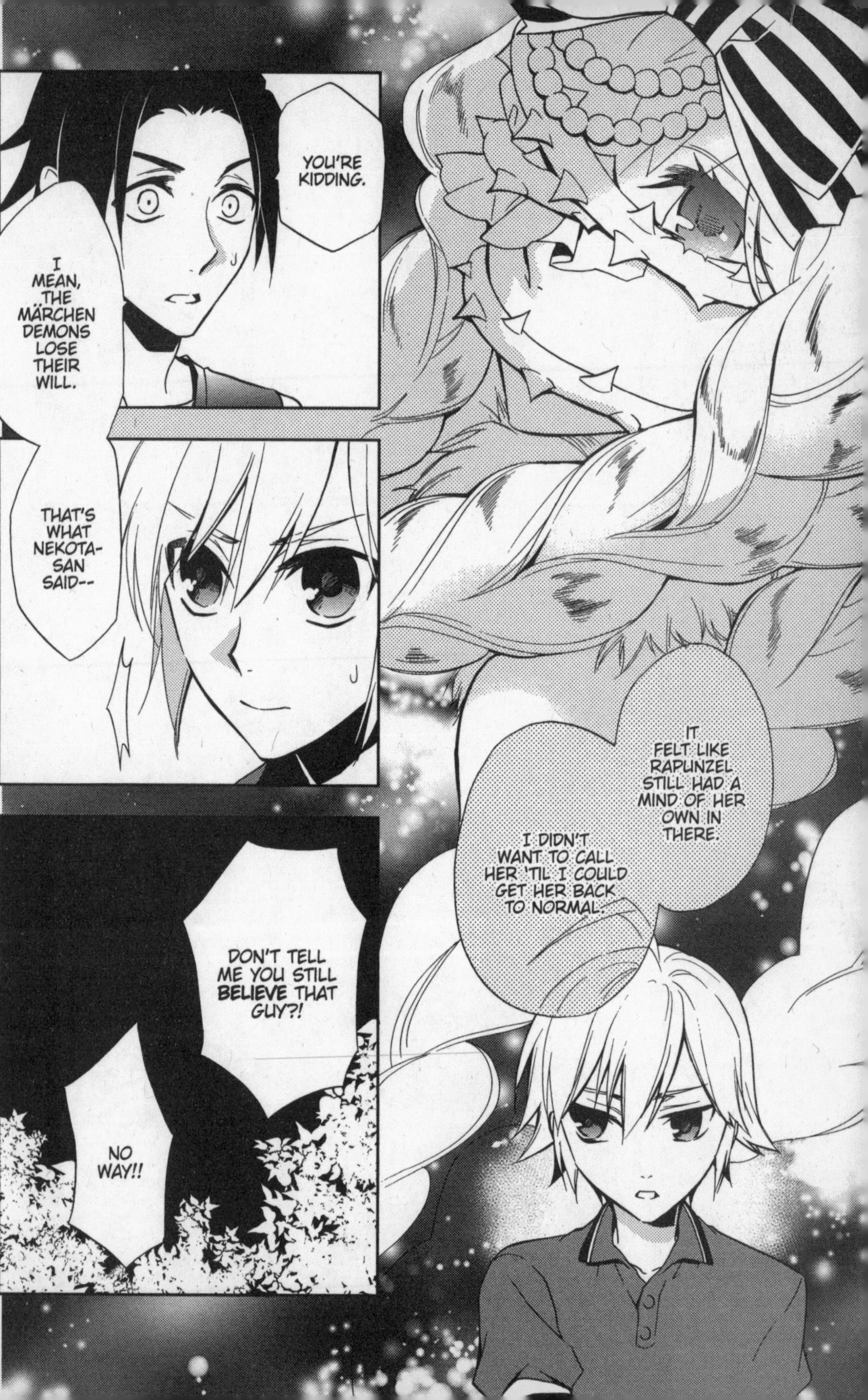
IT FELT LIKE RAPUNZEL STILL HAD A MIND OF HER OWN IN THERE.
I DIDN'T WANT TO CALL HER 'TIL I COULD GET HER BACK TO NORMAL.
YOU'RE KIDDING.
I MEAN, THE MÄRCHEN DEMONS LOSE THEIR WILL.
THAT'S WHAT NEKOTA-SAN SAID--
DON'T TELL ME YOU STILL BELIEVE THAT GUY?!
NO WAY!!

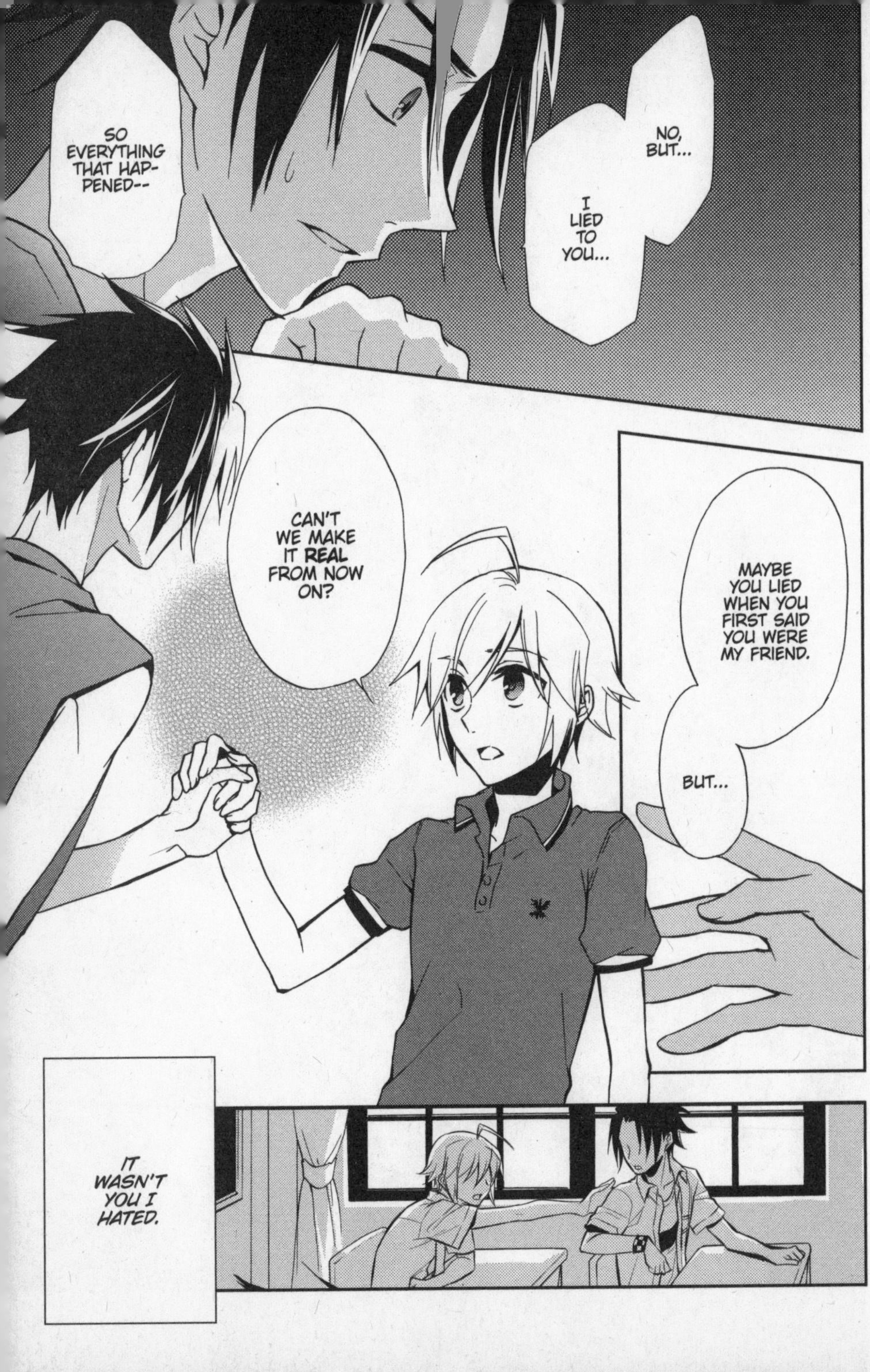
NO, BUT...
I LIED TO YOU...
SO EVERYTHING THAT HAP-PENED--
MAYBE YOU LIED WHEN YOU FIRST SAID YOU WERE MY FRIEND.
BUT...
CAN'T WE MAKE IT REAL FROM NOW ON?
IT WASN'T YOU I HATED.

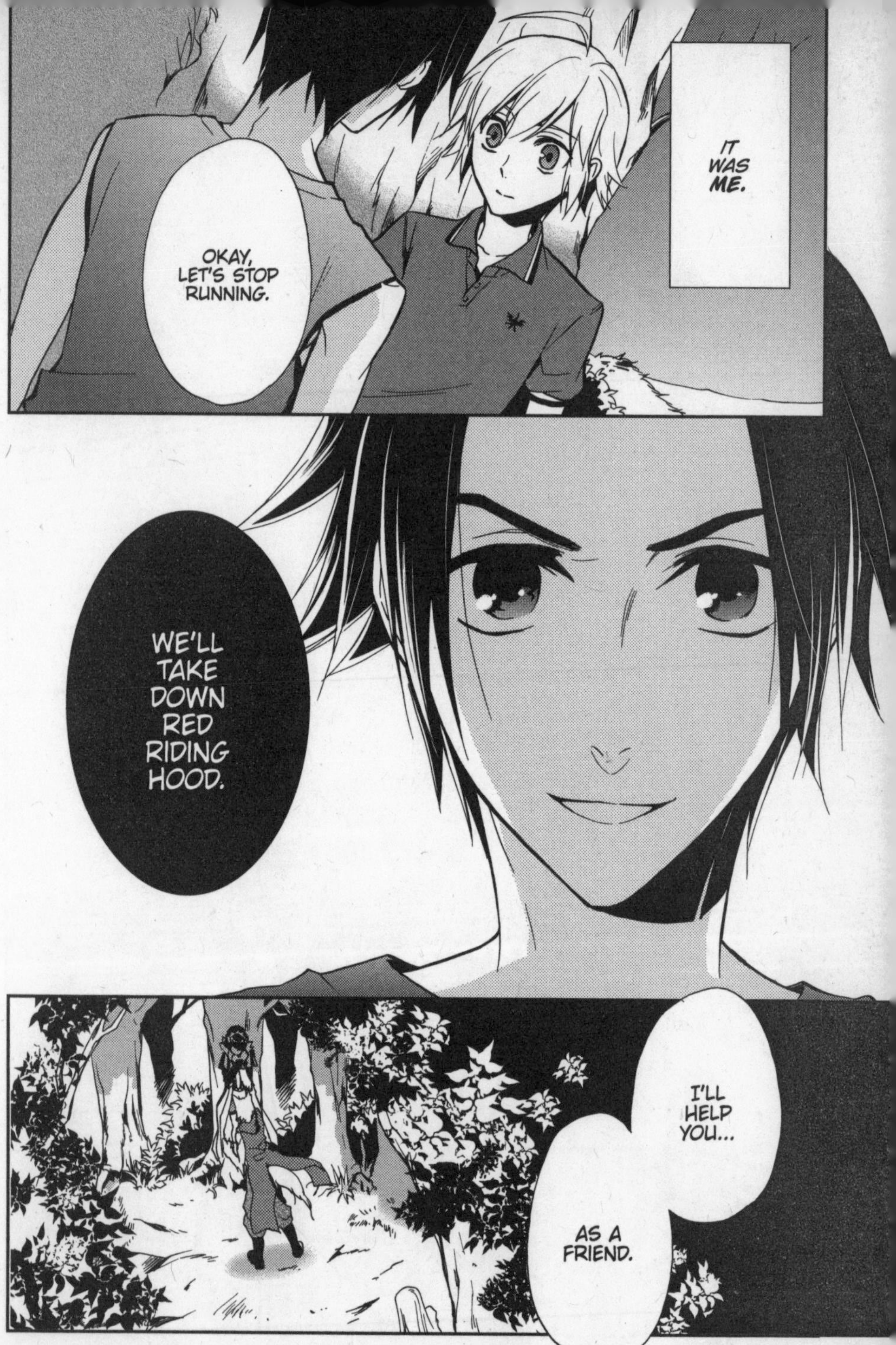
IT WAS ME.
OKAY, LET'S STOP RUNNING.
WE'LL TAKE DOWN RED RIDING HOOD.
I'LL HELP YOU...
AS A FRIEND.

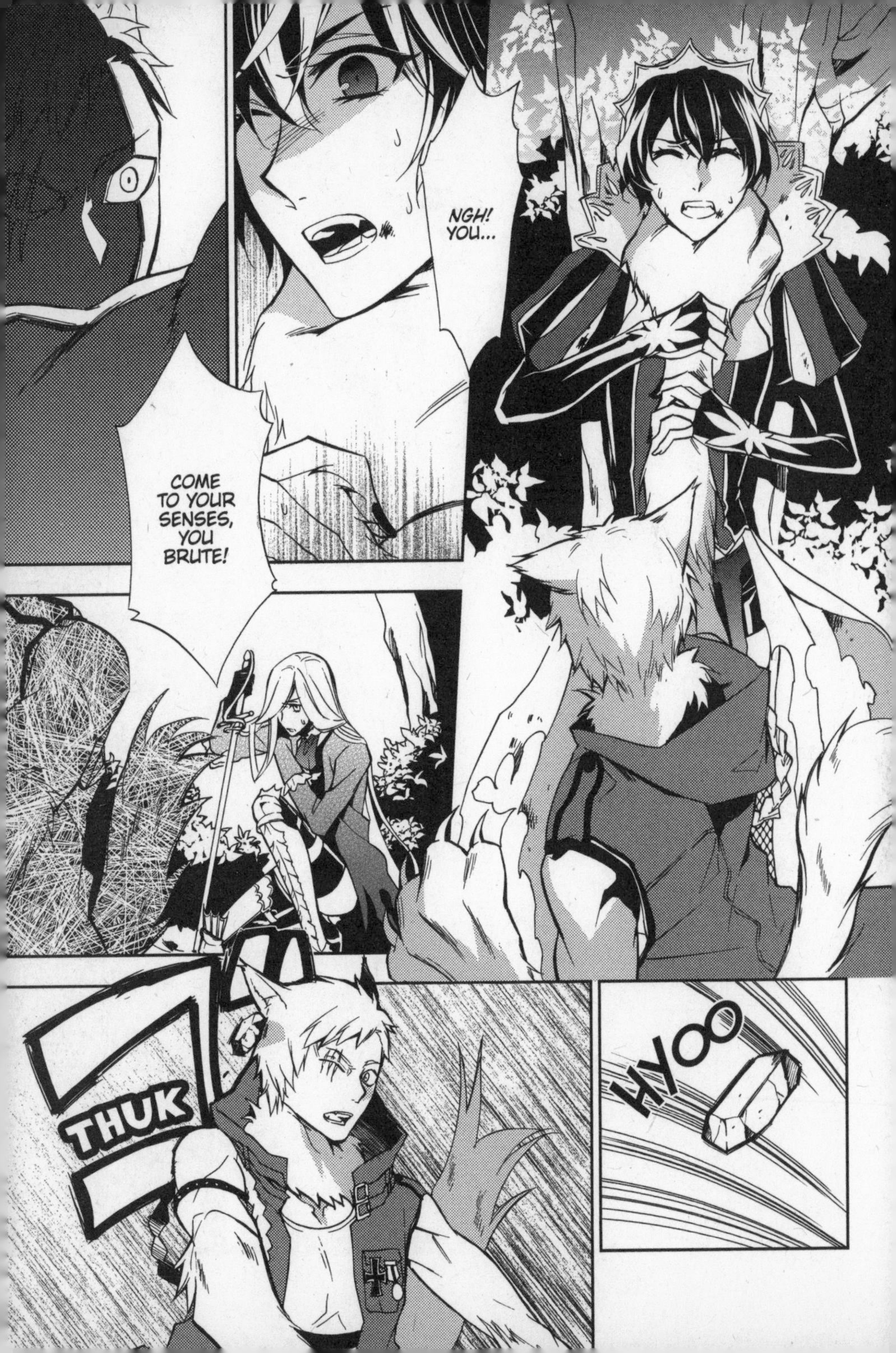
NGH! YOU...
COME TO YOUR SENSES, YOU BRUTE!
HYOO
THUK

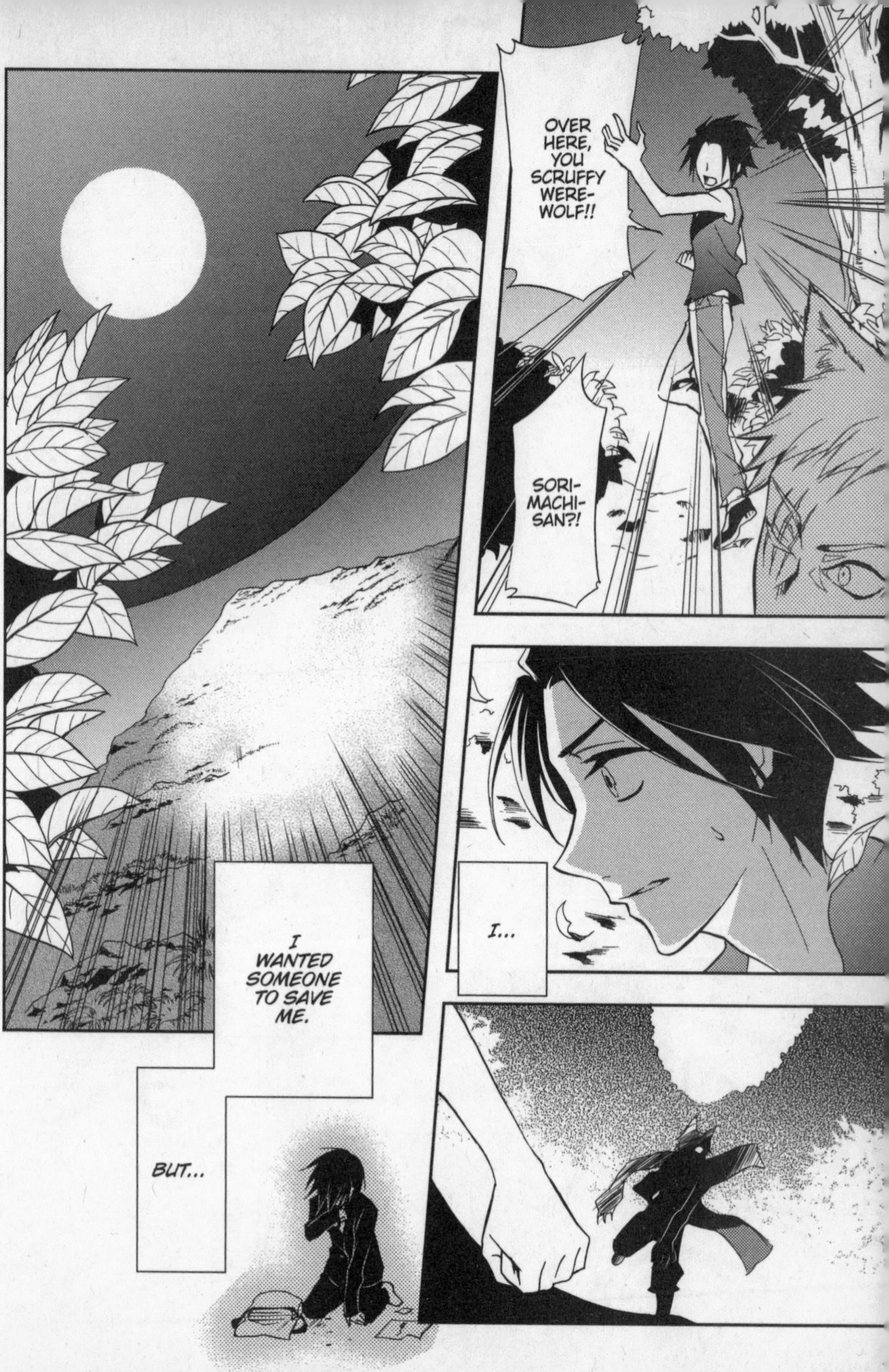
OVER HERE, YOU SCRUFFY WERE-WOLF!!
SORI-MACHI-SAN?!
I...
I WANTED SOMEONE TO SAVE ME.
BUT...

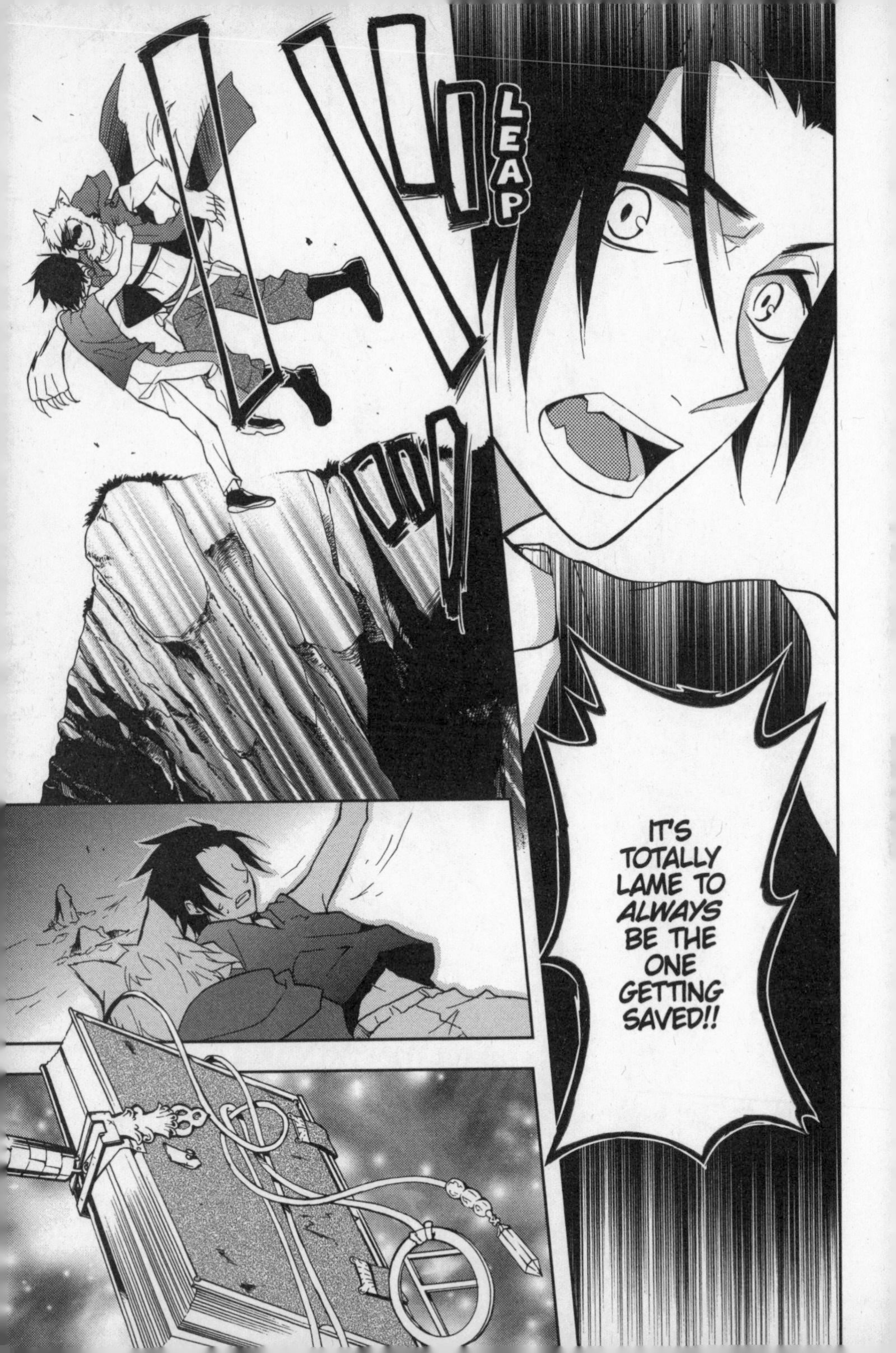
LEAP
IT'S TOTALLY LAME TO ALWAYS BE THE ONE GETTING SAVED!!

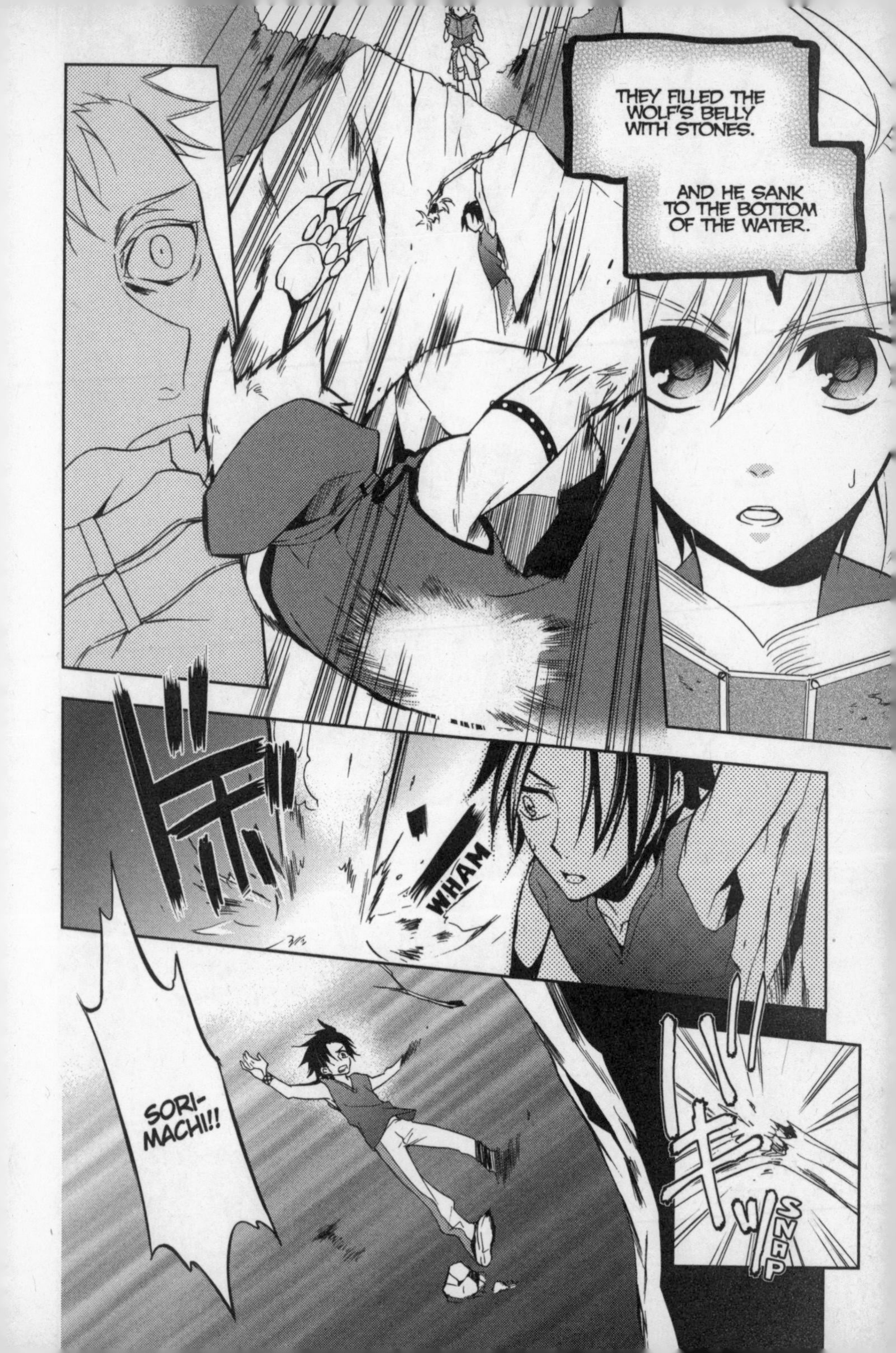
THEY FILLED THE WOLF'S BELLY WITH STONES.
AND HE SANK TO THE BOTTOM OF THE WATER.
WHAM
SNAP
SORI-MACHI!!

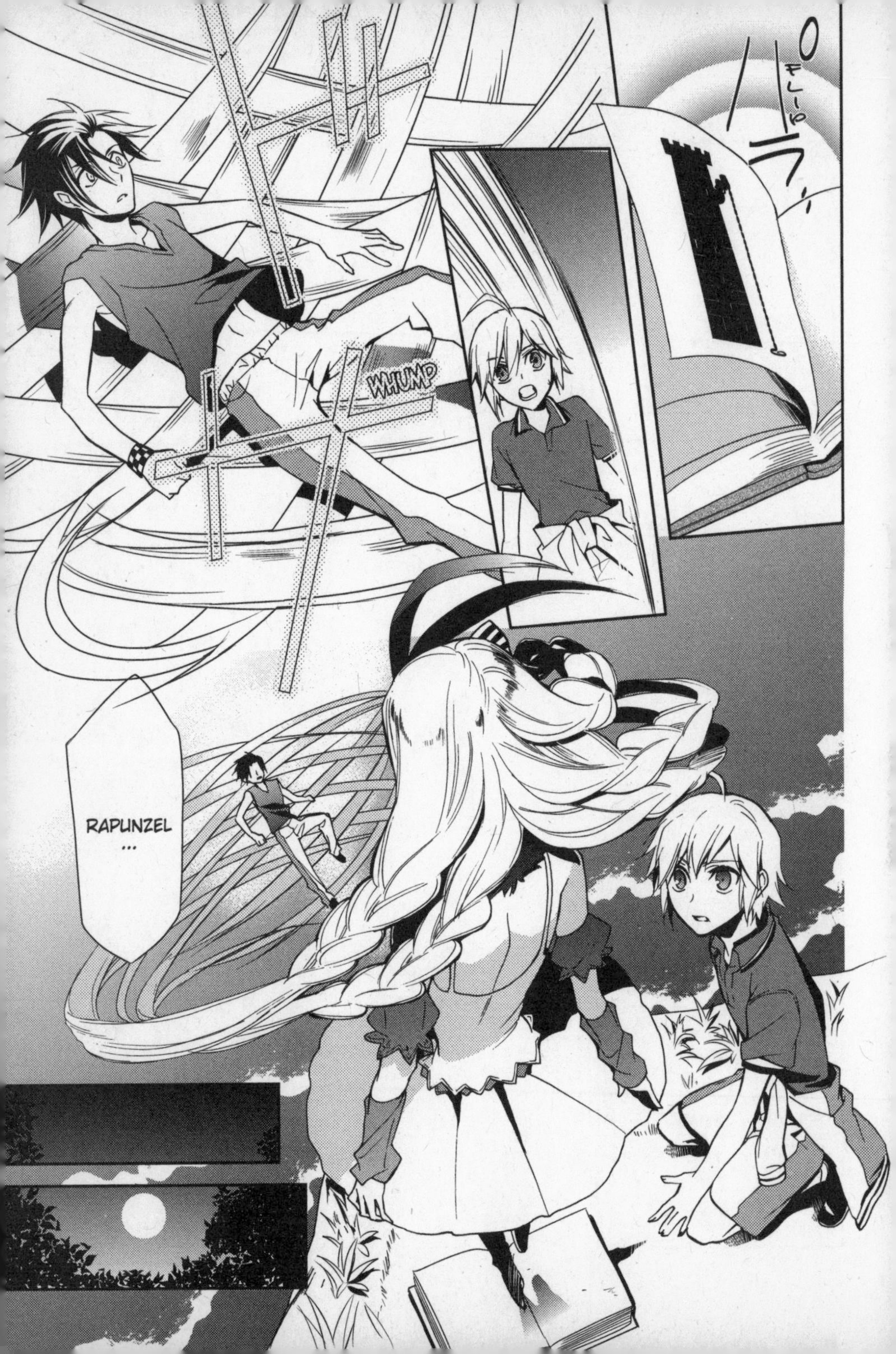
FLIP
WHUMP
RAPUNZEL
...

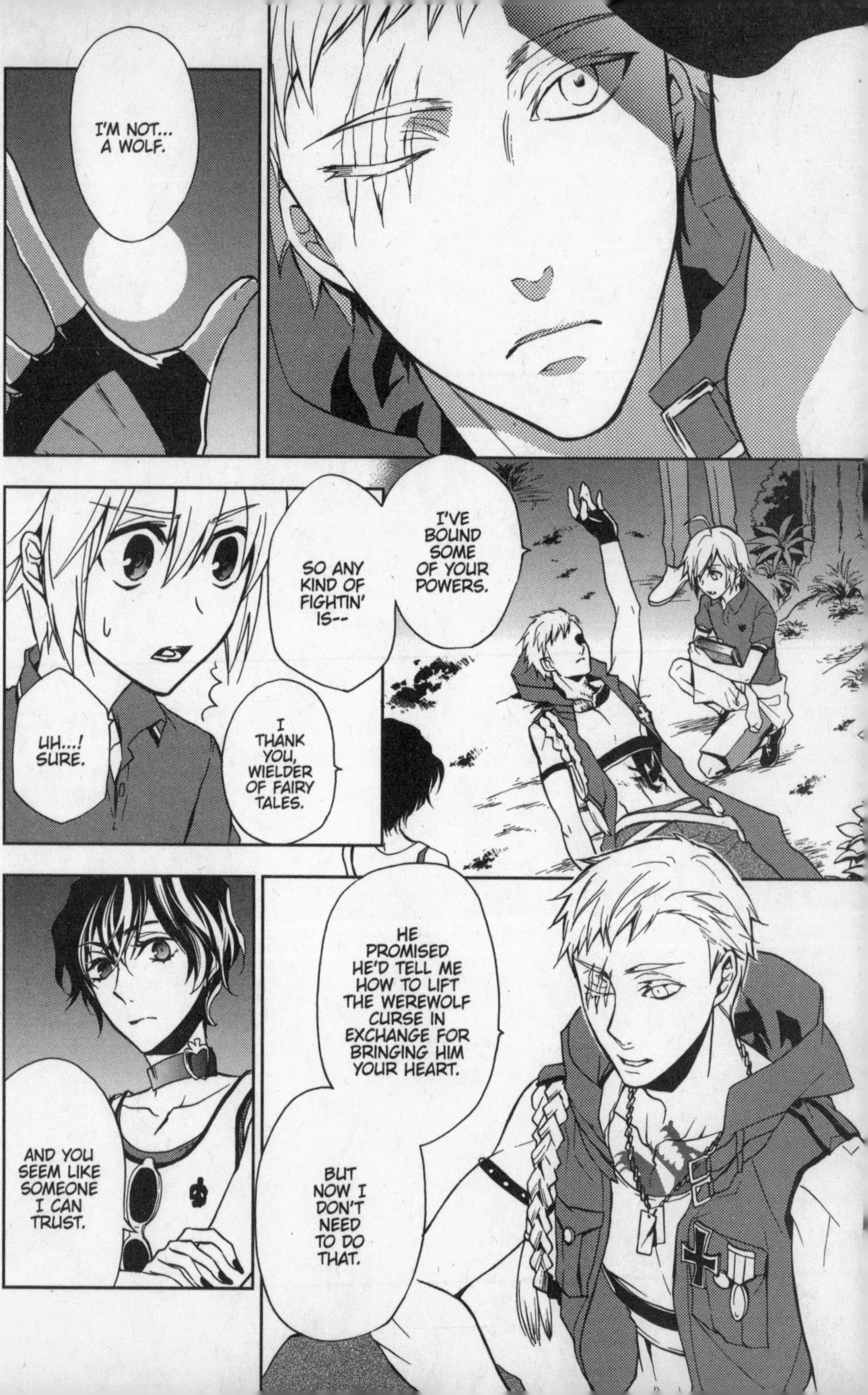
I'M NOT... A WOLF.
I'VE BOUND SOME OF YOUR POWERS.
SO ANY KIND OF FIGHTIN' IS--
I THANK YOU, WIELDER OF FAIRY TALES.
UH...! SURE.
HE PROMISED HE'D TELL ME HOW TO LIFT THE WEREWOLF CURSE IN EXCHANGE FOR BRINGING HIM YOUR HEART.
BUT NOW I DON'T NEED TO DO THAT.
AND YOU SEEM LIKE SOMEONE I CAN TRUST.

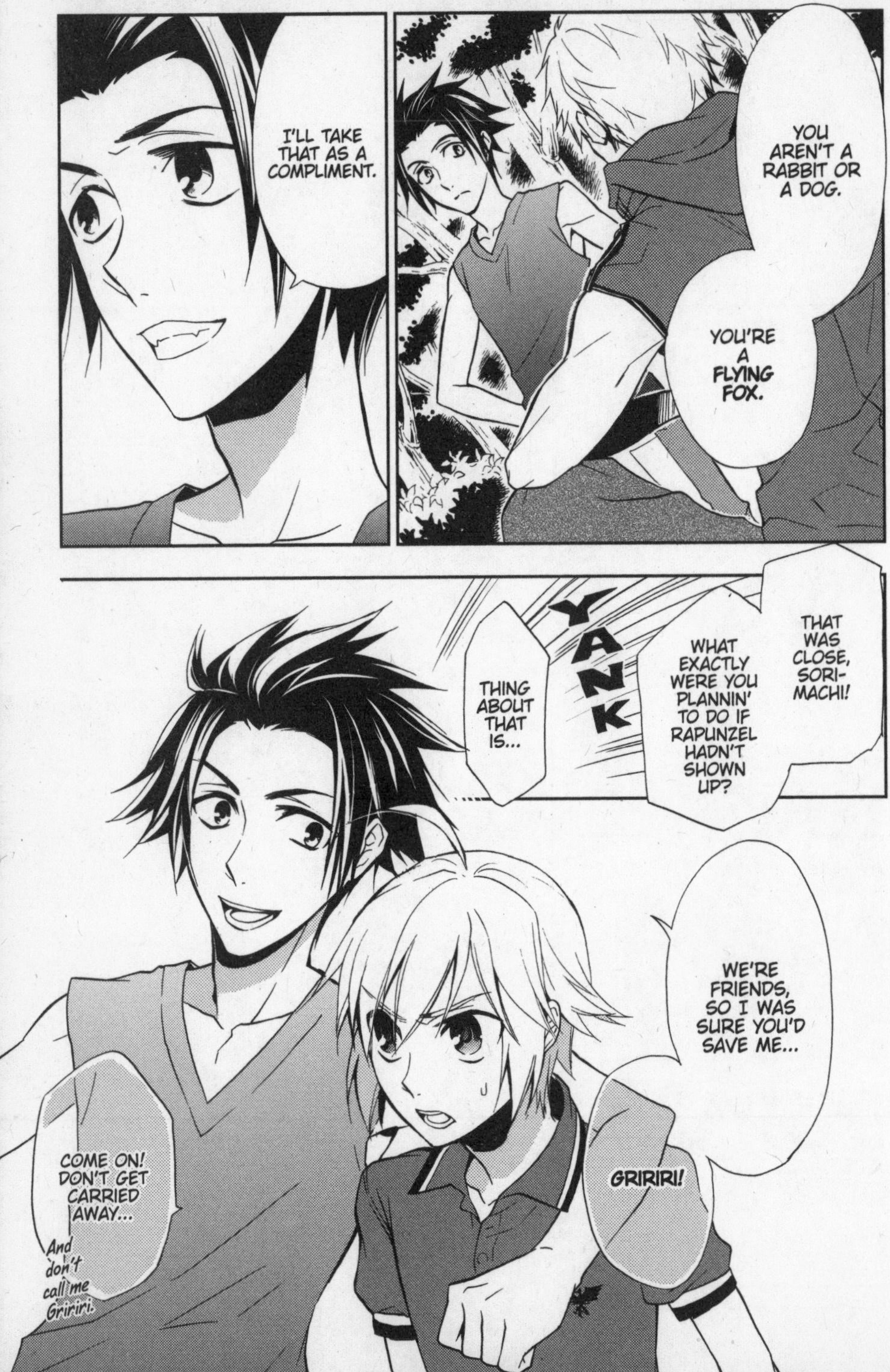
YOU AREN'T A RABBIT OR A DOG.
YOU'RE A FLYING FOX.
I'LL TAKE THAT AS A COMPLIMENT.
THAT WAS CLOSE, SORI-MACHI!
WHAT EXACTLY WERE YOU PLANNIN' TO DO IF RAPUNZEL HADN'T SHOWN UP?
YANK
THING ABOUT THAT IS...
WE'RE FRIENDS, SO I WAS SURE YOU'D SAVE ME...
GRIRIRI!
COME ON! DON'T GET CARRIED AWAY...
And don't call me Griririi.

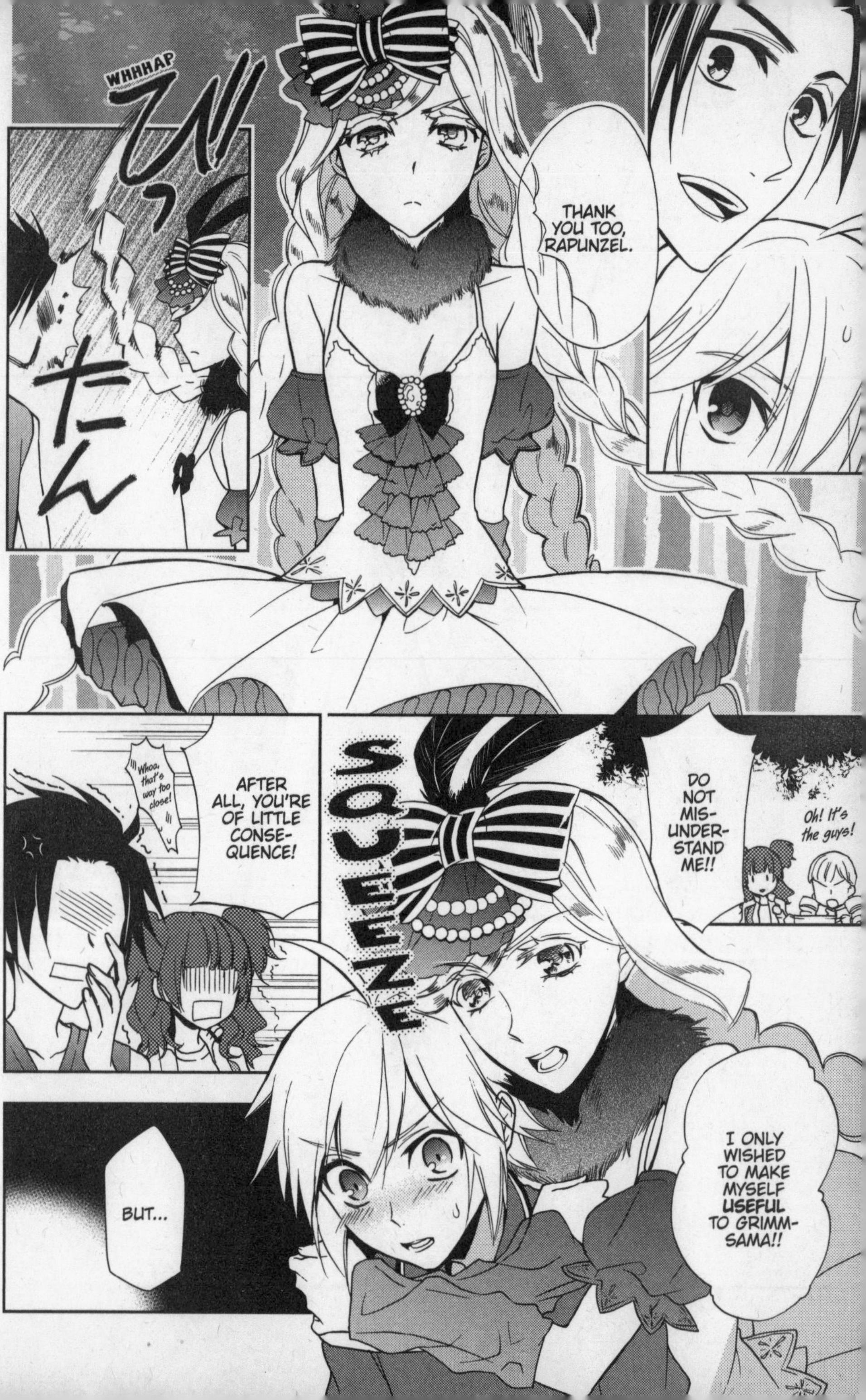
THANK YOU TOO, RAPUNZEL.
WHHHAP
Oh! It's the guys!
DO NOT MIS-UNDER-STAND ME!!
SQUEEZE
I ONLY WISHED TO MAKE MYSELF **USEFUL** TO GRIMM-SAMA!!
AFTER ALL, YOU'RE OF LITTLE CONSE-QUENCE!
Whoa, that's way too close!
BUT...

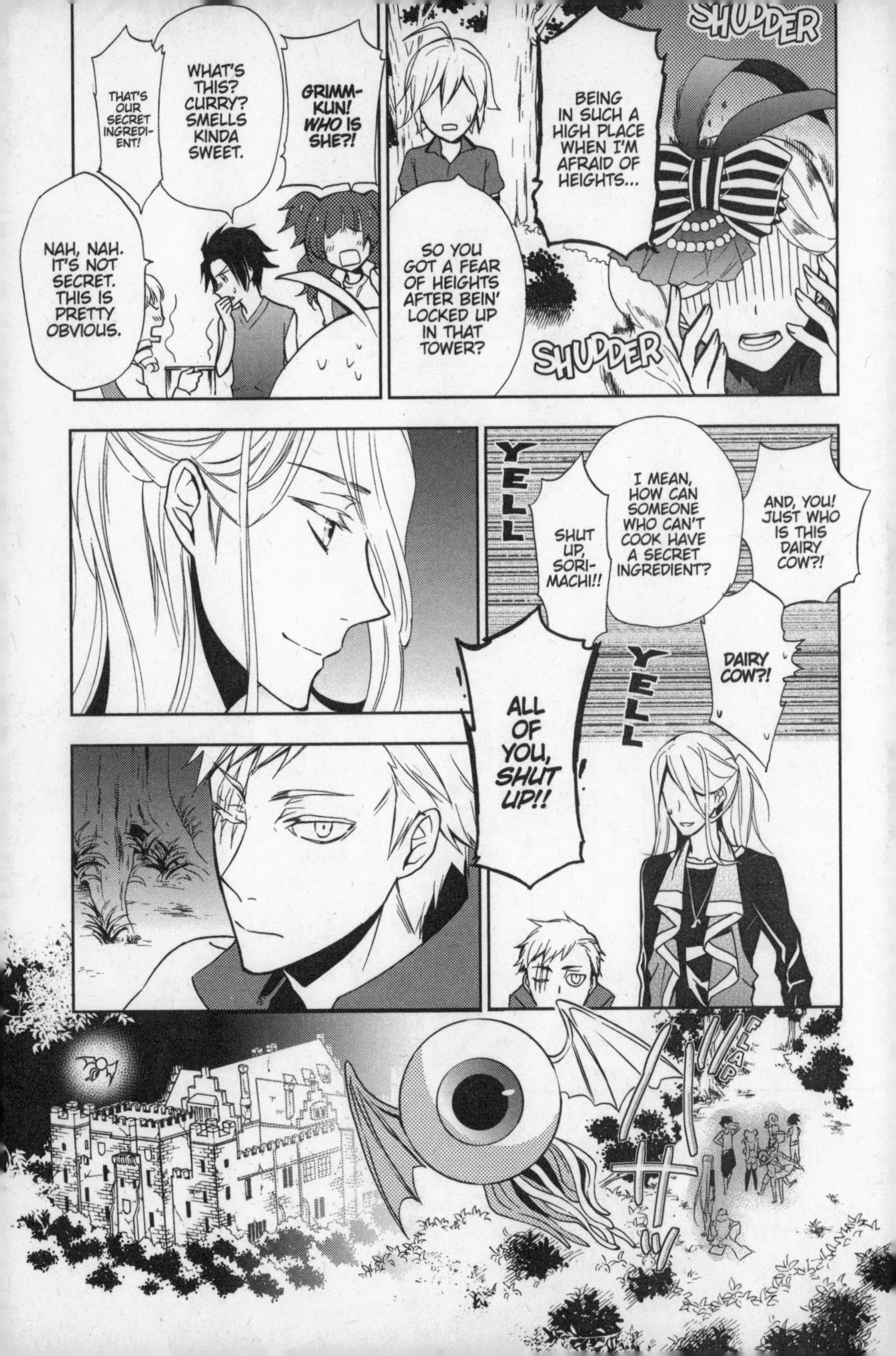
SHUDDER
BEING IN SUCH A HIGH PLACE WHEN I'M AFRAID OF HEIGHTS...
SO YOU GOT A FEAR OF HEIGHTS AFTER BEIN' LOCKED UP IN THAT TOWER?
SHUDDER
GRIMM-KUN! WHO IS SHE?!
WHAT'S THIS? CURRY? SMELLS KINDA SWEET.
THAT'S OUR SECRET INGREDIENT!
NAH, NAH. IT'S NOT SECRET. THIS IS PRETTY OBVIOUS.
AND, YOU! JUST WHO IS THIS DAIRY COW?!
I MEAN, HOW CAN SOMEONE WHO CAN'T COOK HAVE A SECRET INGREDIENT?
YELL
SHUT UP, SORI-MACHI!!
YELL
DAIRY COW?!
ALL OF YOU, SHUT UP!!
FLAP

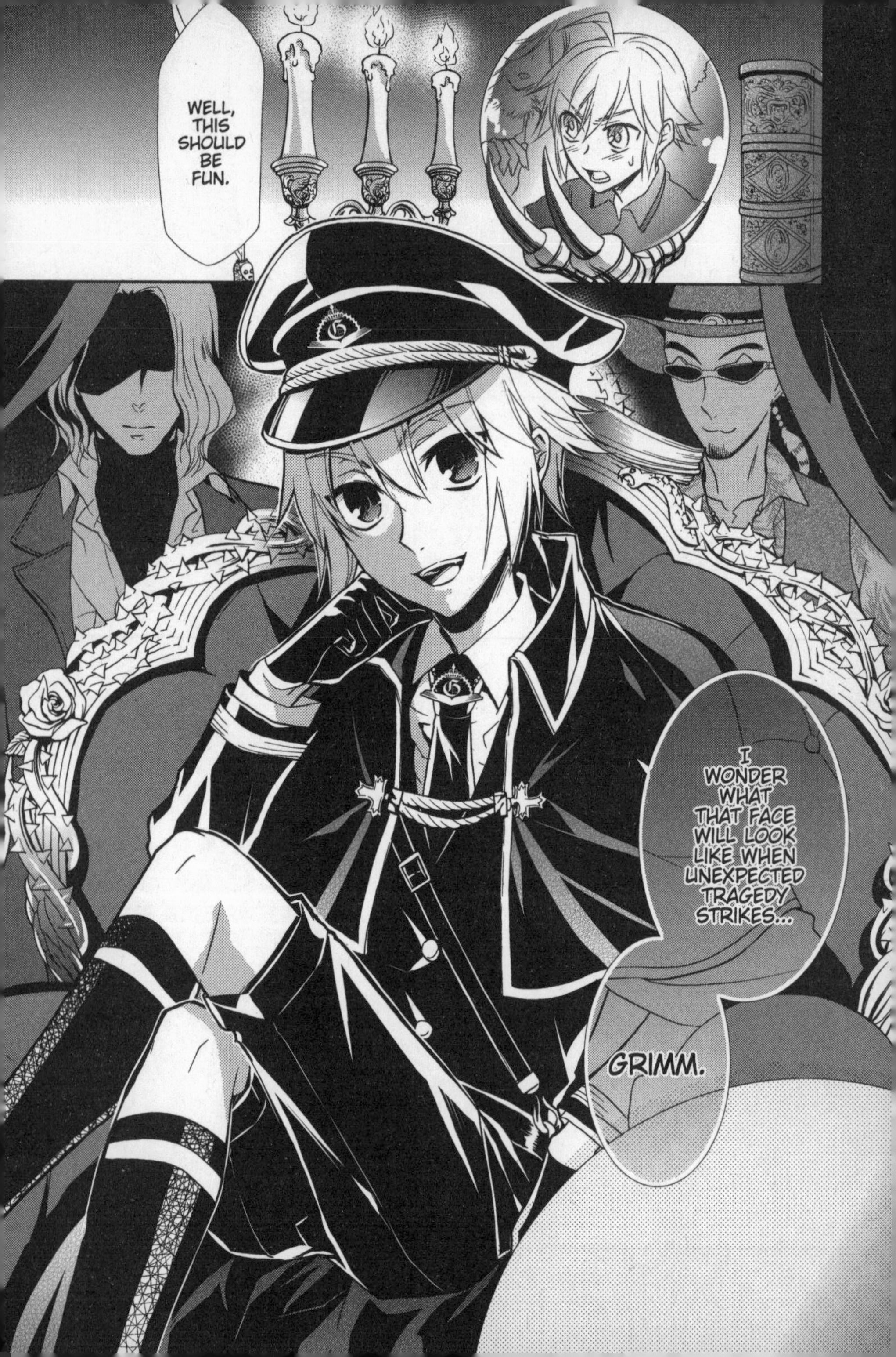
WELL, THIS SHOULD BE FUN.
I WONDER WHAT THAT FACE WILL LOOK LIKE WHEN UNEXPECTED TRAGEDY STRIKES...
GRIMM.

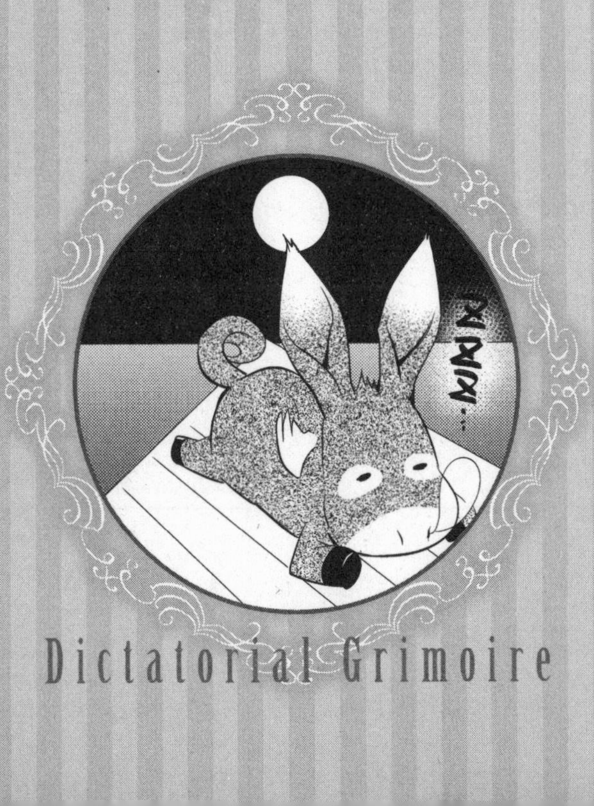
ZZZ...

Dictatorial Grimoire

独裁グリムワール

Dictatorial Grimoire

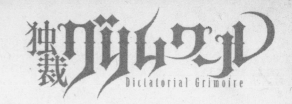

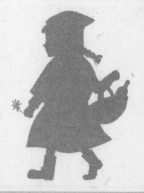

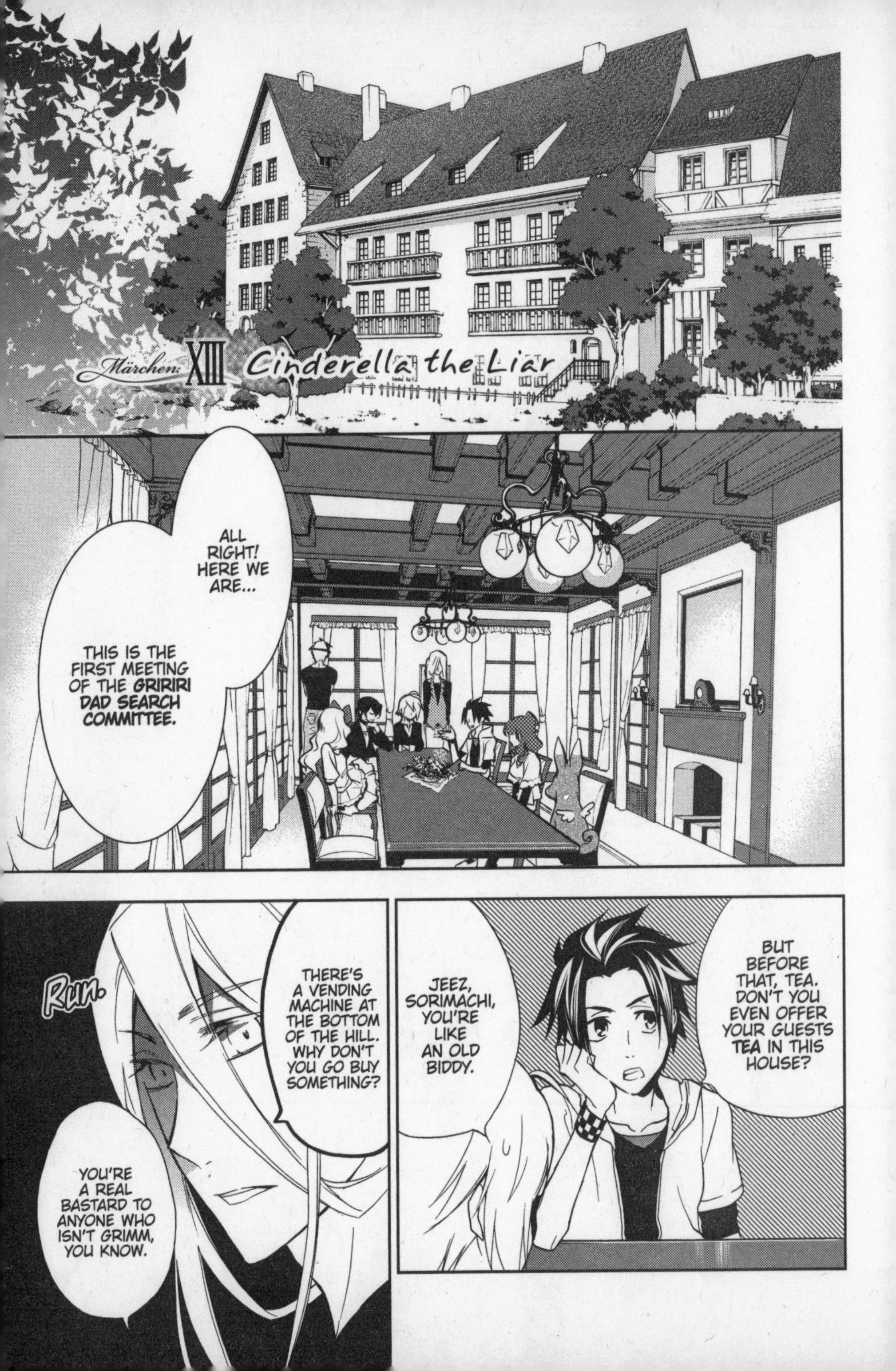
Märchen: XIII Cinderella the Liar
ALL RIGHT! HERE WE ARE...
THIS IS THE FIRST MEETING OF THE GRIRIRI DAD SEARCH COMMITTEE.
BUT BEFORE THAT, TEA. DON'T YOU EVEN OFFER YOUR GUESTS TEA IN THIS HOUSE?
JEEZ, SORIMACHI, YOU'RE LIKE AN OLD BIDDY.
Run.
THERE'S A VENDING MACHINE AT THE BOTTOM OF THE HILL. WHY DON'T YOU GO BUY SOMETHING?
YOU'RE A REAL BASTARD TO ANYONE WHO ISN'T GRIMM, YOU KNOW.

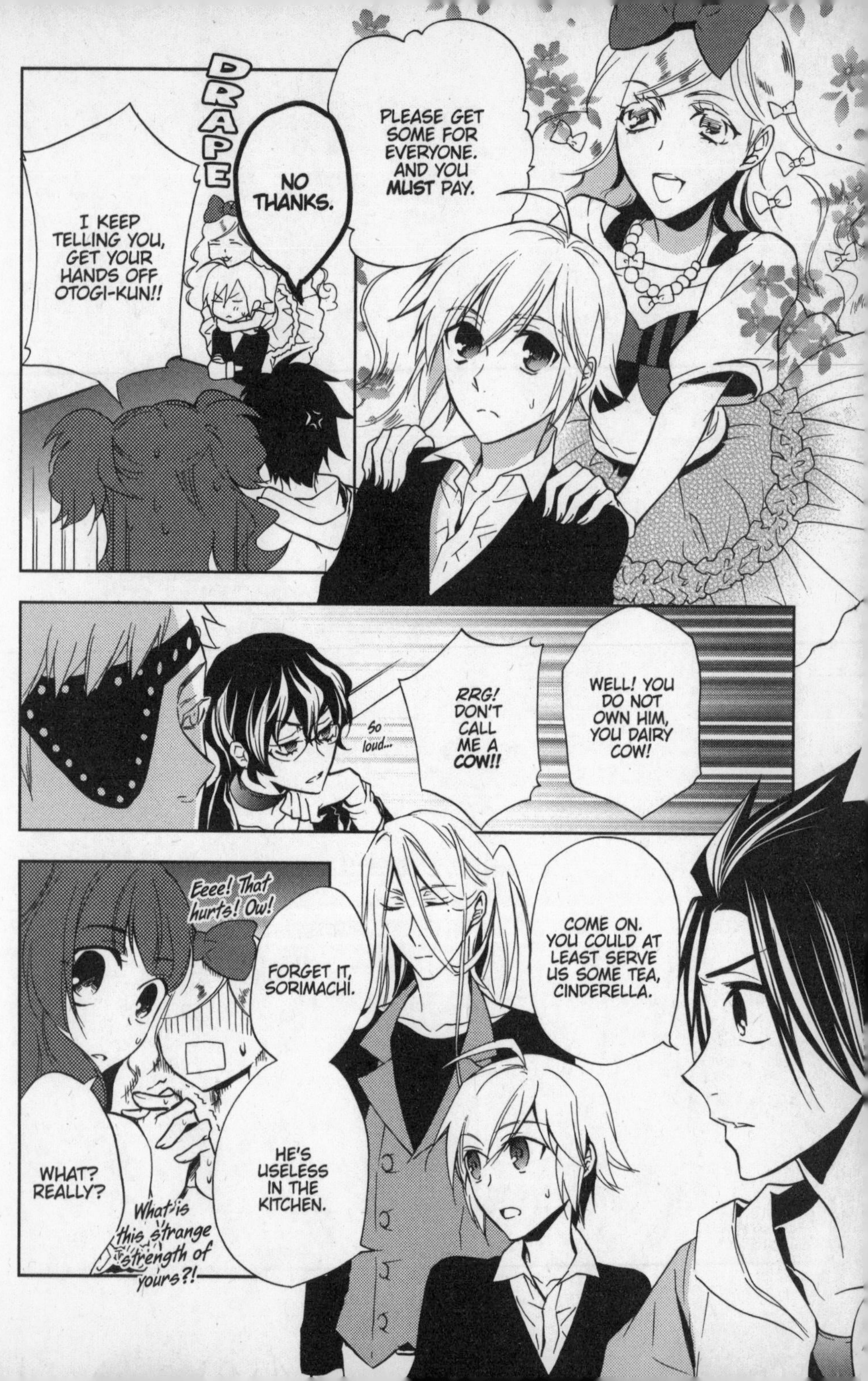
PLEASE GET SOME FOR EVERYONE. AND YOU MUST PAY.
NO THANKS.
DRAPE
I KEEP TELLING YOU, GET YOUR HANDS OFF OTOGI-KUN!!
WELL! YOU DO NOT OWN HIM, YOU DAIRY COW!
RRG! DON'T CALL ME A COW!!
So loud...
COME ON. YOU COULD AT LEAST SERVE US SOME TEA, CINDERELLA.
FORGET IT, SORIMACHI.
HE'S USELESS IN THE KITCHEN.
Eeee! That hurts! Ow!
WHAT? REALLY?
What is this strange strength of yours?!

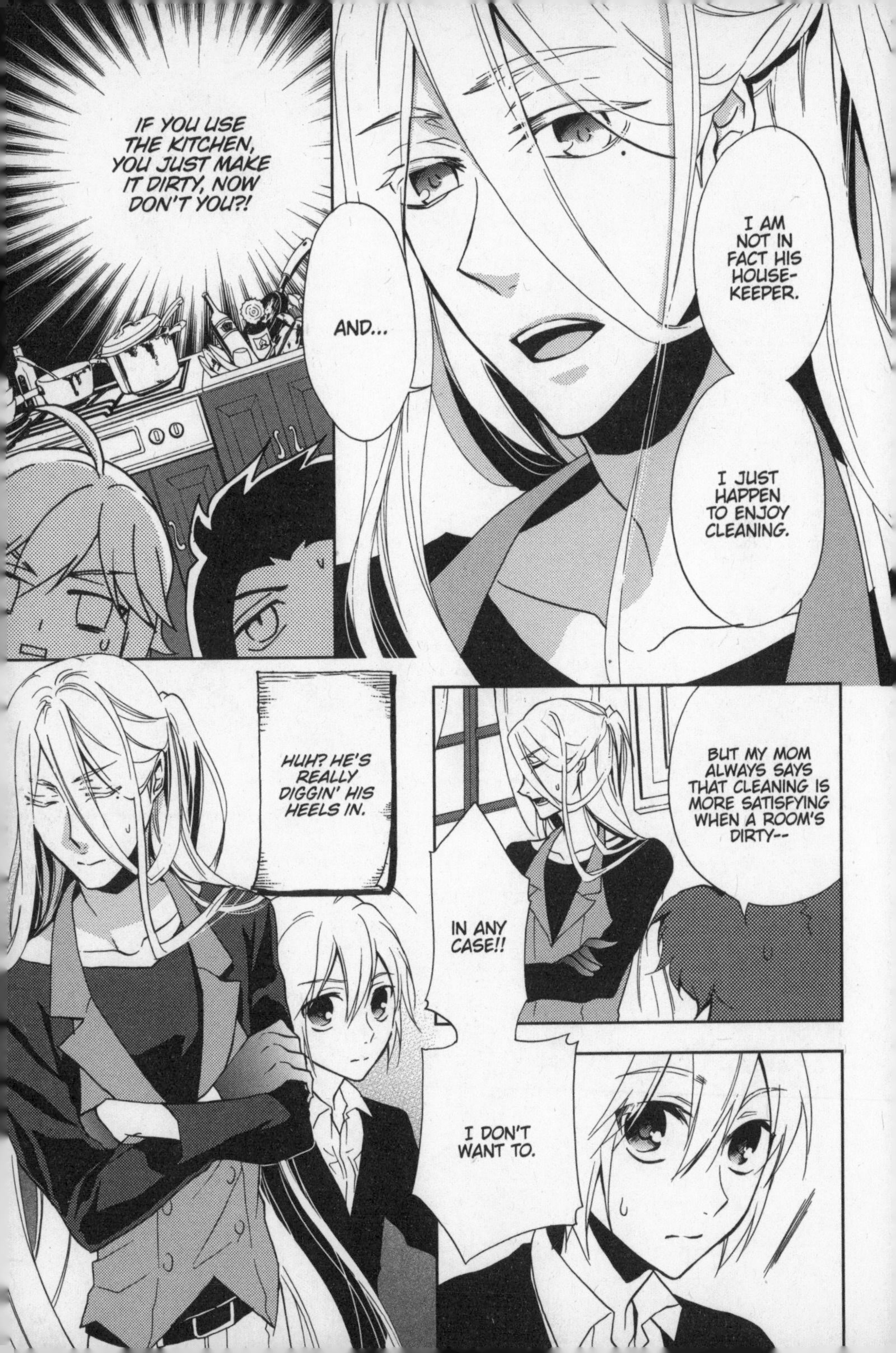
I AM NOT IN FACT HIS HOUSE-KEEPER.
AND...
I JUST HAPPEN TO ENJOY CLEANING.
IF YOU USE THE KITCHEN, YOU JUST MAKE IT DIRTY, NOW DON'T YOU?!
BUT MY MOM ALWAYS SAYS THAT CLEANING IS MORE SATISFYING WHEN A ROOM'S DIRTY--
IN ANY CASE!!
I DON'T WANT TO.
HUH? HE'S REALLY DIGGIN' HIS HEELS IN.

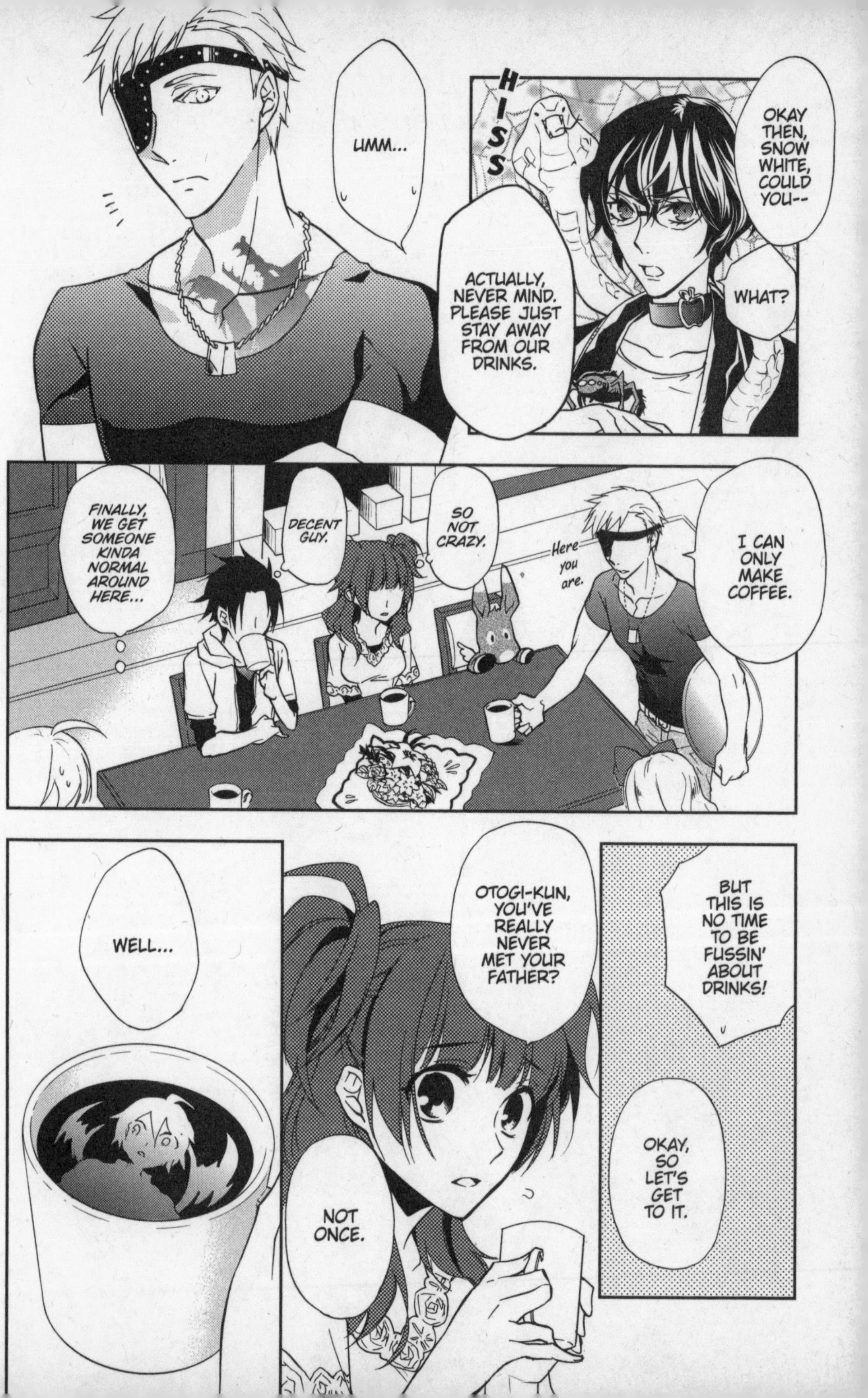
HISS
OKAY THEN, SNOW WHITE, COULD YOU--
WHAT?
ACTUALLY, NEVER MIND. PLEASE JUST STAY AWAY FROM OUR DRINKS.
UMM...
I CAN ONLY MAKE COFFEE.
Here you are.
SO NOT CRAZY.
DECENT GUY.
FINALLY, WE GET SOMEONE KINDA NORMAL AROUND HERE...
BUT THIS IS NO TIME TO BE FUSSIN' ABOUT DRINKS!
OKAY, SO LET'S GET TO IT.
OTOGI-KUN, YOU'VE REALLY NEVER MET YOUR FATHER?
NOT ONCE.
WELL...

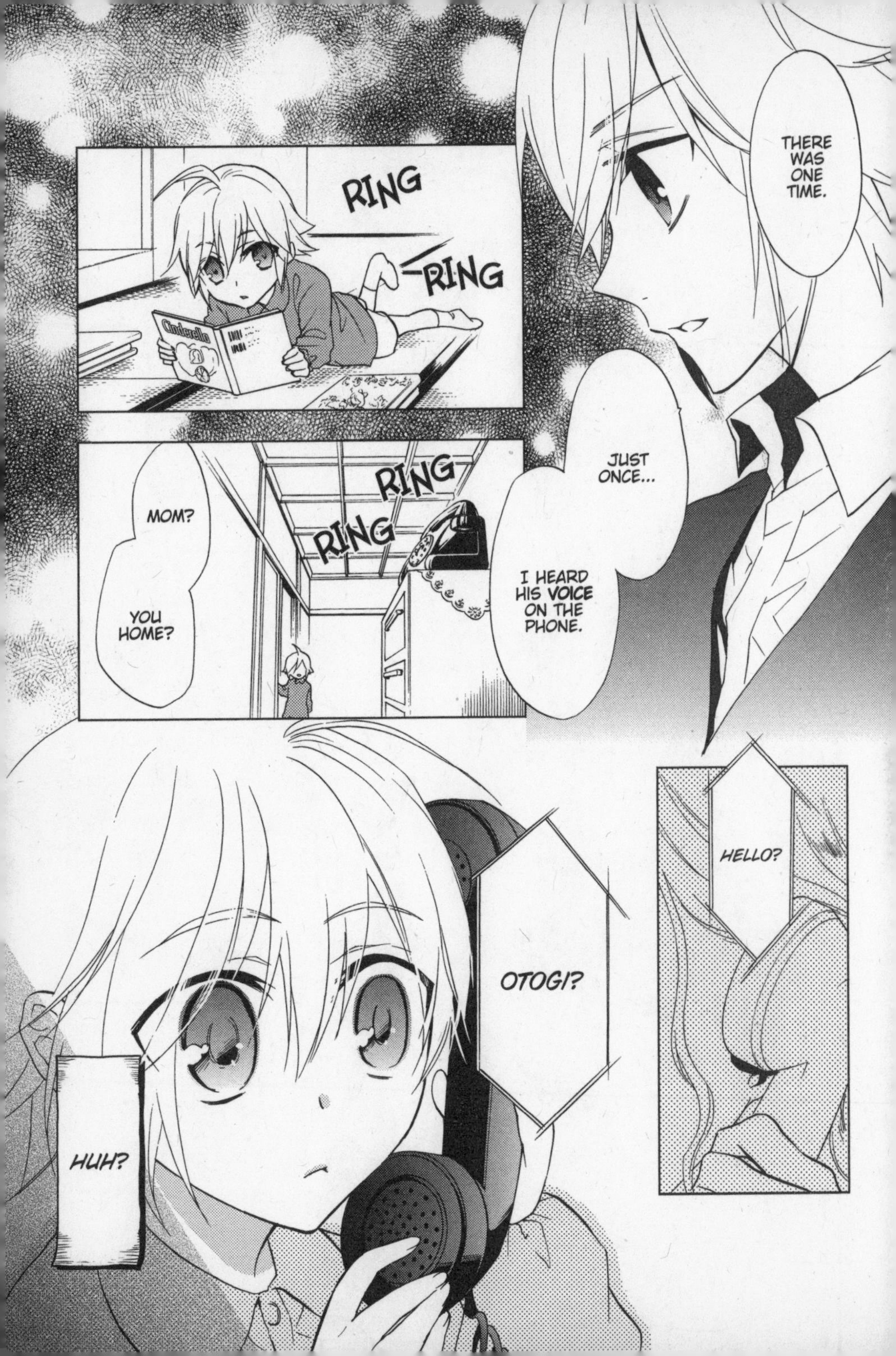

THERE WAS ONE TIME.
JUST ONCE...
I HEARD HIS VOICE ON THE PHONE.
RING
RING
Cinderella
RING
RING
MOM?
YOU HOME?
HELLO?
OTOGI?
HUH?

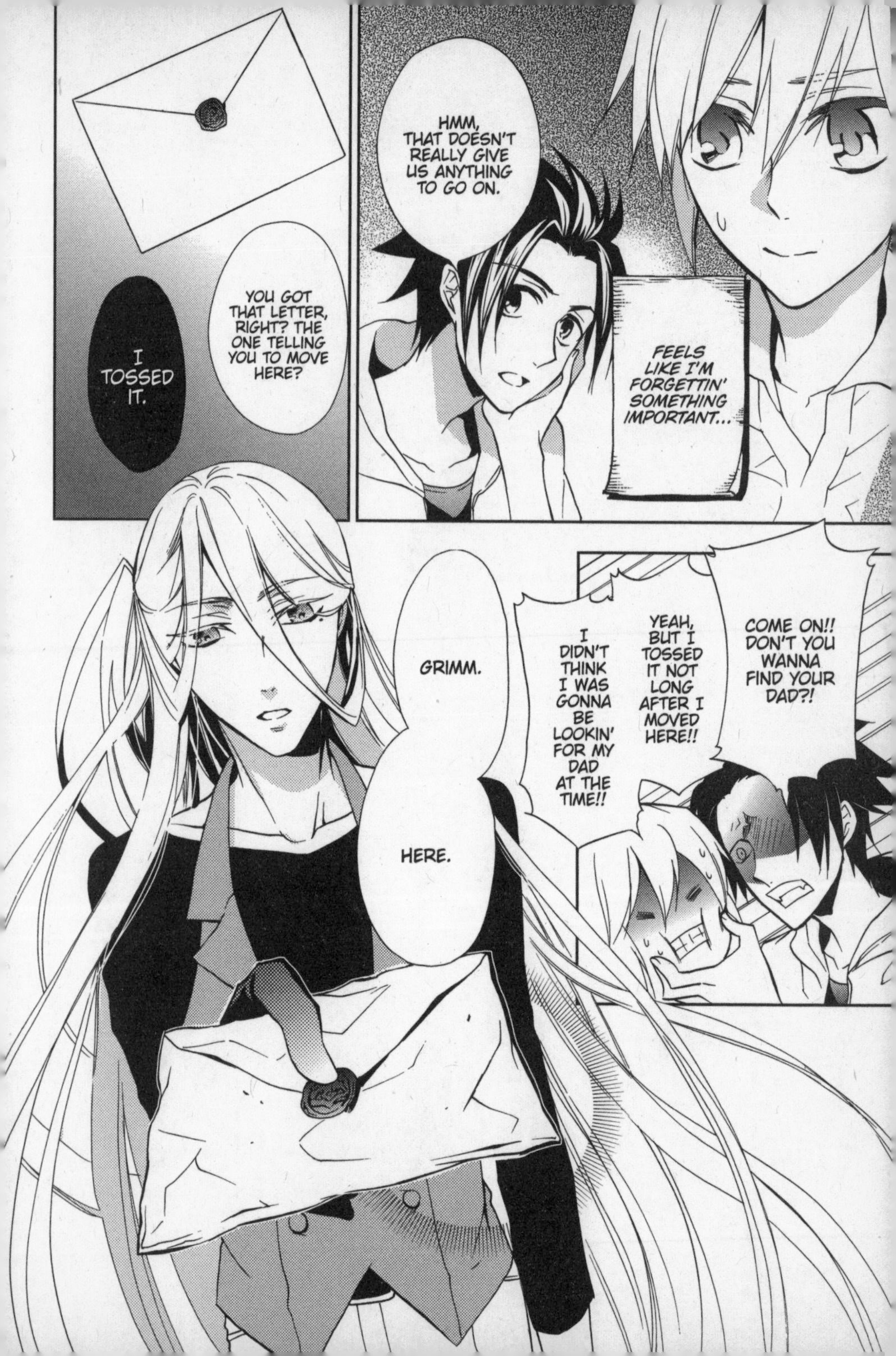
HMM, THAT DOESN'T REALLY GIVE US ANYTHING TO GO ON.
FEELS LIKE I'M FORGETTIN' SOMETHING IMPORTANT...
YOU GOT THAT LETTER, RIGHT? THE ONE TELLING YOU TO MOVE HERE?
I TOSSED IT.
COME ON!! DON'T YOU WANNA FIND YOUR DAD?!
YEAH, BUT I TOSSED IT NOT LONG AFTER I MOVED HERE!!
I DIDN'T THINK I WAS GONNA BE LOOKIN' FOR MY DAD AT THE TIME!!
GRIMM.
HERE.

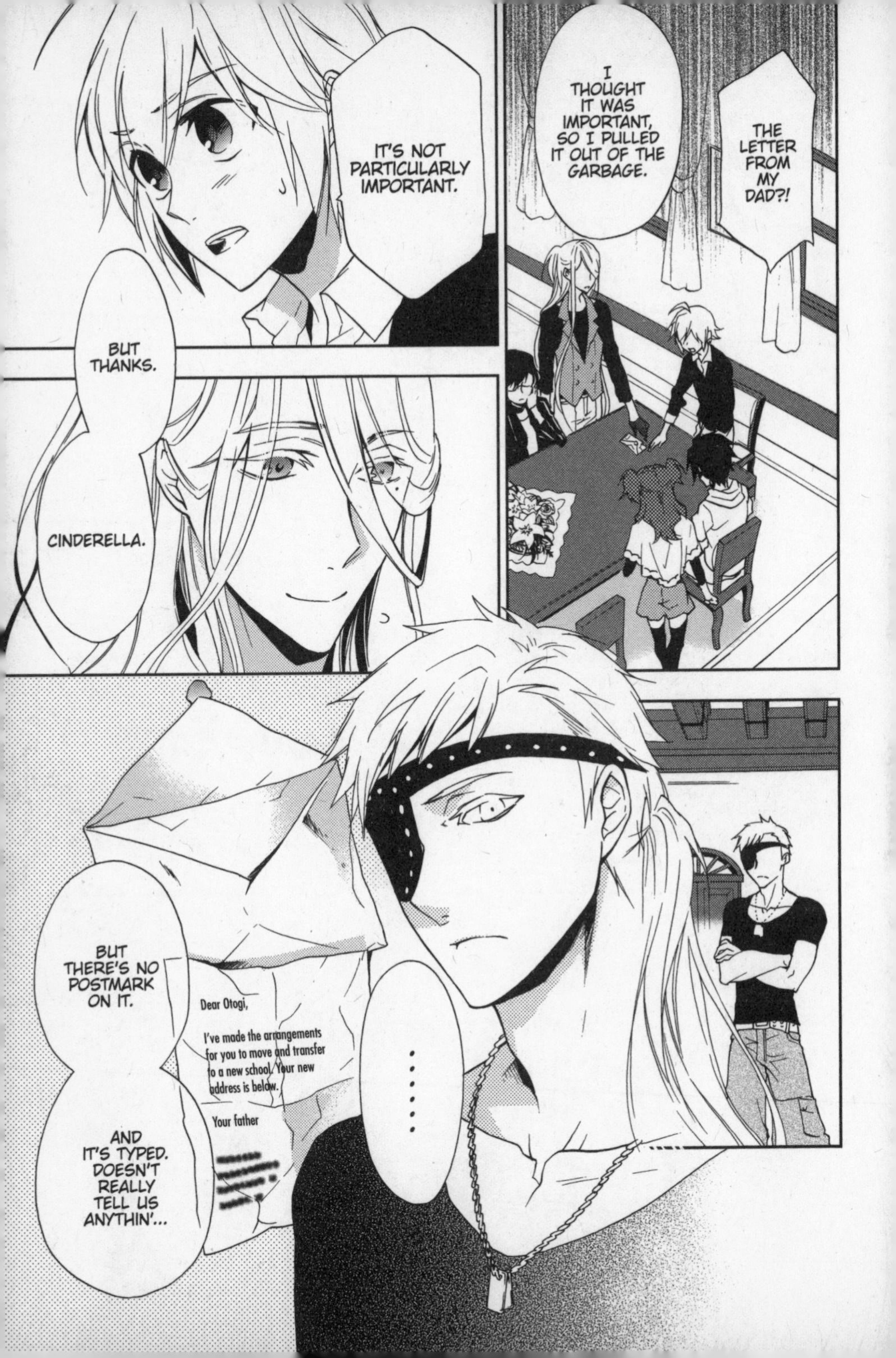
THE LETTER FROM MY DAD?!
I THOUGHT IT WAS IMPORTANT, SO I PULLED IT OUT OF THE GARBAGE.
IT'S NOT PARTICULARLY IMPORTANT.
BUT THANKS.
CINDERELLA.
BUT THERE'S NO POSTMARK ON IT.
Dear Otogi,
I've made the arrangements for you to move and transfer to a new school. Your new address is below.
Your father
AND IT'S TYPED. DOESN'T REALLY TELL US ANYTHIN'...
......

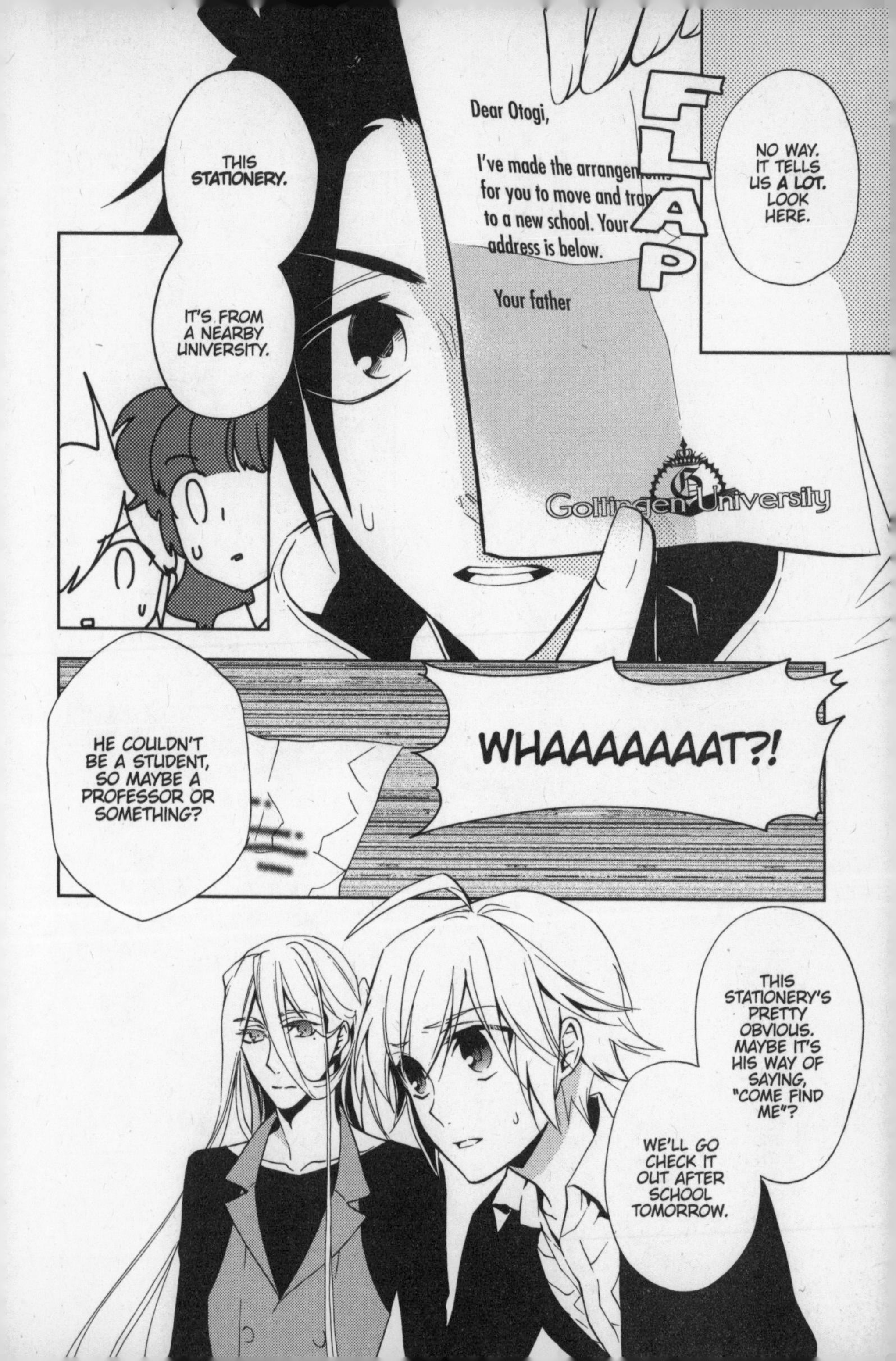

NO WAY. IT TELLS US A LOT. LOOK HERE.
FLAP
Dear Otogi,
I've made the arrangem
for you to move and tra
to a new school. Your
address is below.
Your father
Goltingen University
THIS STATIONERY.
IT'S FROM A NEARBY UNIVERSITY.
WHAAAAAAAT?!
HE COULDN'T BE A STUDENT, SO MAYBE A PROFESSOR OR SOMETHING?
THIS STATIONERY'S PRETTY OBVIOUS. MAYBE IT'S HIS WAY OF SAYING, "COME FIND ME"?
WE'LL GO CHECK IT OUT AFTER SCHOOL TOMORROW.

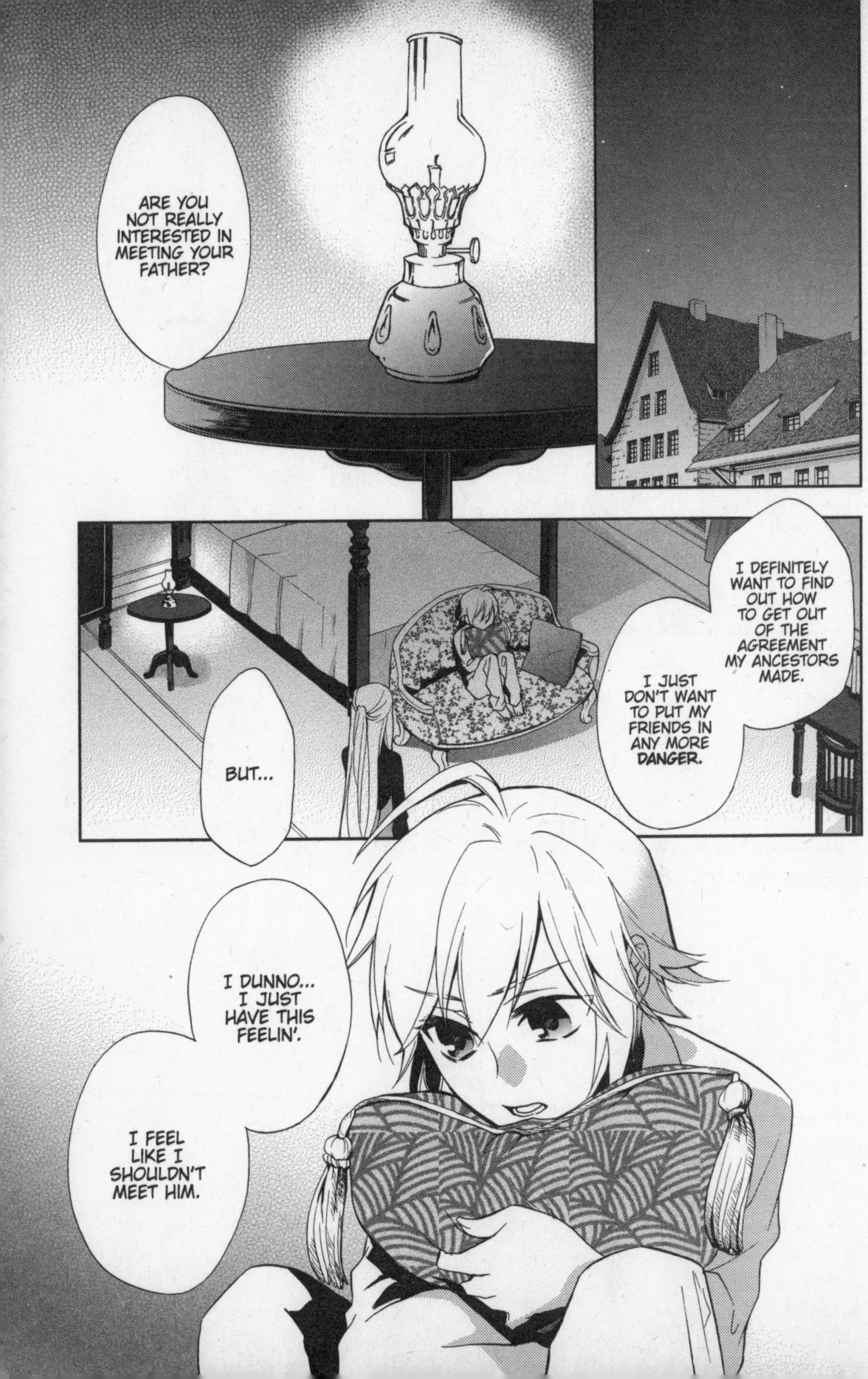
ARE YOU NOT REALLY INTERESTED IN MEETING YOUR FATHER?
I DEFINITELY WANT TO FIND OUT HOW TO GET OUT OF THE AGREEMENT MY ANCESTORS MADE.
I JUST DON'T WANT TO PUT MY FRIENDS IN ANY MORE DANGER.
BUT...
I DUNNO... I JUST HAVE THIS FEELIN'.
I FEEL LIKE I SHOULDN'T MEET HIM.

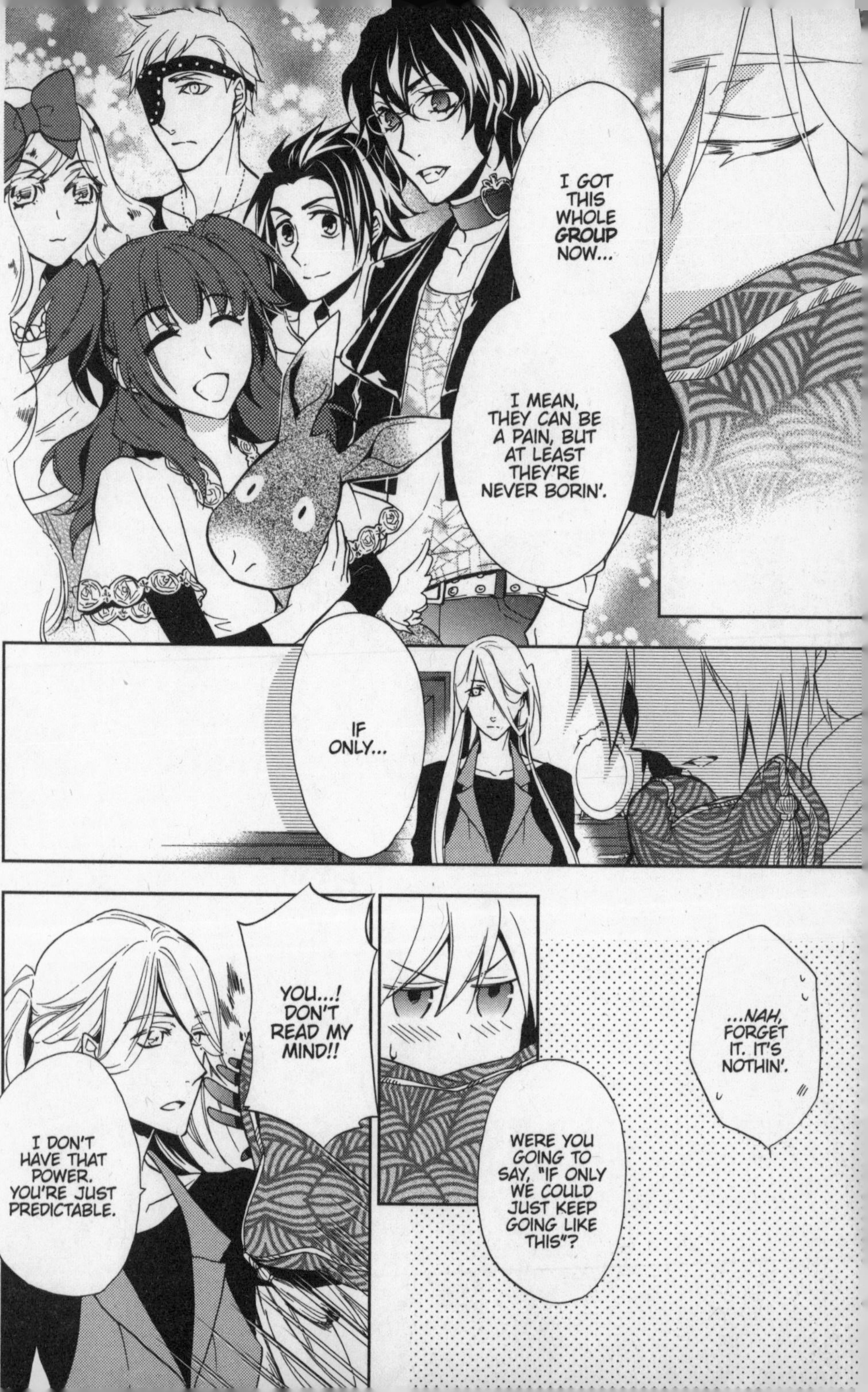
I GOT THIS WHOLE GROUP NOW...
I MEAN, THEY CAN BE A PAIN, BUT AT LEAST THEY'RE NEVER BORIN'.
IF ONLY...
...NAH, FORGET IT. IT'S NOTHIN'.
WERE YOU GOING TO SAY, "IF ONLY WE COULD JUST KEEP GOING LIKE THIS"?
YOU...! DON'T READ MY MIND!!
I DON'T HAVE THAT POWER. YOU'RE JUST PREDICTABLE.

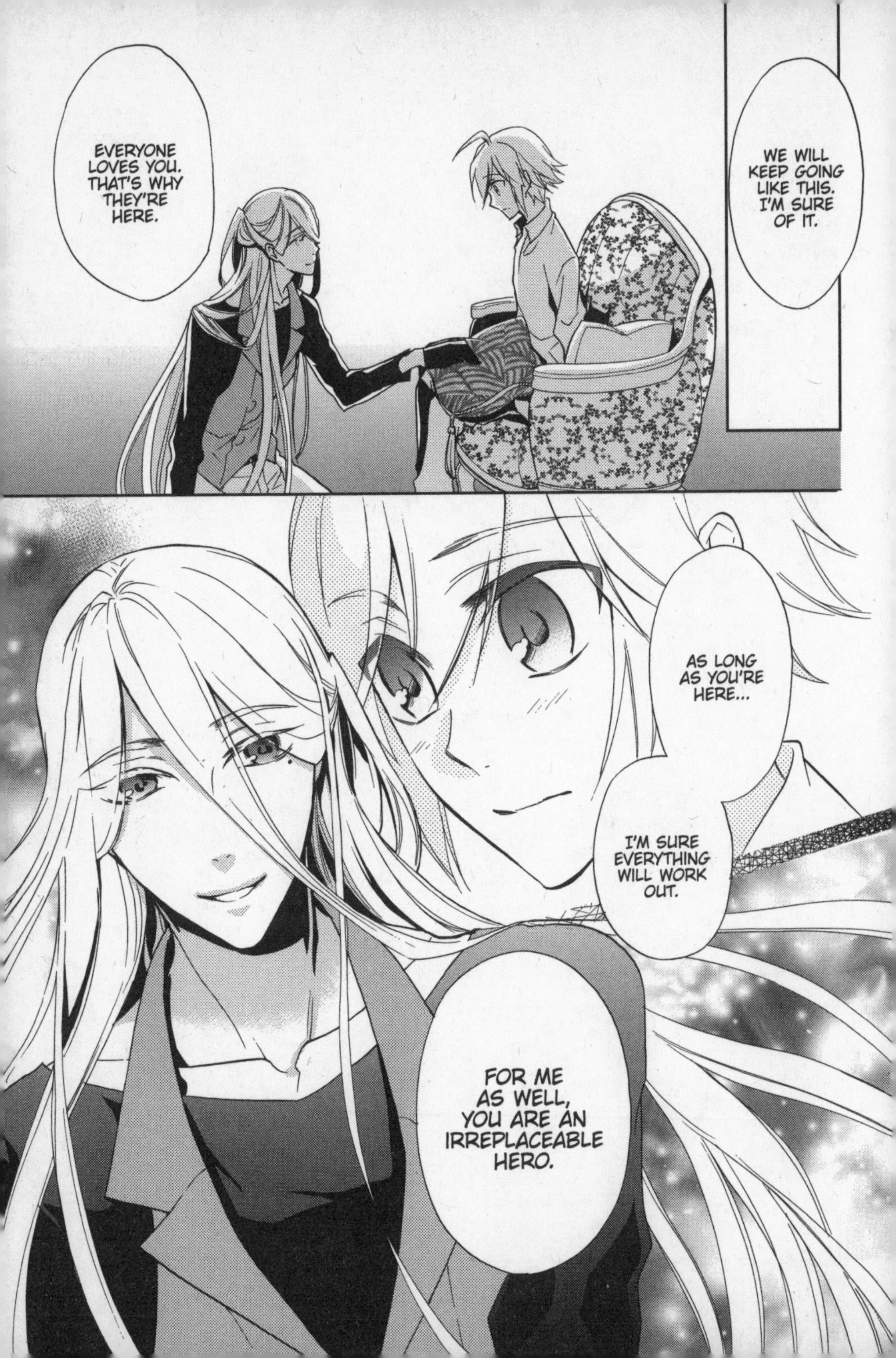
WE WILL KEEP GOING LIKE THIS. I'M SURE OF IT.
EVERYONE LOVES YOU. THAT'S WHY THEY'RE HERE.
AS LONG AS YOU'RE HERE...
I'M SURE EVERYTHING WILL WORK OUT.
FOR ME AS WELL, YOU ARE AN IRREPLACEABLE HERO.

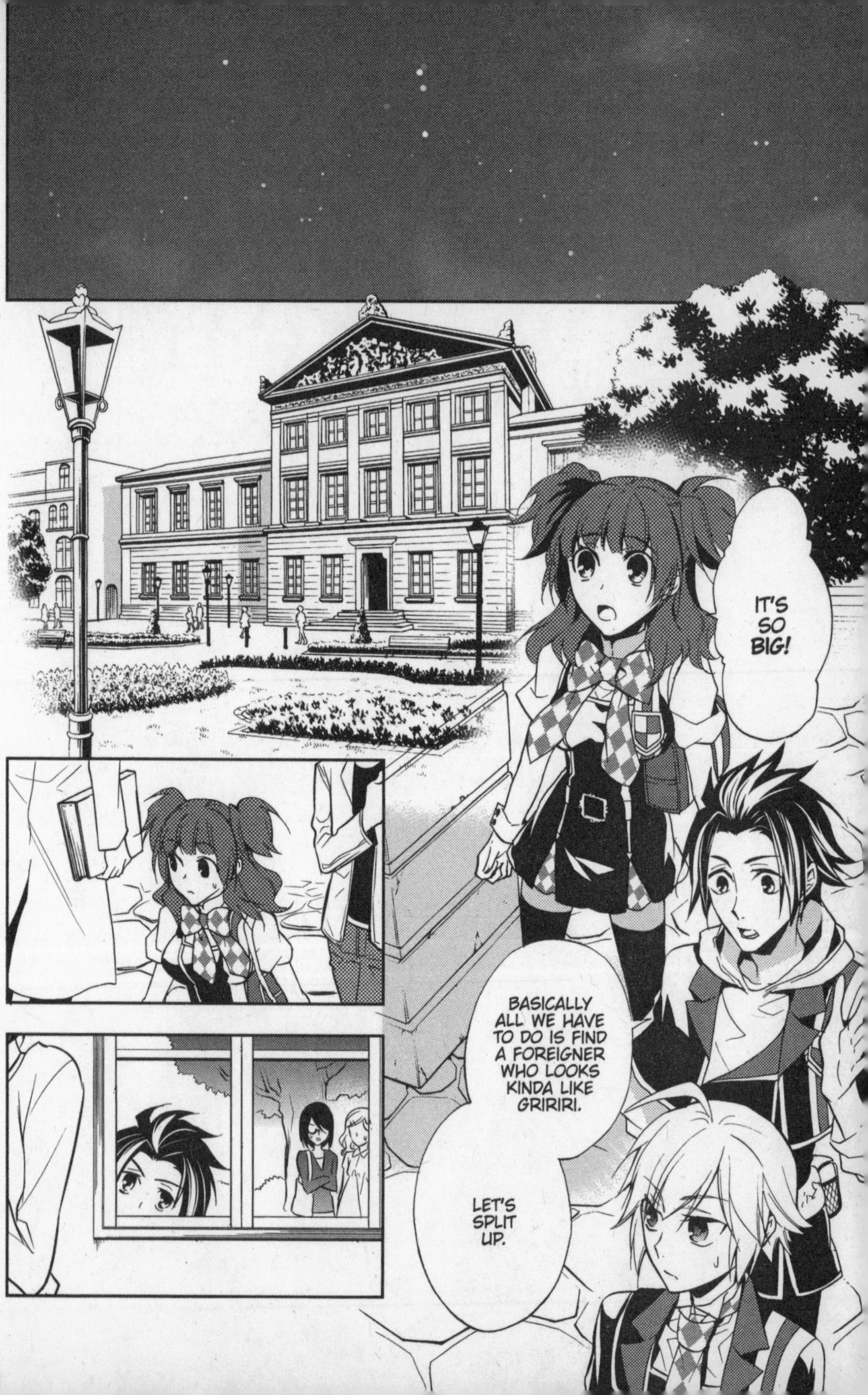
IT'S SO BIG!
BASICALLY ALL WE HAVE TO DO IS FIND A FOREIGNER WHO LOOKS KINDA LIKE GRIRIRI.
LET'S SPLIT UP.

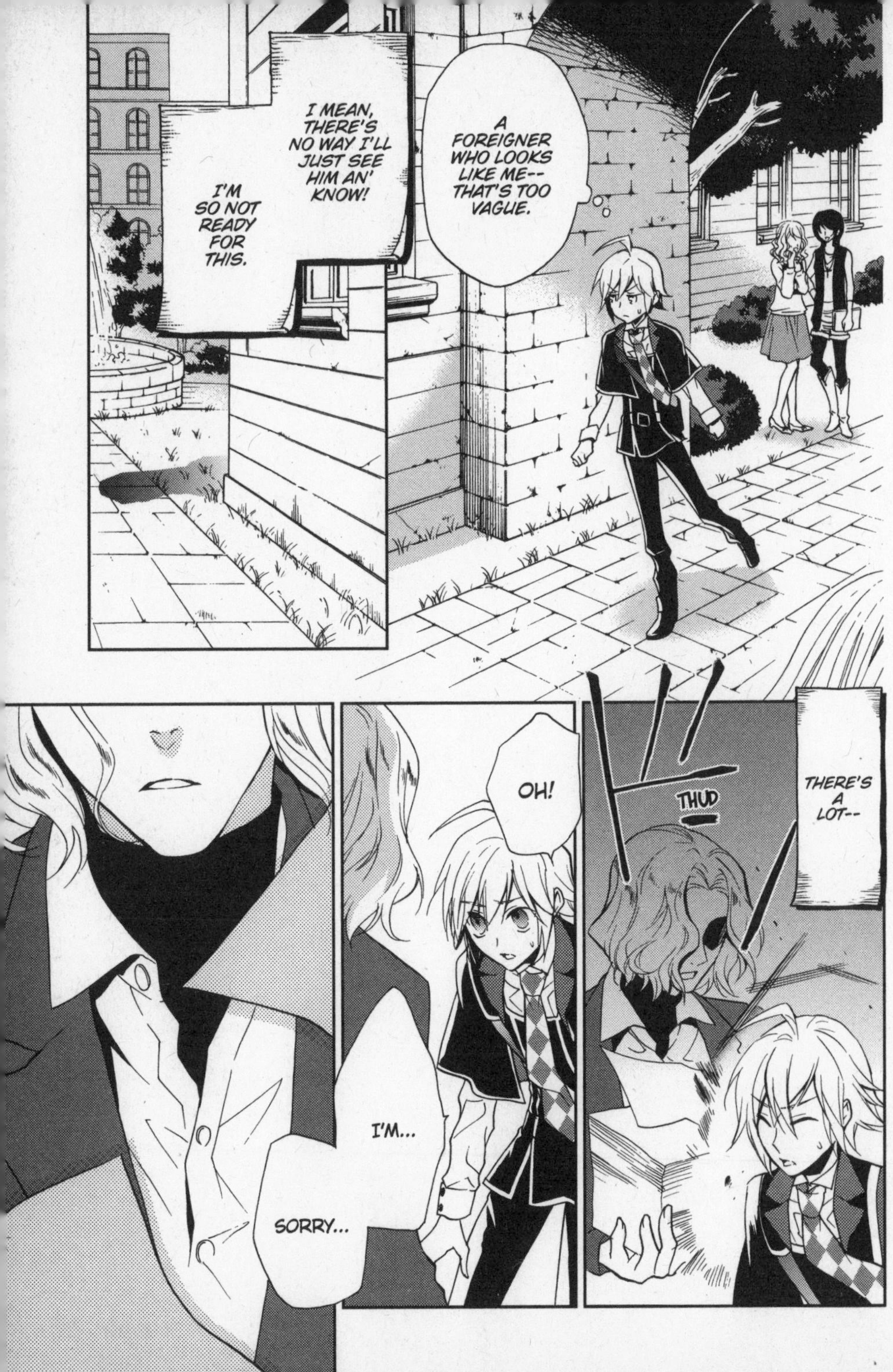
A FOREIGNER WHO LOOKS LIKE ME-- THAT'S TOO VAGUE.
I MEAN, THERE'S NO WAY I'LL JUST SEE HIM AN' KNOW!
I'M SO NOT READY FOR THIS.
THERE'S A LOT--
THUD
OH!
I'M...
SORRY...

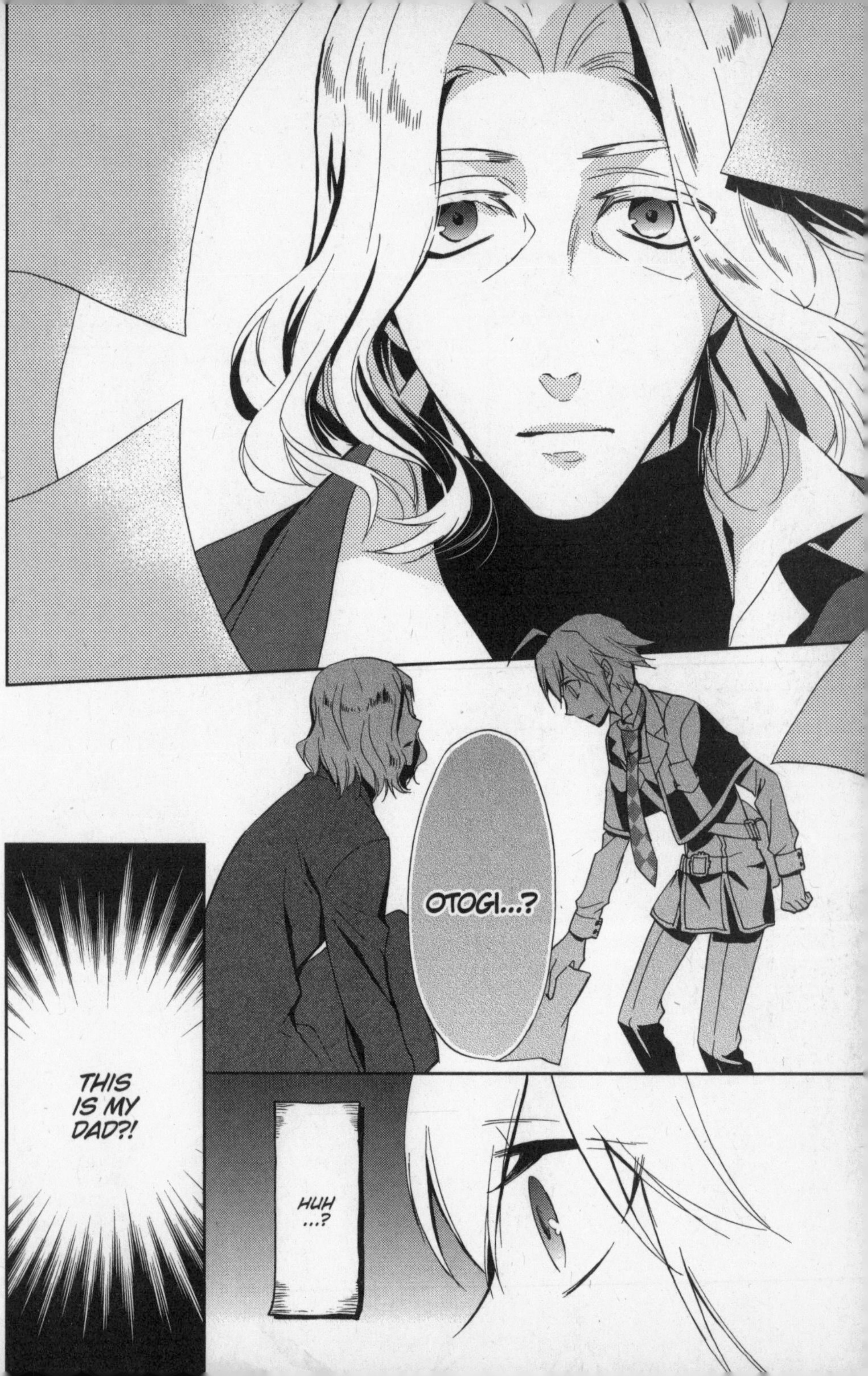
OTOGI...?
HUH ...?
THIS IS MY DAD?!

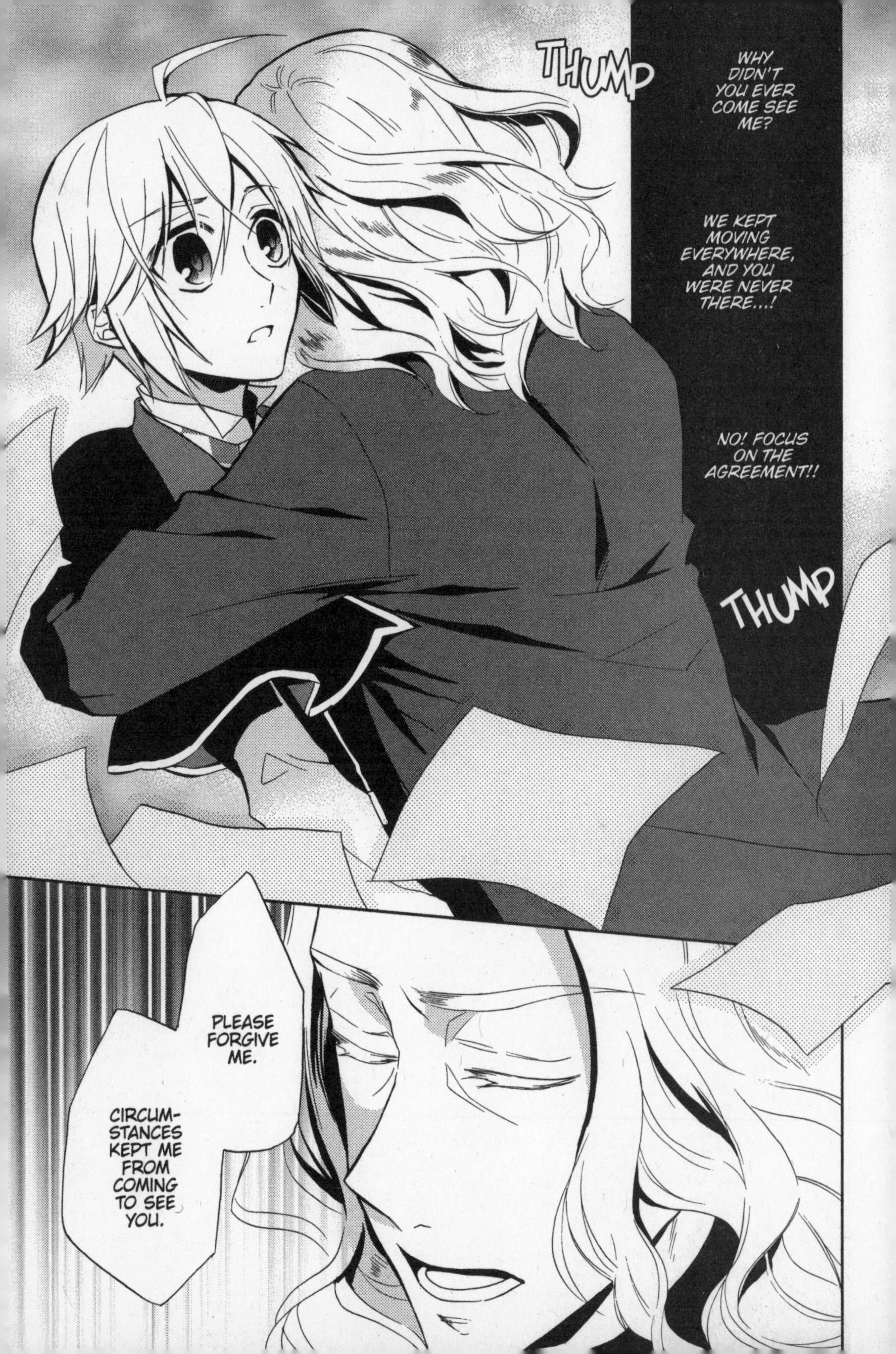
WHY DIDN'T YOU EVER COME SEE ME?
THUMP
WE KEPT MOVING EVERYWHERE, AND YOU WERE NEVER THERE...!
NO! FOCUS ON THE AGREEMENT!!
THUMP
PLEASE FORGIVE ME.
CIRCUM-STANCES KEPT ME FROM COMING TO SEE YOU.

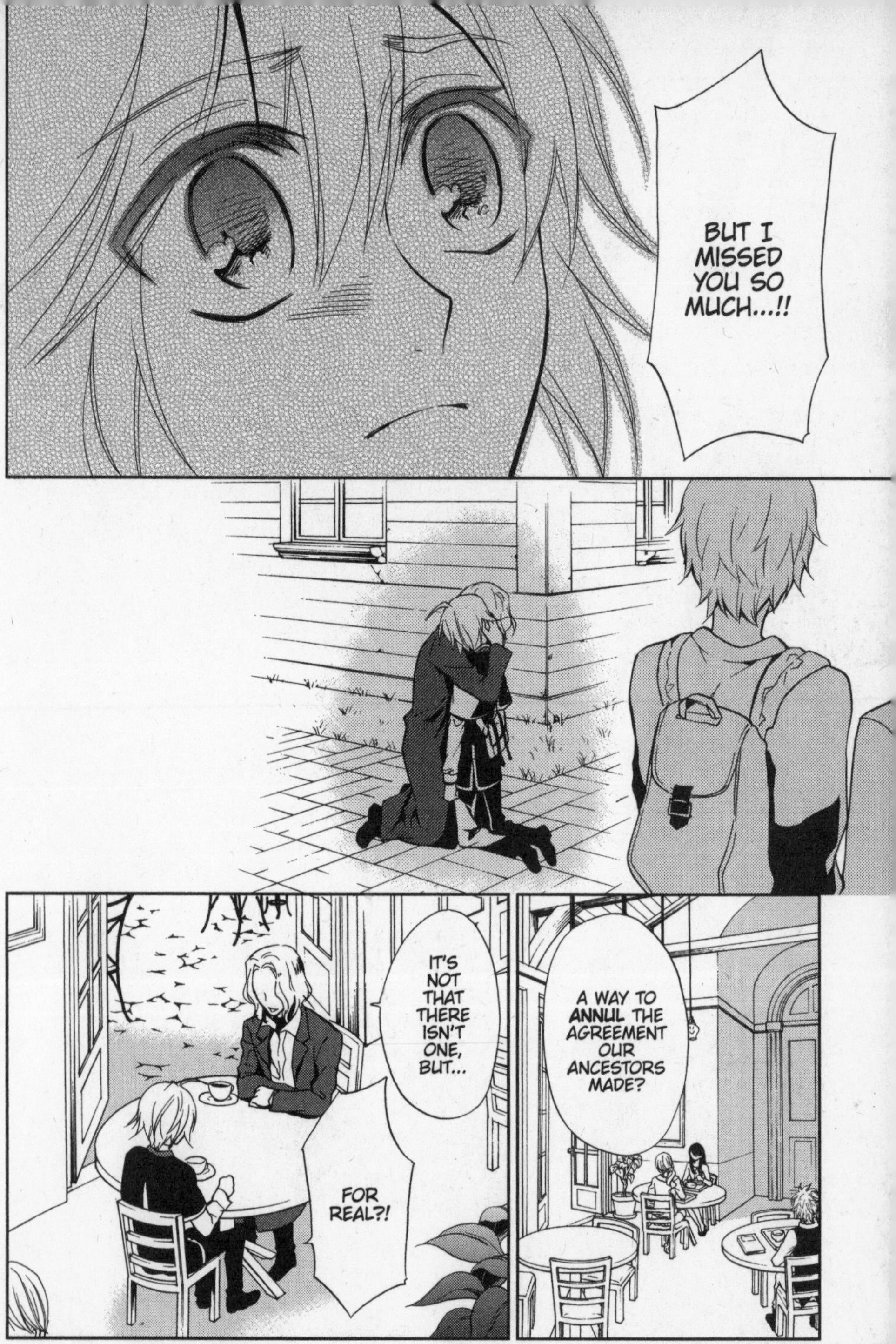
BUT I MISSED YOU SO MUCH...!!
A WAY TO ANNUL THE AGREEMENT OUR ANCESTORS MADE?
IT'S NOT THAT THERE ISN'T ONE, BUT...
FOR REAL?!

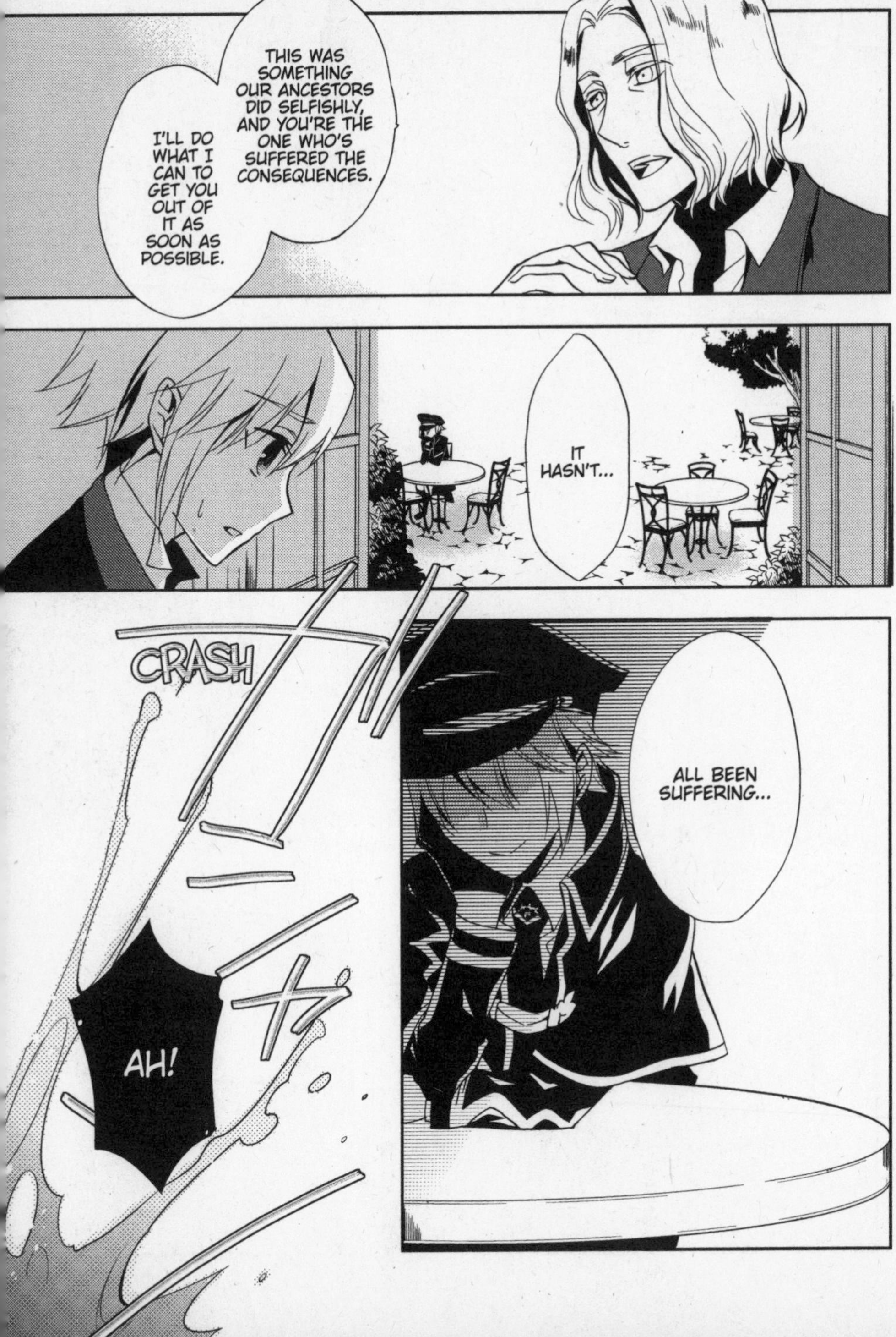
THIS WAS SOMETHING OUR ANCESTORS DID SELFISHLY, AND YOU'RE THE ONE WHO'S SUFFERED THE CONSEQUENCES.
I'LL DO WHAT I CAN TO GET YOU OUT OF IT AS SOON AS POSSIBLE.
IT HASN'T...
ALL BEEN SUFFERING...
CRASH
AH!

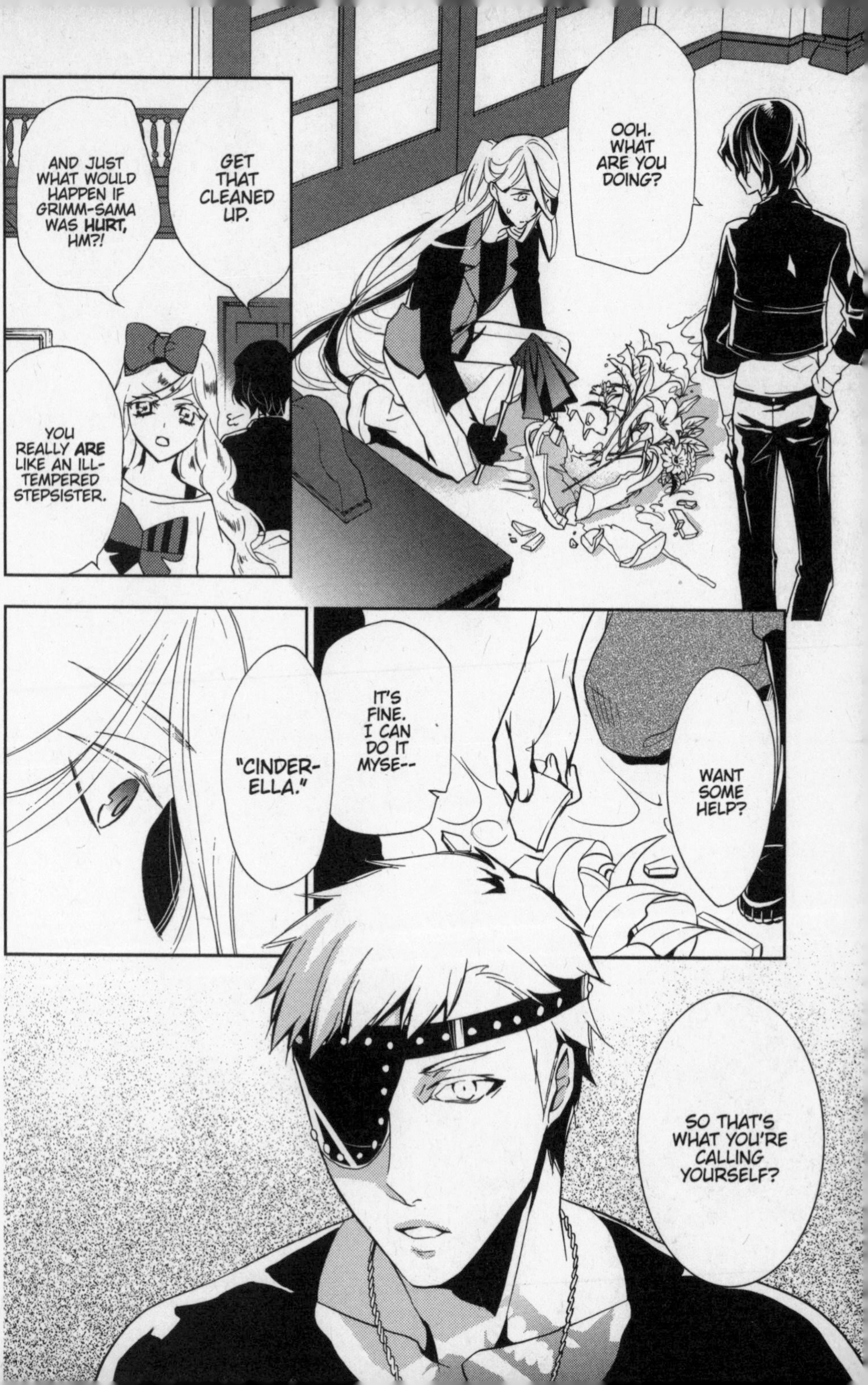
OOH. WHAT ARE YOU DOING?
GET THAT CLEANED UP.
AND JUST WHAT WOULD HAPPEN IF GRIMM-SAMA WAS **HURT**, HM?!
YOU REALLY **ARE** LIKE AN ILL-TEMPERED STEPSISTER.
WANT SOME HELP?
IT'S FINE. I CAN DO IT MYSE--
"CINDER-ELLA."
SO THAT'S WHAT YOU'RE CALLING YOURSELF?

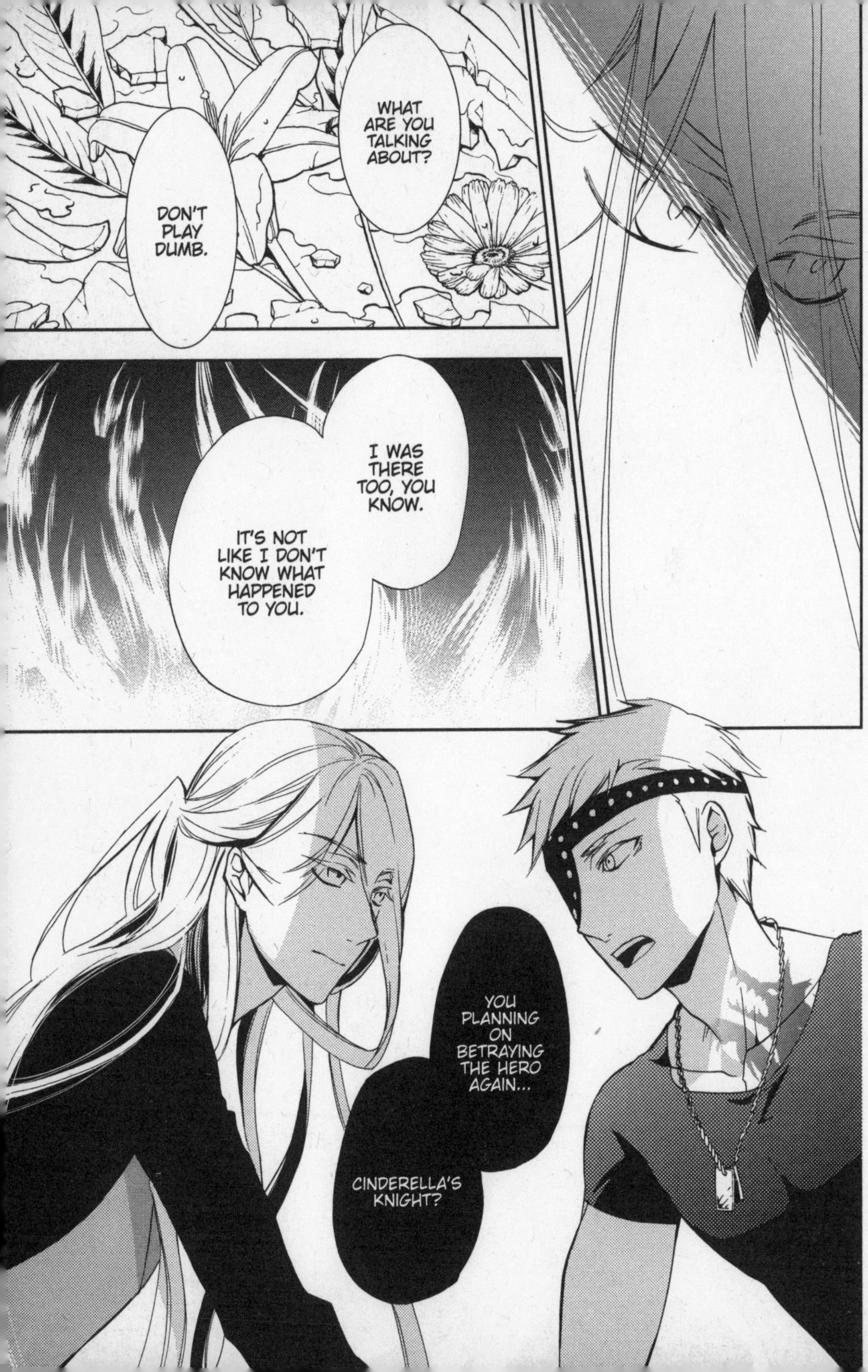
WHAT ARE YOU TALKING ABOUT?
DON'T PLAY DUMB.
I WAS THERE TOO, YOU KNOW.
IT'S NOT LIKE I DON'T KNOW WHAT HAPPENED TO YOU.
YOU PLANNING ON BETRAYING THE HERO AGAIN...
CINDERELLA'S KNIGHT?

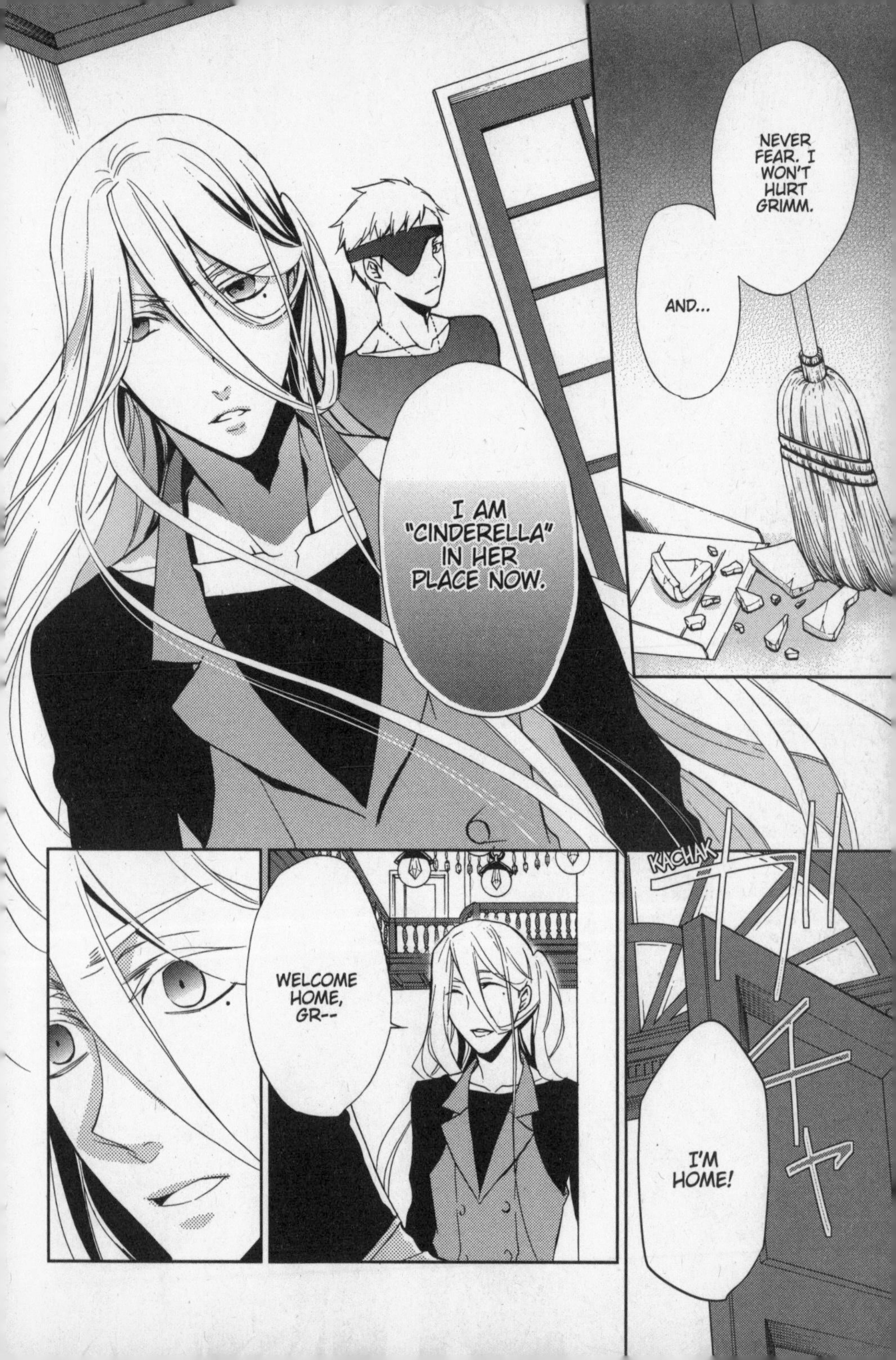
NEVER FEAR. I WON'T HURT GRIMM.
AND...
I AM "CINDERELLA" IN HER PLACE NOW.
KACHAK
I'M HOME!
WELCOME HOME, GR--

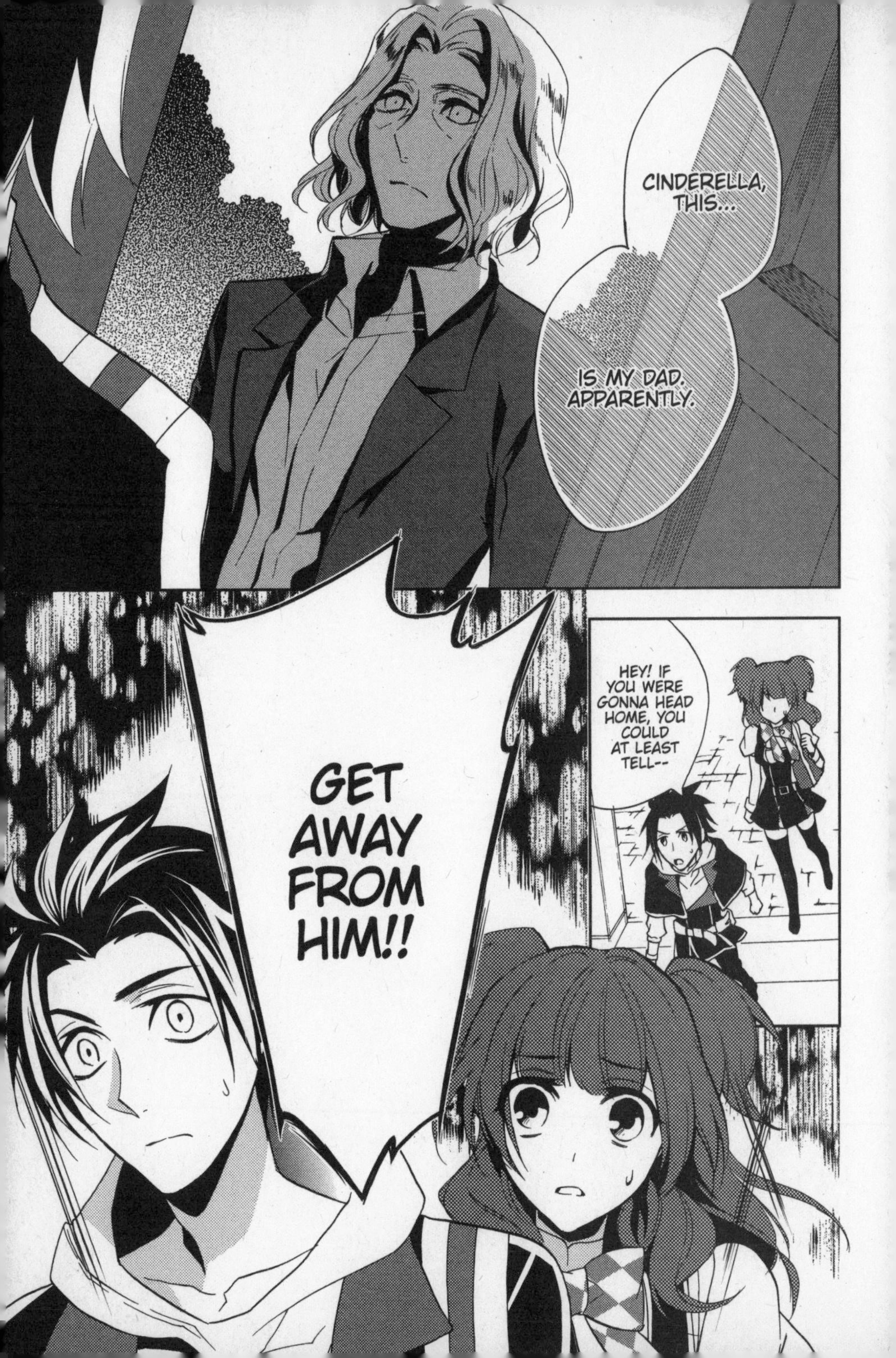
CINDERELLA, THIS...
IS MY DAD. APPARENTLY.
HEY! IF YOU WERE GONNA HEAD HOME, YOU COULD AT LEAST TELL--
GET AWAY FROM HIM!!

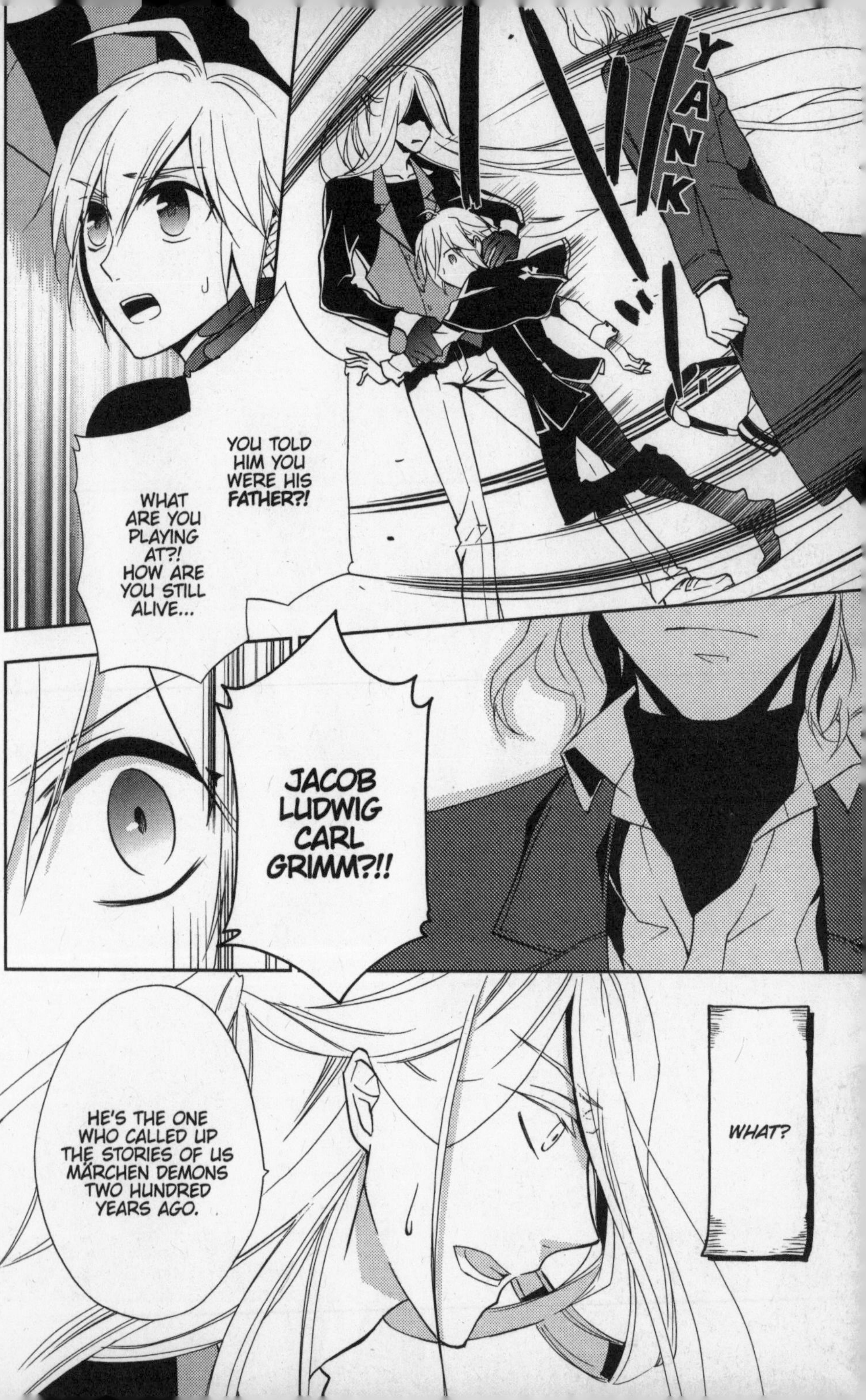
YANK
YOU TOLD HIM YOU WERE HIS FATHER?!
WHAT ARE YOU PLAYING AT?! HOW ARE YOU STILL ALIVE...
JACOB LUDWIG CARL GRIMM?!!
WHAT?
HE'S THE ONE WHO CALLED UP THE STORIES OF US MÄRCHEN DEMONS TWO HUNDRED YEARS AGO.

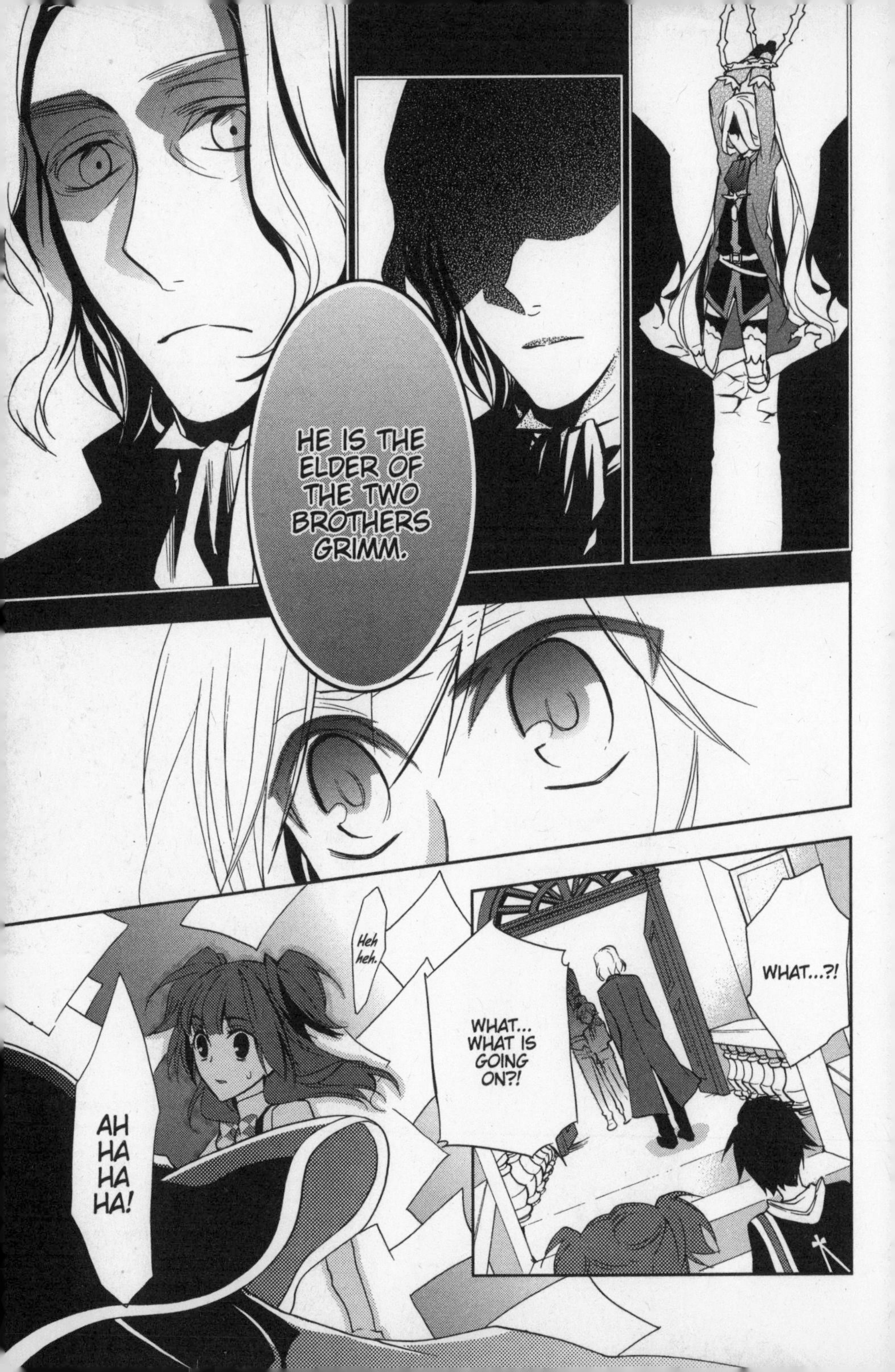

HE IS THE ELDER OF THE TWO BROTHERS GRIMM.
WHAT...?!
WHAT... WHAT IS GOING ON?!
Heh heh.
AH HA HA HA HA!

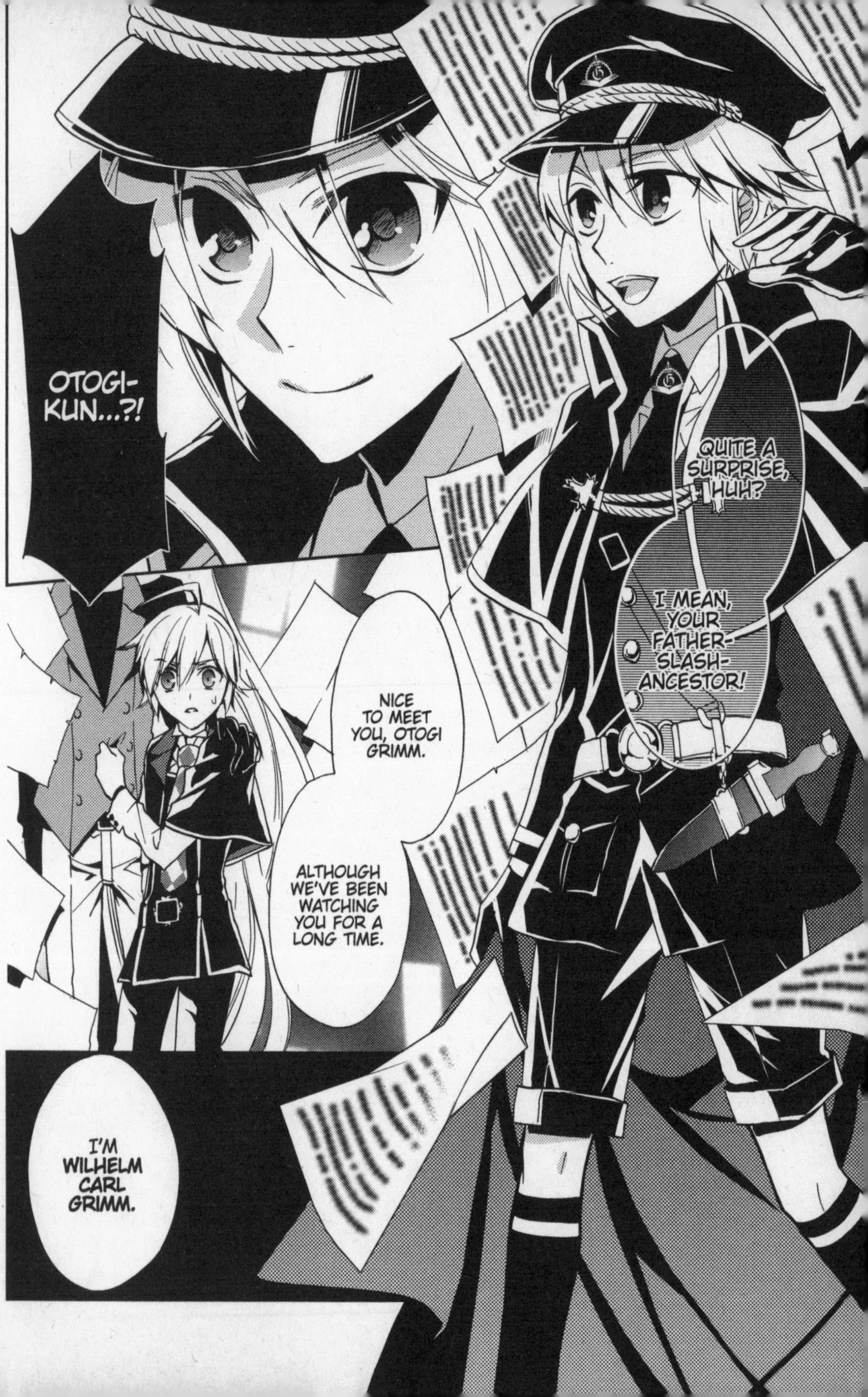
QUITE A SURPRISE, HUH?
I MEAN, YOUR FATHER-SLASH-ANCESTOR!
OTOGI-KUN...?!
NICE TO MEET YOU, OTOGI GRIMM.
ALTHOUGH WE'VE BEEN WATCHING YOU FOR A LONG TIME.
I'M WILHELM CARL GRIMM.

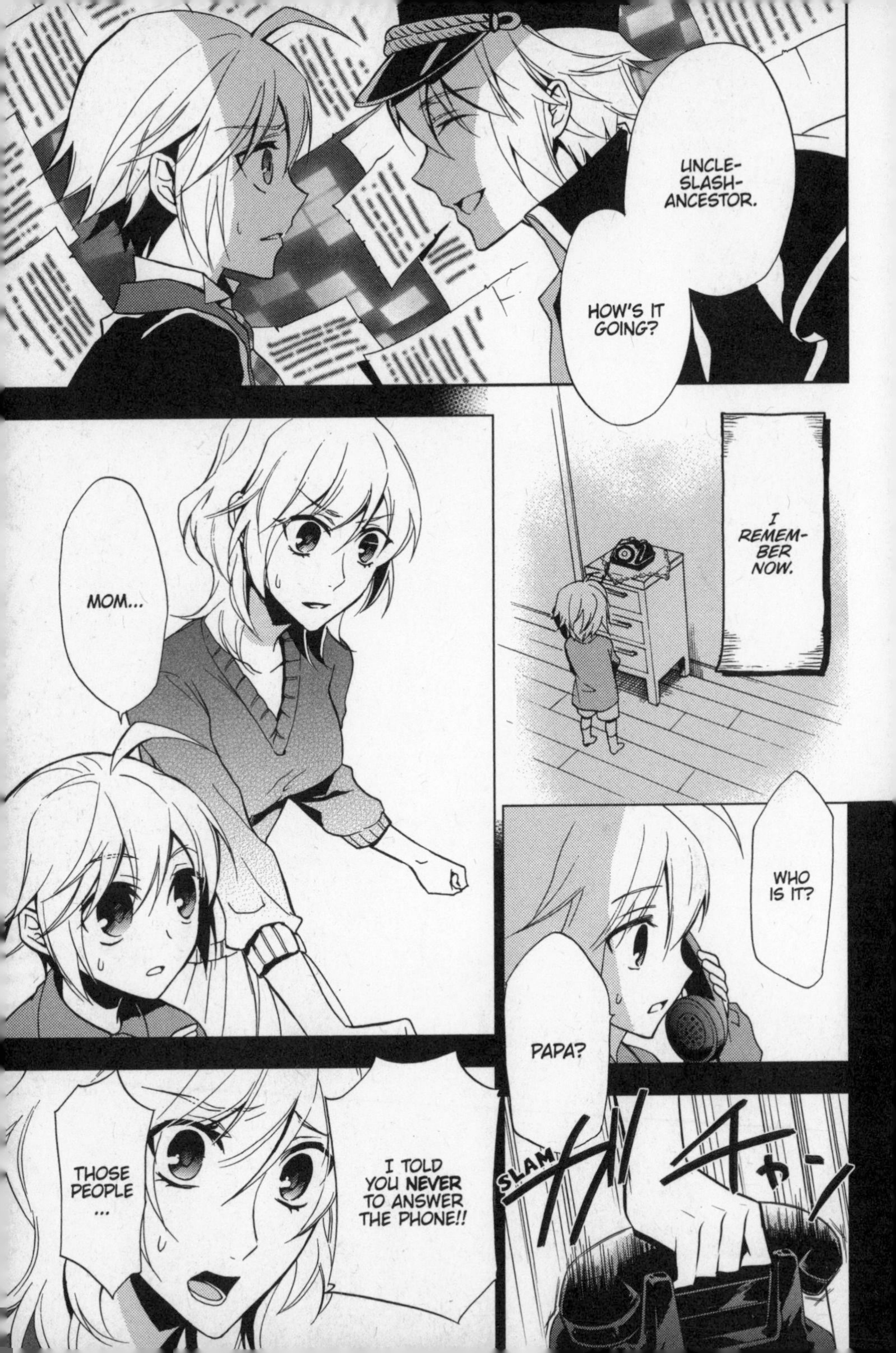
UNCLE-SLASH-ANCESTOR.
HOW'S IT GOING?
I REMEMBER NOW.
WHO IS IT?
PAPA?
SLAM
MOM...
I TOLD YOU **NEVER** TO ANSWER THE PHONE!!
THOSE PEOPLE ...

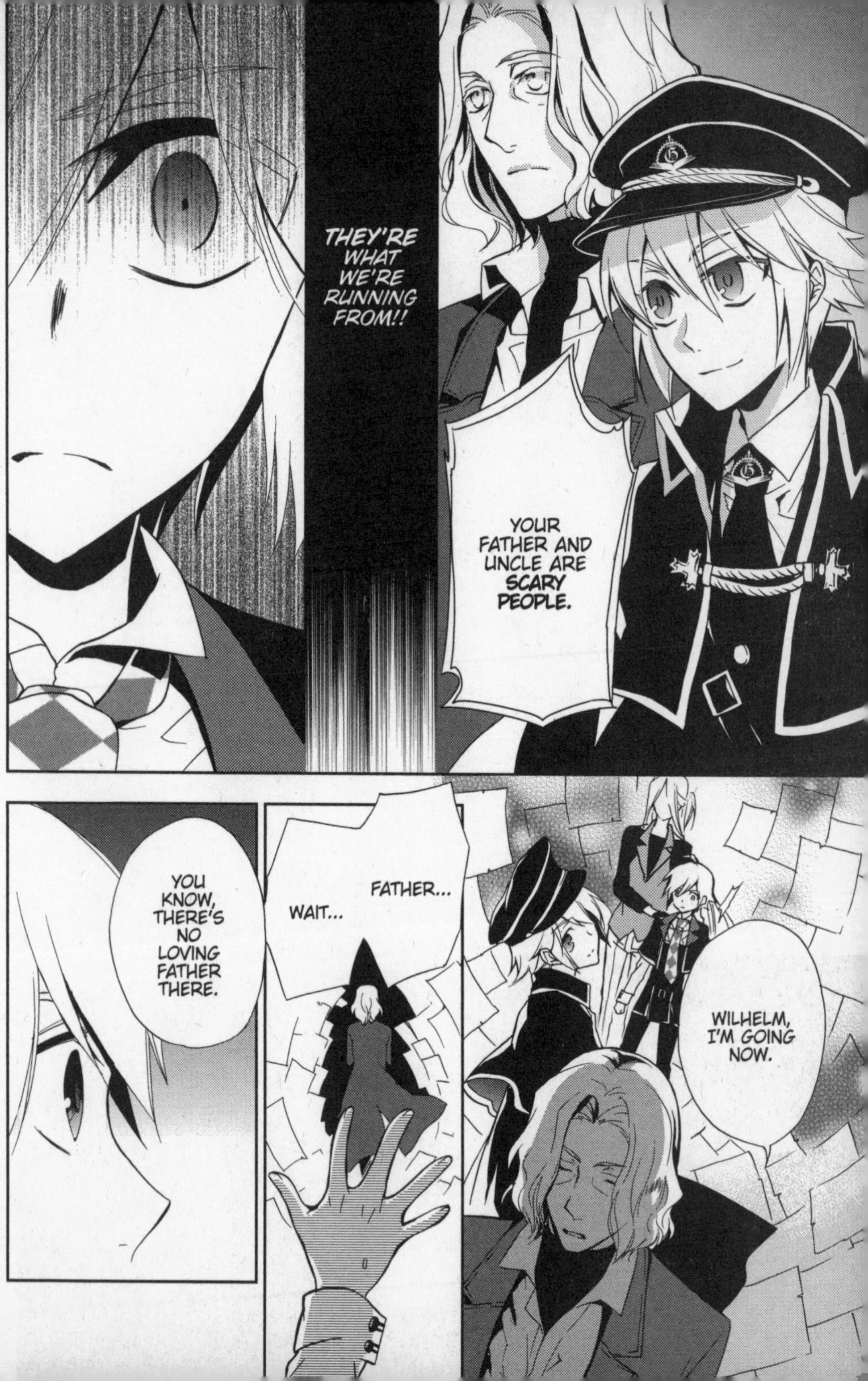
YOUR FATHER AND UNCLE ARE SCARY PEOPLE.
THEY'RE WHAT WE'RE RUNNING FROM!!
WILHELM, I'M GOING NOW.
FATHER...
WAIT...
YOU KNOW, THERE'S NO LOVING FATHER THERE.

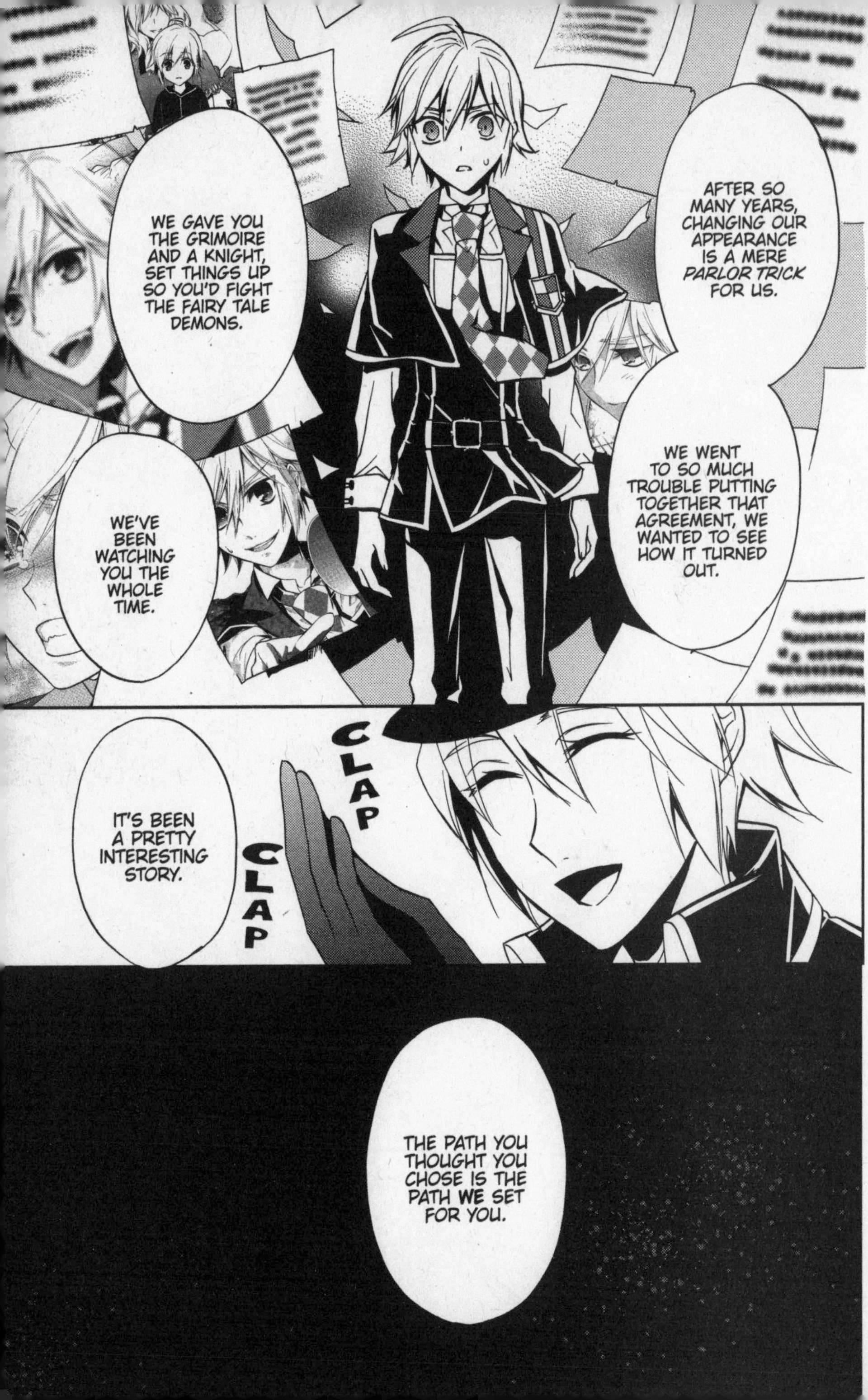

AFTER SO MANY YEARS, CHANGING OUR APPEARANCE IS A MERE *PARLOR TRICK* FOR US.
WE GAVE YOU THE GRIMOIRE AND A KNIGHT, SET THINGS UP SO YOU'D FIGHT THE FAIRY TALE DEMONS.
WE WENT TO SO MUCH TROUBLE PUTTING TOGETHER THAT AGREEMENT, WE WANTED TO SEE HOW IT TURNED OUT.
WE'VE BEEN WATCHING YOU THE WHOLE TIME.
CLAP
CLAP
IT'S BEEN A PRETTY INTERESTING STORY.
THE PATH YOU THOUGHT YOU CHOSE IS THE PATH WE SET FOR YOU.

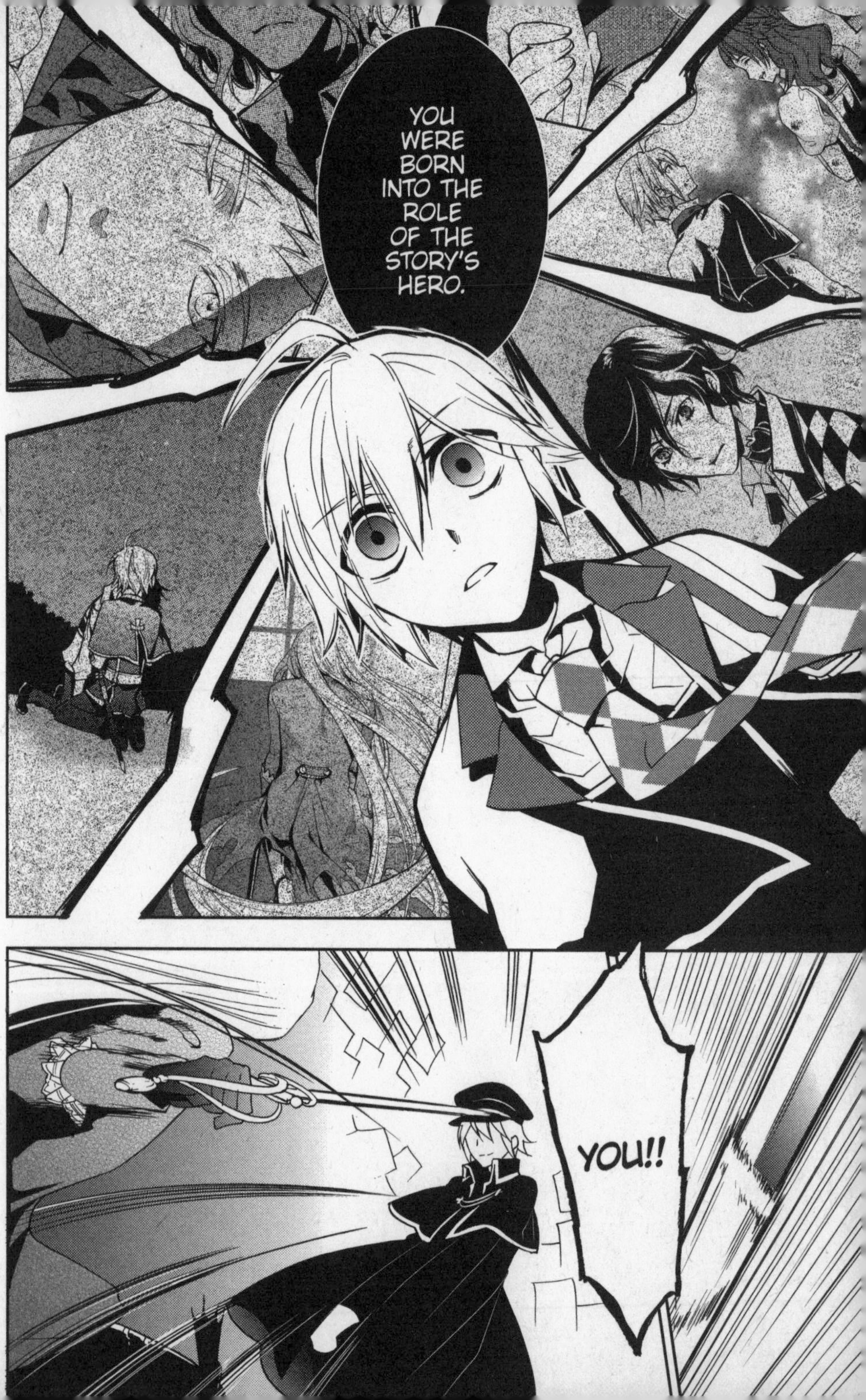
YOU WERE BORN INTO THE ROLE OF THE STORY'S HERO.
YOU!!

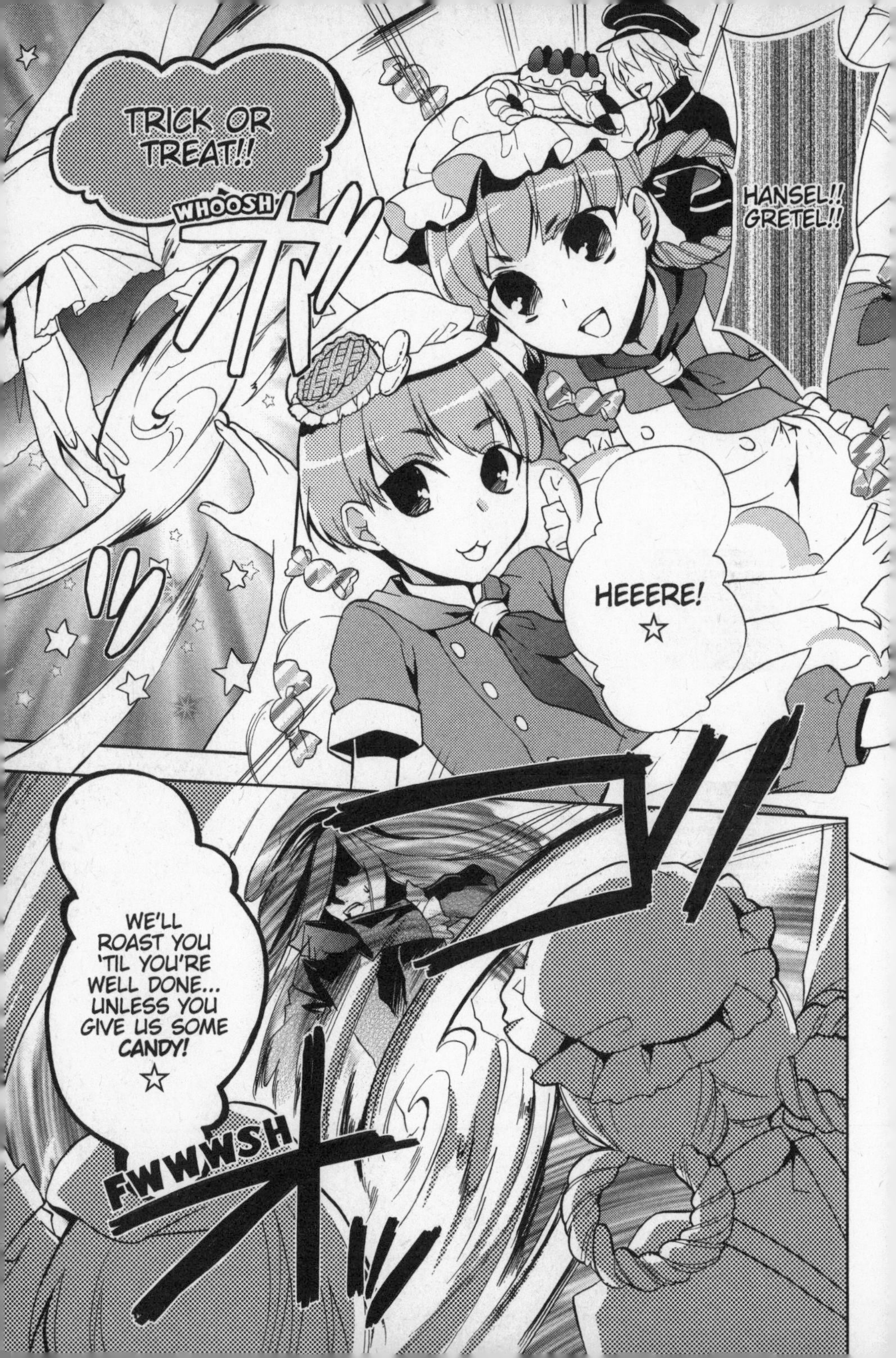
HANSEL!! GRETEL!!
TRICK OR TREAT!!
WHOOSH
HEEERE! ☆
WE'LL ROAST YOU 'TIL YOU'RE WELL DONE... UNLESS YOU GIVE US SOME CANDY! ☆
FWWWSH

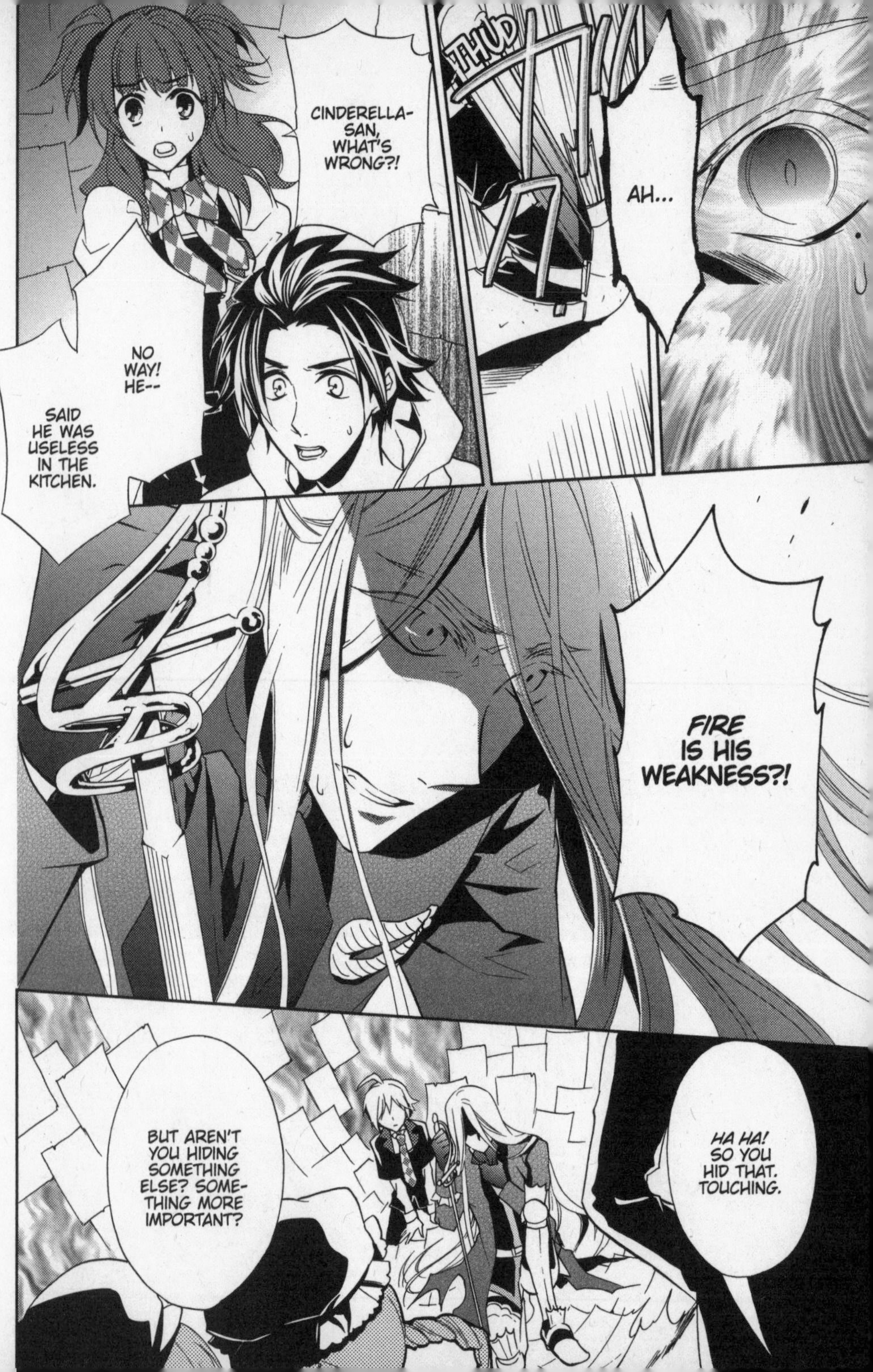
AH...
THUD
CINDERELLA-SAN, WHAT'S WRONG?!
NO WAY! HE--
SAID HE WAS USELESS IN THE KITCHEN.
FIRE IS HIS WEAKNESS?!
HA HA! SO YOU HID THAT. TOUCHING.
BUT AREN'T YOU HIDING SOMETHING ELSE? SOME-THING MORE IMPORTANT?

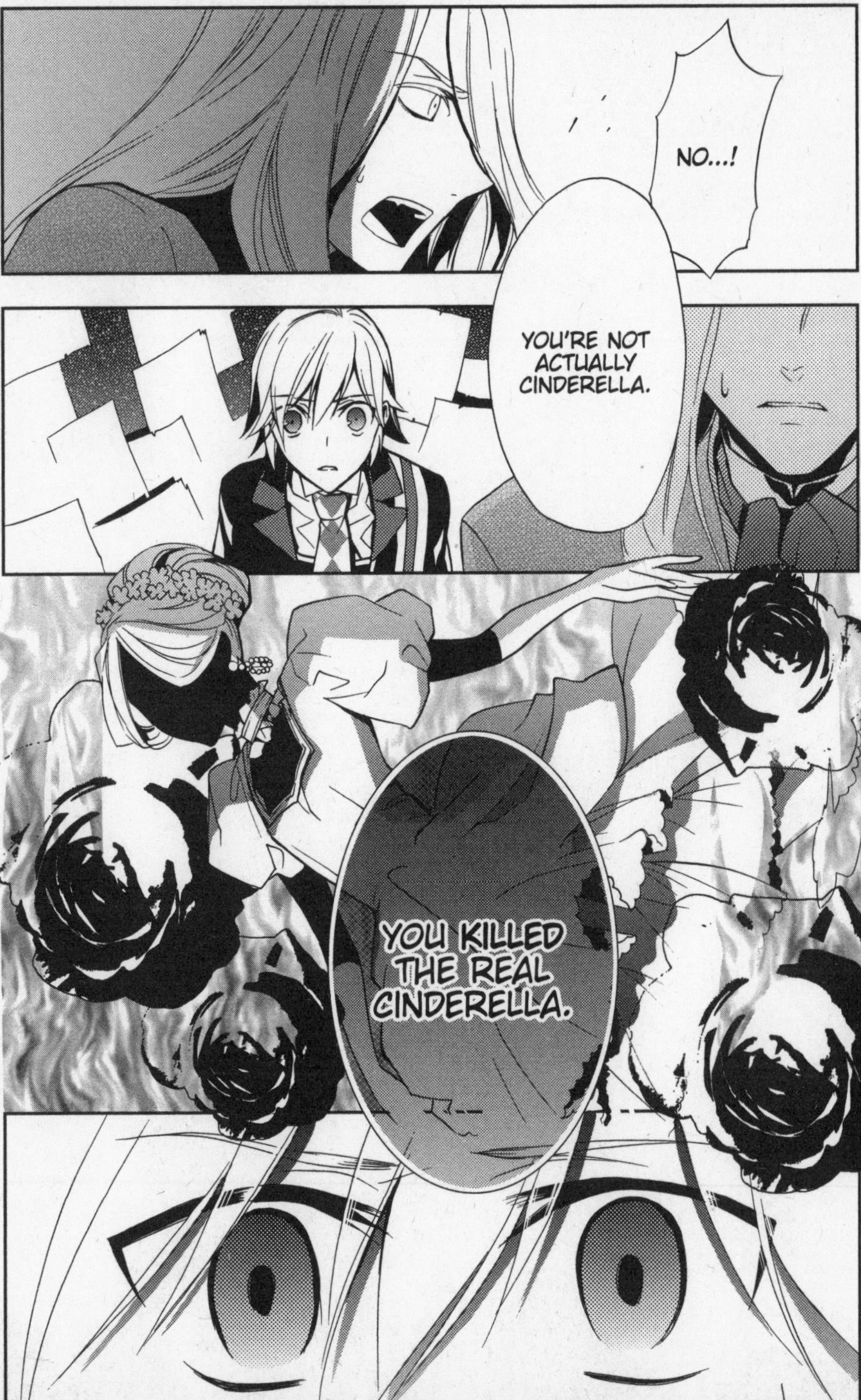
NO...!
YOU'RE NOT ACTUALLY CINDERELLA.
YOU KILLED THE REAL CINDERELLA.

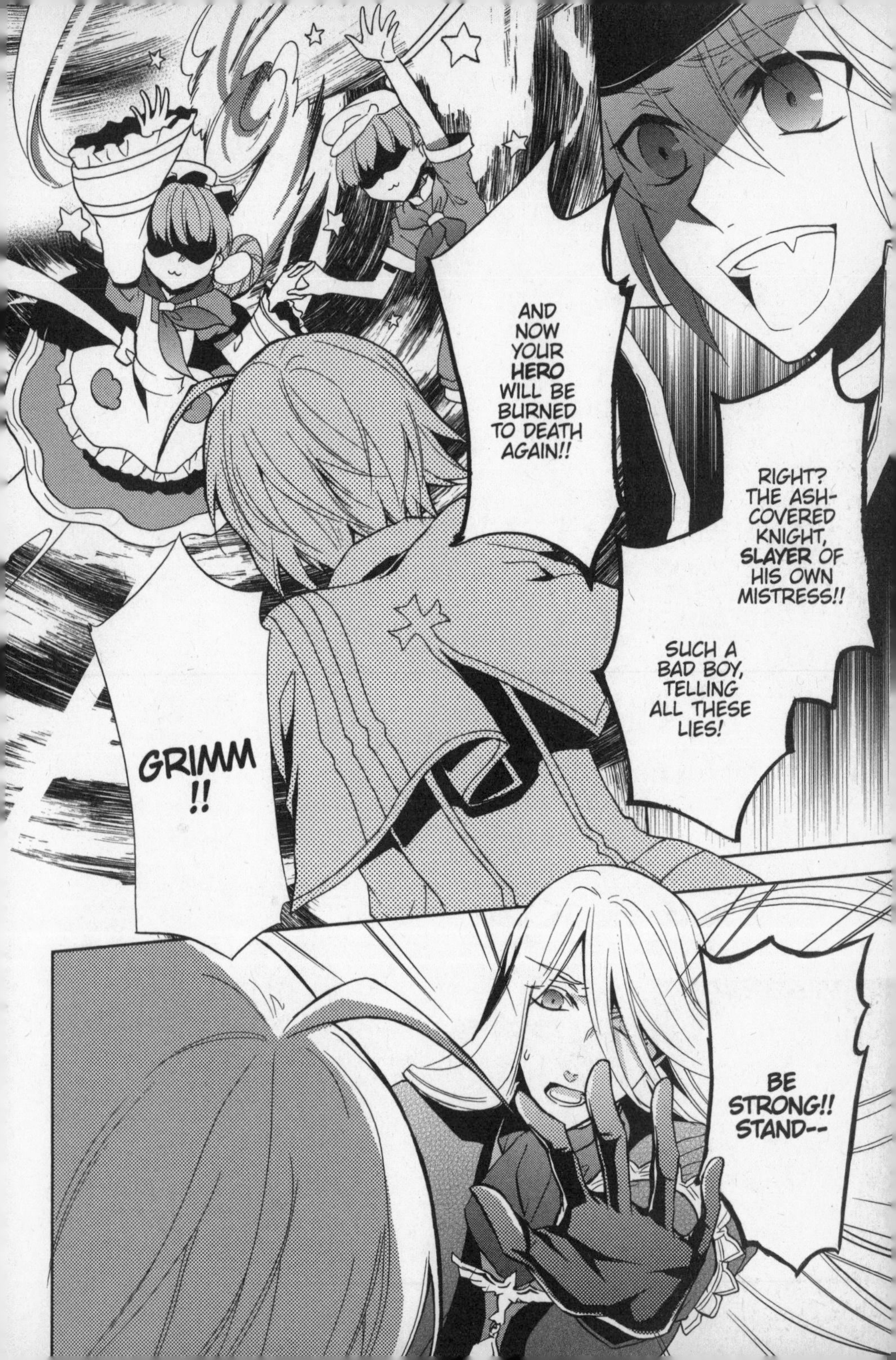
AND NOW YOUR HERO WILL BE BURNED TO DEATH AGAIN!!
RIGHT? THE ASH-COVERED KNIGHT, SLAYER OF HIS OWN MISTRESS!!
SUCH A BAD BOY, TELLING ALL THESE LIES!
GRIMM!!
BE STRONG!! STAND--

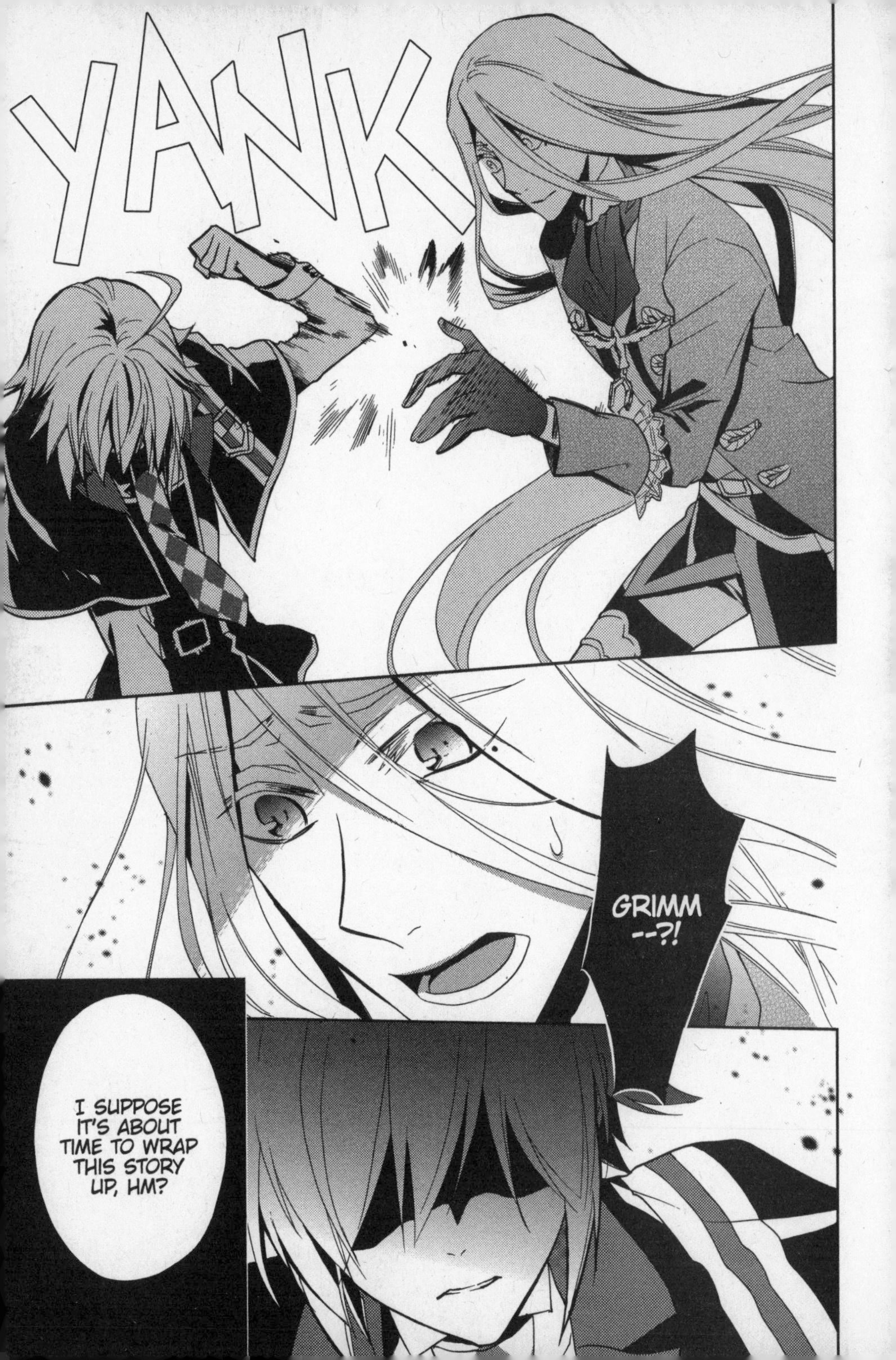
YANK
GRIMM --?!
I SUPPOSE IT'S ABOUT TIME TO WRAP THIS STORY UP, HM?

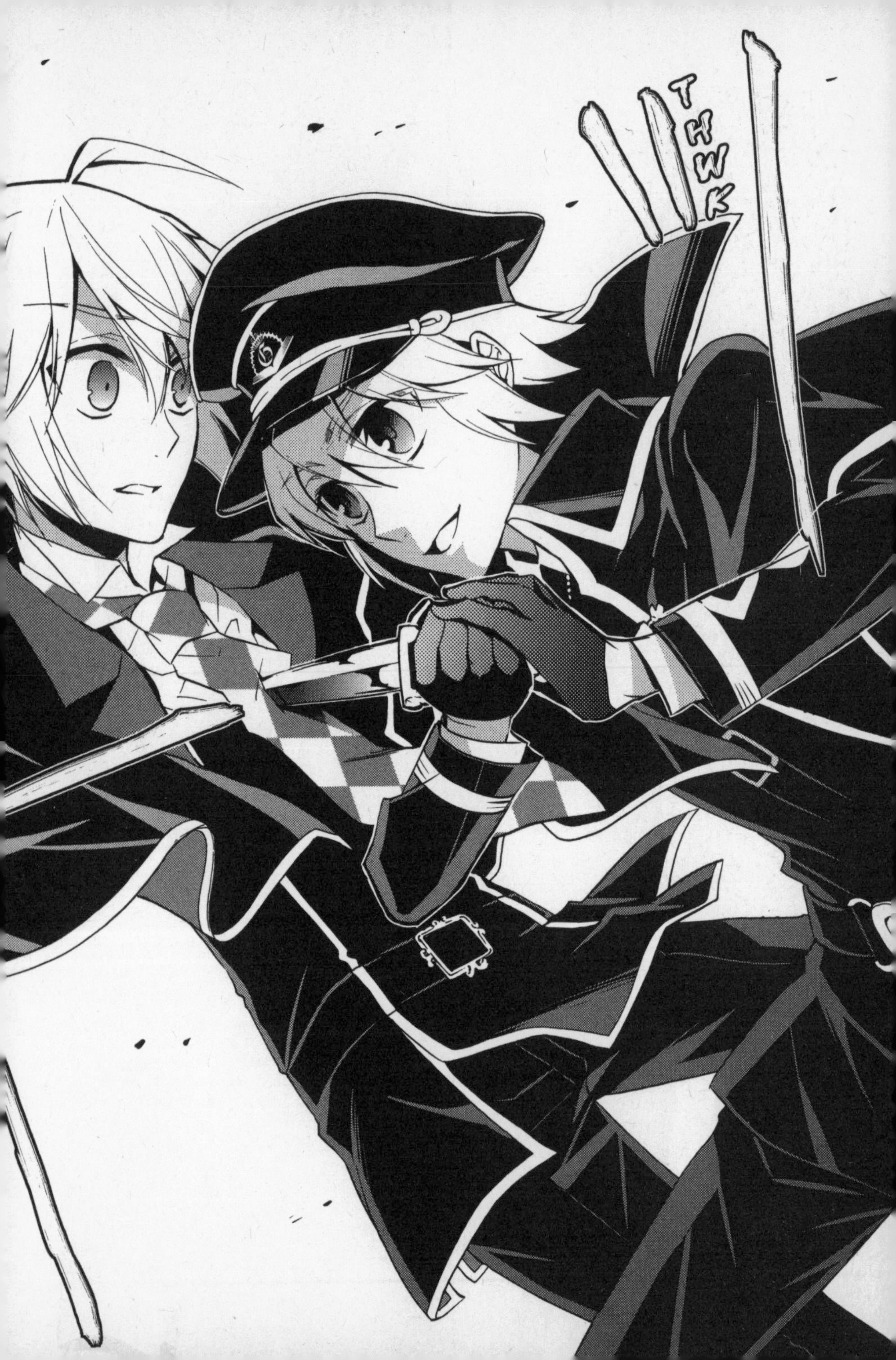
THWK

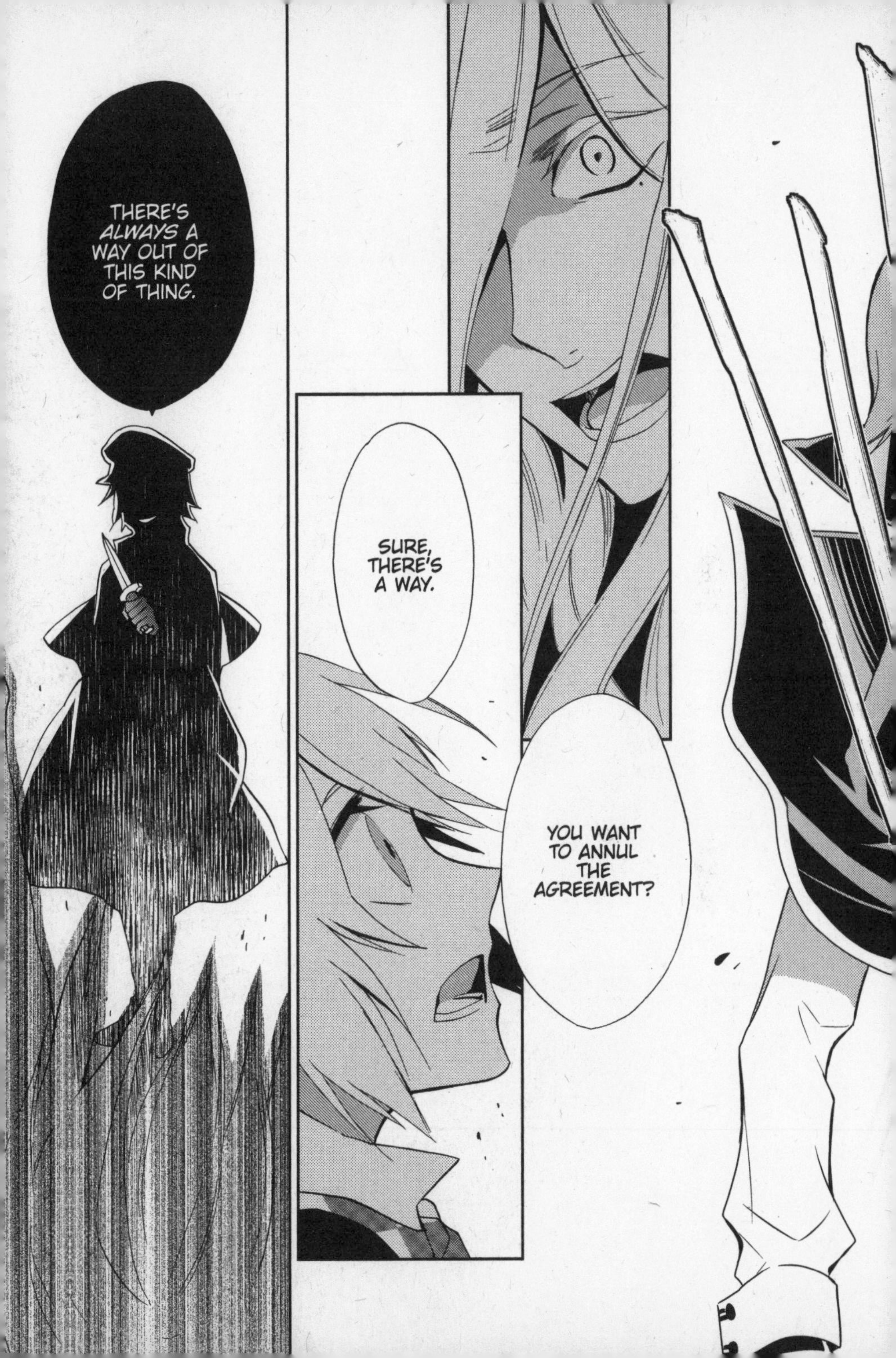
YOU WANT TO ANNUL THE AGREEMENT?
SURE, THERE'S A WAY.
THERE'S *ALWAYS* A WAY OUT OF THIS KIND OF THING.

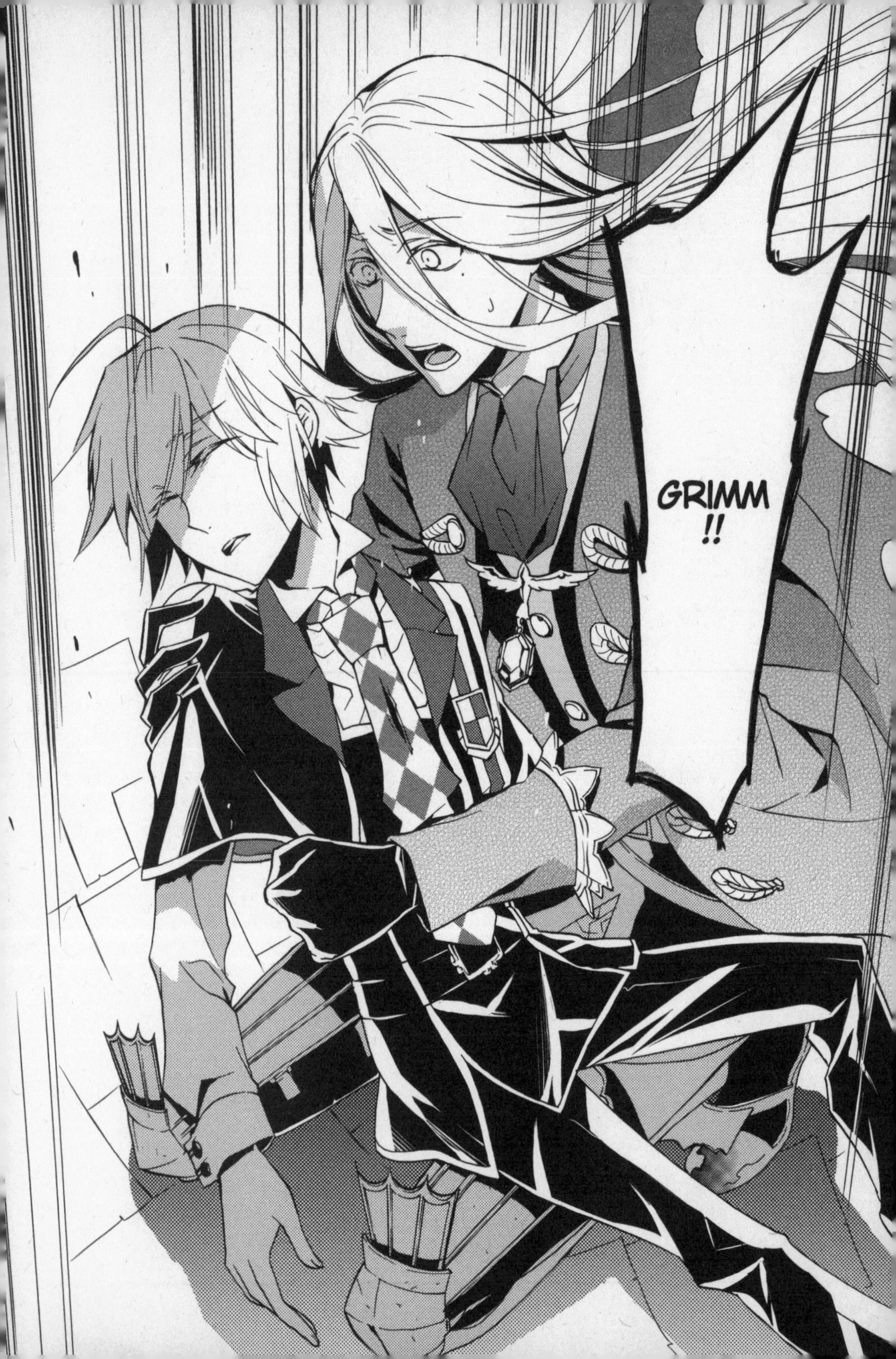
GRIMM !!

Dictatorial Grimoire

独裁グリムワール

Dictatorial Grimoire

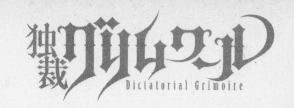

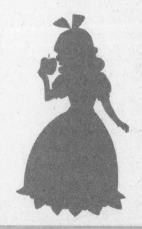

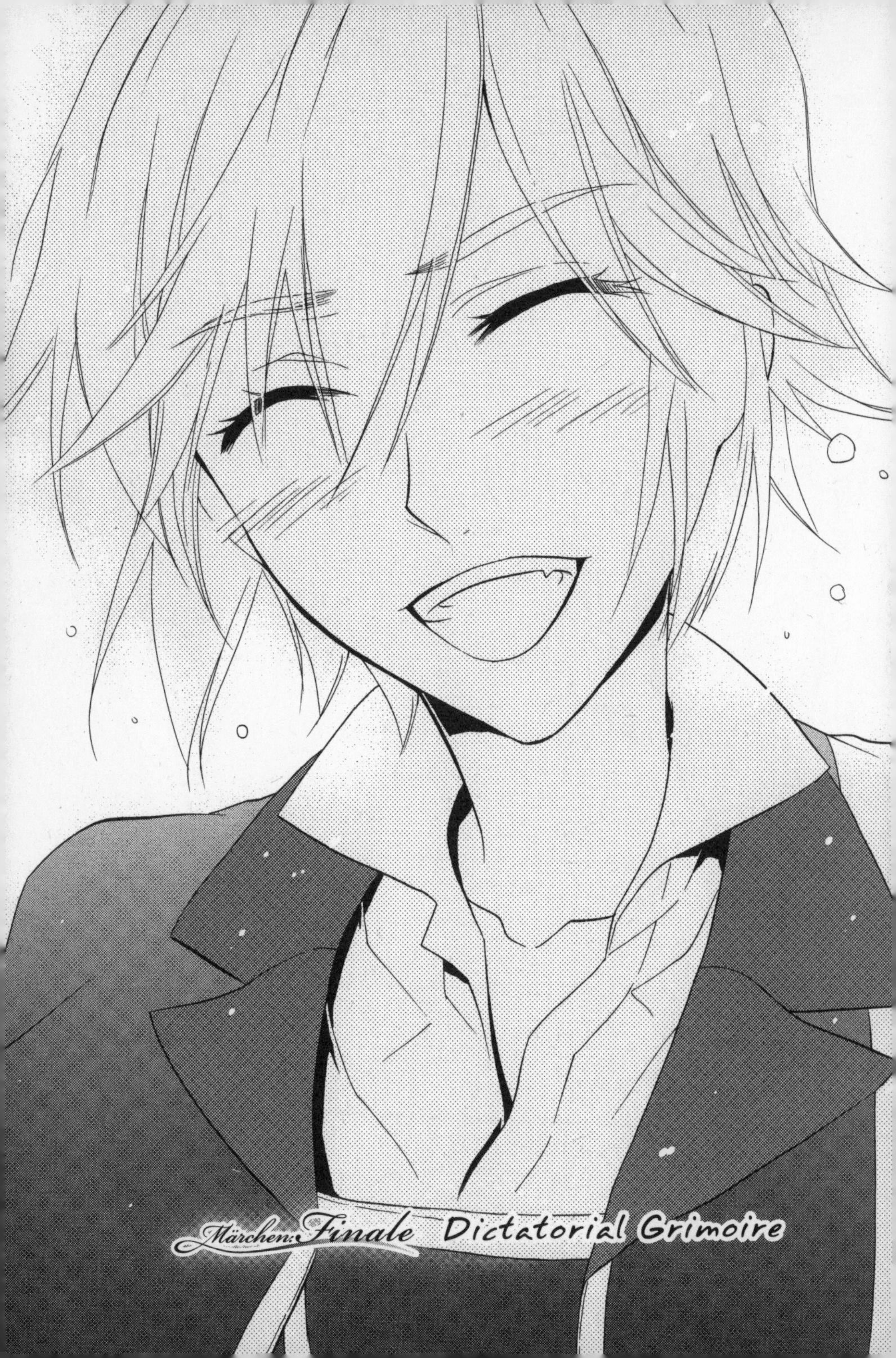
Märchen: Finale Dictatorial Grimoire

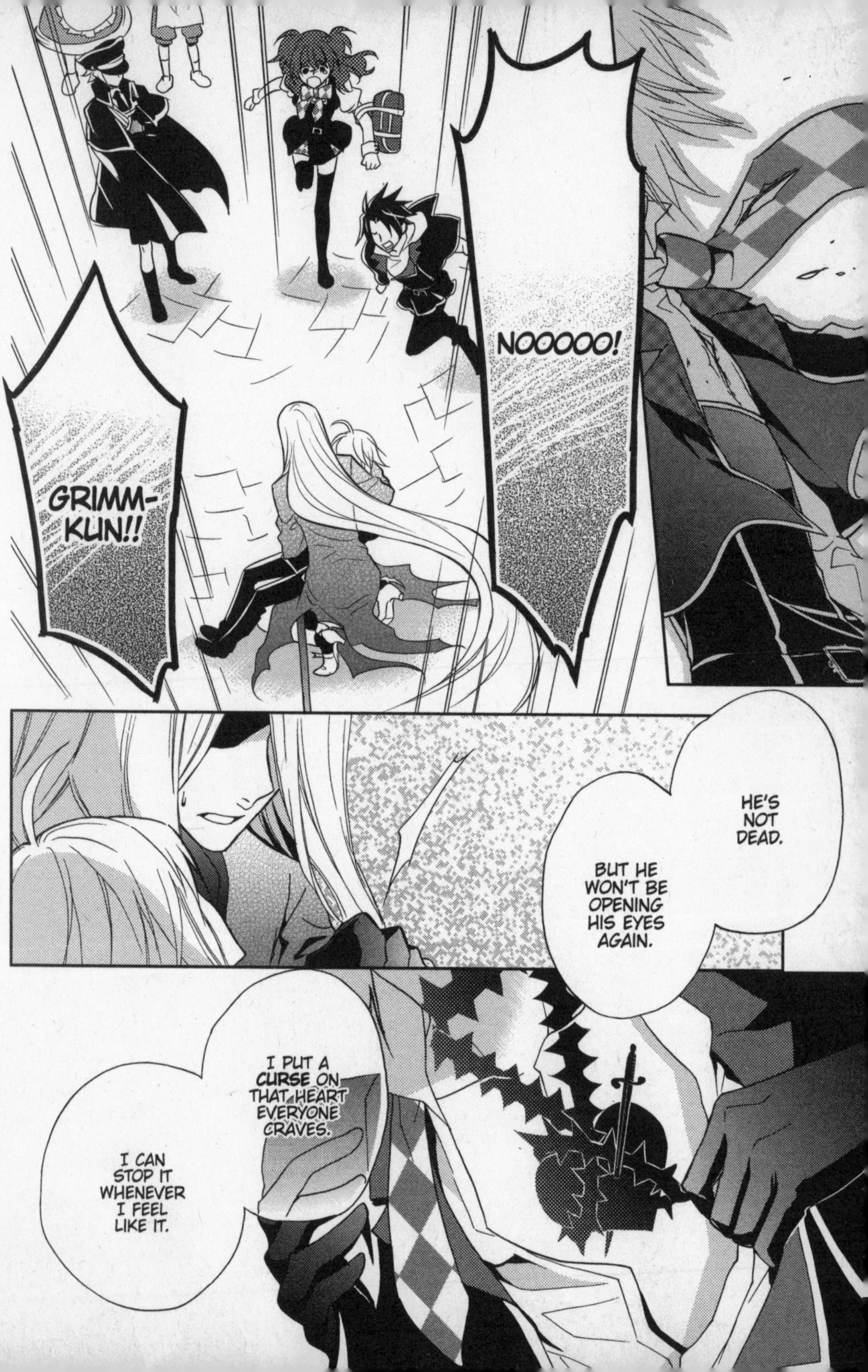
NOOOOO!
GRIMM-KUN!!
HE'S NOT DEAD.
BUT HE WON'T BE OPENING HIS EYES AGAIN.
I PUT A CURSE ON THAT HEART EVERYONE CRAVES.
I CAN STOP IT WHENEVER I FEEL LIKE IT.

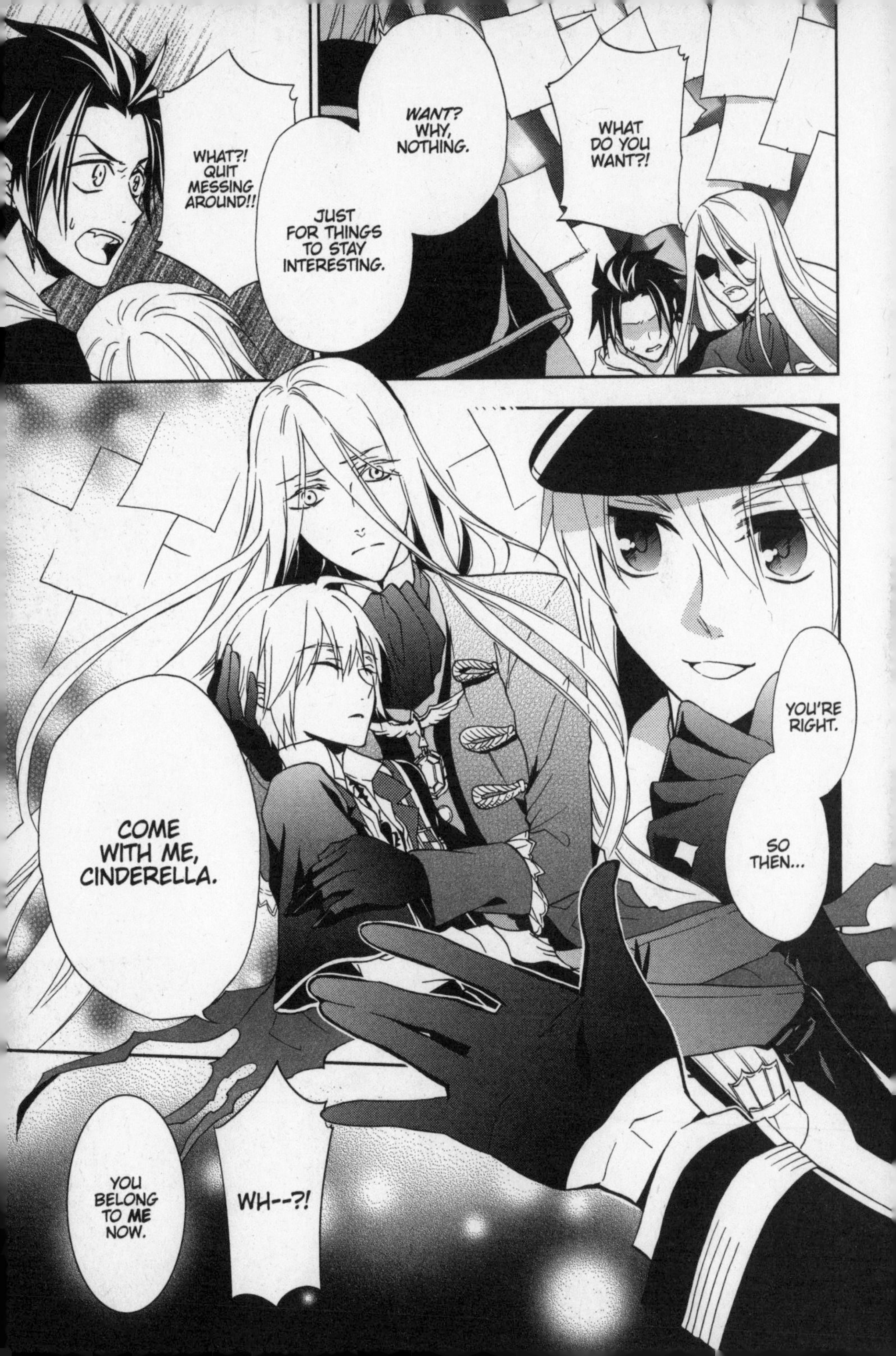
WHAT DO YOU WANT?!
WANT? WHY, NOTHING.
JUST FOR THINGS TO STAY INTERESTING.
WHAT?! QUIT MESSING AROUND!!
YOU'RE RIGHT.
SO THEN...
COME WITH ME, CINDERELLA.
WH--?!
YOU BELONG TO ME NOW.

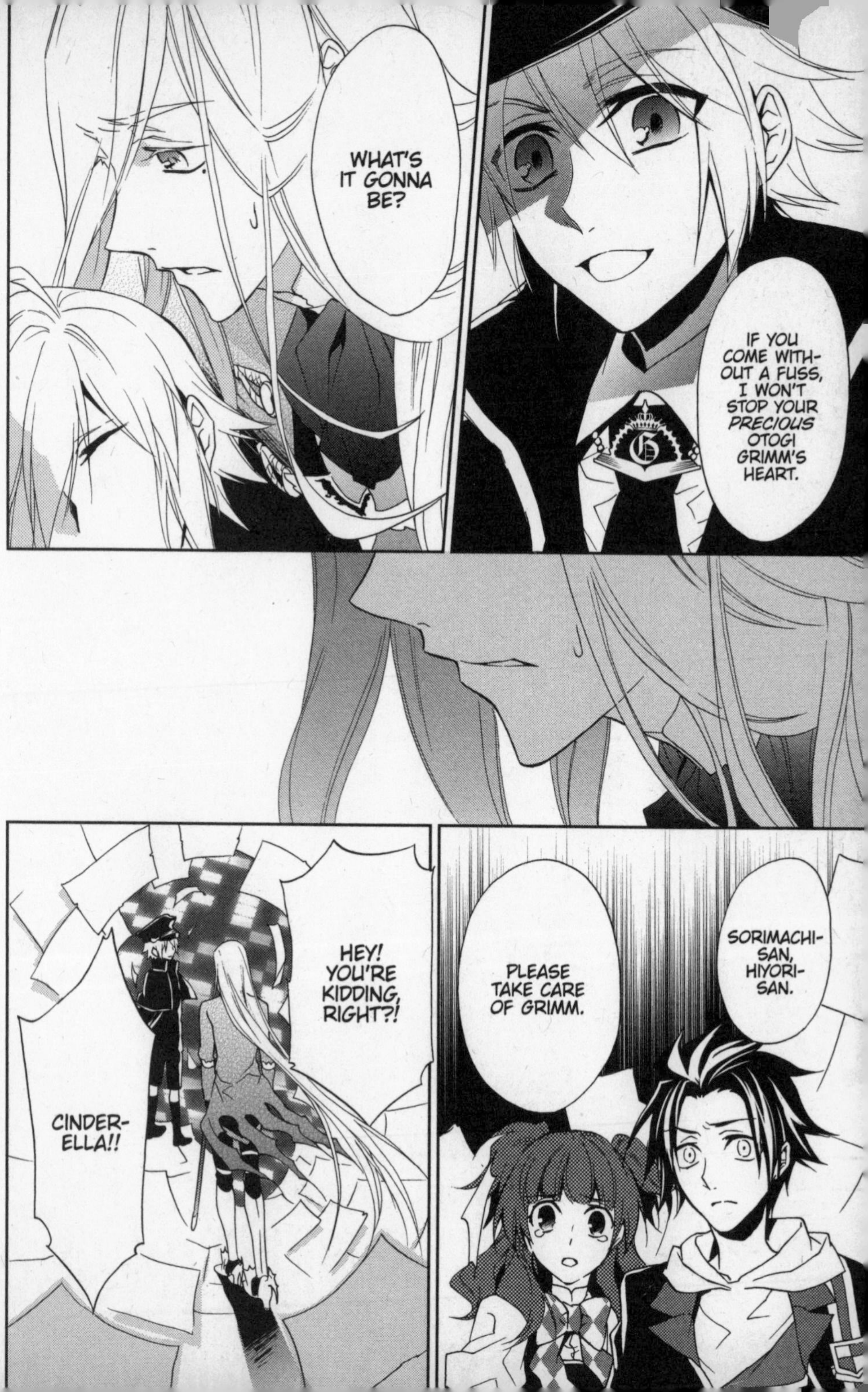
IF YOU COME WITH-OUT A FUSS, I WON'T STOP YOUR *PRECIOUS* OTOGI GRIMM'S HEART.
WHAT'S IT GONNA BE?
SORIMACHI-SAN, HIYORI-SAN.
PLEASE TAKE CARE OF GRIMM.
HEY! YOU'RE KIDDING, RIGHT?!
CINDER-ELLA!!

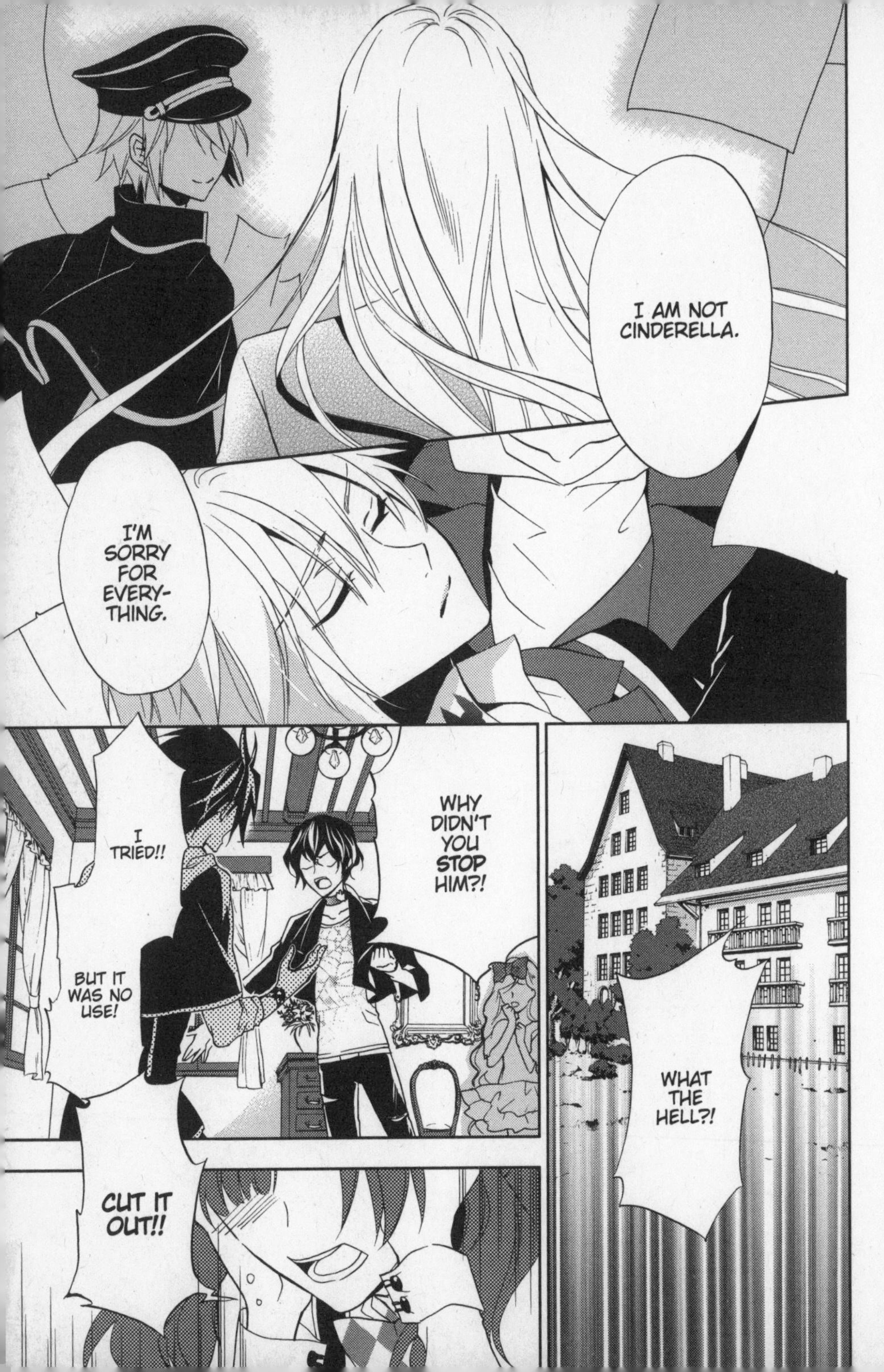
I AM NOT CINDERELLA.
I'M SORRY FOR EVERYTHING.
WHAT THE HELL?!
WHY DIDN'T YOU STOP HIM?!
I TRIED!!
BUT IT WAS NO USE!
CUT IT OUT!!

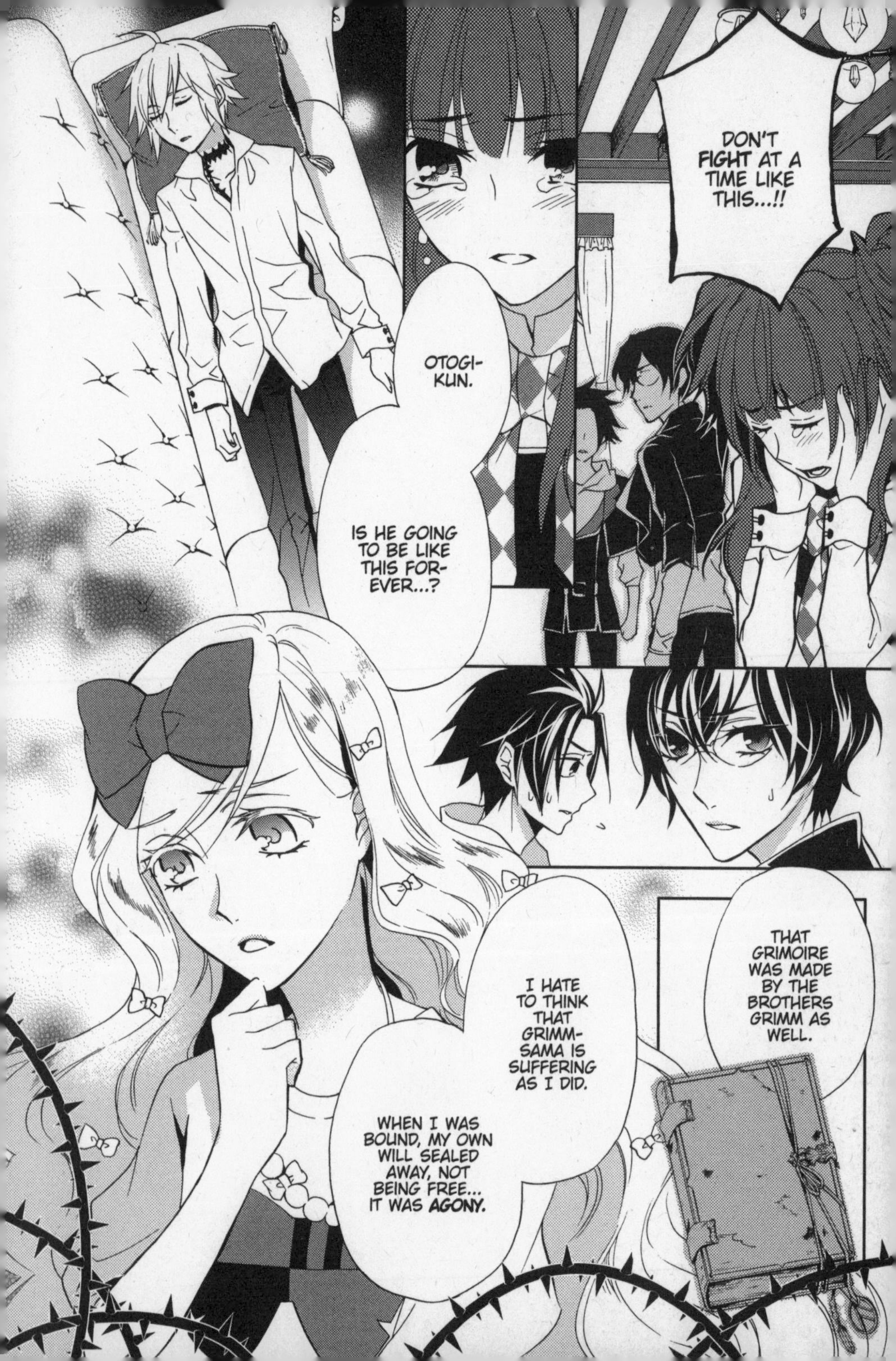
DON'T FIGHT AT A TIME LIKE THIS...!!
OTOGI-KUN.
IS HE GOING TO BE LIKE THIS FOR-EVER...?
THAT GRIMOIRE WAS MADE BY THE BROTHERS GRIMM AS WELL.
I HATE TO THINK THAT GRIMM-SAMA IS SUFFERING AS I DID.
WHEN I WAS BOUND, MY OWN WILL SEALED AWAY, NOT BEING FREE... IT WAS AGONY.

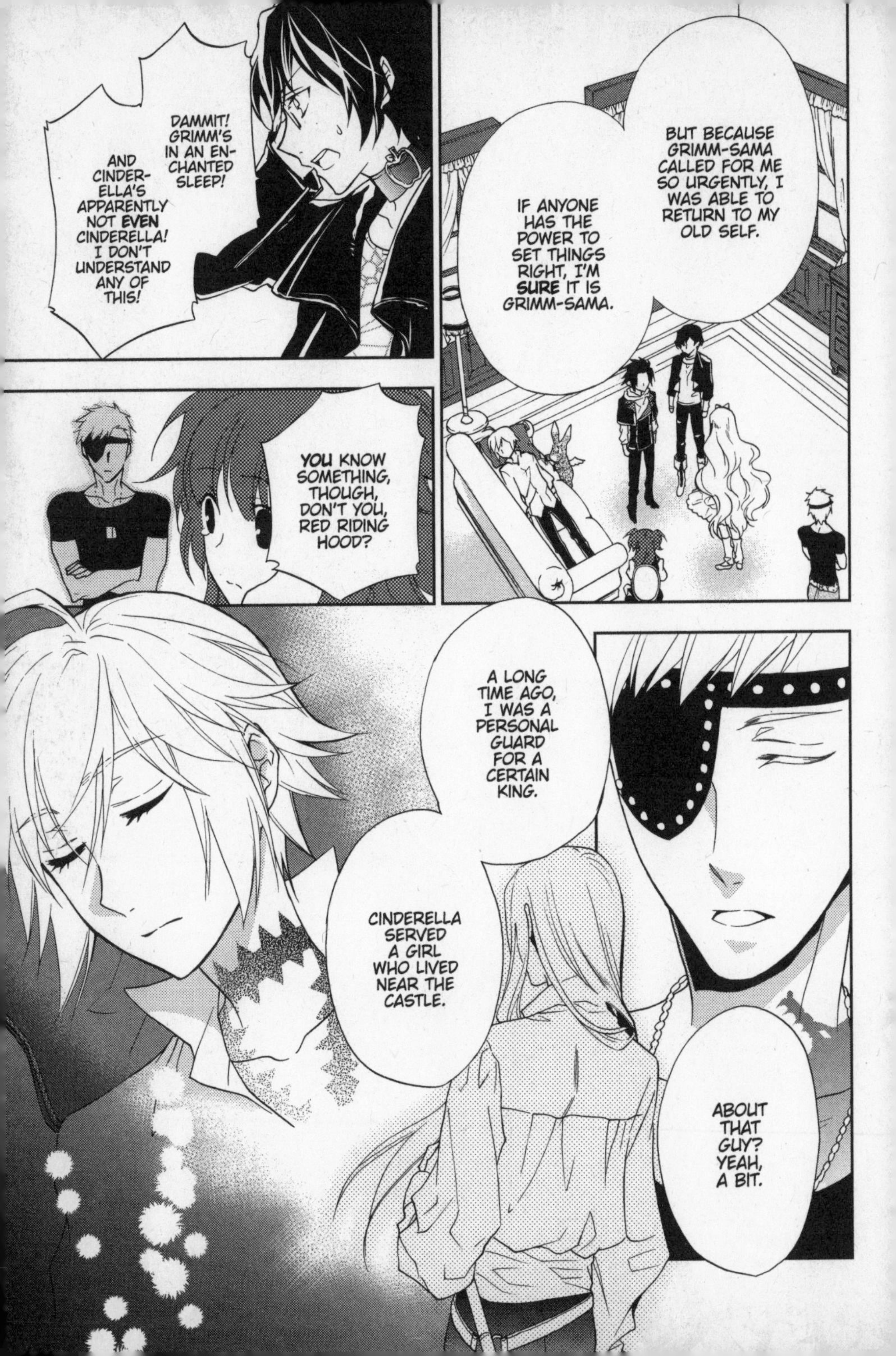

BUT BECAUSE GRIMM-SAMA CALLED FOR ME SO URGENTLY, I WAS ABLE TO RETURN TO MY OLD SELF.
IF ANYONE HAS THE POWER TO SET THINGS RIGHT, I'M **SURE** IT IS GRIMM-SAMA.
DAMMIT! GRIMM'S IN AN EN-CHANTED SLEEP!
AND CINDER-ELLA'S APPARENTLY NOT **EVEN** CINDERELLA! I DON'T UNDERSTAND ANY OF THIS!
**YOU** KNOW SOMETHING, THOUGH, DON'T YOU, RED RIDING HOOD?
ABOUT THAT GUY? YEAH, A BIT.
A LONG TIME AGO, I WAS A PERSONAL GUARD FOR A CERTAIN KING.
CINDERELLA SERVED A GIRL WHO LIVED NEAR THE CASTLE.

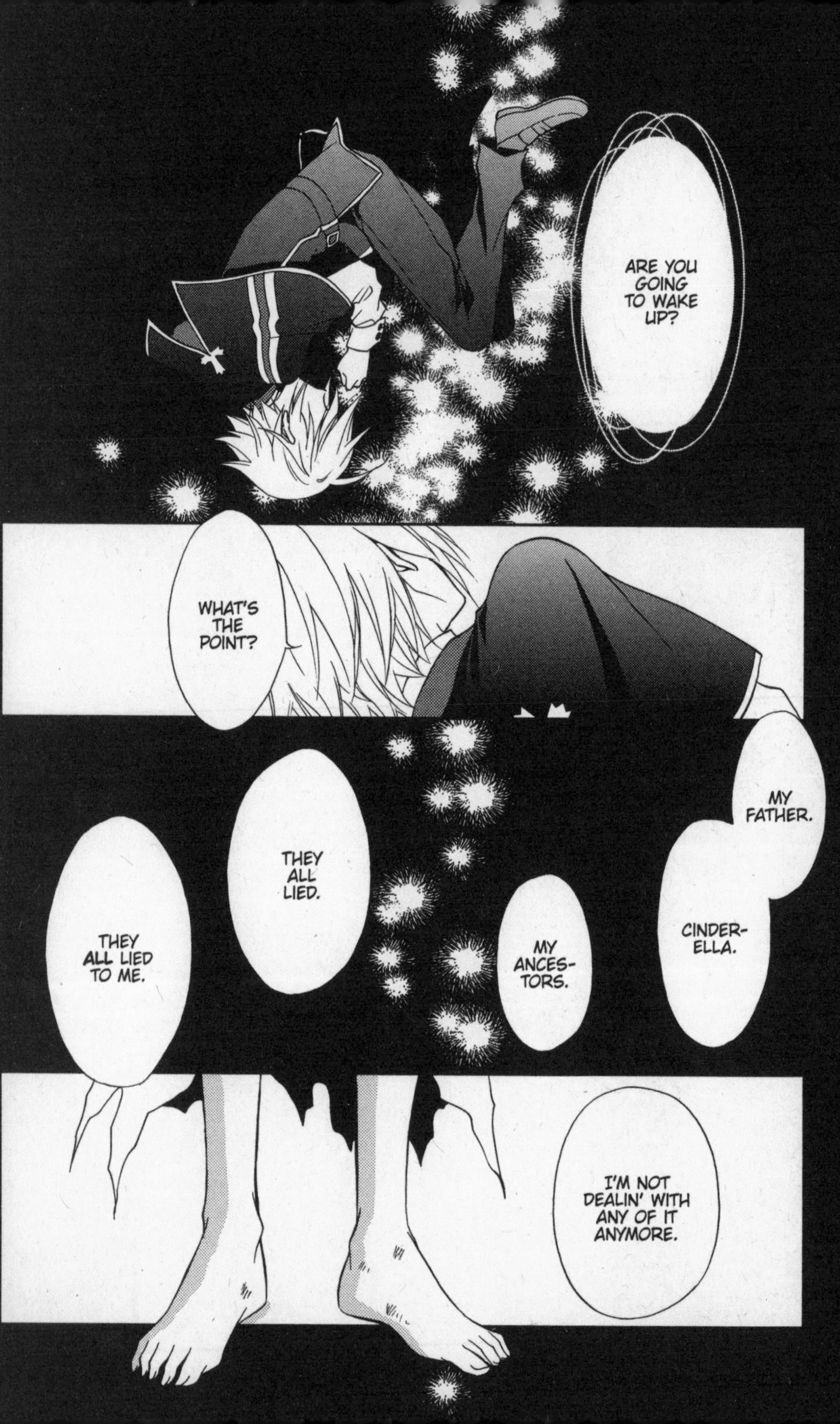
ARE YOU GOING TO WAKE UP?
WHAT'S THE POINT?
MY FATHER.
CINDER-ELLA.
MY ANCES-TORS.
THEY ALL LIED.
THEY ALL LIED TO ME.
I'M NOT DEALIN' WITH ANY OF IT ANYMORE.

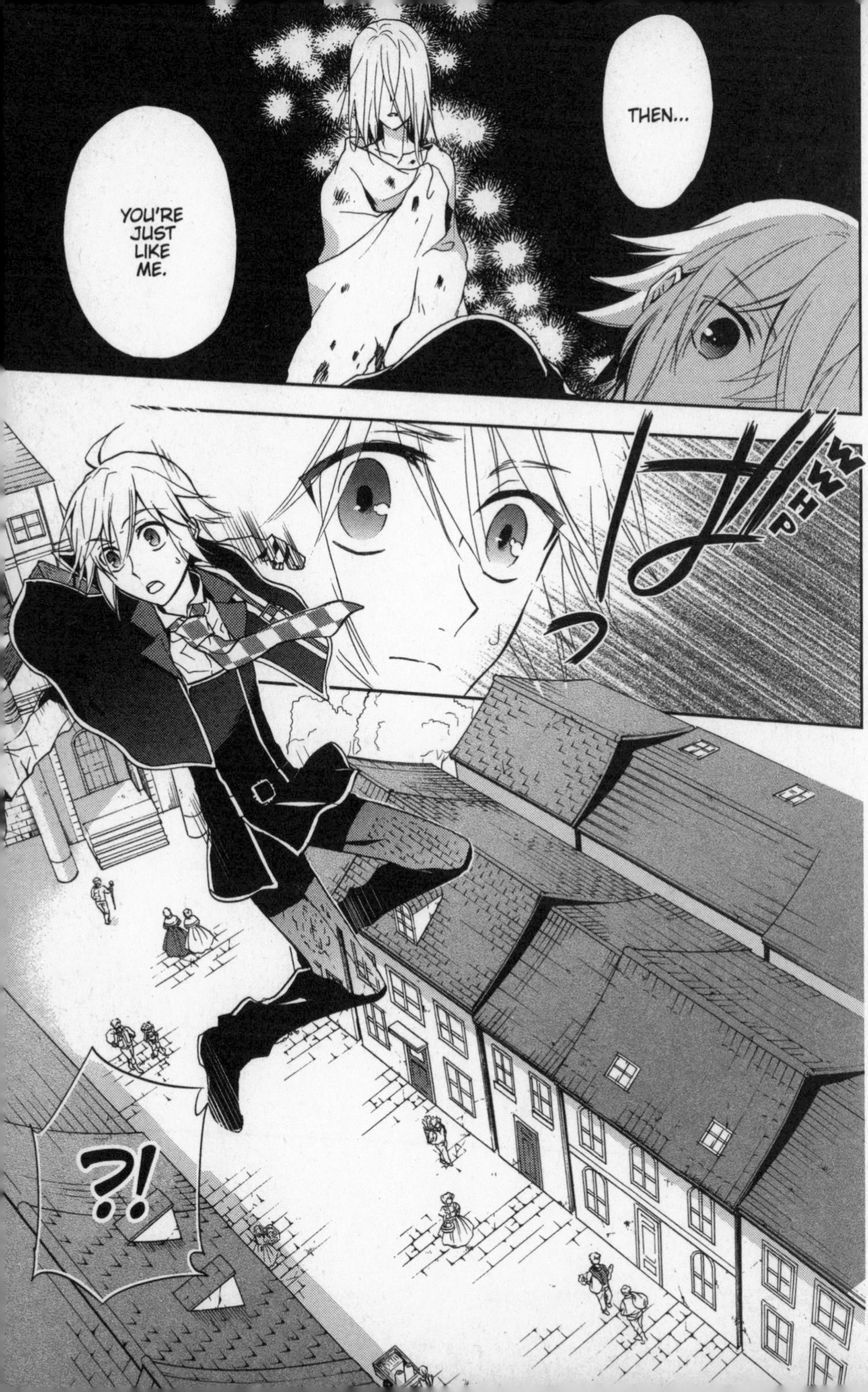
THEN...
YOU'RE JUST LIKE ME.
WWHP
?!

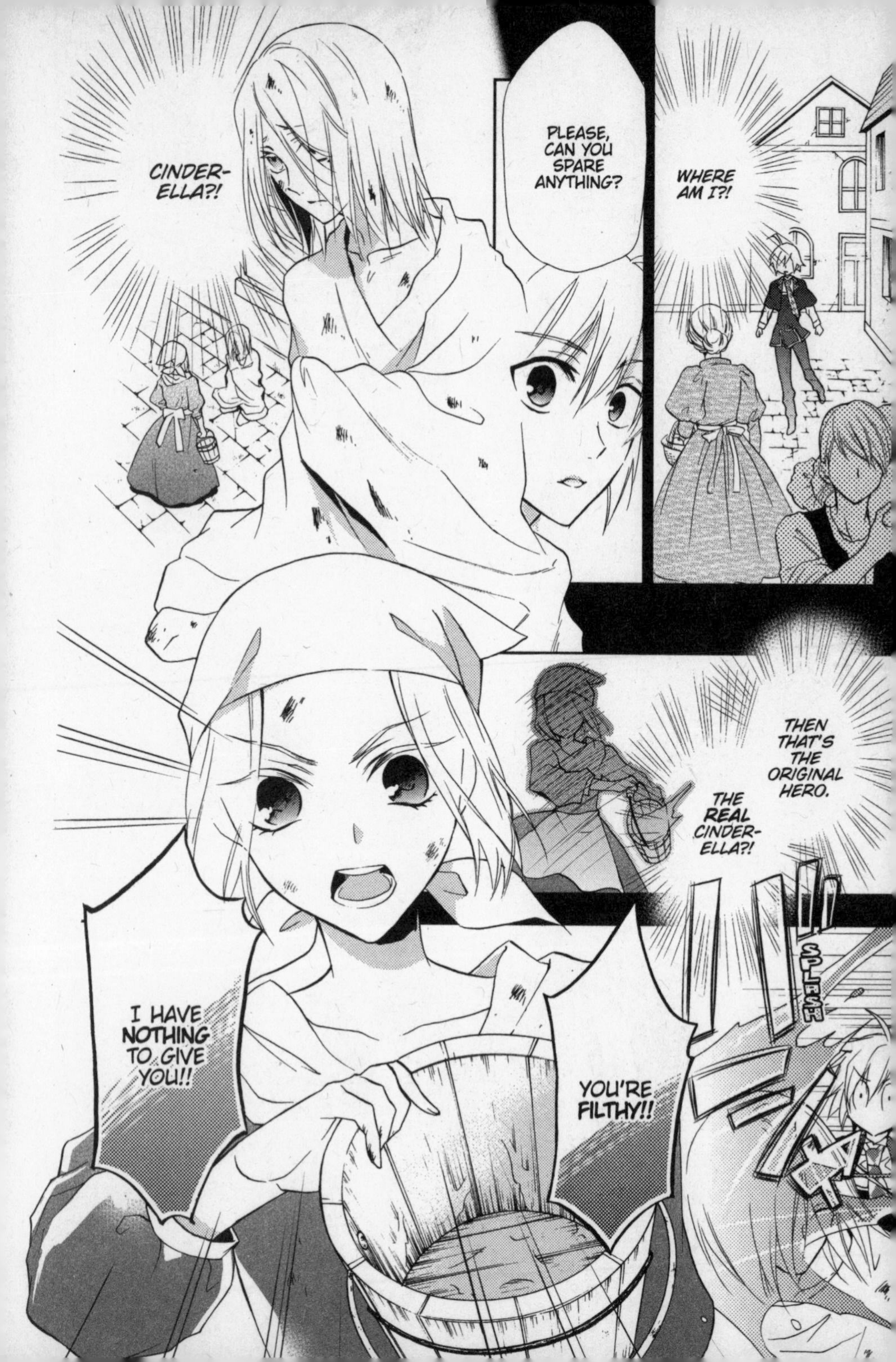
WHERE AM I?!
PLEASE, CAN YOU SPARE ANYTHING?
CINDER-ELLA?!
THEN THAT'S THE ORIGINAL HERO.
THE REAL CINDER-ELLA?!
SPLASH
YOU'RE FILTHY!!
I HAVE NOTHING TO GIVE YOU!!

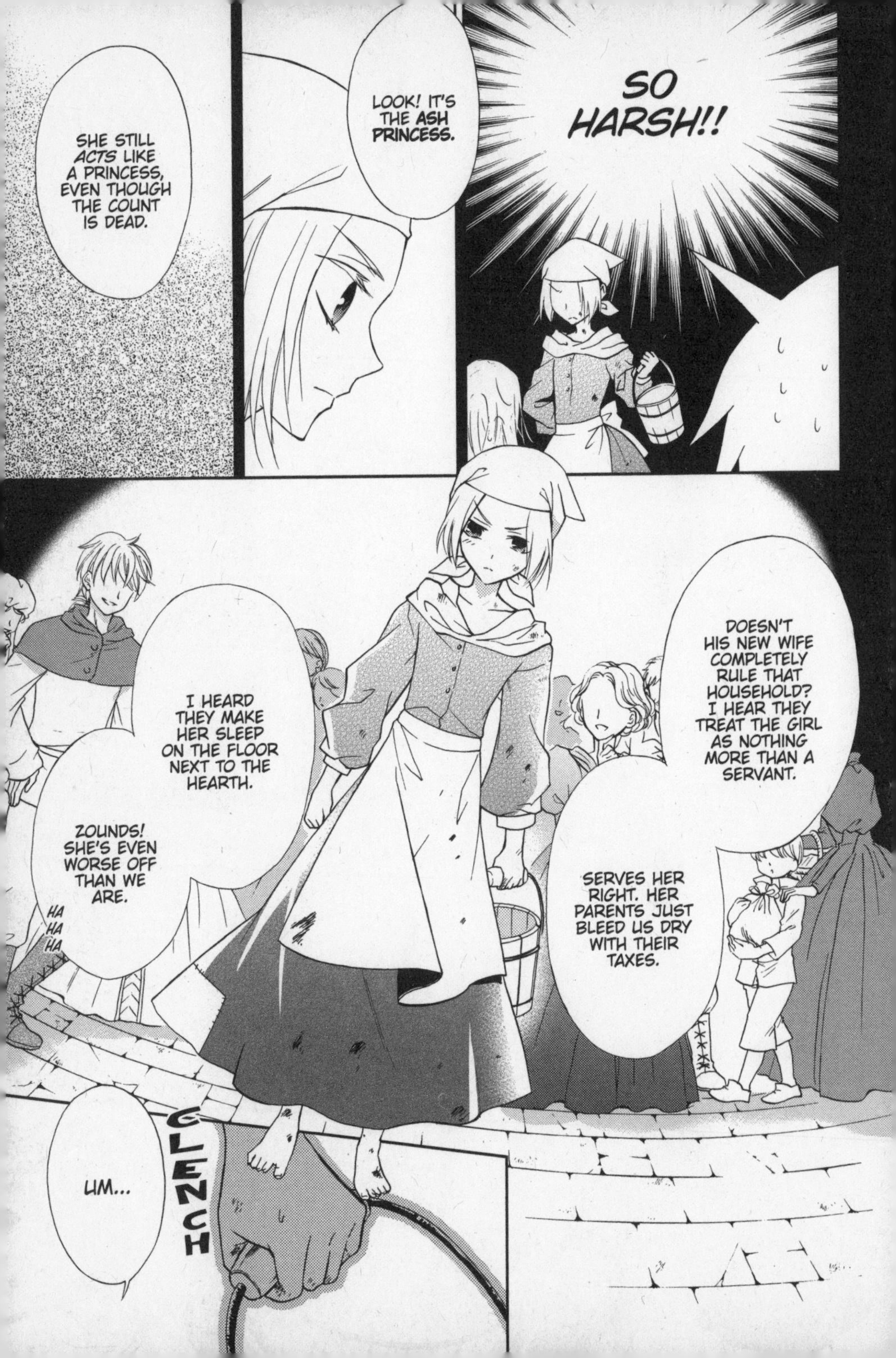
SO HARSH!!
LOOK! IT'S THE ASH PRINCESS.
SHE STILL ACTS LIKE A PRINCESS, EVEN THOUGH THE COUNT IS DEAD.
DOESN'T HIS NEW WIFE COMPLETELY RULE THAT HOUSEHOLD? I HEAR THEY TREAT THE GIRL AS NOTHING MORE THAN A SERVANT.
I HEARD THEY MAKE HER SLEEP ON THE FLOOR NEXT TO THE HEARTH.
SERVES HER RIGHT. HER PARENTS JUST BLEED US DRY WITH THEIR TAXES.
ZOUNDS! SHE'S EVEN WORSE OFF THAN WE ARE.
HA HA HA
CLENCH
UM...

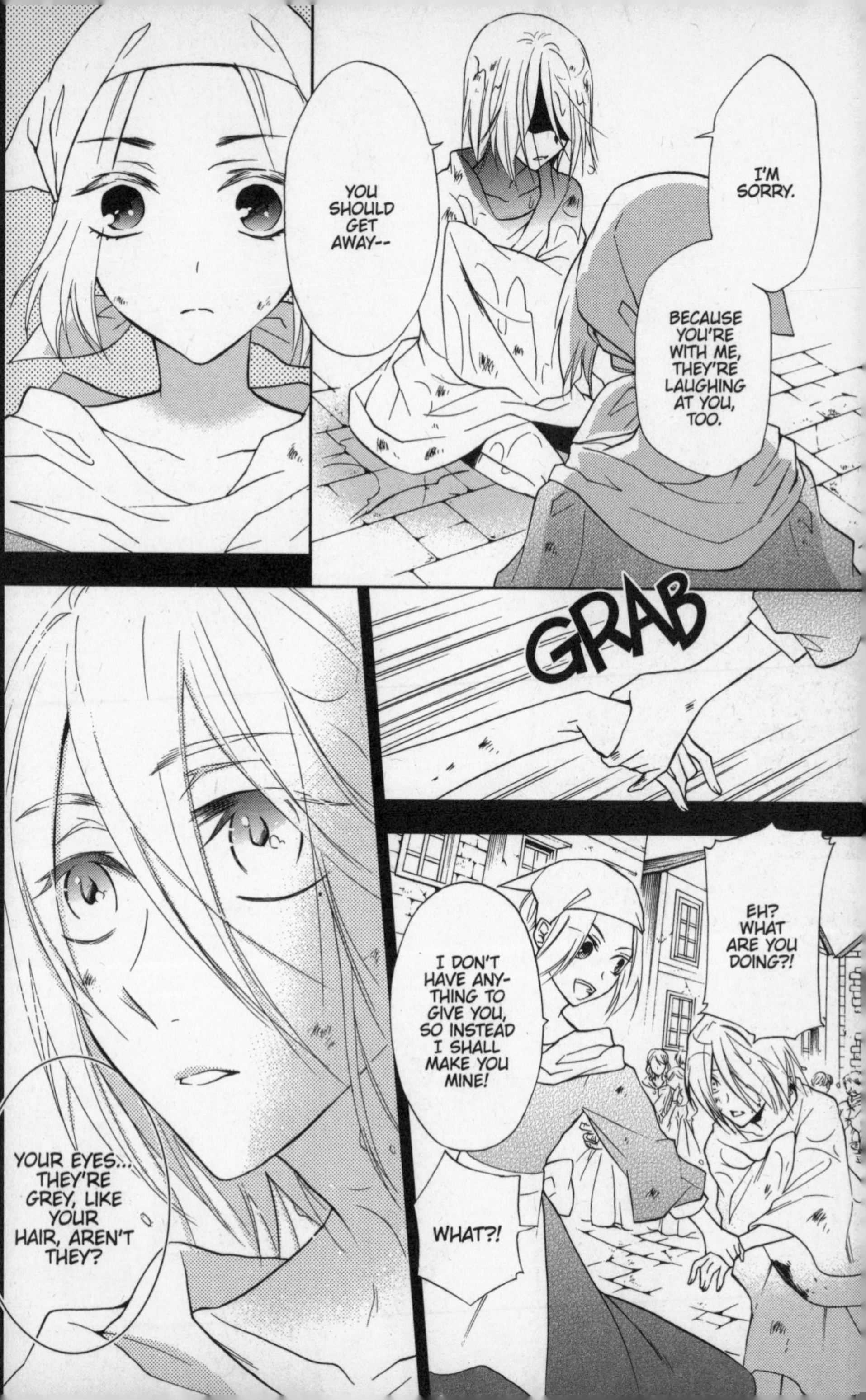
I'M SORRY.
BECAUSE YOU'RE WITH ME, THEY'RE LAUGHING AT YOU, TOO.
YOU SHOULD GET AWAY--
GRAB
EH? WHAT ARE YOU DOING?!
I DON'T HAVE ANY-THING TO GIVE YOU, SO INSTEAD I SHALL MAKE YOU MINE!
WHAT?!
YOUR EYES... THEY'RE GREY, LIKE YOUR HAIR, AREN'T THEY?

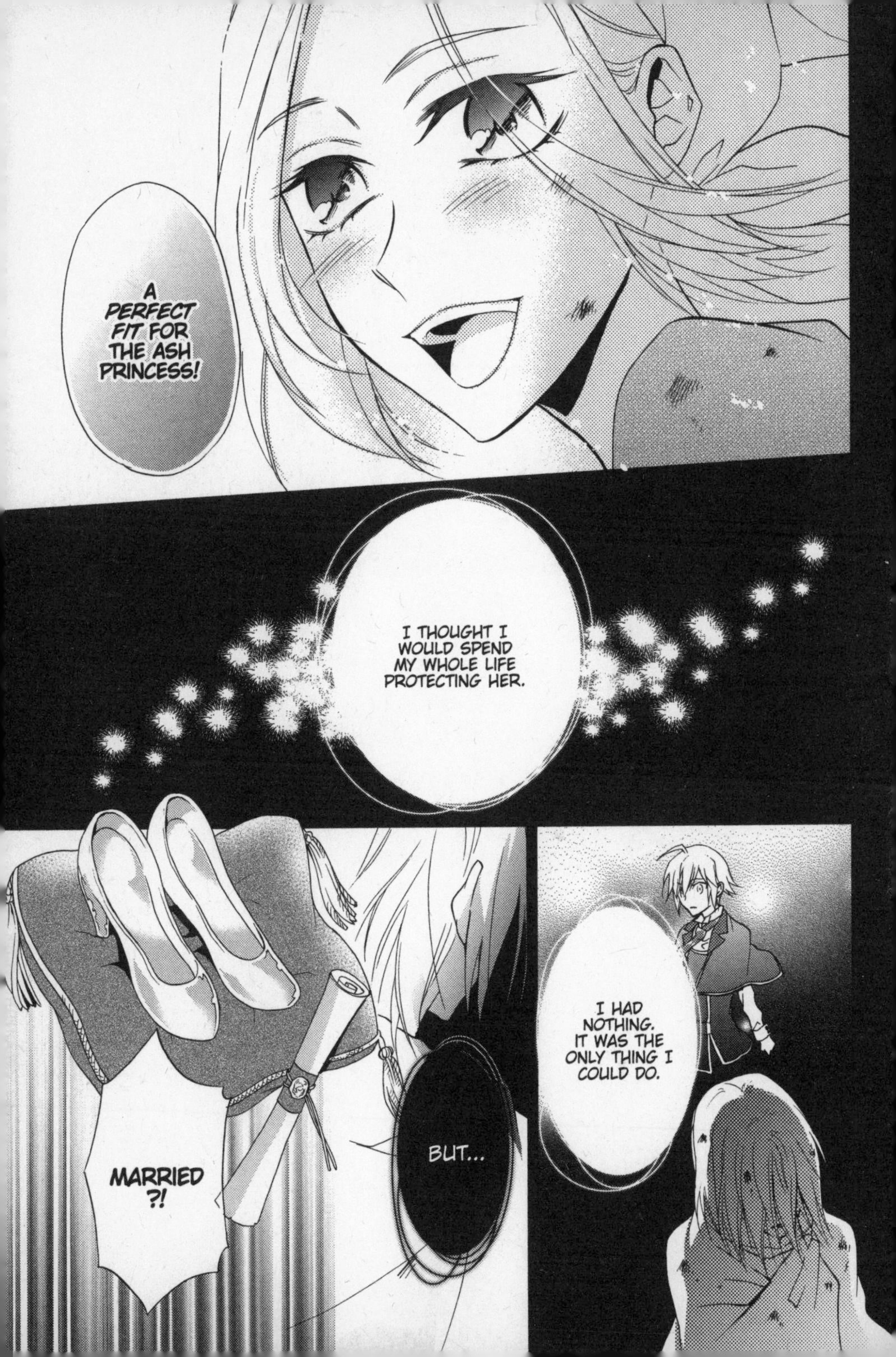
A PERFECT FIT FOR THE ASH PRINCESS!
I THOUGHT I WOULD SPEND MY WHOLE LIFE PROTECTING HER.
I HAD NOTHING. IT WAS THE ONLY THING I COULD DO.
BUT...
MARRIED?!

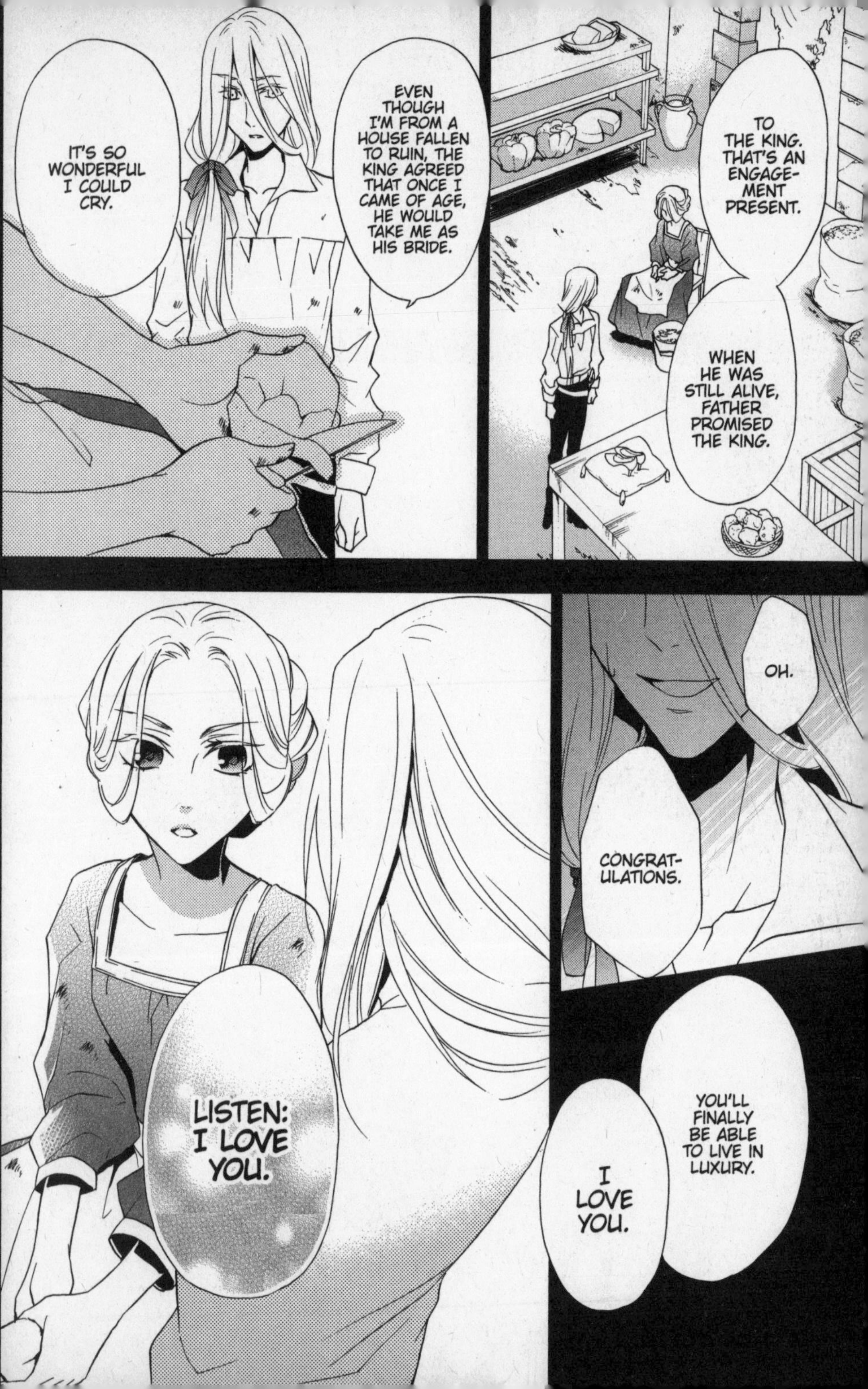
TO THE KING. THAT'S AN ENGAGE-MENT PRESENT.
WHEN HE WAS STILL ALIVE, FATHER PROMISED THE KING.
EVEN THOUGH I'M FROM A HOUSE FALLEN TO RUIN, THE KING AGREED THAT ONCE I CAME OF AGE, HE WOULD TAKE ME AS HIS BRIDE.
IT'S SO WONDERFUL I COULD CRY.
OH.
CONGRAT-ULATIONS.
YOU'LL FINALLY BE ABLE TO LIVE IN LUXURY.
I LOVE YOU.
LISTEN: I LOVE YOU.

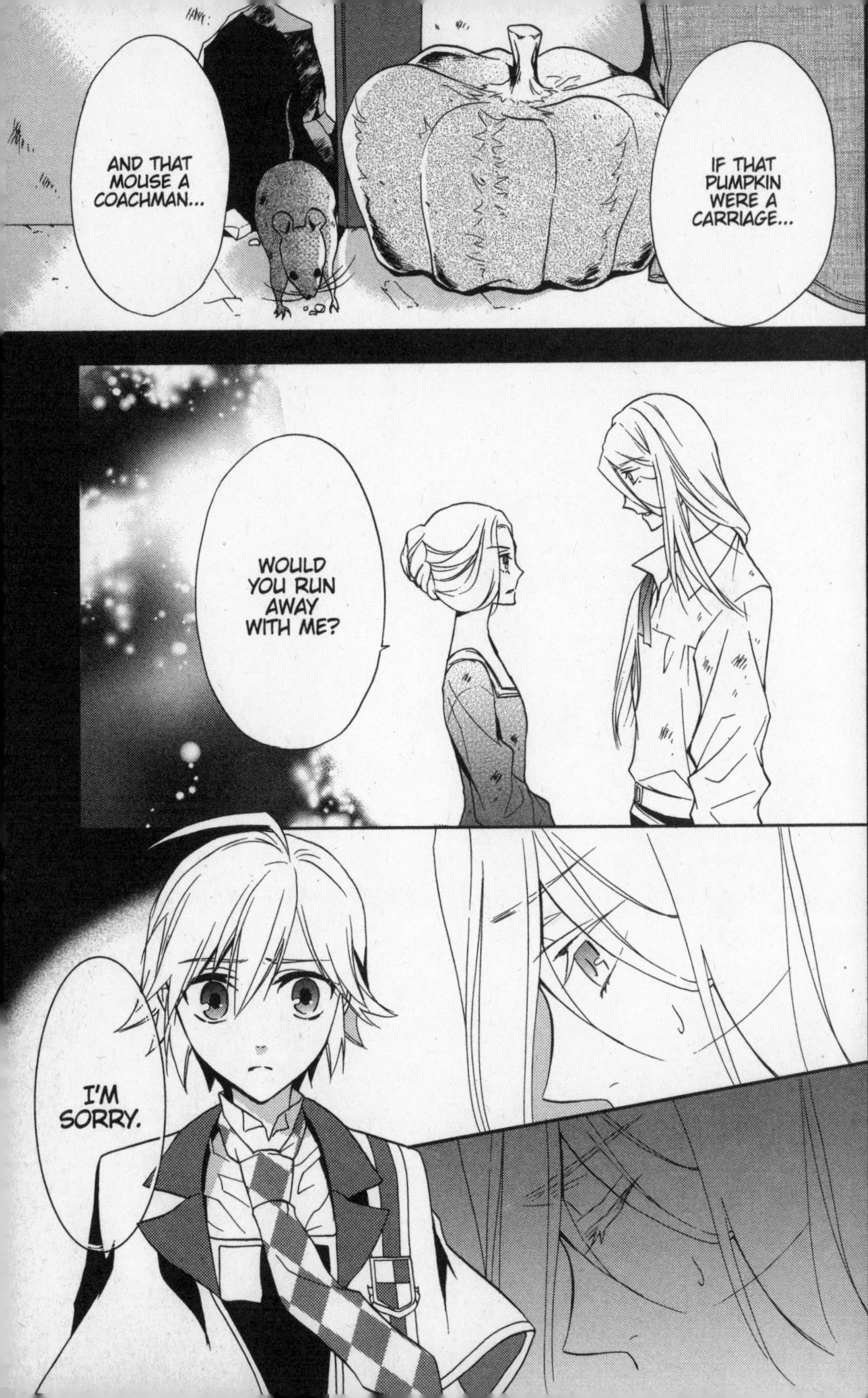
IF THAT PUMPKIN WERE A CARRIAGE...
AND THAT MOUSE A COACHMAN...
WOULD YOU RUN AWAY WITH ME?
I'M SORRY.

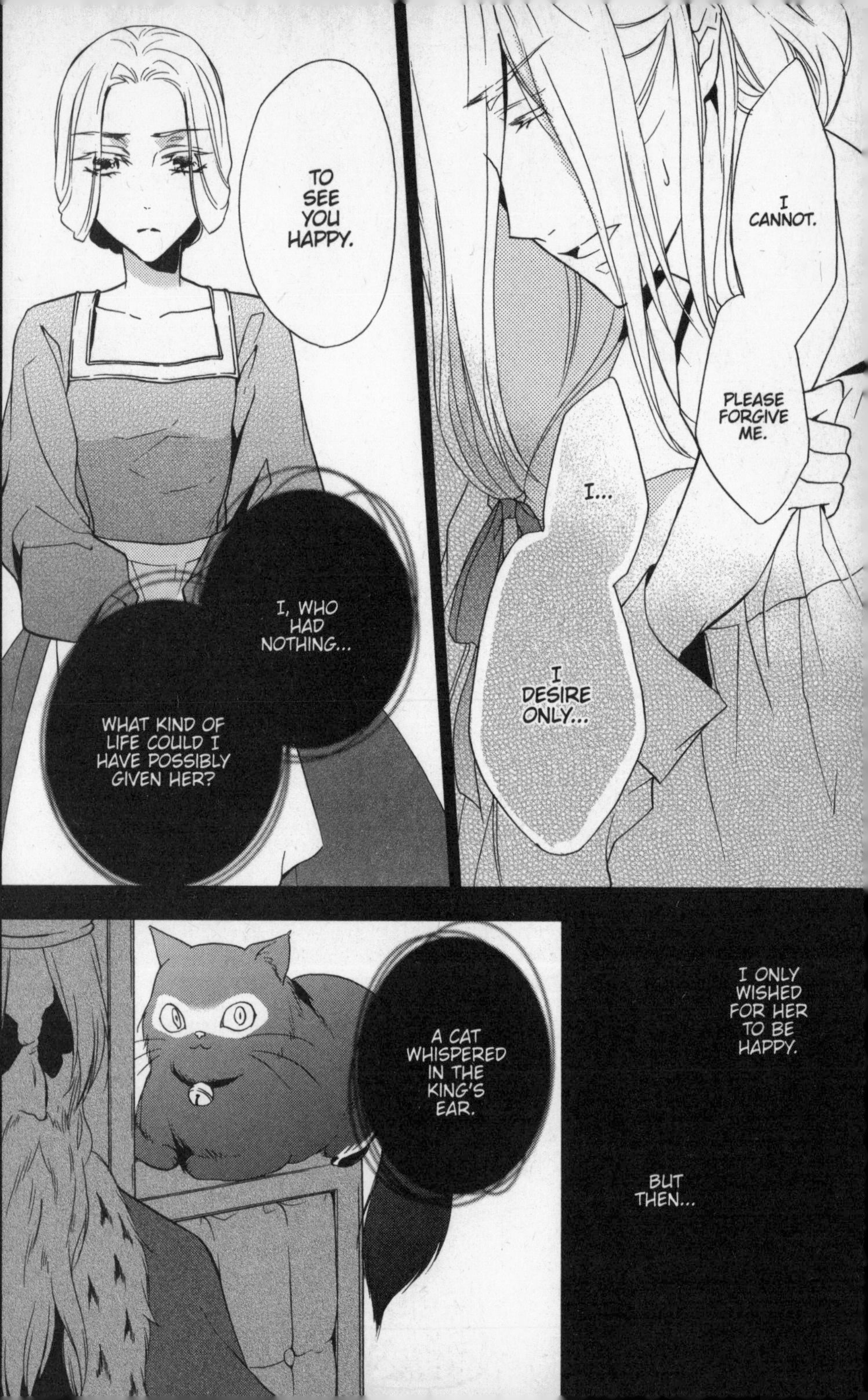
I CANNOT.
PLEASE FORGIVE ME.
I...
I DESIRE ONLY...
TO SEE YOU HAPPY.
I, WHO HAD NOTHING...
WHAT KIND OF LIFE COULD I HAVE POSSIBLY GIVEN HER?
I ONLY WISHED FOR HER TO BE HAPPY.
BUT THEN...
A CAT WHISPERED IN THE KING'S EAR.

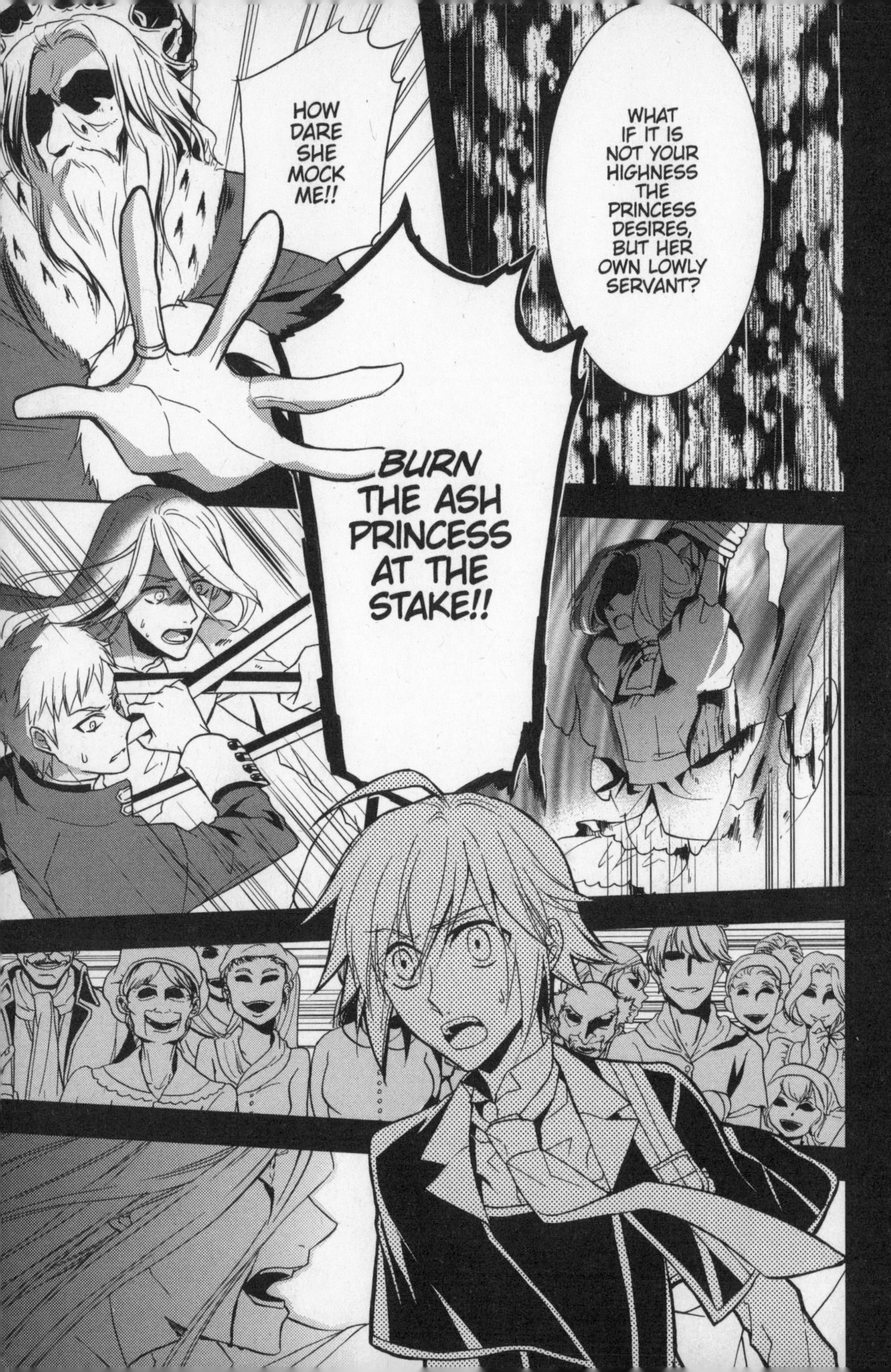
WHAT IF IT IS NOT YOUR HIGHNESS THE PRINCESS DESIRES, BUT HER OWN LOWLY SERVANT?
HOW DARE SHE MOCK ME!!
BURN THE ASH PRINCESS AT THE STAKE!!

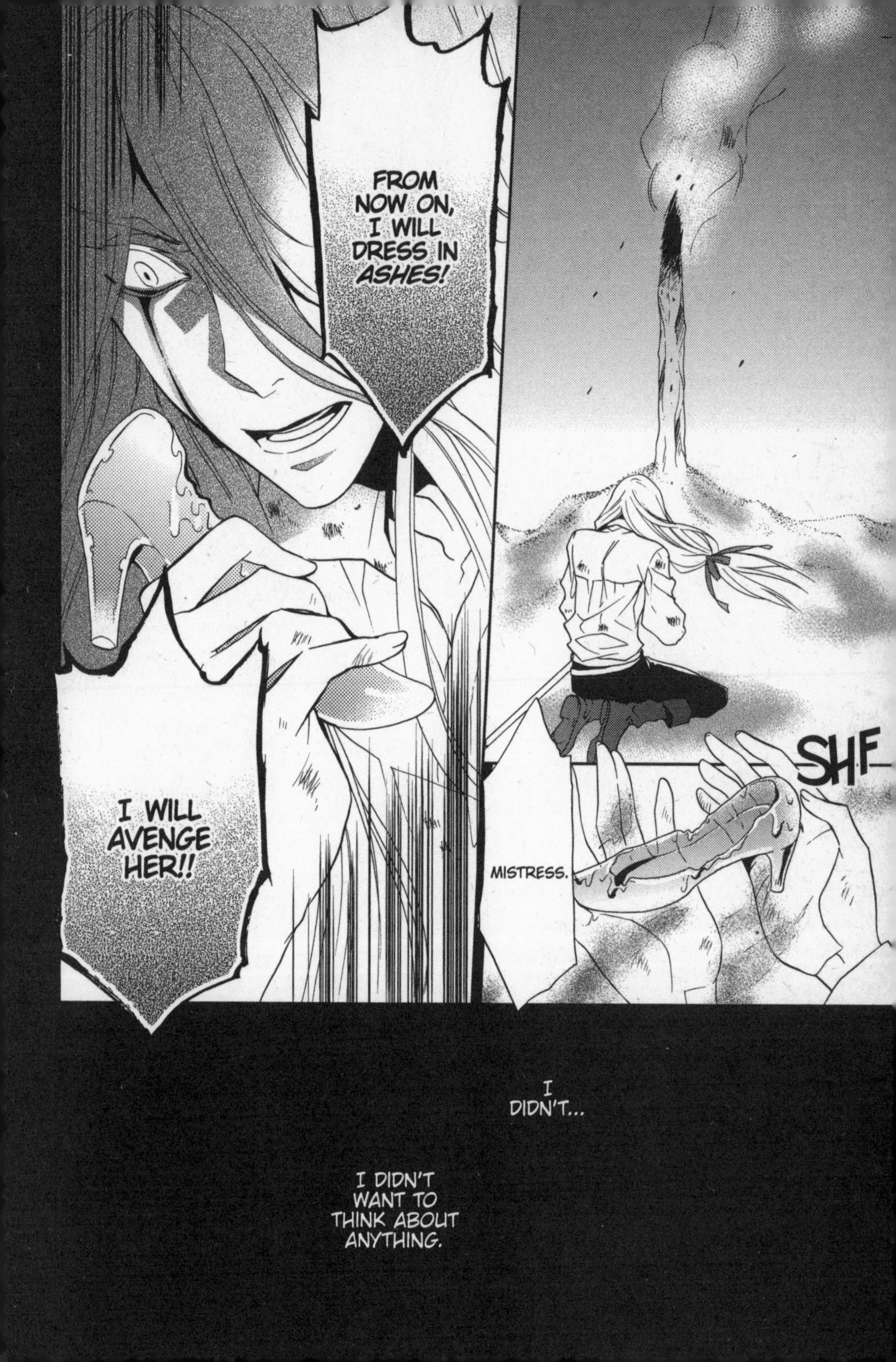
SHF
MISTRESS.
FROM NOW ON, I WILL DRESS IN *ASHES!*
I WILL AVENGE HER!!
I DIDN'T...
I DIDN'T WANT TO THINK ABOUT ANYTHING.

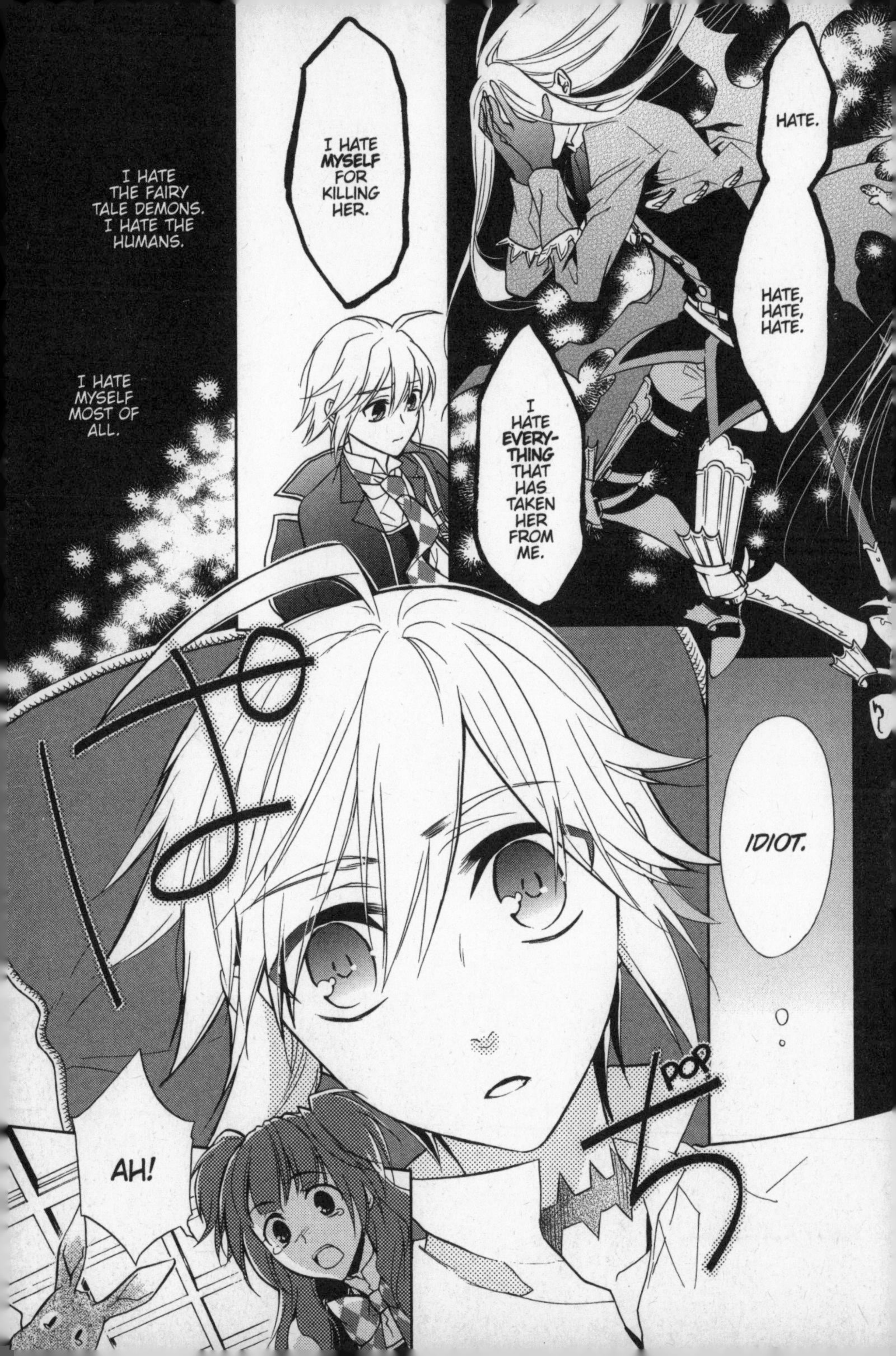
HATE.
HATE, HATE, HATE.
I HATE EVERYTHING THAT HAS TAKEN HER FROM ME.
I HATE MYSELF FOR KILLING HER.
I HATE THE FAIRY TALE DEMONS. I HATE THE HUMANS.
I HATE MYSELF MOST OF ALL.
IDIOT.
POP
AH!

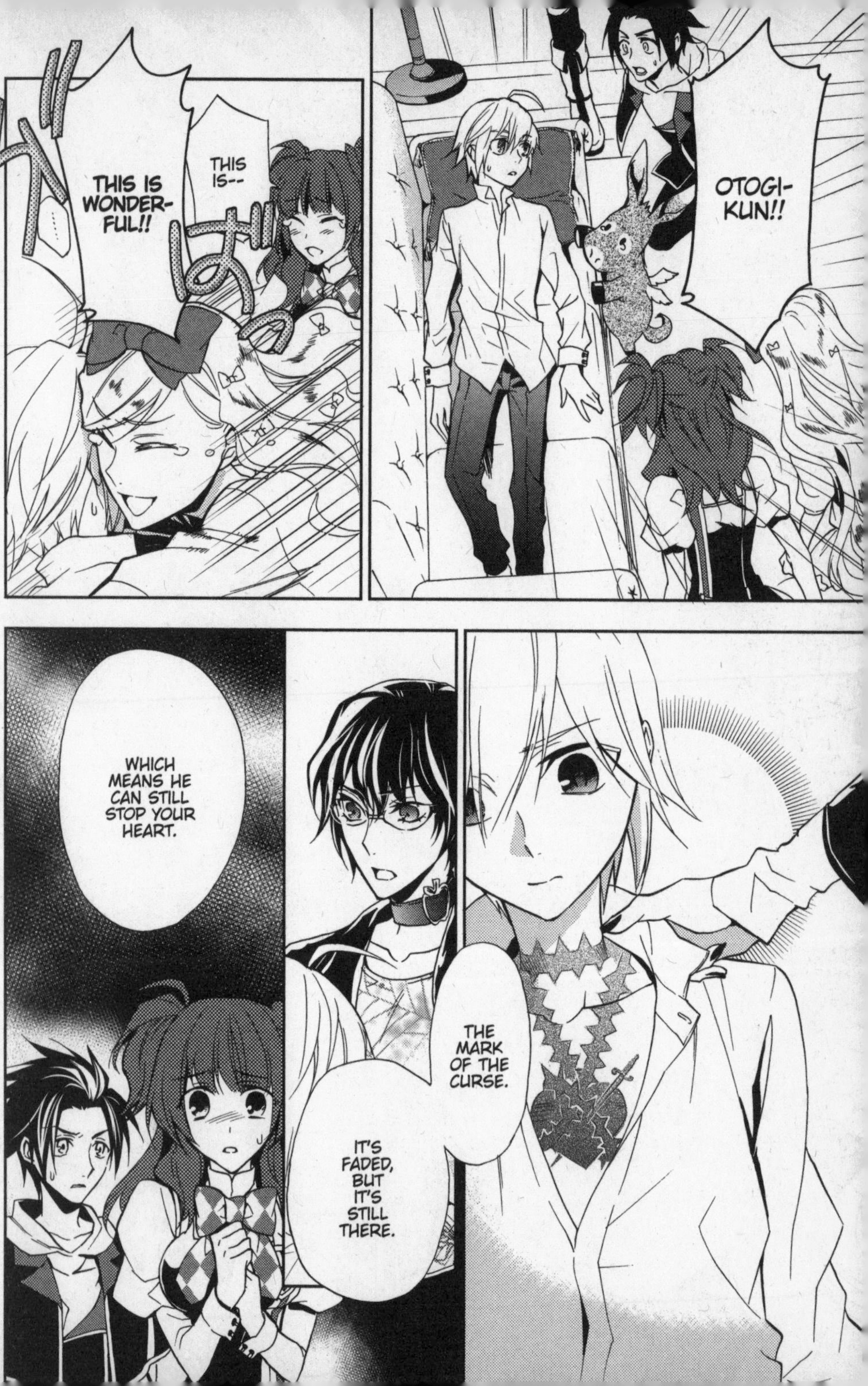
OTOGI-KUN!!
THIS IS--
THIS IS WONDERFUL!!
......
THE MARK OF THE CURSE.
IT'S FADED, BUT IT'S STILL THERE.
WHICH MEANS HE CAN STILL STOP YOUR HEART.

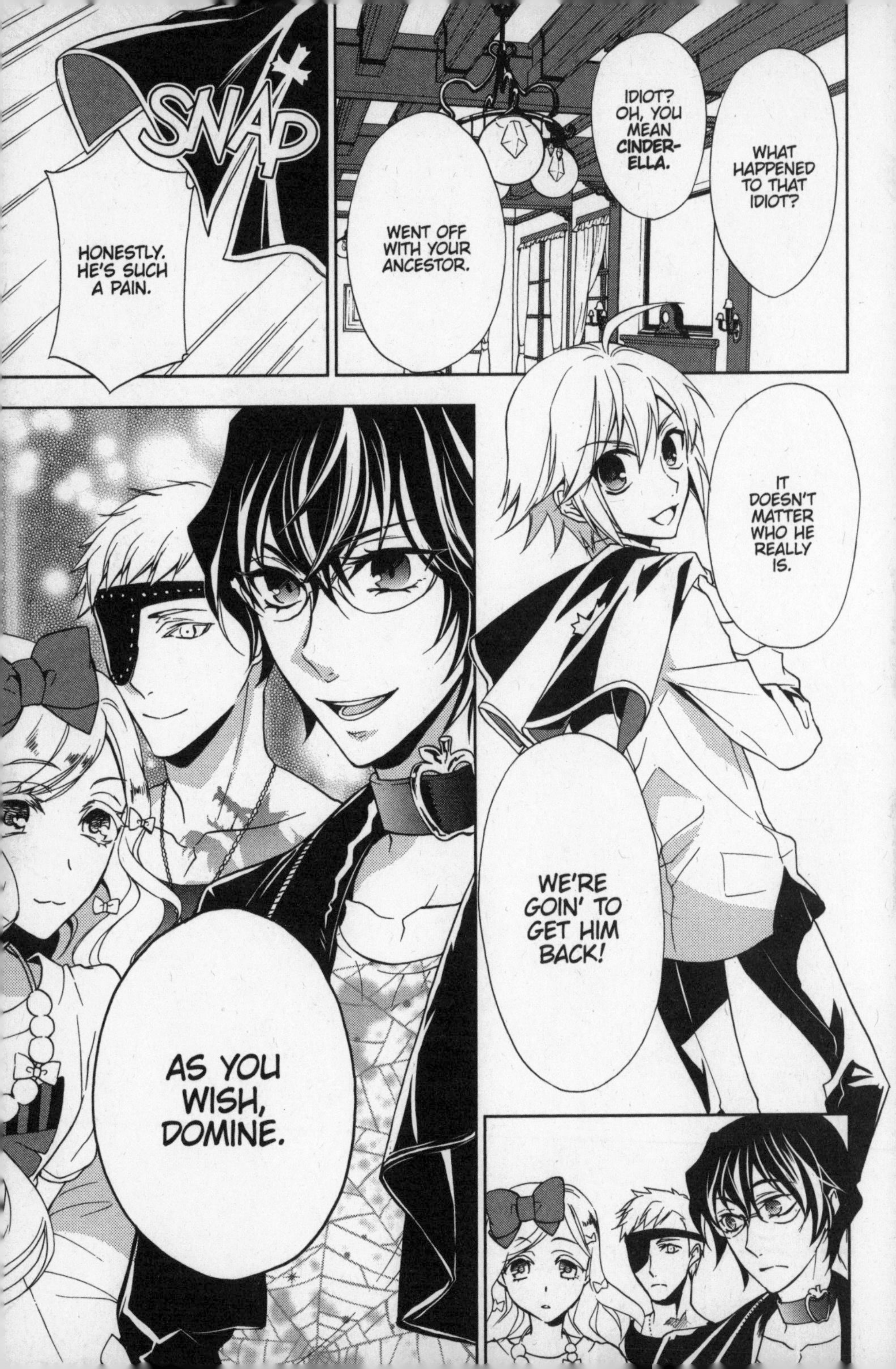
WHAT HAPPENED TO THAT IDIOT?
IDIOT? OH, YOU MEAN CINDERELLA.
WENT OFF WITH YOUR ANCESTOR.
SWAP
HONESTLY. HE'S SUCH A PAIN.
IT DOESN'T MATTER WHO HE REALLY IS.
WE'RE GOIN' TO GET HIM BACK!
AS YOU WISH, DOMINE.

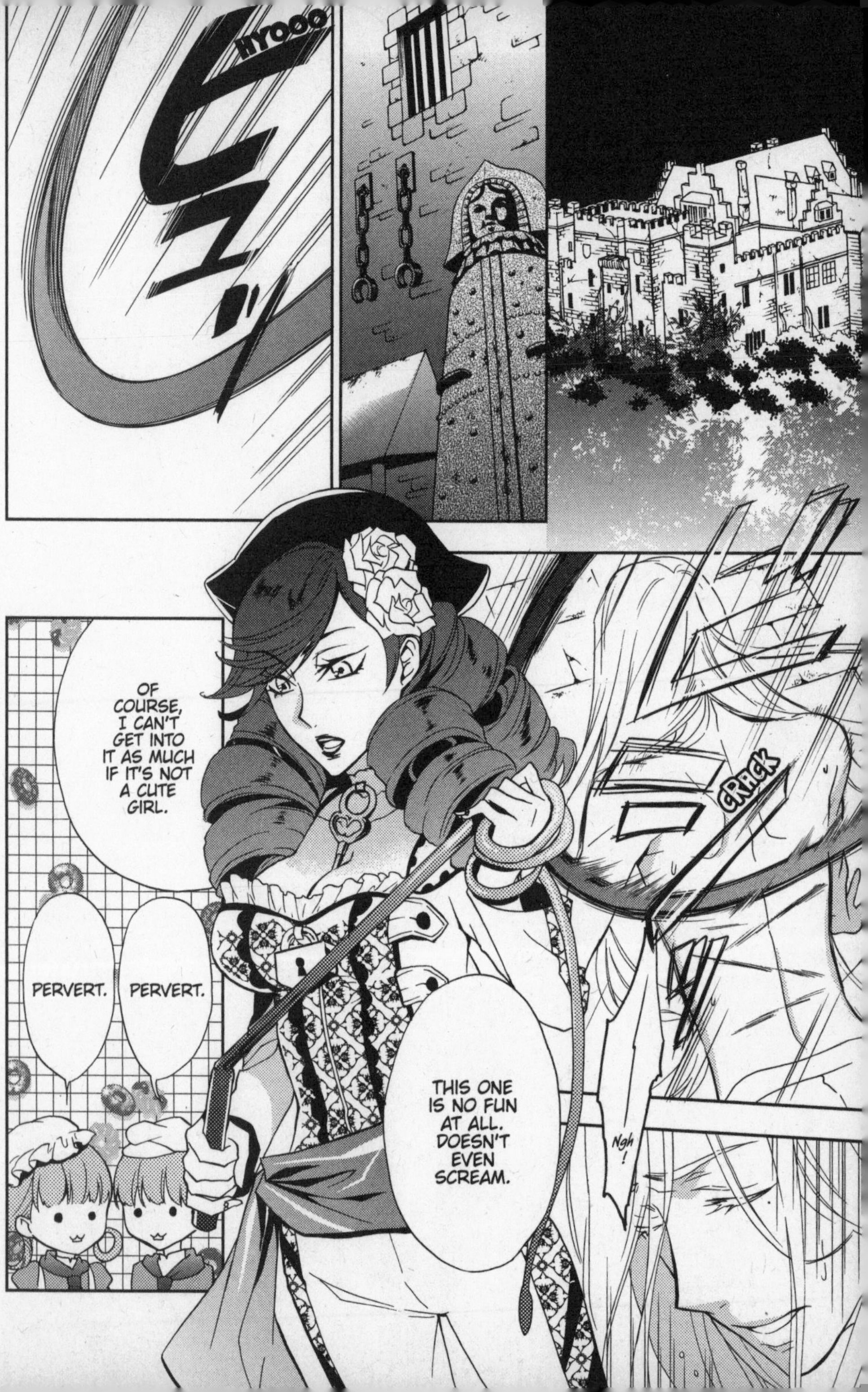
HYOOO
CRACK
THIS ONE IS NO FUN AT ALL. DOESN'T EVEN SCREAM.
Ngh!
OF COURSE, I CAN'T GET INTO IT AS MUCH IF IT'S NOT A CUTE GIRL.
PERVERT.
PERVERT.

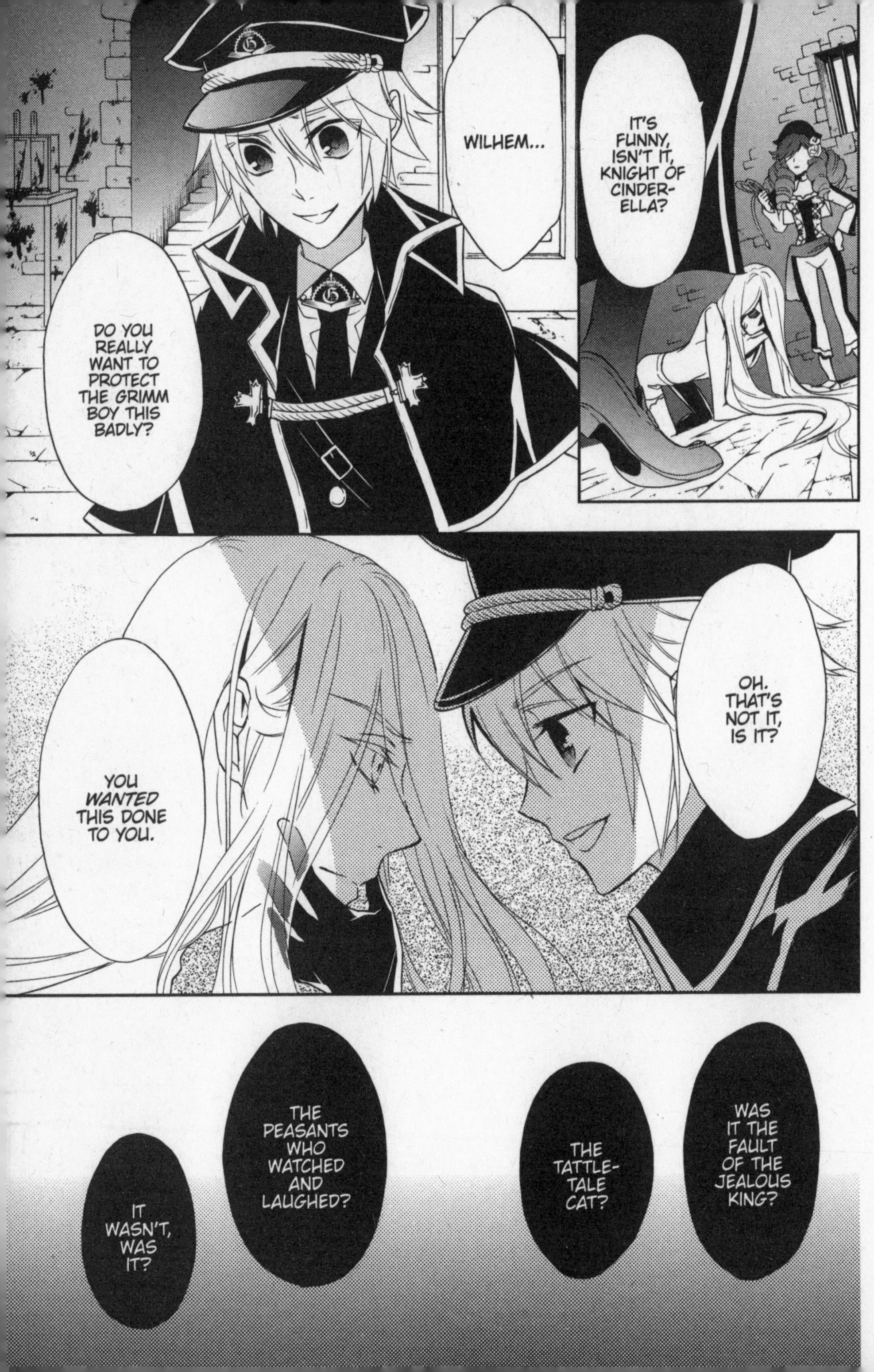
IT'S FUNNY, ISN'T IT, KNIGHT OF CINDER-ELLA?
WILHEM...
DO YOU REALLY WANT TO PROTECT THE GRIMM BOY THIS BADLY?
OH. THAT'S NOT IT, IS IT?
YOU *WANTED* THIS DONE TO YOU.
WAS IT THE FAULT OF THE JEALOUS KING?
THE TATTLE-TALE CAT?
THE PEASANTS WHO WATCHED AND LAUGHED?
IT WASN'T, WAS IT?

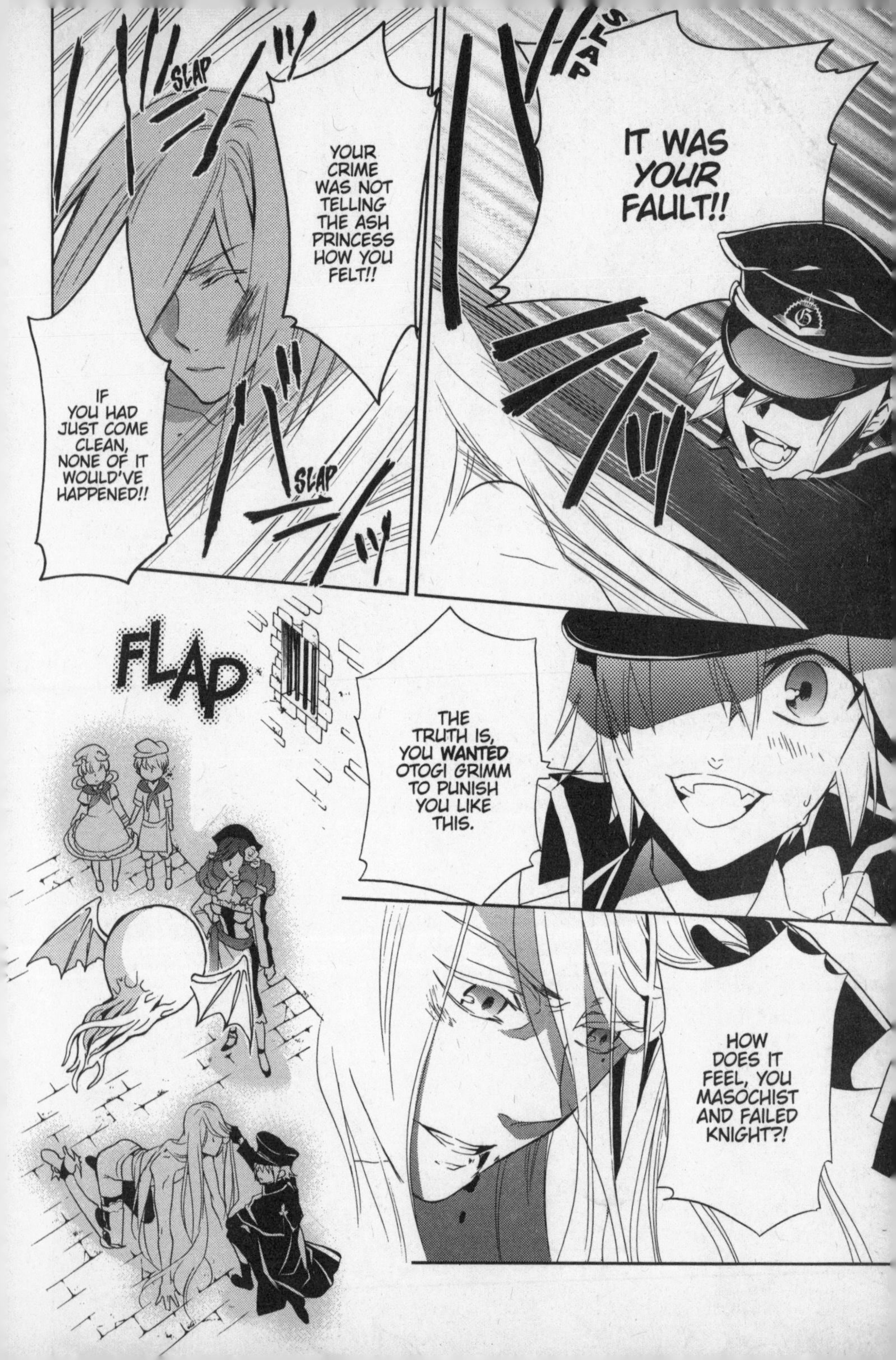
SLAP
IT WAS YOUR FAULT!!
SLAP
YOUR CRIME WAS NOT TELLING THE ASH PRINCESS HOW YOU FELT!!
SLAP
IF YOU HAD JUST COME CLEAN, NONE OF IT WOULD'VE HAPPENED!!
THE TRUTH IS, YOU WANTED OTOGI GRIMM TO PUNISH YOU LIKE THIS.
HOW DOES IT FEEL, YOU MASOCHIST AND FAILED KNIGHT?!
FLAP

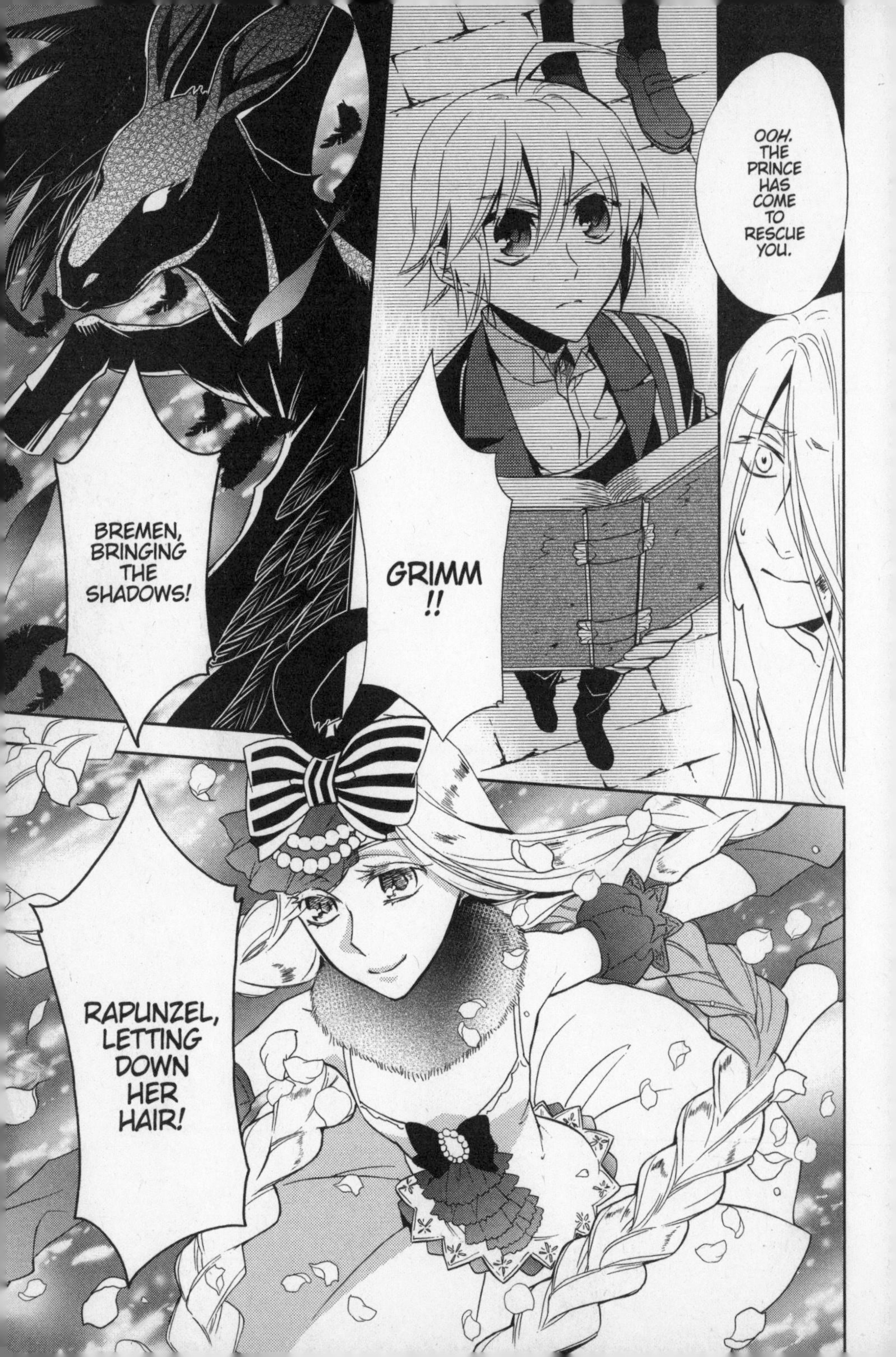
OOH. THE PRINCE HAS COME TO RESCUE YOU.
GRIMM !!
BREMEN, BRINGING THE SHADOWS!
RAPUNZEL, LETTING DOWN HER HAIR!

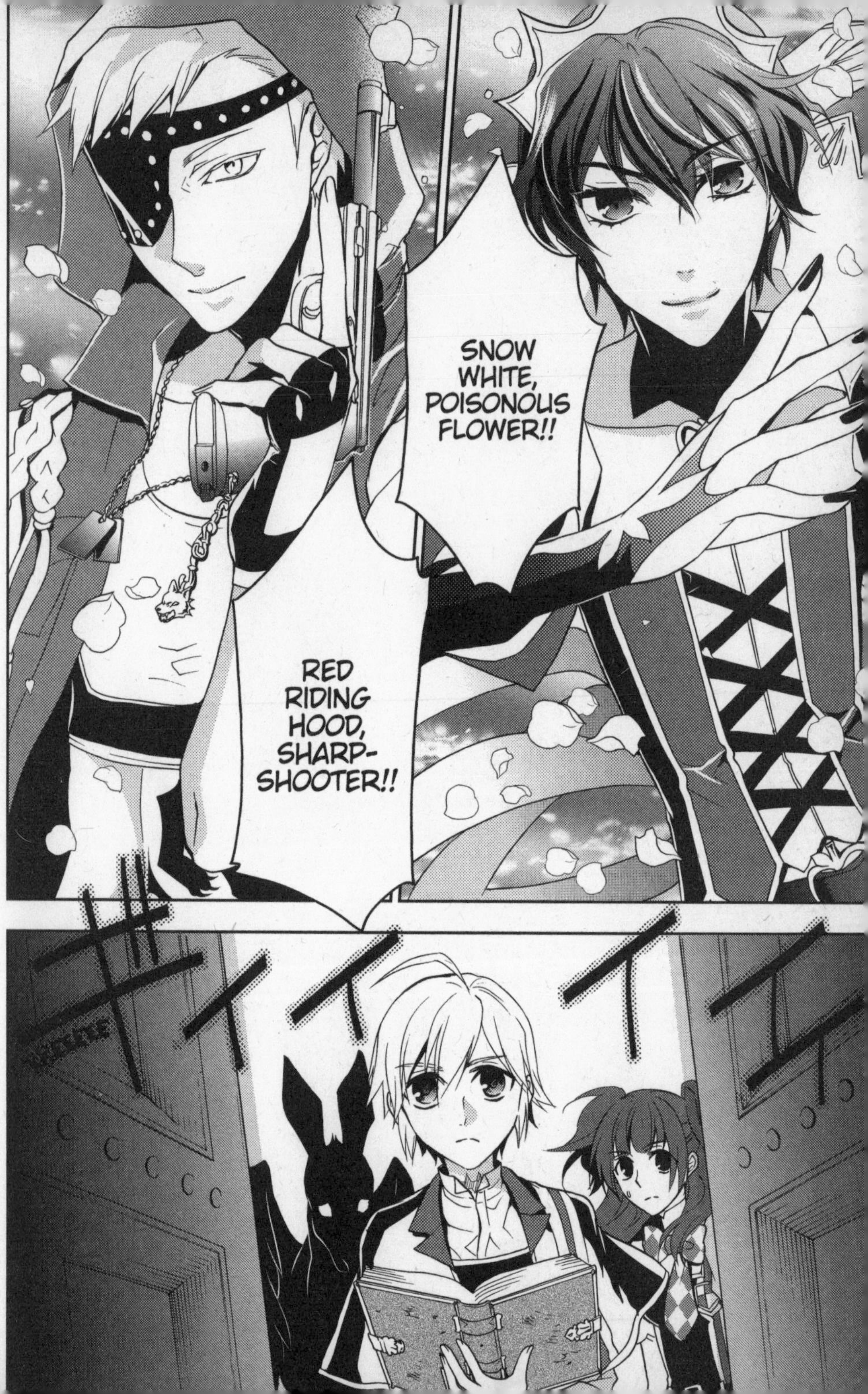
SNOW WHITE, POISONOUS FLOWER!!
RED RIDING HOOD, SHARP-SHOOTER!!

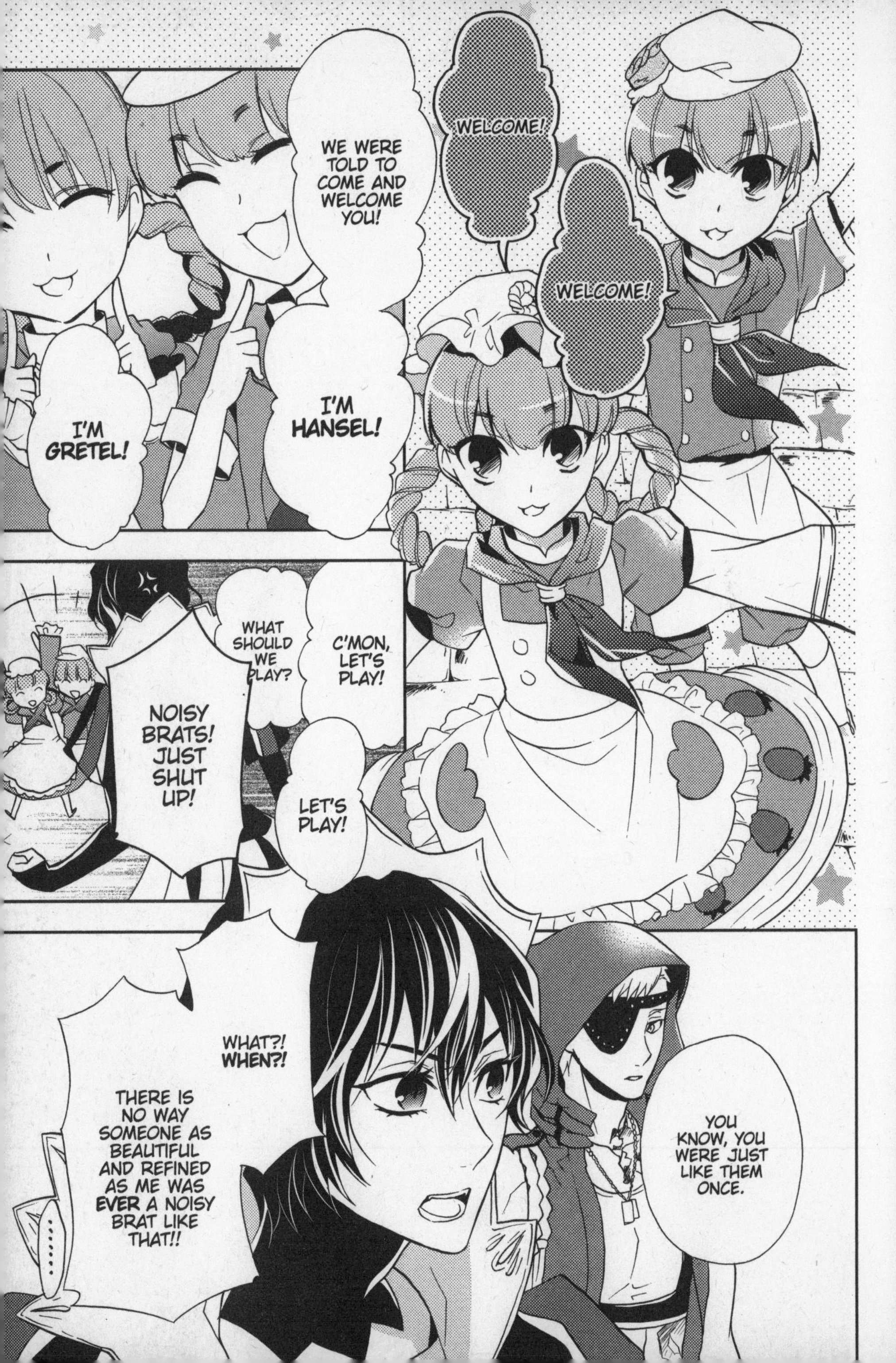

WELCOME!
WELCOME!
WE WERE TOLD TO COME AND WELCOME YOU!
I'M HANSEL!
I'M GRETEL!
C'MON, LET'S PLAY!
WHAT SHOULD WE PLAY?
LET'S PLAY!
NOISY BRATS! JUST SHUT UP!
YOU KNOW, YOU WERE JUST LIKE THEM ONCE.
WHAT?! WHEN?!
THERE IS NO WAY SOMEONE AS BEAUTIFUL AND REFINED AS ME WAS EVER A NOISY BRAT LIKE THAT!!

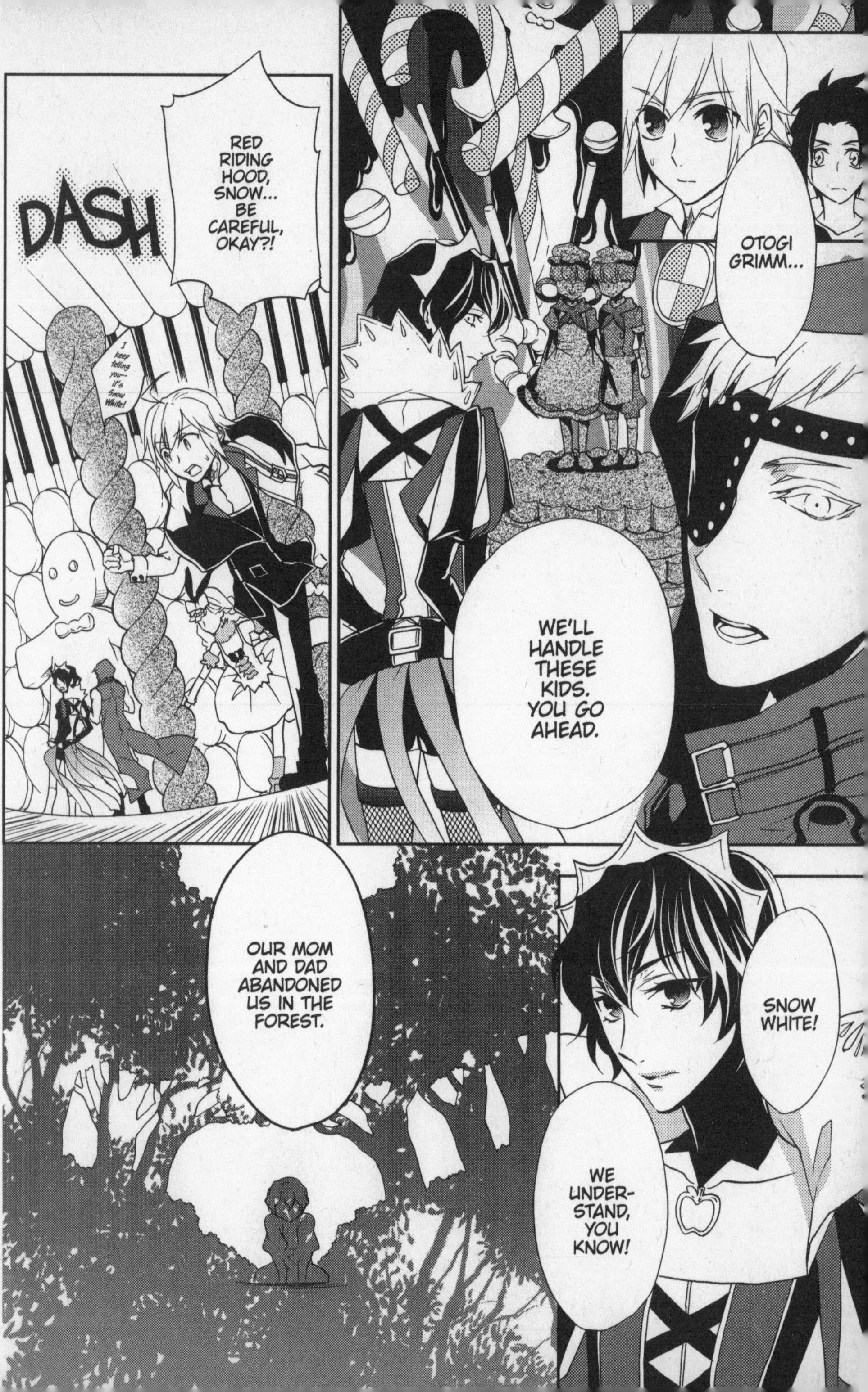

OTOGI GRIMM...
WE'LL HANDLE THESE KIDS. YOU GO AHEAD.
DASH
RED RIDING HOOD, SNOW... BE CAREFUL, OKAY?!
I keep telling you— it's Snow White!
SNOW WHITE!
WE UNDER-STAND, YOU KNOW!
OUR MOM AND DAD ABANDONED US IN THE FOREST.

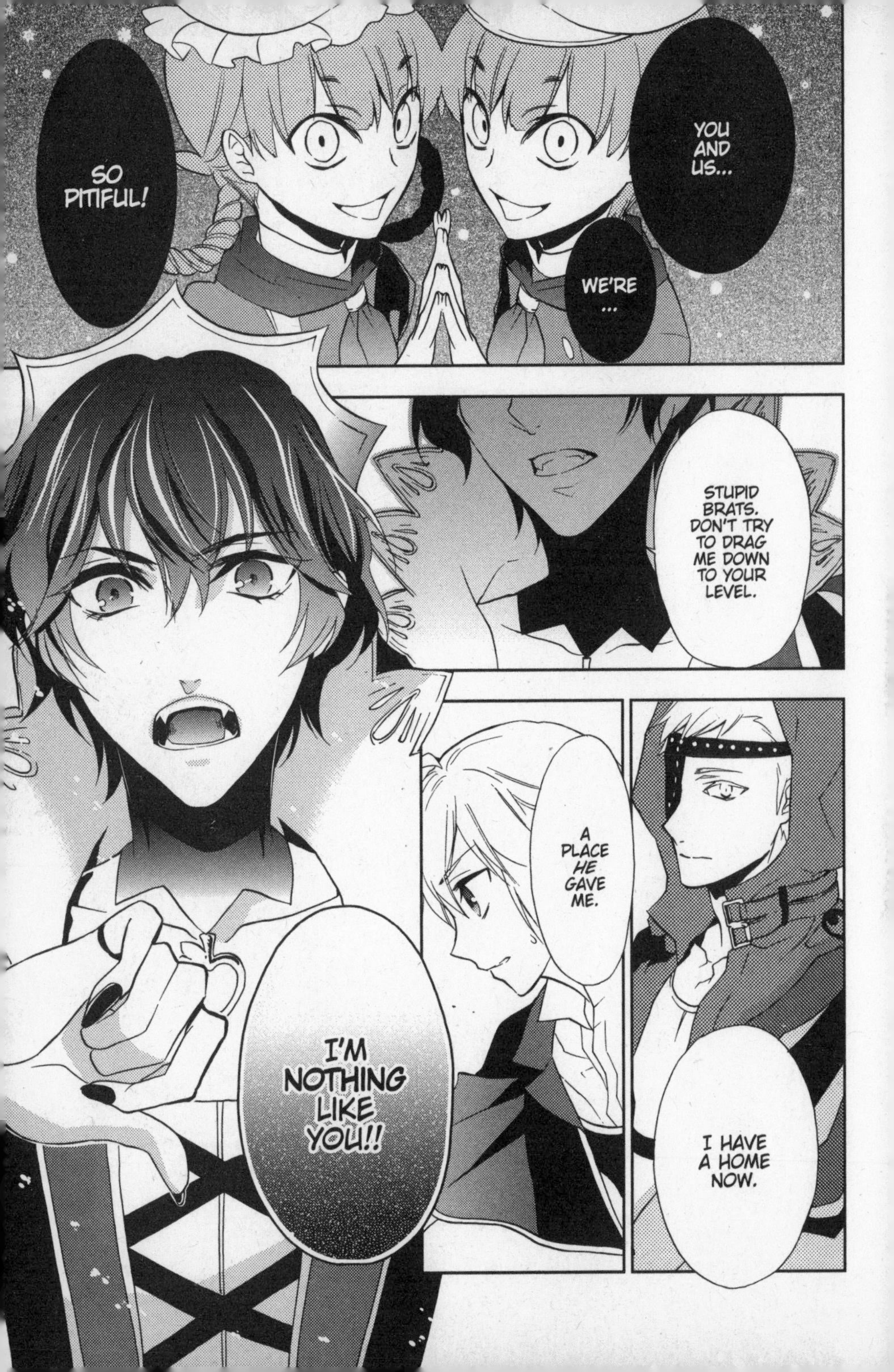

YOU AND US...
WE'RE ...
SO PITIFUL!
STUPID BRATS. DON'T TRY TO DRAG ME DOWN TO YOUR LEVEL.
I HAVE A HOME NOW.
A PLACE HE GAVE ME.
I'M NOTHING LIKE YOU!!

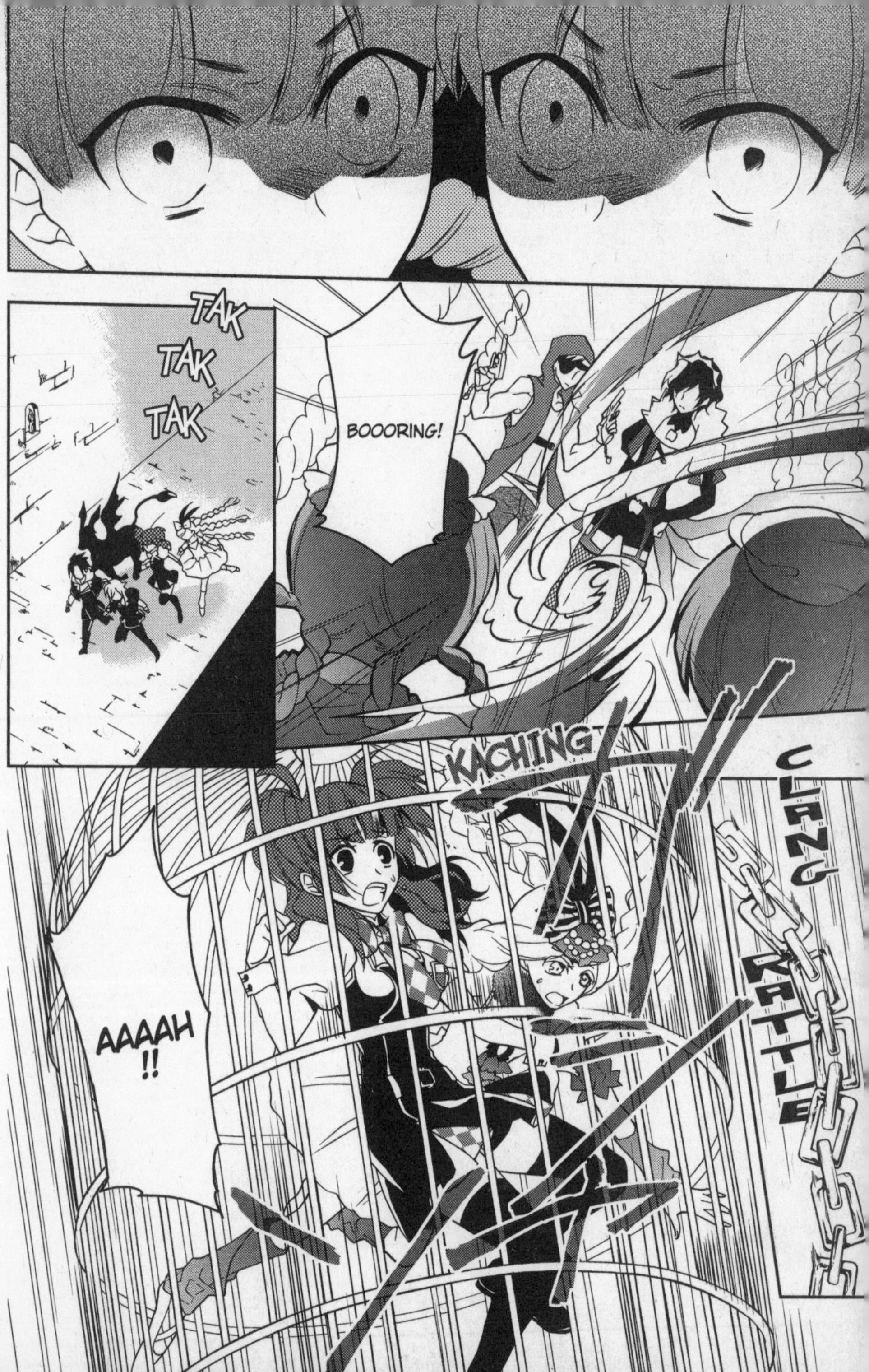
BOOORING!
TAK
TAK
TAK
CLANG
KACHING
RATTLE
AAAAH!!

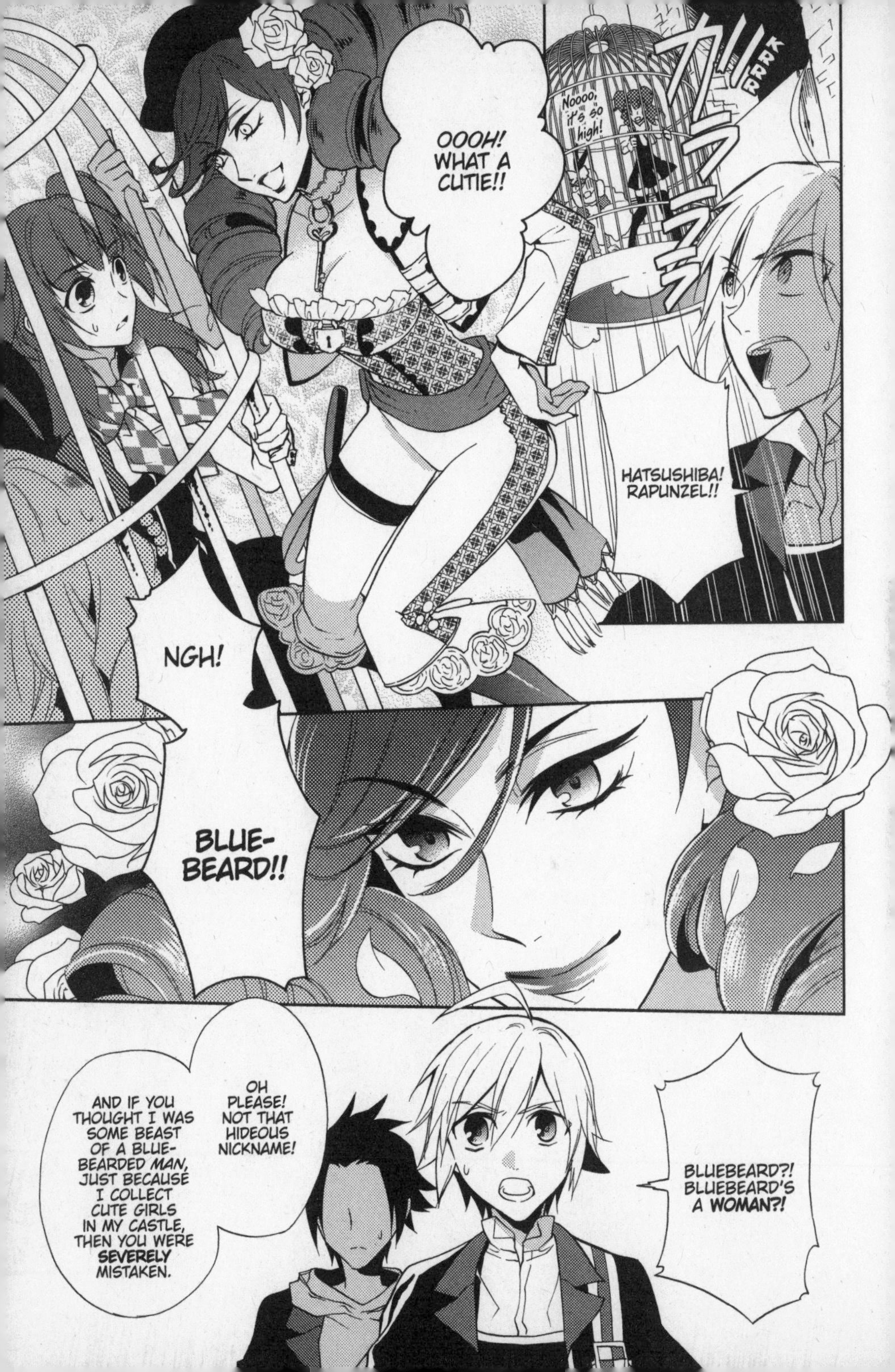
KRRR
"Noooo, it's so high!
HATSUSHIBA! RAPUNZEL!!
OOOH! WHAT A CUTIE!!
NGH!
BLUE-BEARD!!
BLUEBEARD?! BLUEBEARD'S A WOMAN?!
OH PLEASE! NOT THAT HIDEOUS NICKNAME!
AND IF YOU THOUGHT I WAS SOME BEAST OF A BLUE-BEARDED MAN, JUST BECAUSE I COLLECT CUTE GIRLS IN MY CASTLE, THEN YOU WERE SEVERELY MISTAKEN.

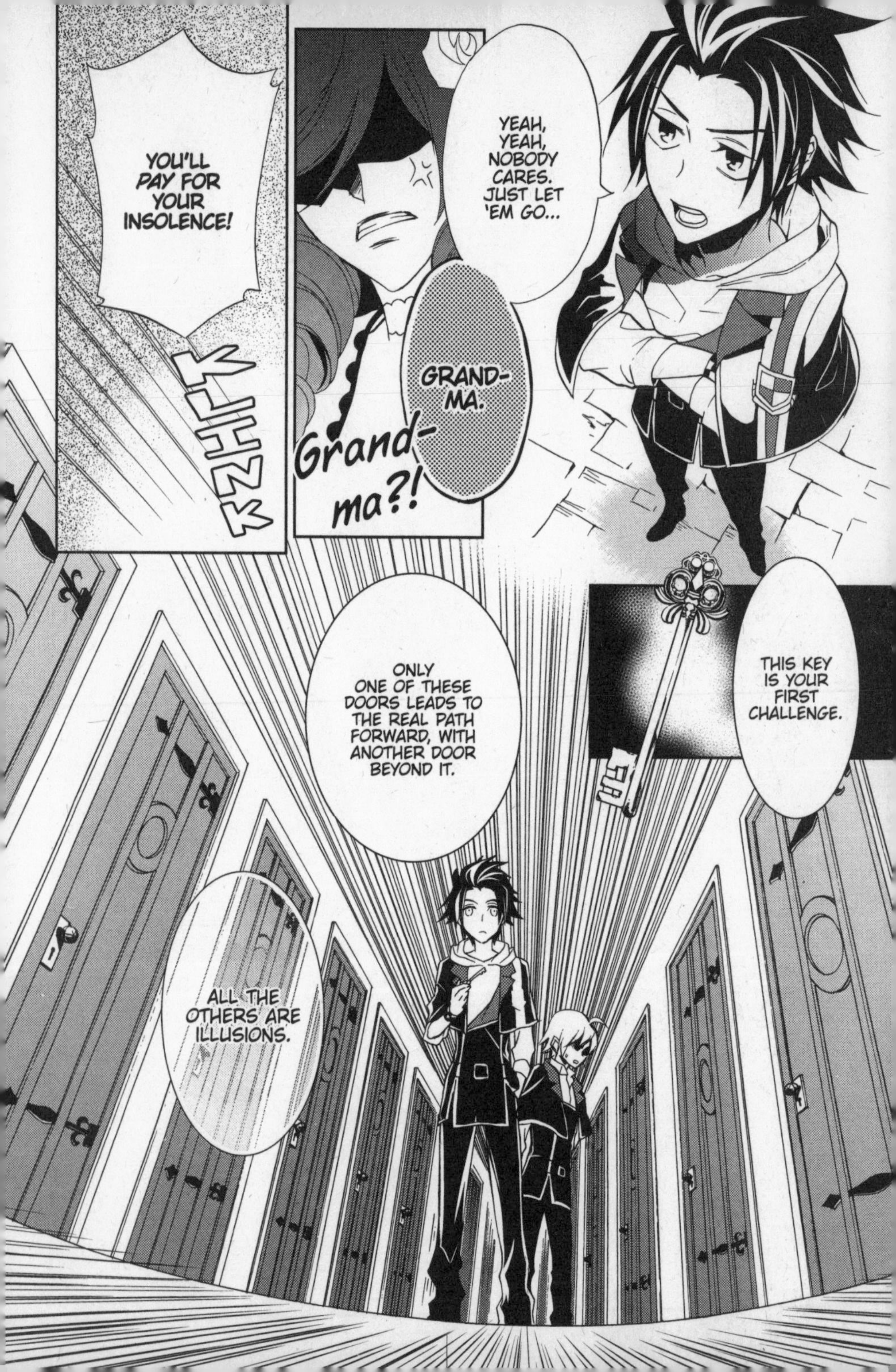
YEAH, YEAH, NOBODY CARES. JUST LET 'EM GO...
GRAND-MA.
Grand-ma?!
YOU'LL PAY FOR YOUR INSOLENCE!
KLINK
THIS KEY IS YOUR FIRST CHALLENGE.
ONLY ONE OF THESE DOORS LEADS TO THE REAL PATH FORWARD, WITH ANOTHER DOOR BEYOND IT.
ALL THE OTHERS ARE ILLUSIONS.

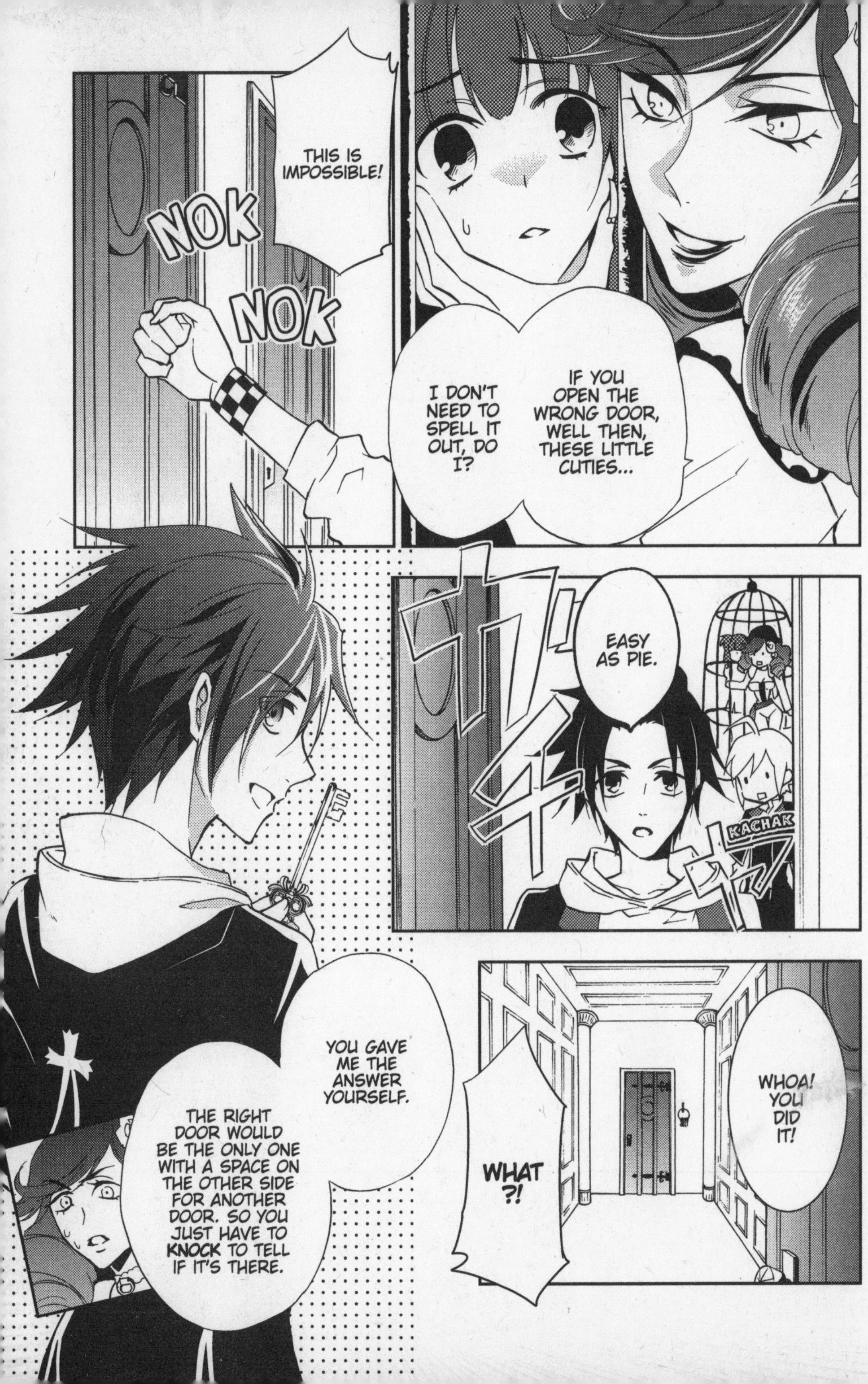
IF YOU OPEN THE WRONG DOOR, WELL THEN, THESE LITTLE CUTIES...
I DON'T NEED TO SPELL IT OUT, DO I?
THIS IS IMPOSSIBLE!
NOK
NOK
EASY AS PIE.
KACHAK
WHOA! YOU DID IT!
WHAT?!
YOU GAVE ME THE ANSWER YOURSELF.
THE RIGHT DOOR WOULD BE THE ONLY ONE WITH A SPACE ON THE OTHER SIDE FOR ANOTHER DOOR. SO YOU JUST HAVE TO **KNOCK** TO TELL IF IT'S THERE.

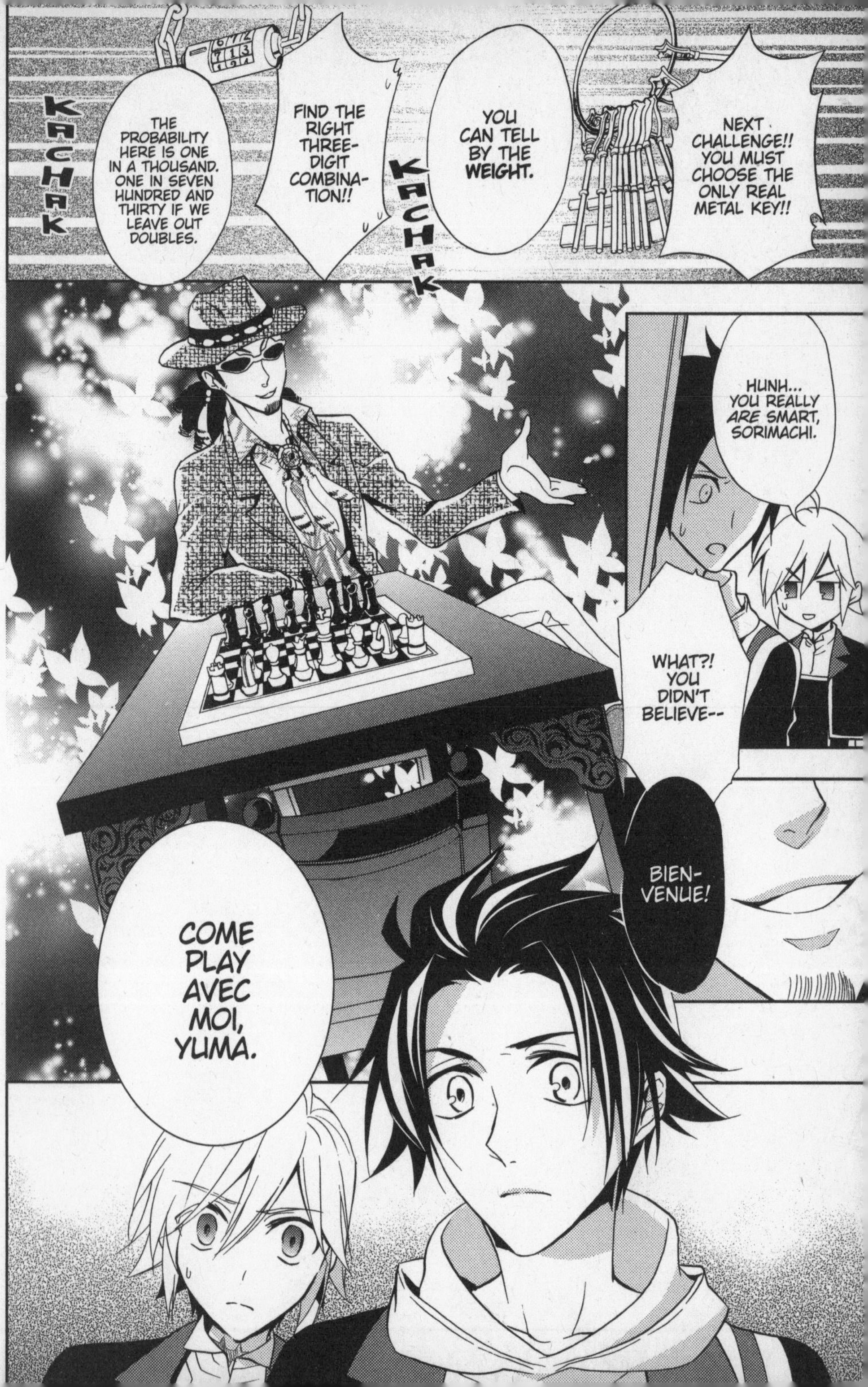
NEXT CHALLENGE!! YOU MUST CHOOSE THE ONLY REAL METAL KEY!!
YOU CAN TELL BY THE WEIGHT.
KACHAK
FIND THE RIGHT THREE-DIGIT COMBINATION!!
THE PROBABILITY HERE IS ONE IN A THOUSAND. ONE IN SEVEN HUNDRED AND THIRTY IF WE LEAVE OUT DOUBLES.
KACHAK
HUNH... YOU REALLY ARE SMART, SORIMACHI.
WHAT?! YOU DIDN'T BELIEVE--
BIEN-VENUE!
COME PLAY AVEC MOI, YUMA.

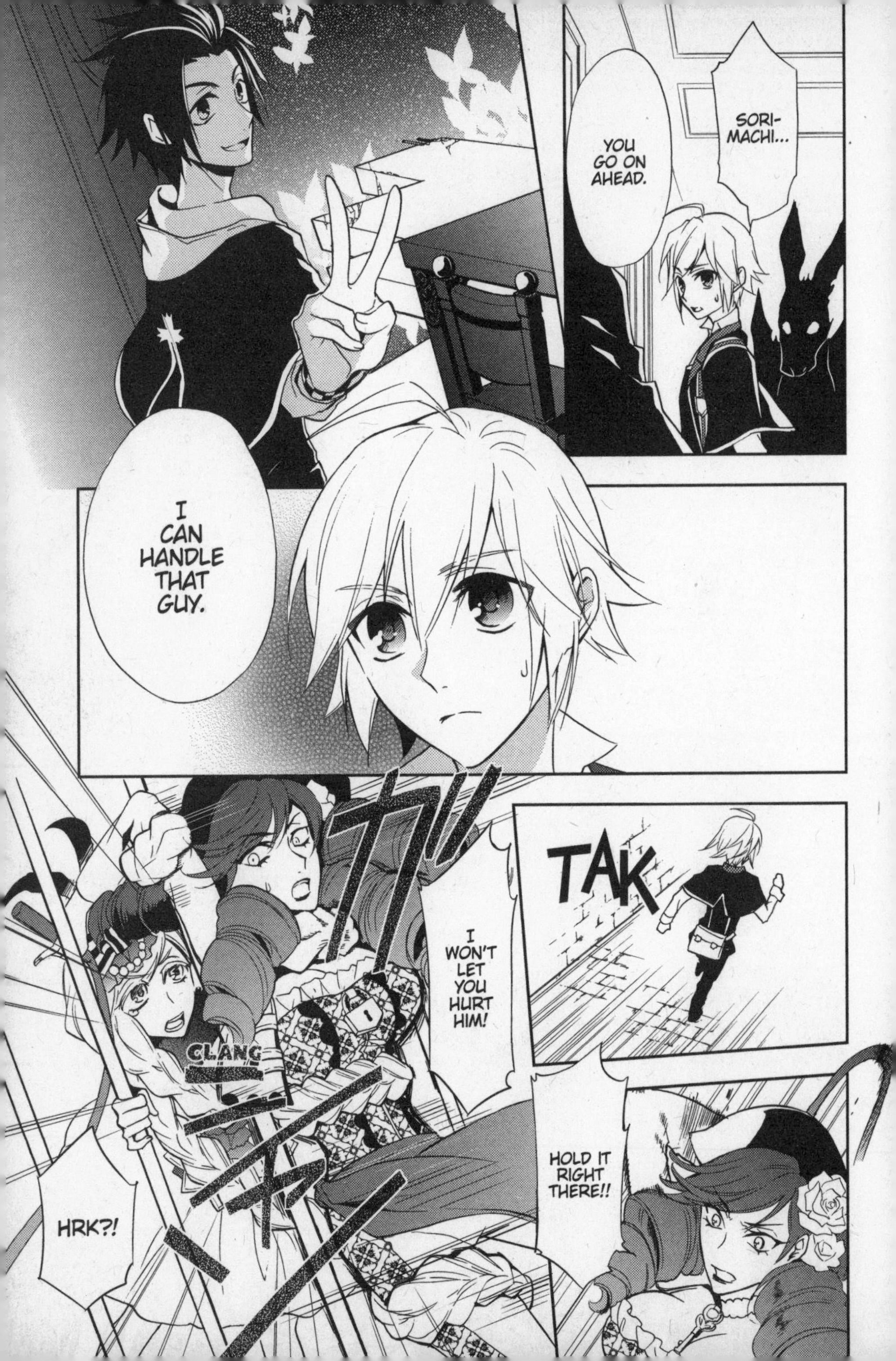
SORI-MACHI...
YOU GO ON AHEAD.
I CAN HANDLE THAT GUY.
TAK
I WON'T LET YOU HURT HIM!
CLANG
HOLD IT RIGHT THERE!!
HRK?!

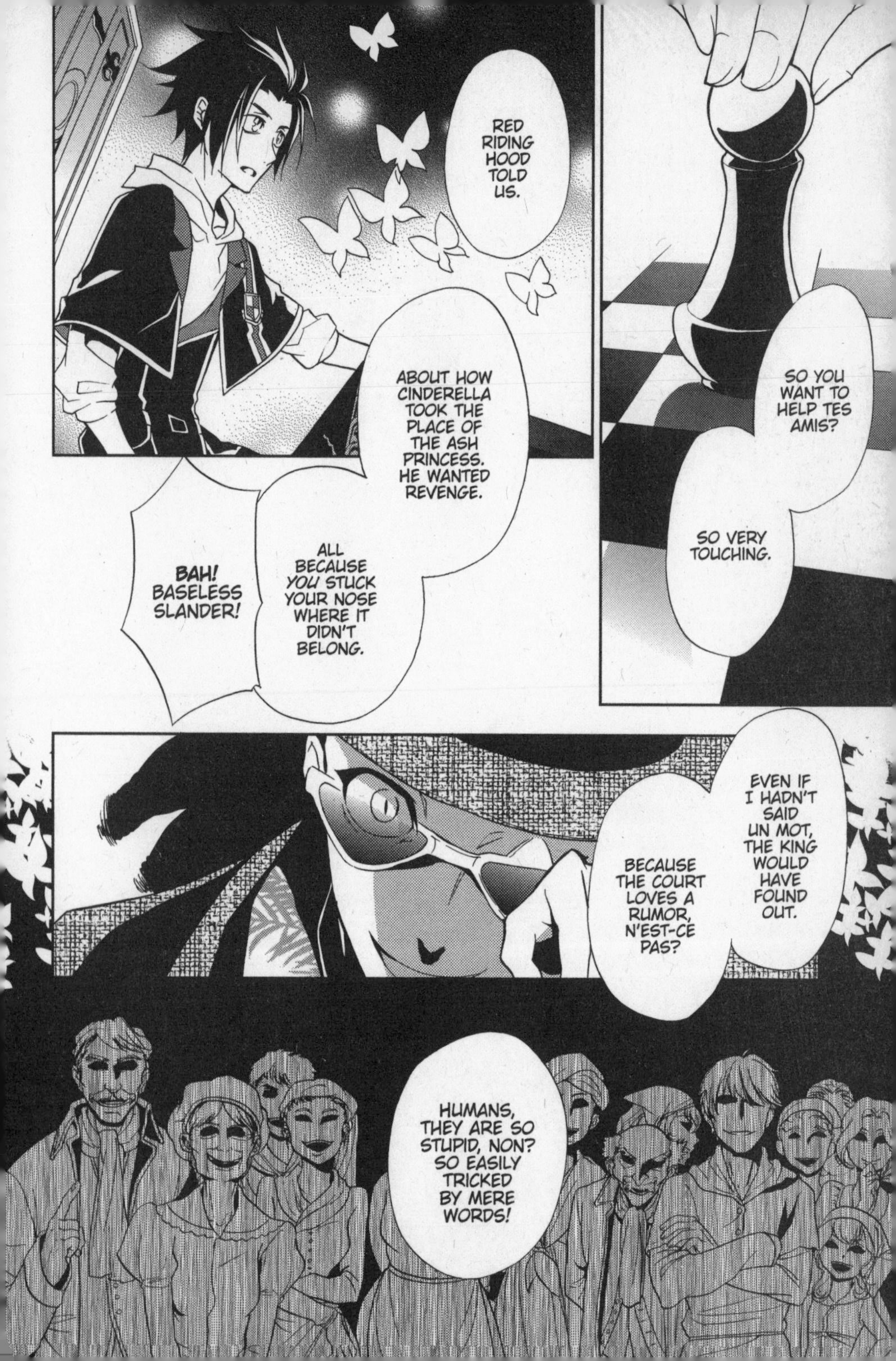
SO YOU WANT TO HELP TES AMIS?
SO VERY TOUCHING.
RED RIDING HOOD TOLD US.
ABOUT HOW CINDERELLA TOOK THE PLACE OF THE ASH PRINCESS. HE WANTED REVENGE.
ALL BECAUSE *YOU* STUCK YOUR NOSE WHERE IT DIDN'T BELONG.
BAH! BASELESS SLANDER!
EVEN IF I HADN'T SAID UN MOT, THE KING WOULD HAVE FOUND OUT.
BECAUSE THE COURT LOVES A RUMOR, N'EST-CE PAS?
HUMANS, THEY ARE SO STUPID, NON? SO EASILY TRICKED BY MERE WORDS!

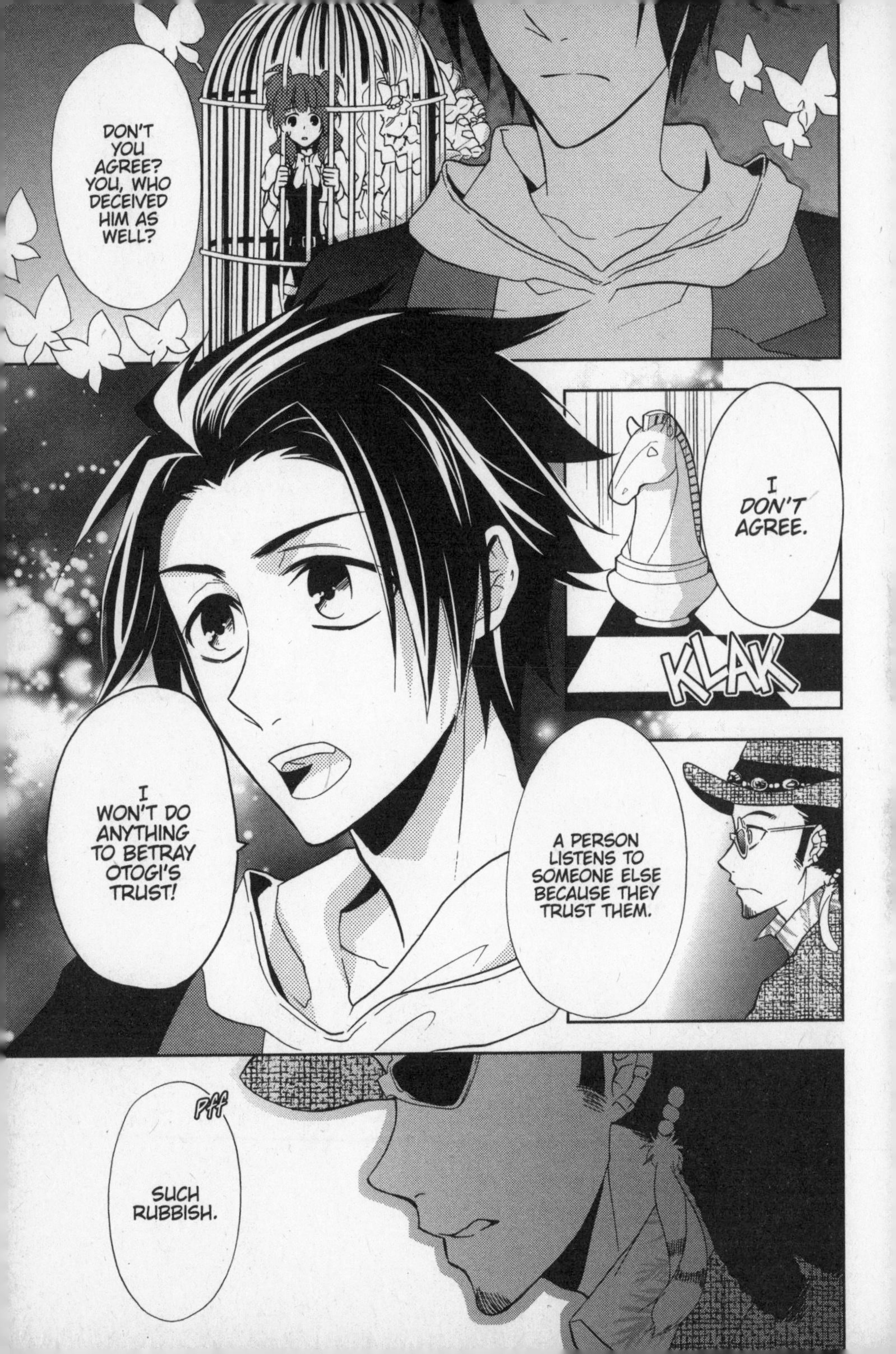
DON'T YOU AGREE? YOU, WHO DECEIVED HIM AS WELL?
I DON'T AGREE.
KLAK
A PERSON LISTENS TO SOMEONE ELSE BECAUSE THEY TRUST THEM.
I WON'T DO ANYTHING TO BETRAY OTOGI'S TRUST!
Pff
SUCH RUBBISH.

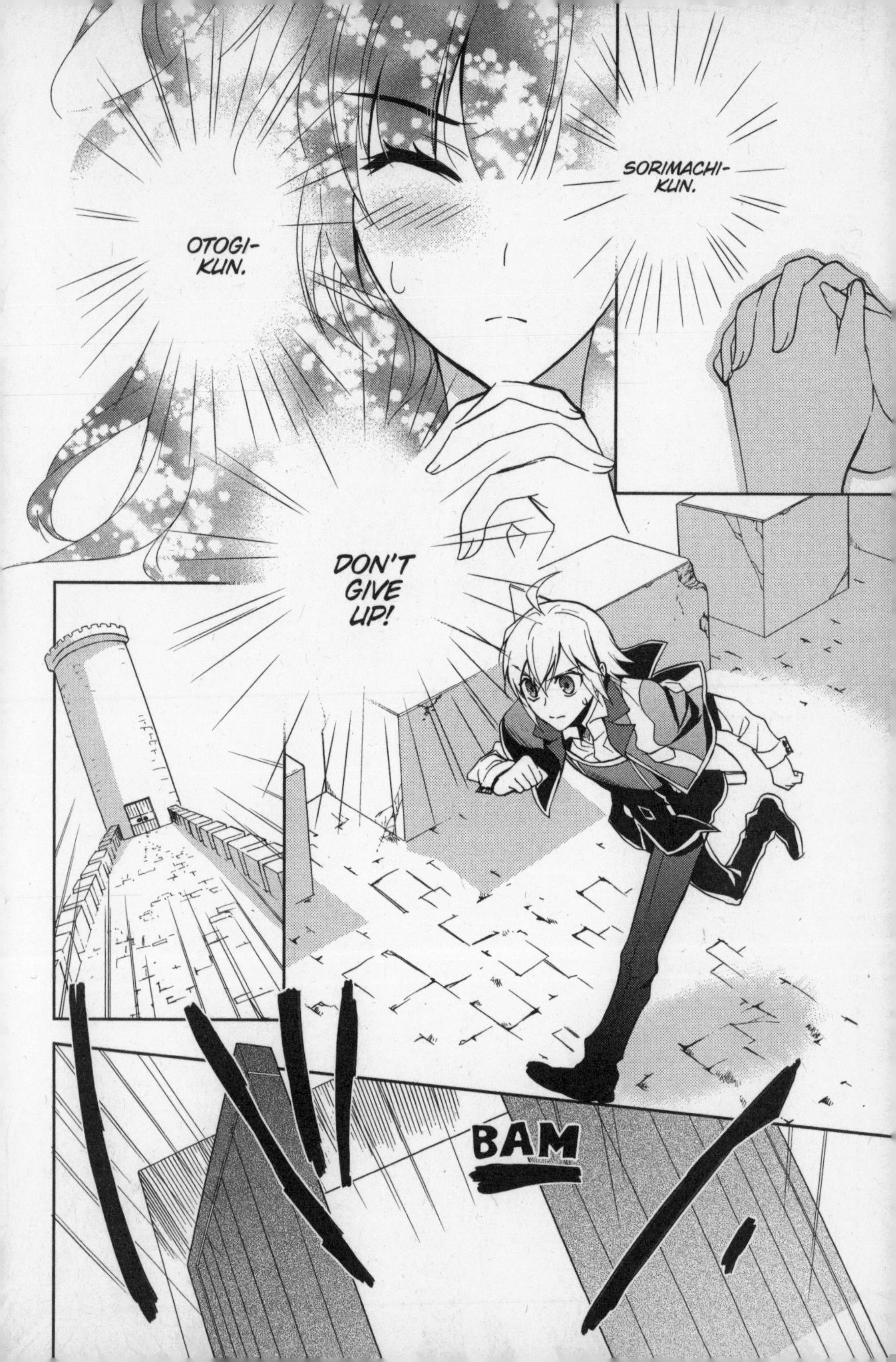
SORIMACHI-KUN.
OTOGI-KUN.
DON'T GIVE UP!
BAM

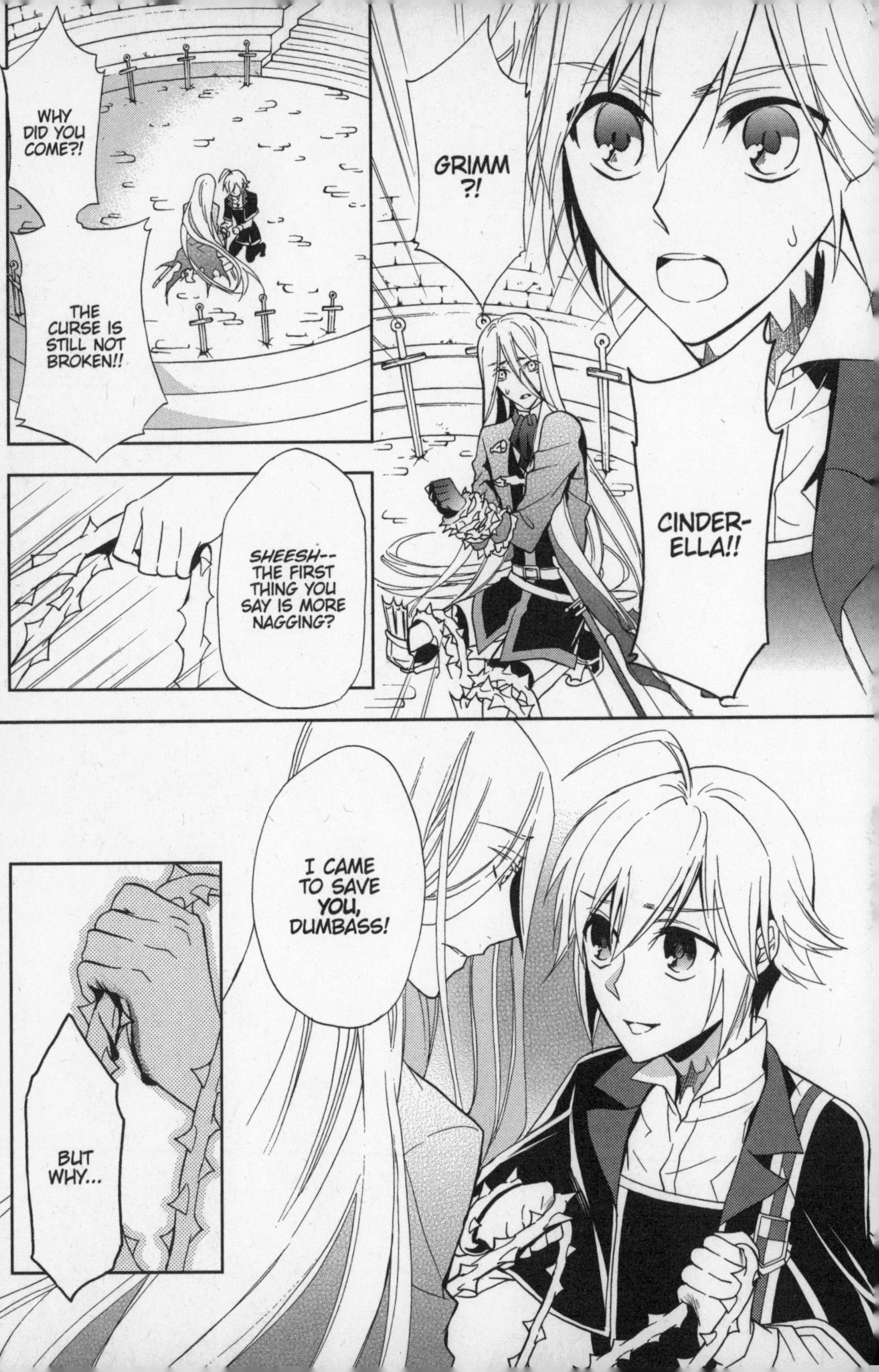
GRIMM ?!
CINDER-ELLA!!
WHY DID YOU COME?!
THE CURSE IS STILL NOT BROKEN!!
SHEESH-- THE FIRST THING YOU SAY IS MORE NAGGING?
I CAME TO SAVE YOU, DUMBASS!
BUT WHY...

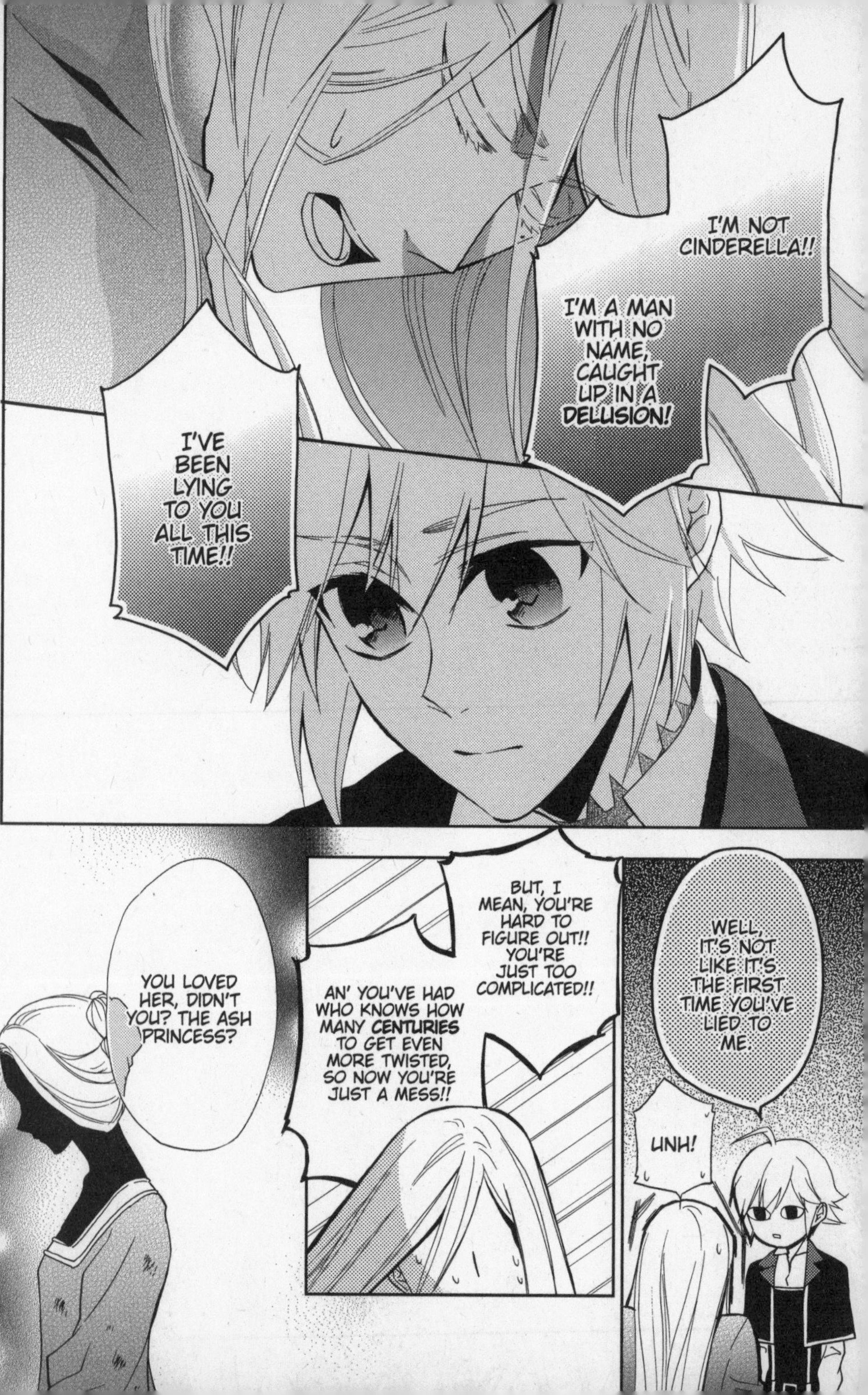
I'M NOT CINDERELLA!!
I'M A MAN WITH NO NAME, CAUGHT UP IN A DELUSION!
I'VE BEEN LYING TO YOU ALL THIS TIME!!
WELL, IT'S NOT LIKE IT'S THE FIRST TIME YOU'VE LIED TO ME.
UNH!
BUT, I MEAN, YOU'RE HARD TO FIGURE OUT!! YOU'RE JUST TOO COMPLICATED!!
AN' YOU'VE HAD WHO KNOWS HOW MANY CENTURIES TO GET EVEN MORE TWISTED, SO NOW YOU'RE JUST A MESS!!
YOU LOVED HER, DIDN'T YOU? THE ASH PRINCESS?

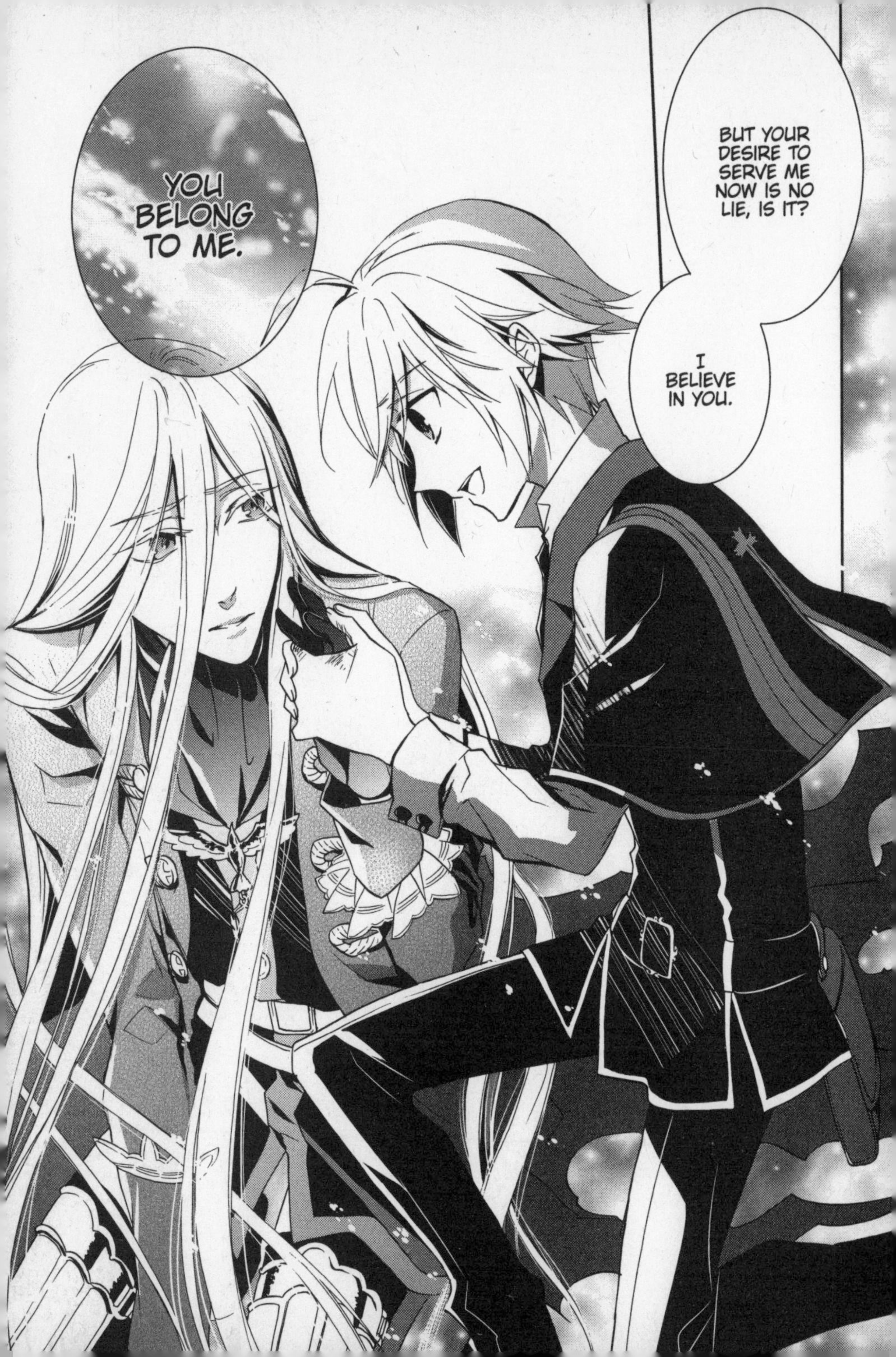
BUT YOUR DESIRE TO SERVE ME NOW IS NO LIE, IS IT?
I BELIEVE IN YOU.
YOU BELONG TO ME.

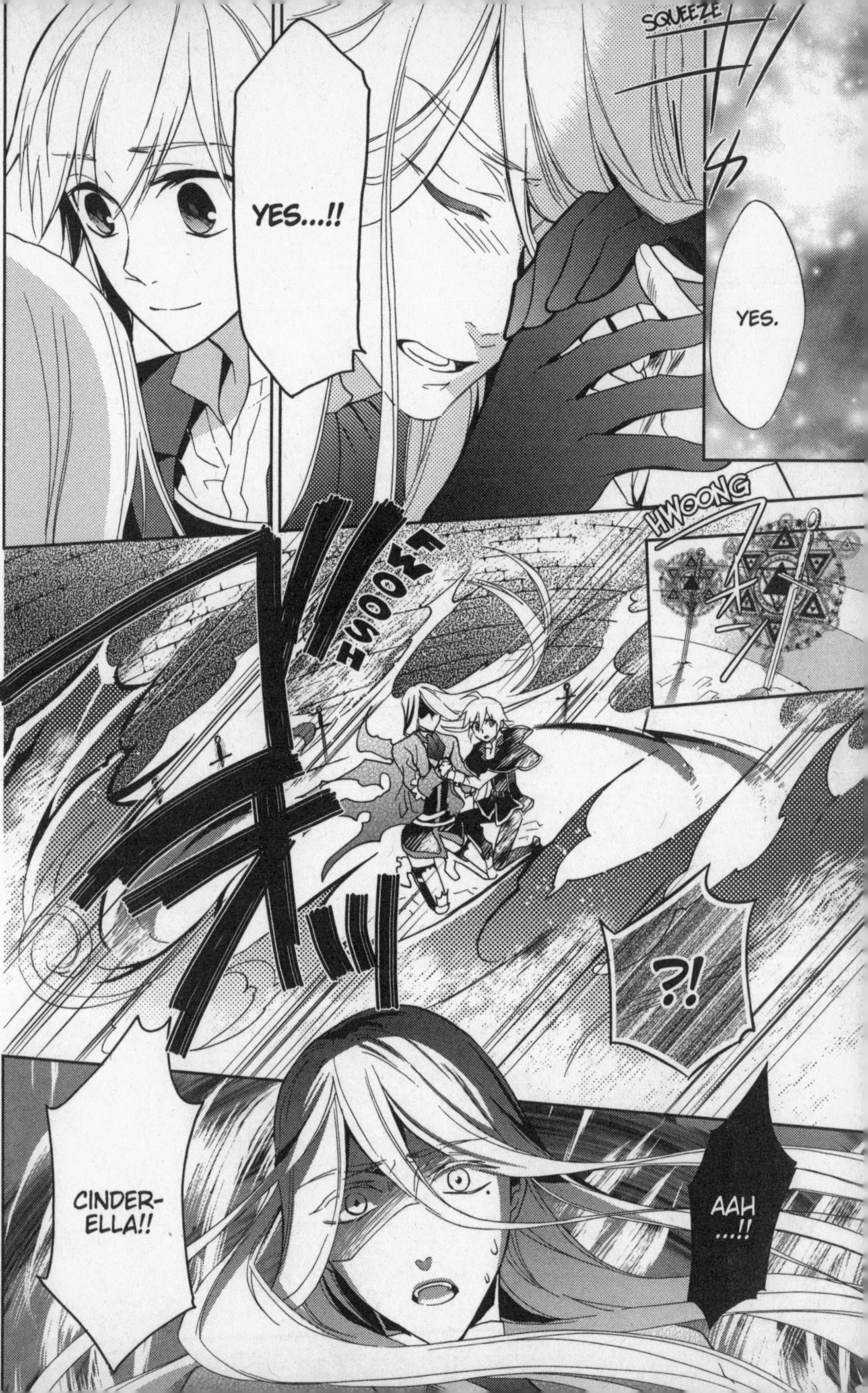
SQUEEZE
YES.
YES...!!
HWOONG
FWOOSH
?!
AAH ...!!
CINDER-ELLA!!

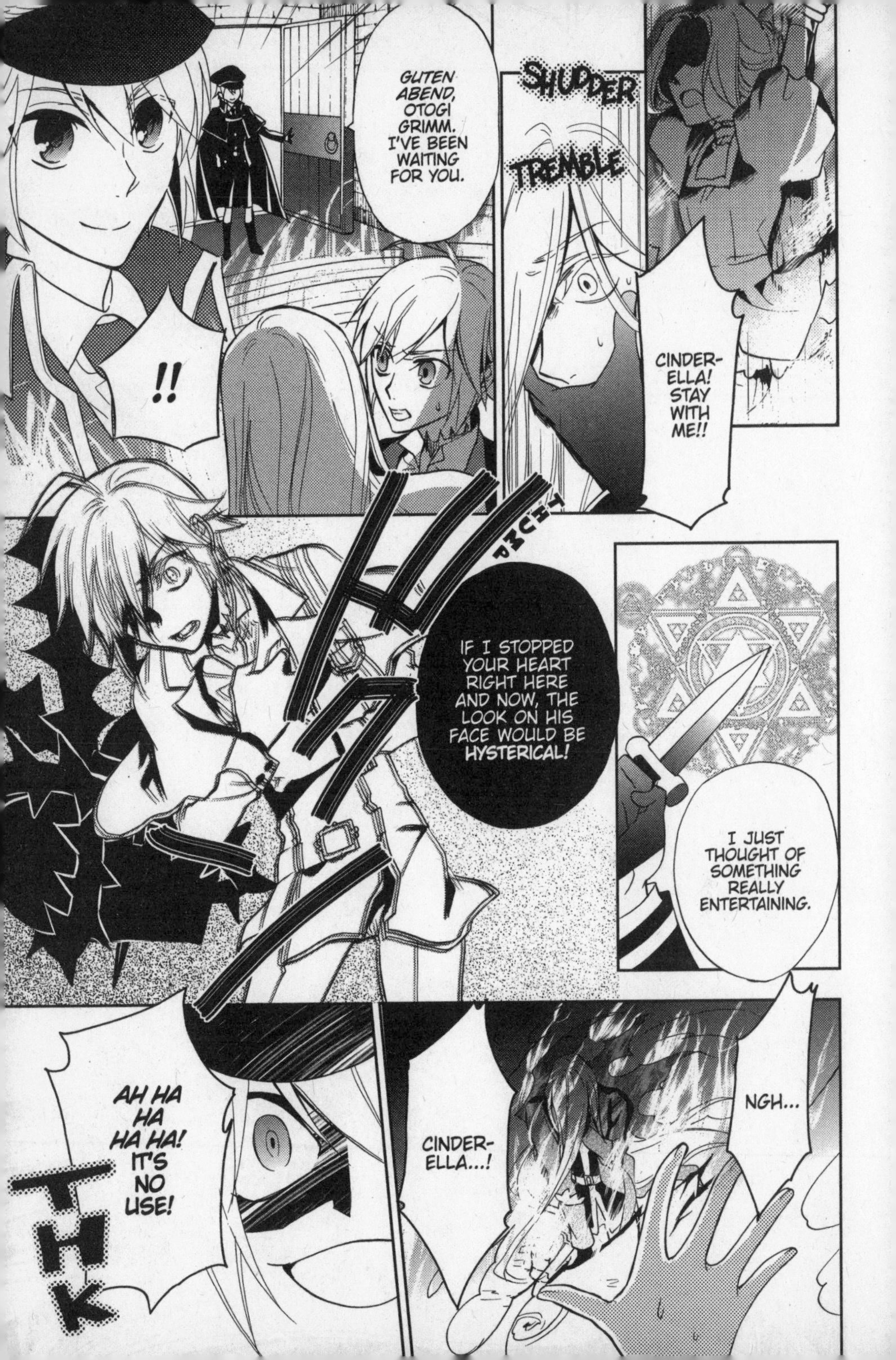
CINDER-ELLA! STAY WITH ME!!
SHUDDER
TREMBLE
GUTEN ABEND, OTOGI GRIMM. I'VE BEEN WAITING FOR YOU.
!!
I JUST THOUGHT OF SOMETHING REALLY ENTERTAINING.
IF I STOPPED YOUR HEART RIGHT HERE AND NOW, THE LOOK ON HIS FACE WOULD BE HYSTERICAL!
NGH...
CINDER-ELLA...!
AH HA HA HA HA! IT'S NO USE!
THK

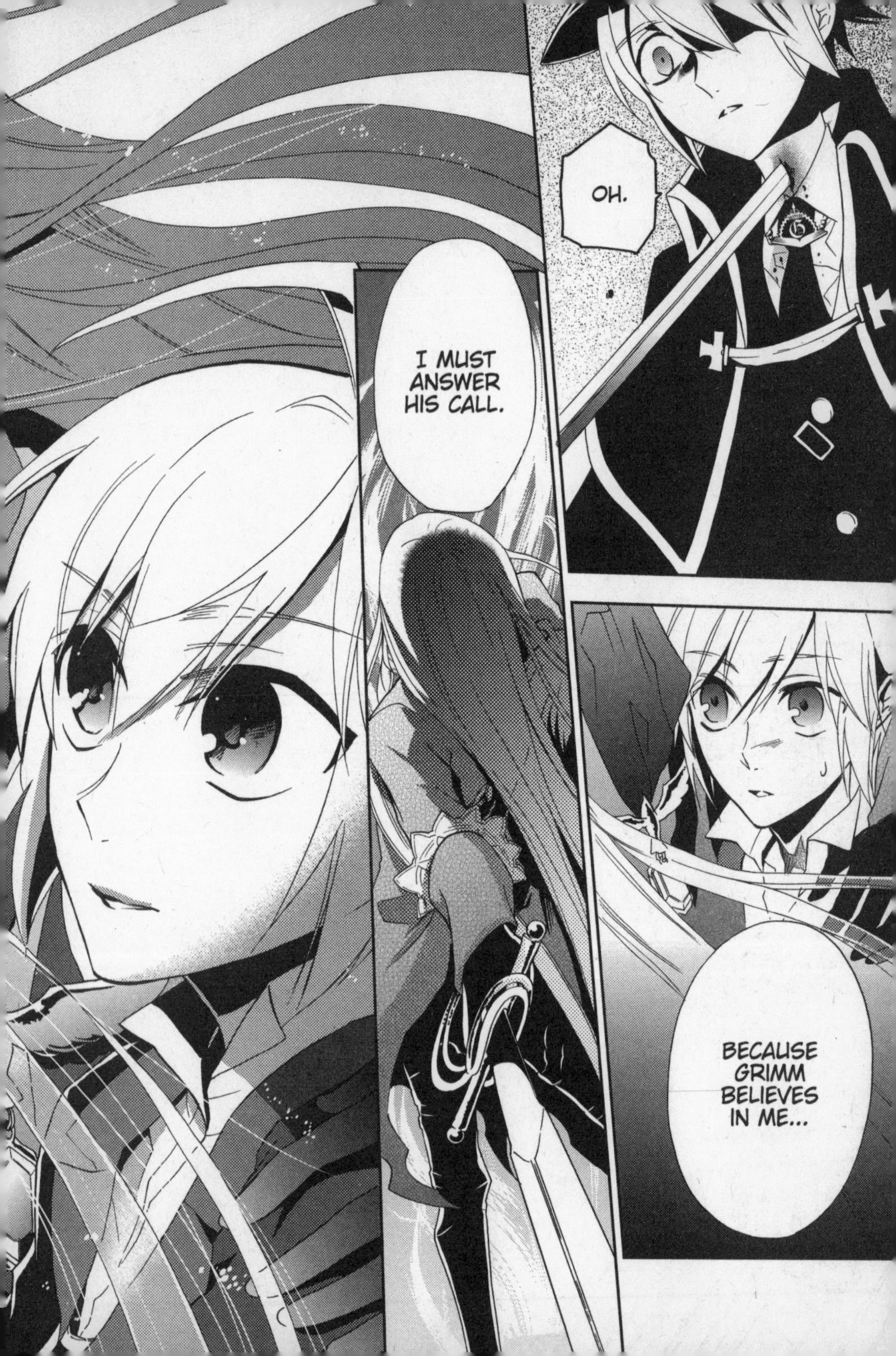
OH.
BECAUSE GRIMM BELIEVES IN ME...
I MUST ANSWER HIS CALL.

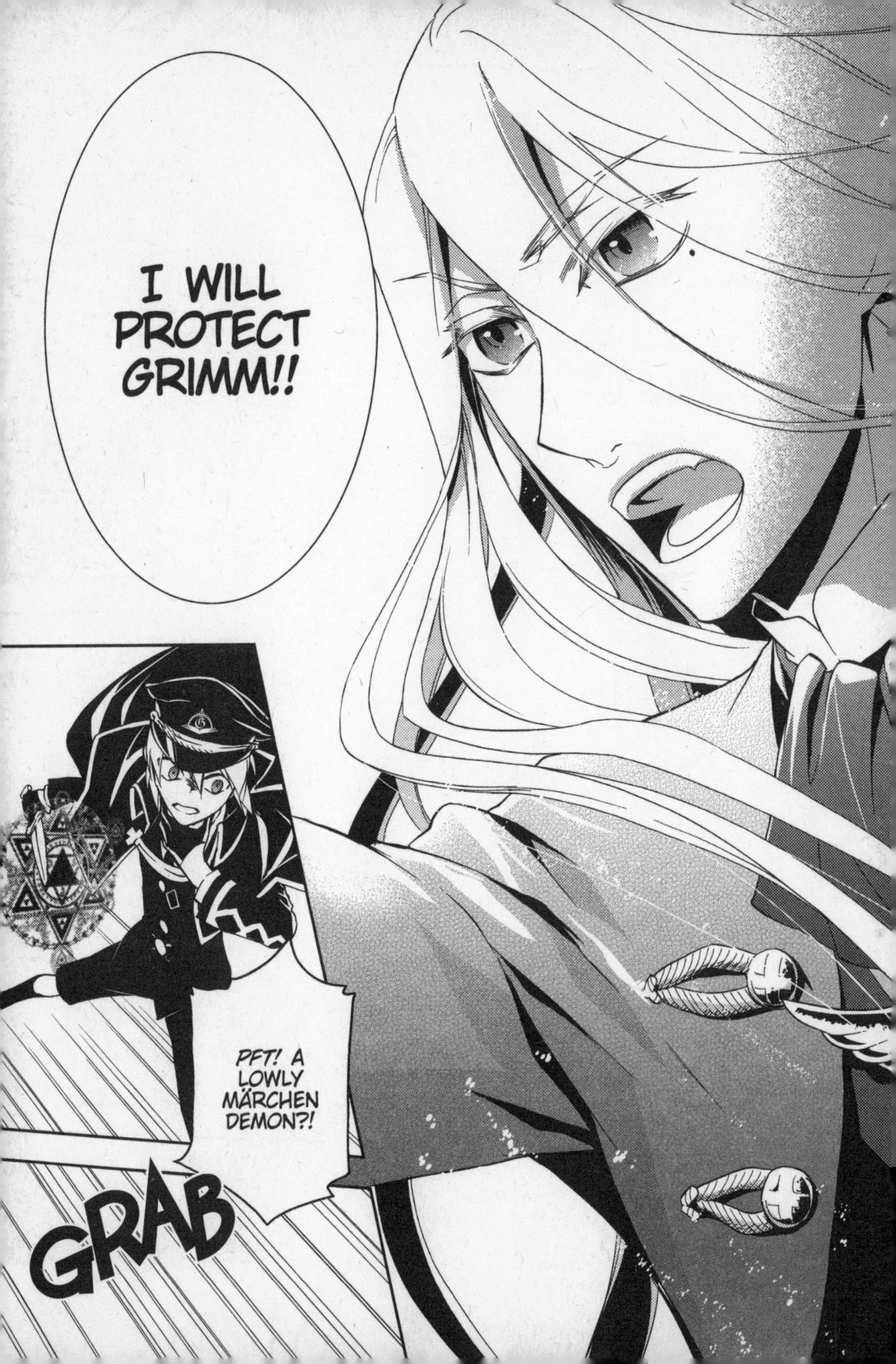
I WILL PROTECT GRIMM!!
PFT! A LOWLY MÄRCHEN DEMON?!
GRAB

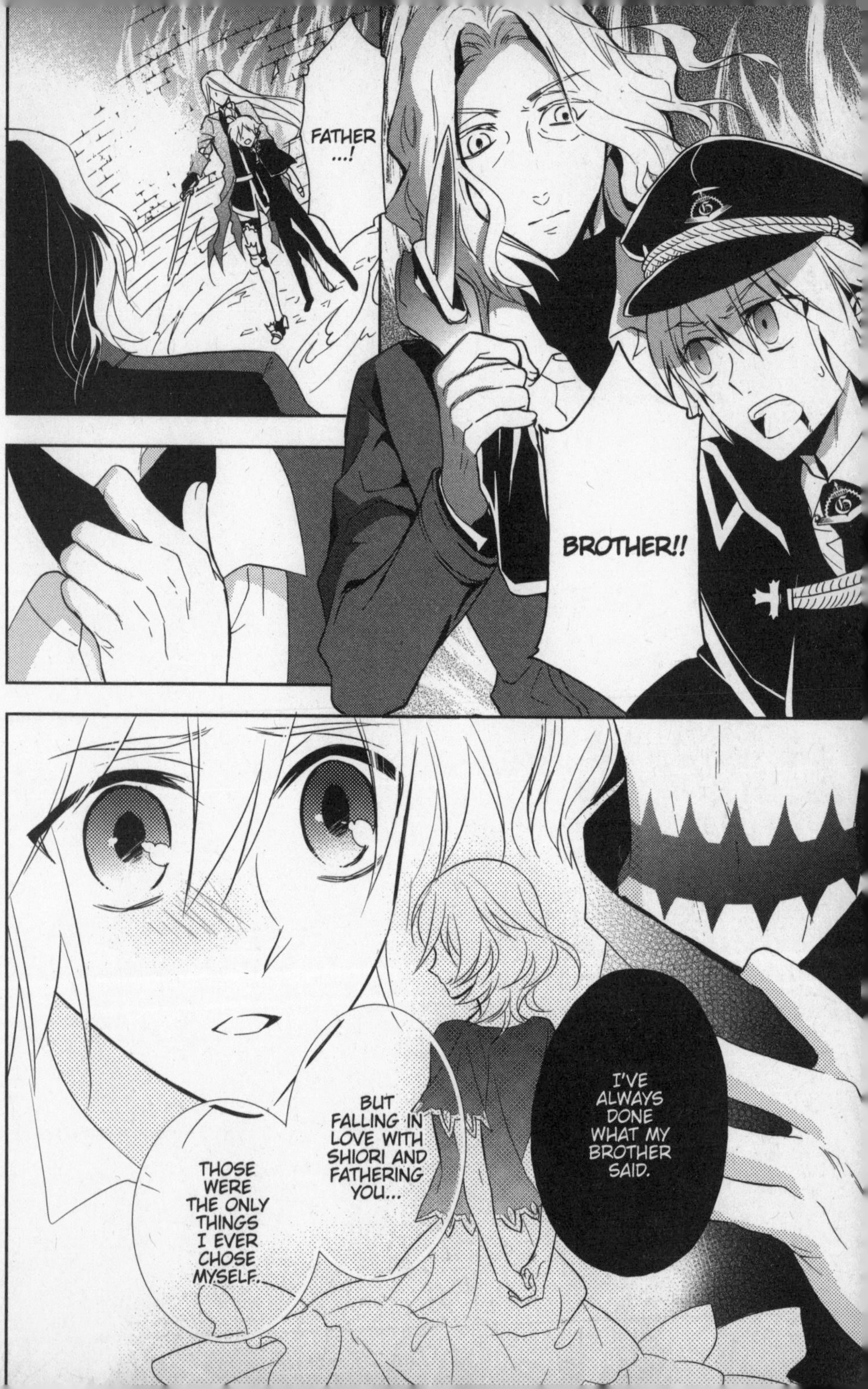
BROTHER!!
FATHER ...!
I'VE ALWAYS DONE WHAT MY BROTHER SAID.
BUT FALLING IN LOVE WITH SHIORI AND FATHERING YOU...
THOSE WERE THE ONLY THINGS I EVER CHOSE MYSELF..

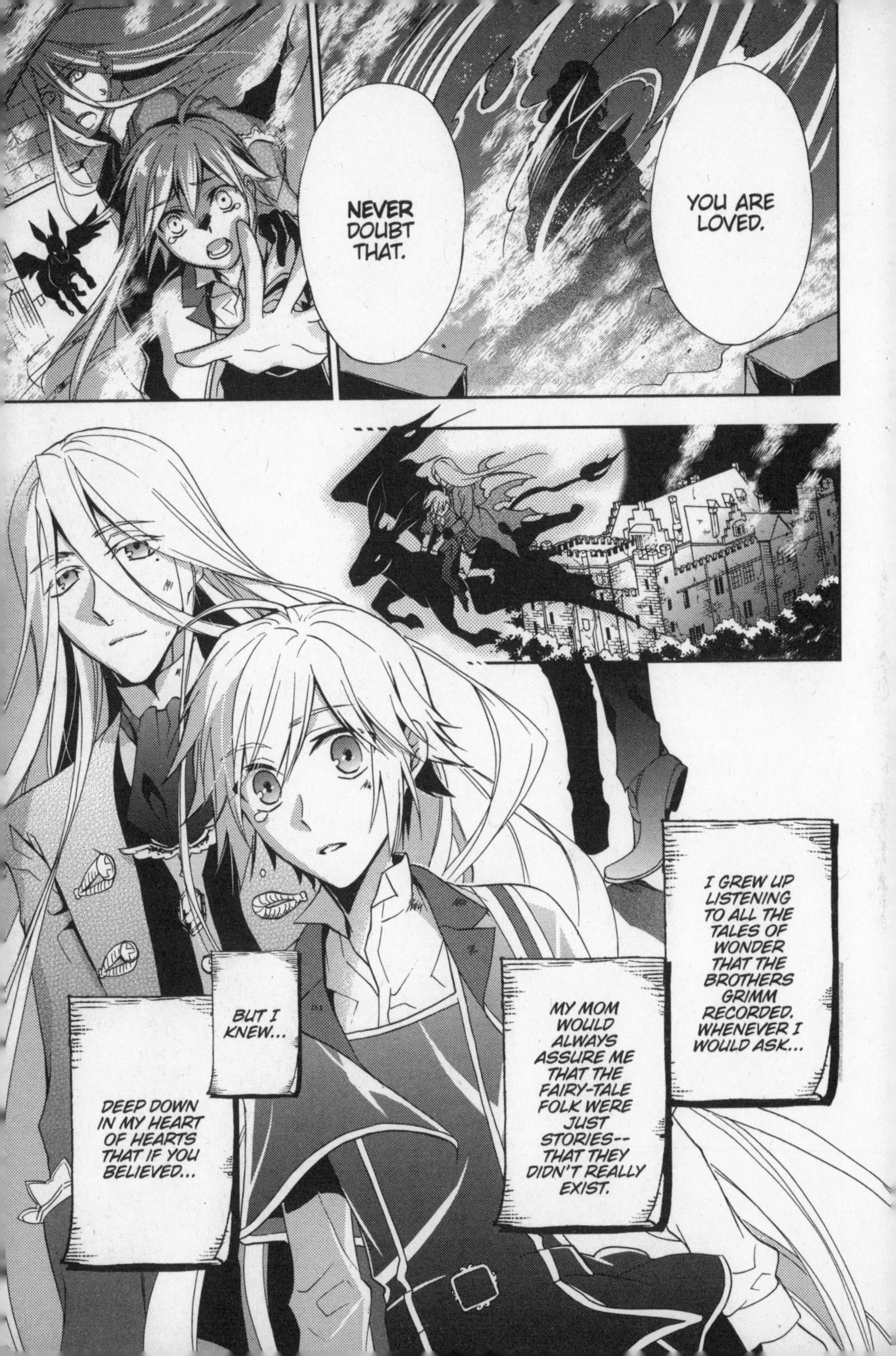
YOU ARE LOVED.
NEVER DOUBT THAT.
I GREW UP LISTENING TO ALL THE TALES OF WONDER THAT THE BROTHERS GRIMM RECORDED. WHENEVER I WOULD ASK...
MY MOM WOULD ALWAYS ASSURE ME THAT THE FAIRY-TALE FOLK WERE JUST STORIES-- THAT THEY DIDN'T REALLY EXIST.
BUT I KNEW...
DEEP DOWN IN MY HEART OF HEARTS THAT IF YOU BELIEVED...

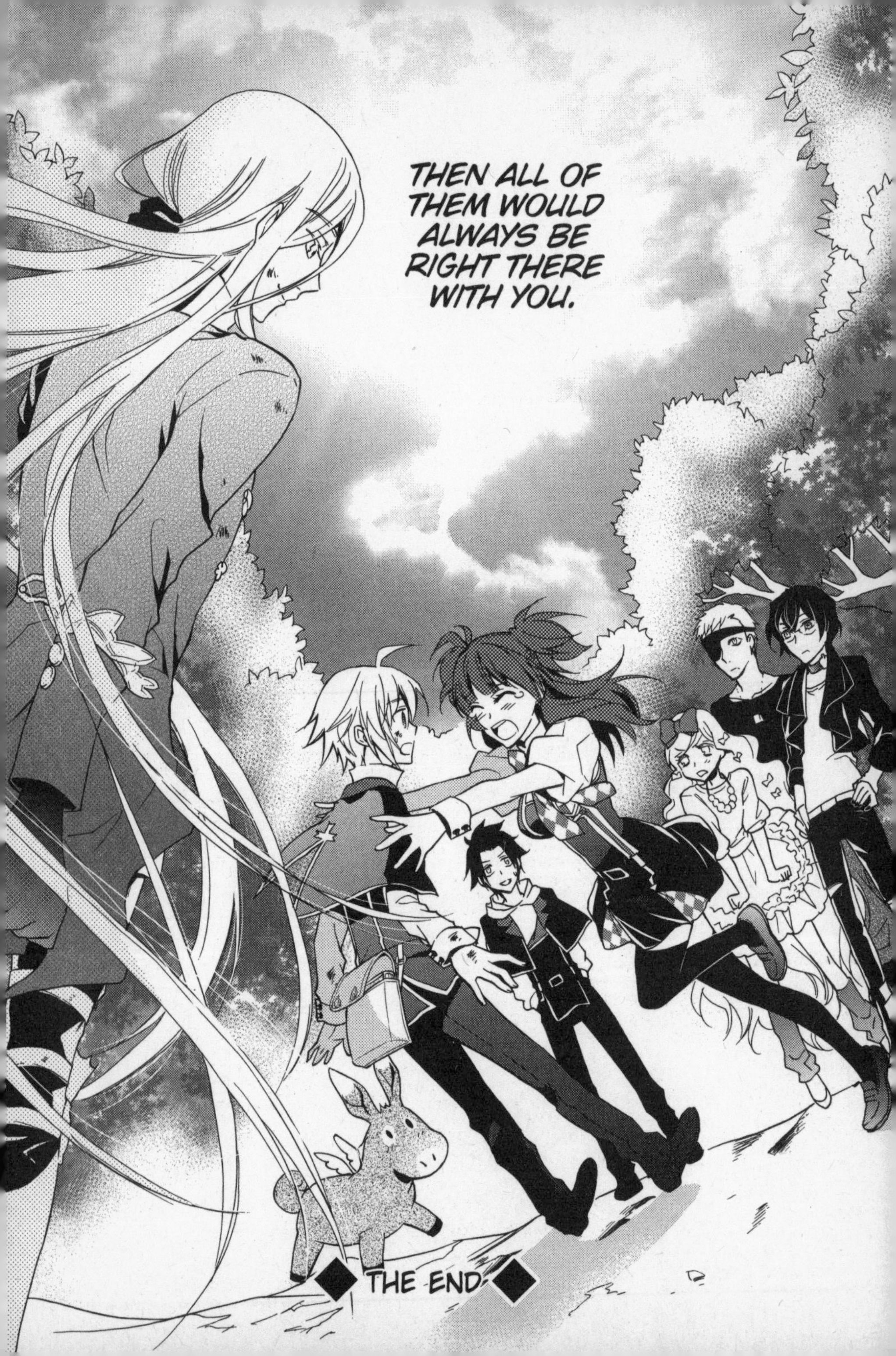
THEN ALL OF THEM WOULD ALWAYS BE RIGHT THERE WITH YOU.
THE END

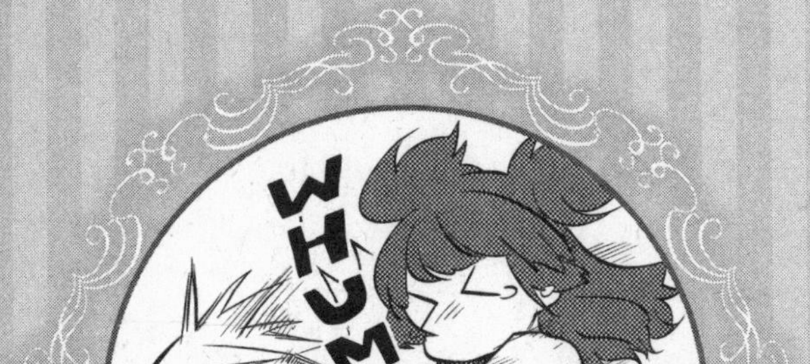
WHUMP

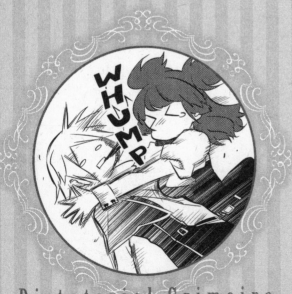

Dictatorial Grimoire

独裁グリムワール
Dictatorial Grimoire

← A BONUS CHAPTER PUBLISHED IN COMIC GENE STARTS ON THE NEXT PAGE! IT CONTINUES THE STORY, TELLING WHAT HAPPENED AFTER CHAPTER 11! ENJOY!!

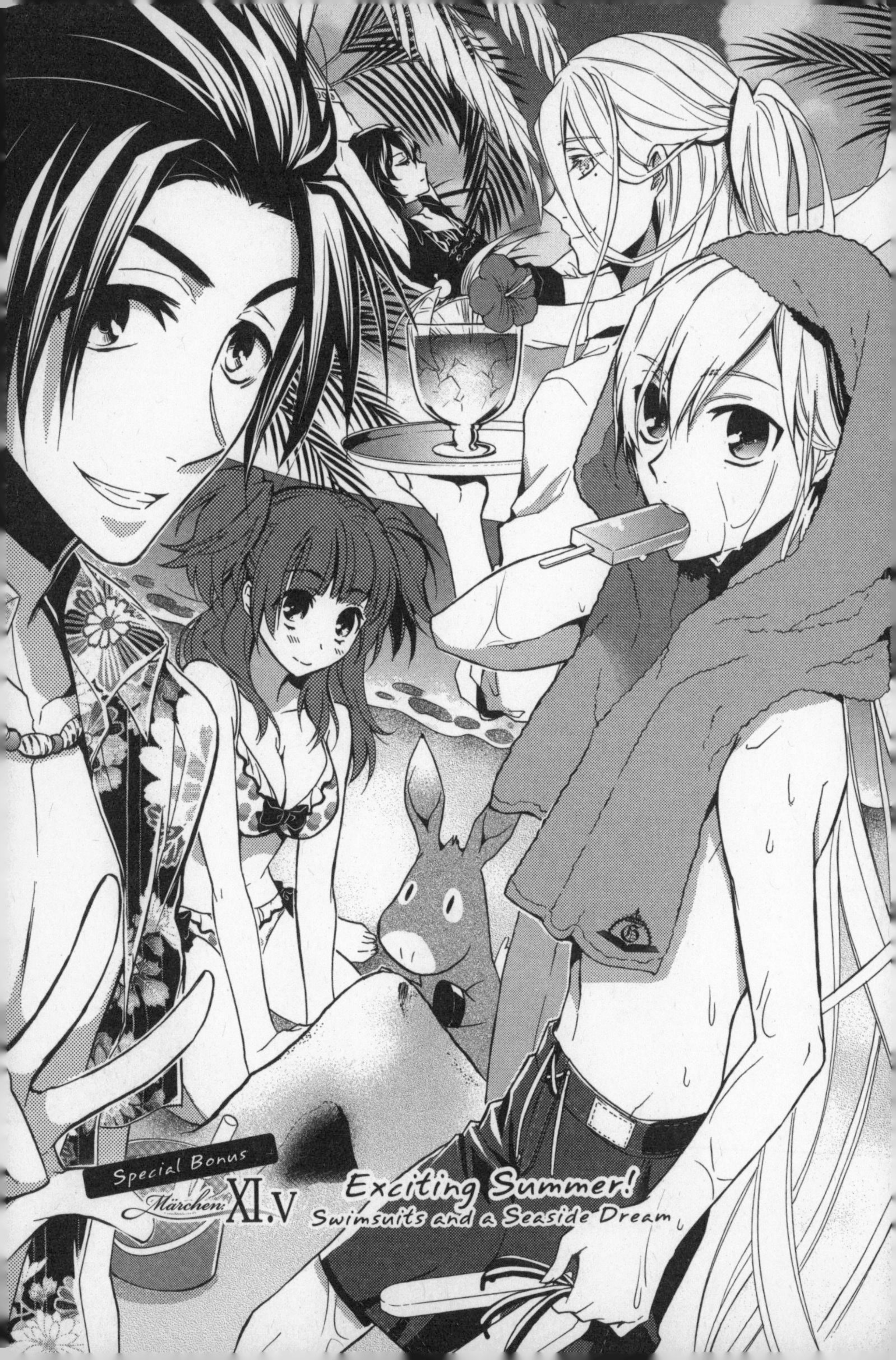
Special Bonus
Märchen: XI.V
Exciting Summer!
Swimsuits and a Seaside Dream

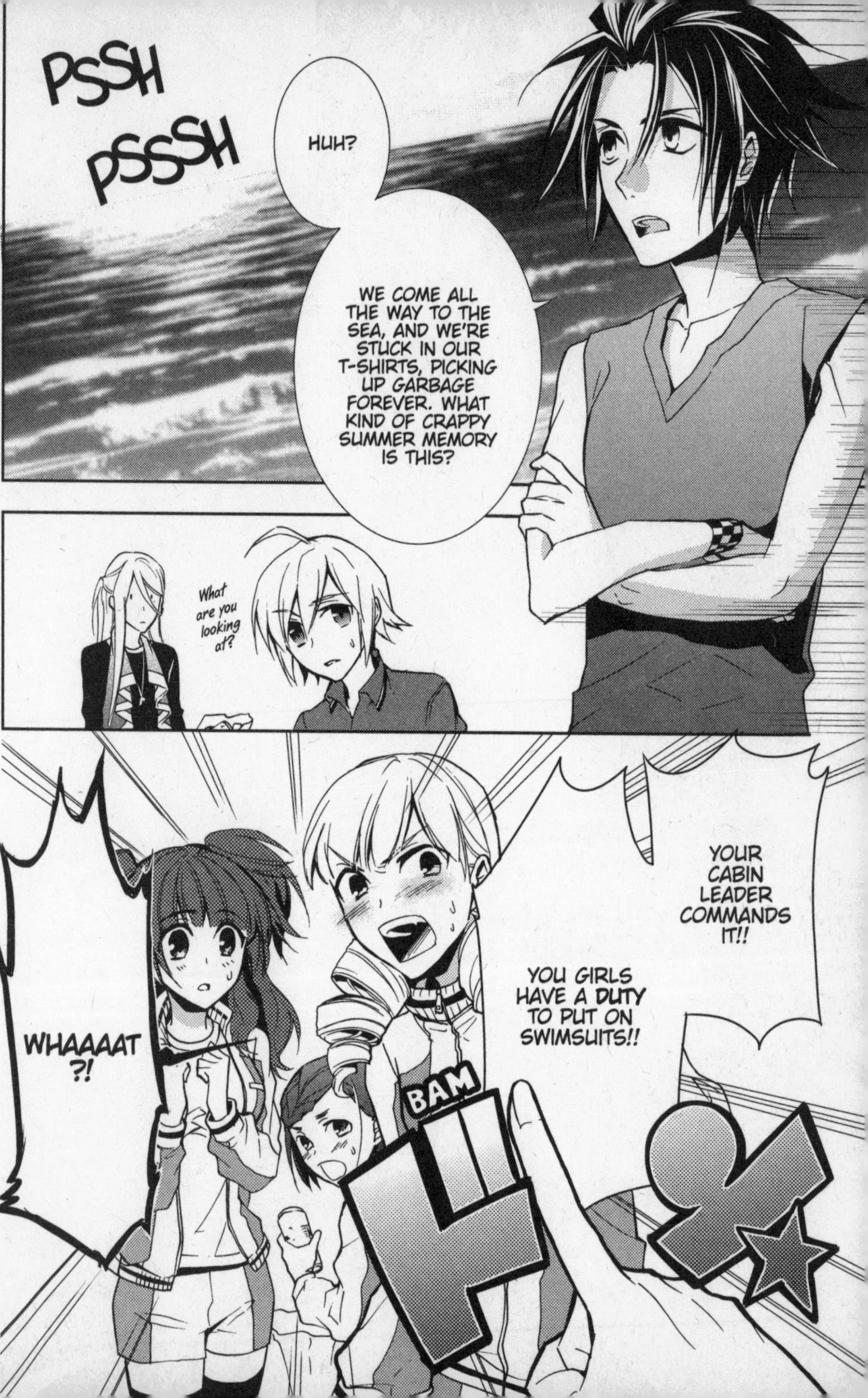
PSSH
PSSSH
HUH?
WE COME ALL THE WAY TO THE SEA, AND WE'RE STUCK IN OUR T-SHIRTS, PICKING UP GARBAGE FOREVER. WHAT KIND OF CRAPPY SUMMER MEMORY IS THIS?
What are you looking at?
YOUR CABIN LEADER COMMANDS IT!!
YOU GIRLS HAVE A DUTY TO PUT ON SWIMSUITS!!
BAM
WHAAAAT ?!

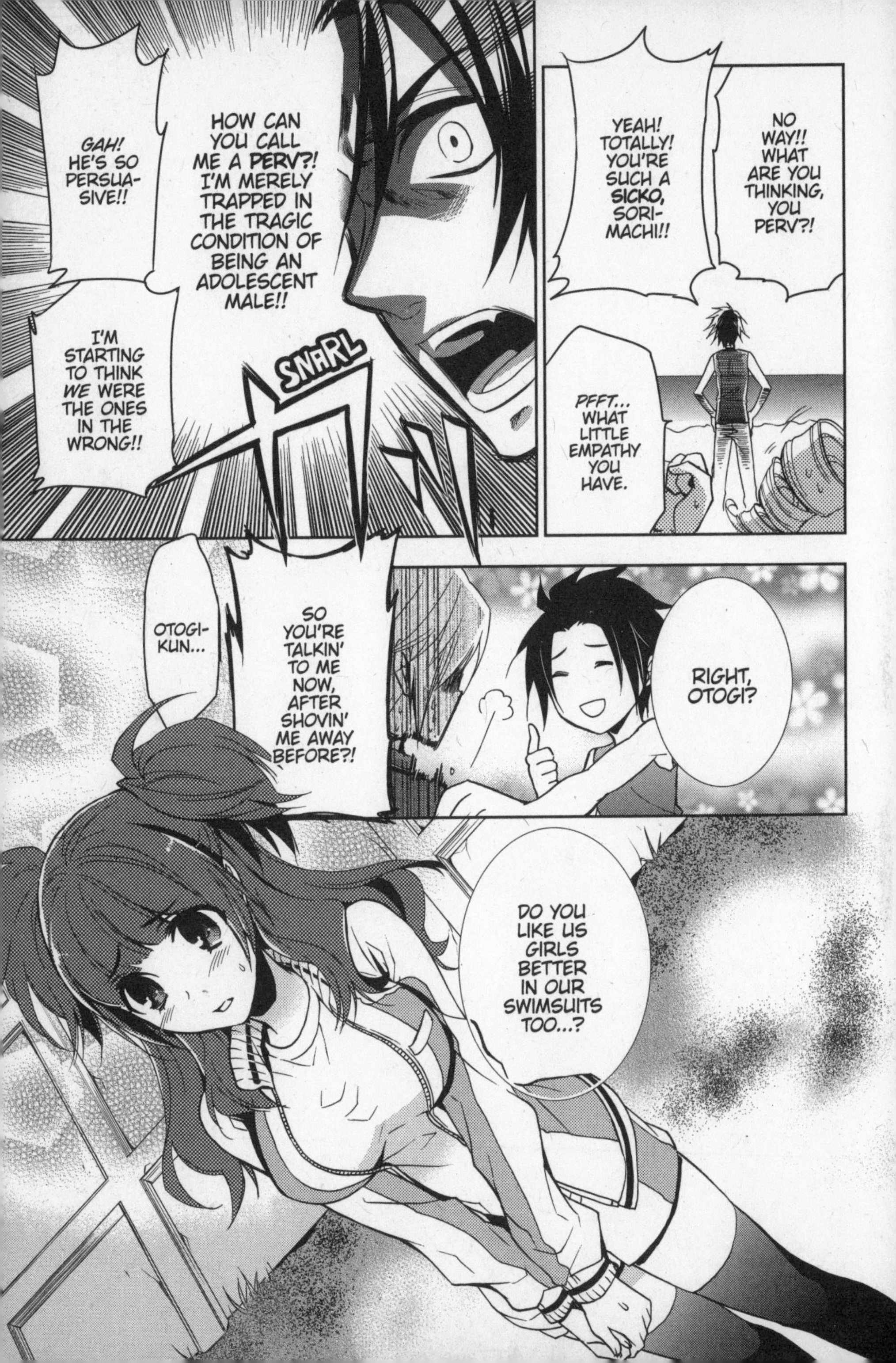
NO WAY!! WHAT ARE YOU THINKING, YOU PERV?!
YEAH! TOTALLY! YOU'RE SUCH A SICKO, SORI-MACHI!!
PFFT... WHAT LITTLE EMPATHY YOU HAVE.
HOW CAN YOU CALL ME A PERV?! I'M MERELY TRAPPED IN THE TRAGIC CONDITION OF BEING AN ADOLESCENT MALE!!
GAH! HE'S SO PERSUA-SIVE!!
SNARL
I'M STARTING TO THINK WE WERE THE ONES IN THE WRONG!!
RIGHT, OTOGI?
SO YOU'RE TALKIN' TO ME NOW, AFTER SHOVIN' ME AWAY BEFORE?!
OTOGI-KUN...
DO YOU LIKE US GIRLS BETTER IN OUR SWIMSUITS TOO...?

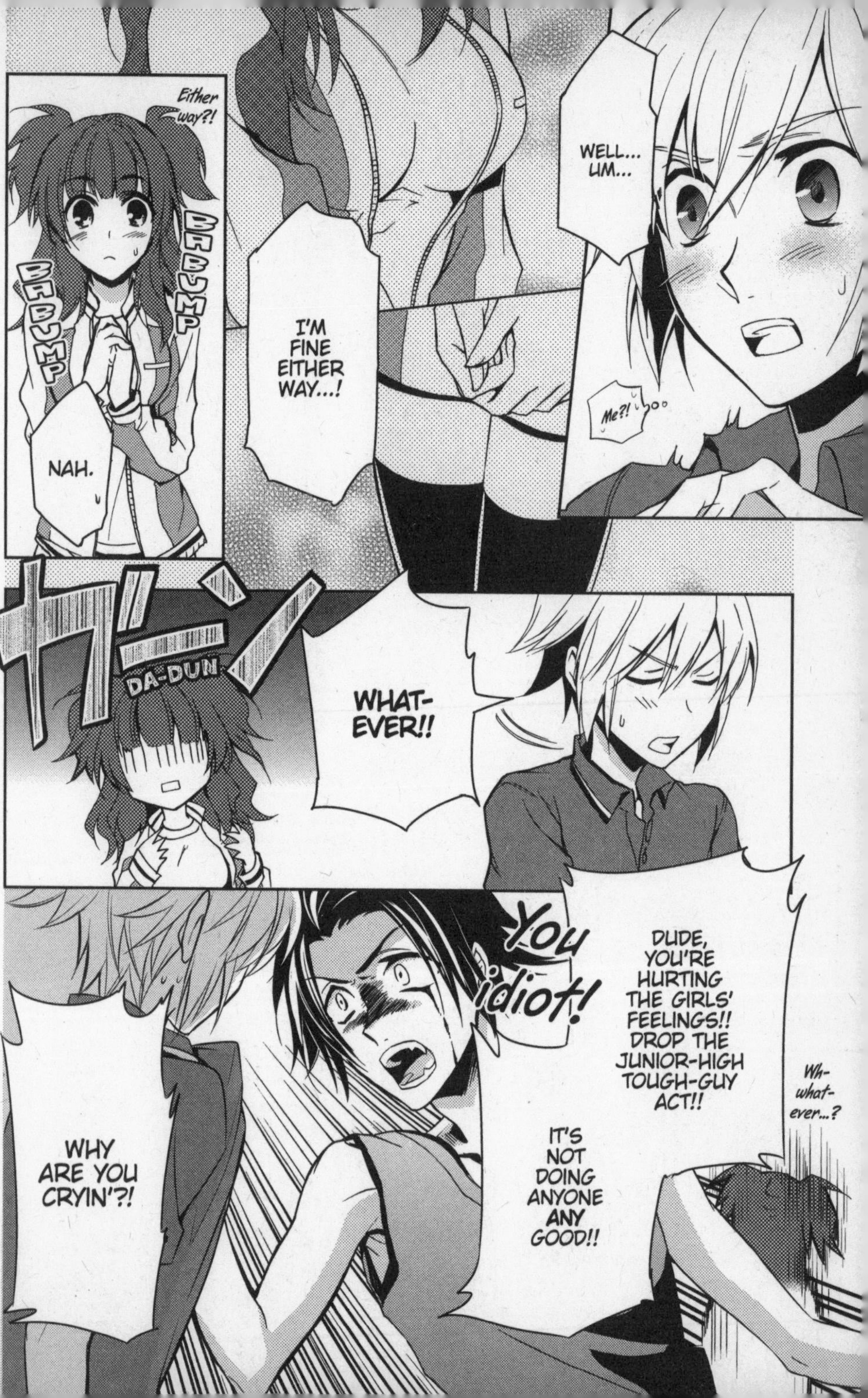
WELL... UM...
Me?!
I'M FINE EITHER WAY...!
Either way?!
BABUMP
BABUMP
NAH.
WHAT-EVER!!
DA-DUN
Wh-what-ever...?
DUDE, YOU'RE HURTING THE GIRLS' FEELINGS!! DROP THE JUNIOR-HIGH TOUGH-GUY ACT!!
You idiot!
IT'S NOT DOING ANYONE ANY GOOD!!
WHY ARE YOU CRYIN'?!

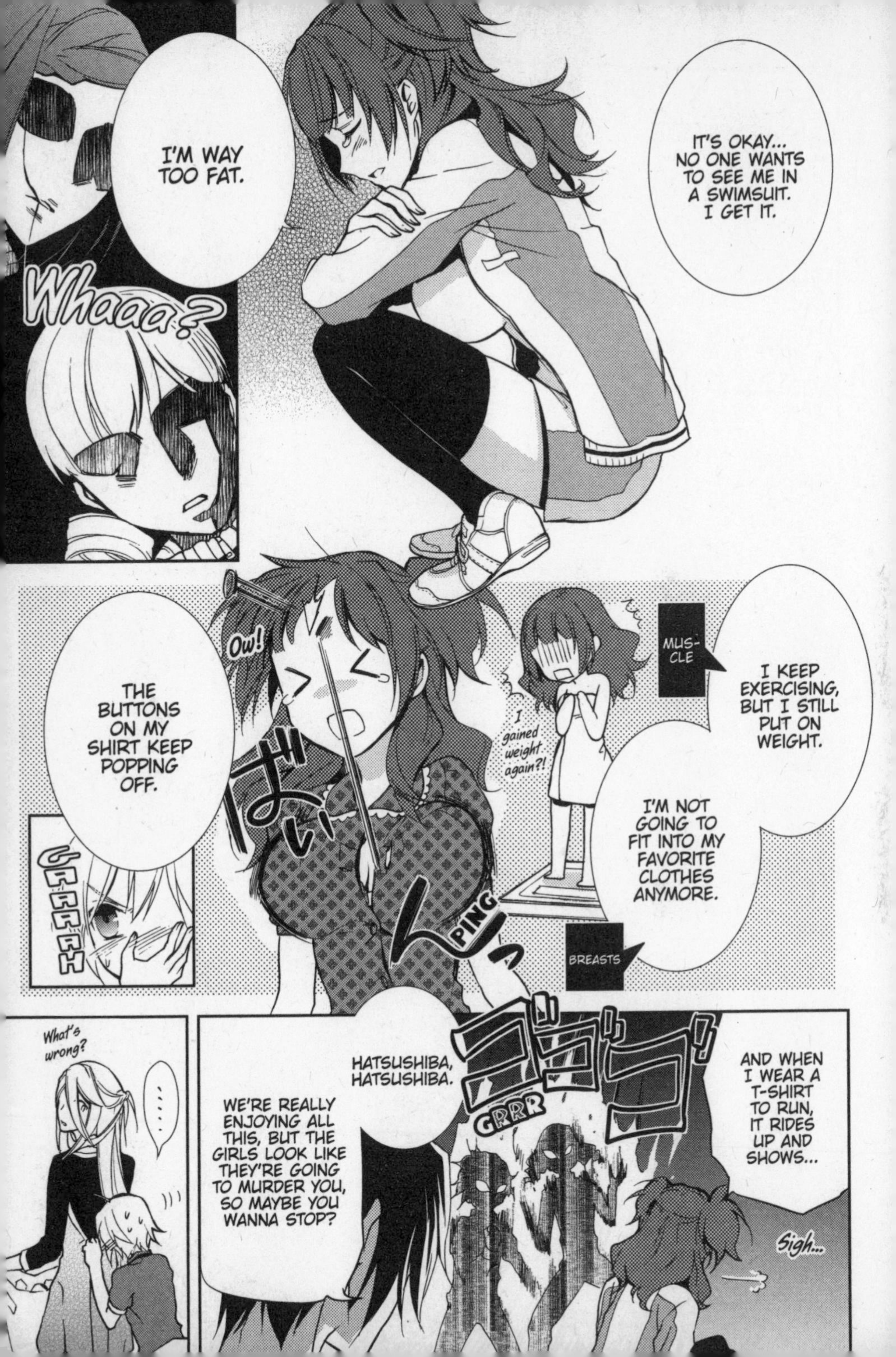
IT'S OKAY... NO ONE WANTS TO SEE ME IN A SWIMSUIT. I GET IT.
I'M WAY TOO FAT.
Whaaa?
I KEEP EXERCISING, BUT I STILL PUT ON WEIGHT.
MUS-CLE
I gained weight again?!
I'M NOT GOING TO FIT INTO MY FAVORITE CLOTHES ANYMORE.
BREASTS
Ow!
THE BUTTONS ON MY SHIRT KEEP POPPING OFF.
PING
GRAAAAH
AND WHEN I WEAR A T-SHIRT TO RUN, IT RIDES UP AND SHOWS...
Sigh...
GRRR
HATSUSHIBA, HATSUSHIBA.
WE'RE REALLY ENJOYING ALL THIS, BUT THE GIRLS LOOK LIKE THEY'RE GOING TO MURDER YOU, SO MAYBE YOU WANNA STOP?
What's wrong?
......

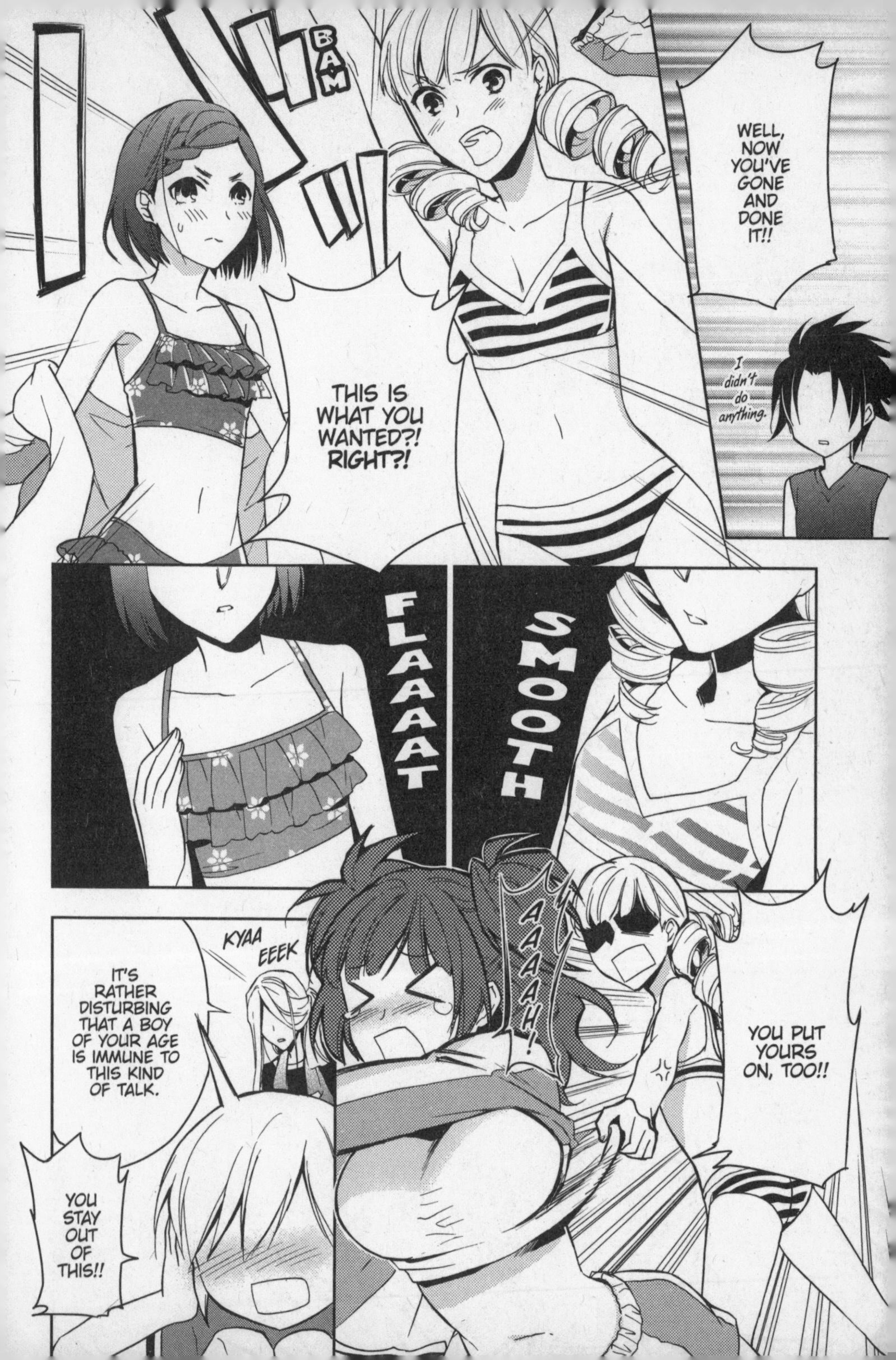
WELL, NOW YOU'VE GONE AND DONE IT!!
I didn't do anything.
BAM
THIS IS WHAT YOU WANTED?! RIGHT?!
SMOOTH
FLAAAAT
YOU PUT YOURS ON, TOO!!
AAAAAH!
KYAA EEEK
IT'S RATHER DISTURBING THAT A BOY OF YOUR AGE IS IMMUNE TO THIS KIND OF TALK.
YOU STAY OUT OF THIS!!

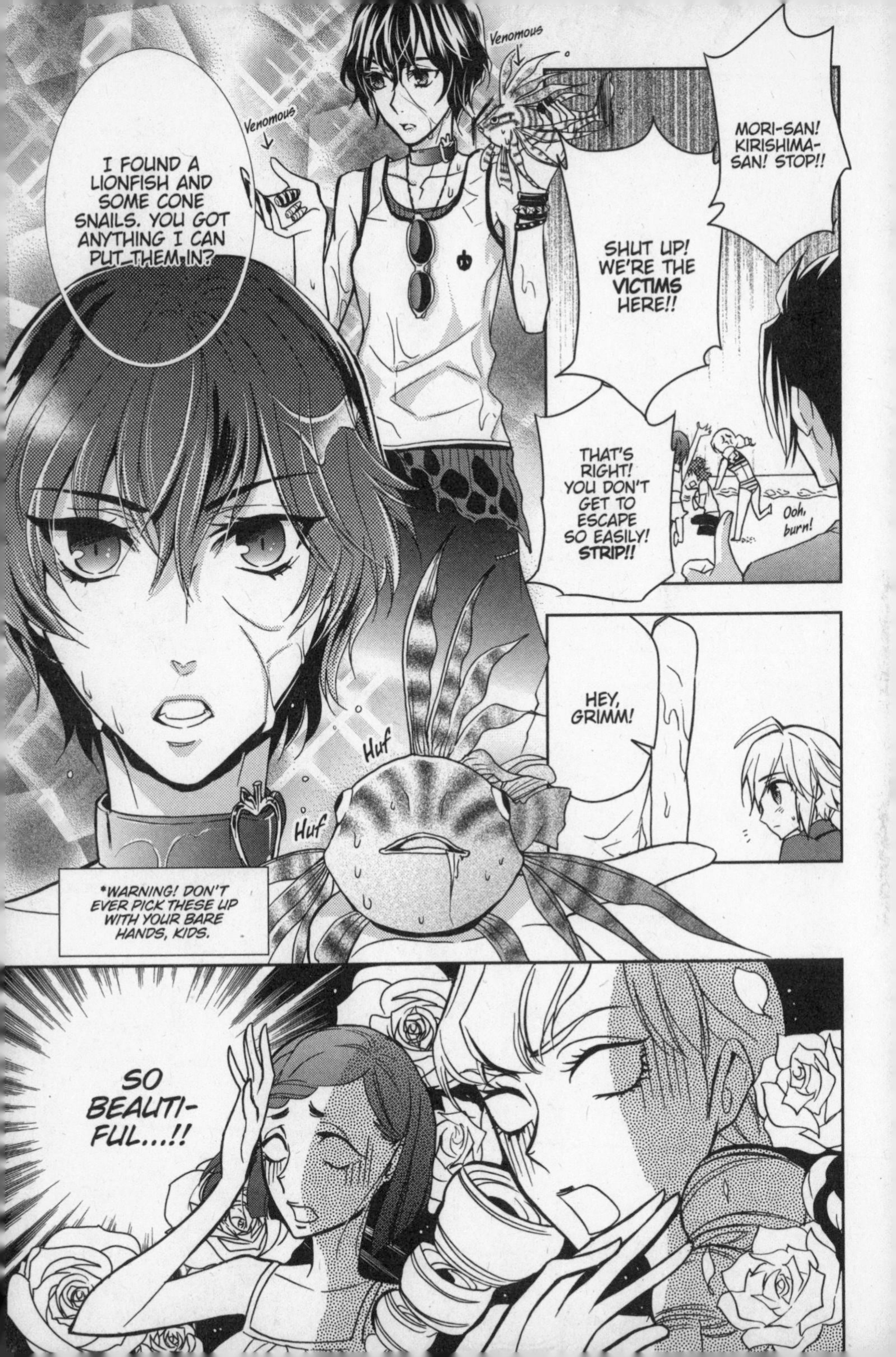
MORI-SAN! KIRISHIMA-SAN! STOP!!
SHUT UP! WE'RE THE VICTIMS HERE!!
THAT'S RIGHT! YOU DON'T GET TO ESCAPE SO EASILY! STRIP!!
Ooh, burn!
HEY, GRIMM!
Venomous
Venomous
I FOUND A LIONFISH AND SOME CONE SNAILS. YOU GOT ANYTHING I CAN PUT THEM IN?
Huf
Huf
*WARNING! DON'T EVER PICK THESE UP WITH YOUR BARE HANDS, KIDS.
SO BEAUTI-FUL...!!

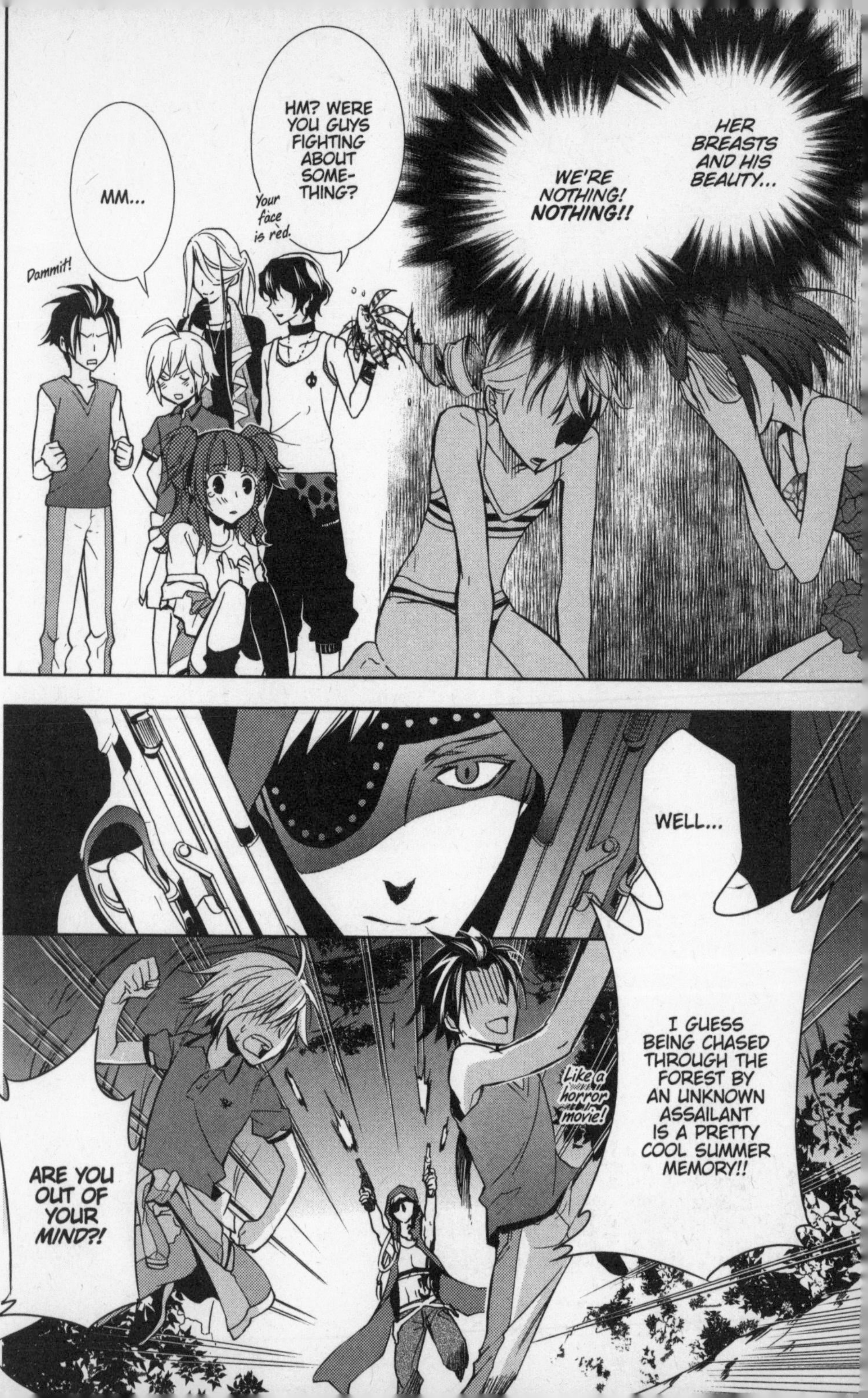
HER BREASTS AND HIS BEAUTY...
WE'RE NOTHING! NOTHING!!
HM? WERE YOU GUYS FIGHTING ABOUT SOME-THING?
Your face is red.
MM...
Dammit!
WELL...
I GUESS BEING CHASED THROUGH THE FOREST BY AN UNKNOWN ASSAILANT IS A PRETTY COOL SUMMER MEMORY!!
Like a horror movie!
ARE YOU OUT OF YOUR MIND?!

DICTATORIAL GRIMOIRE

FIN

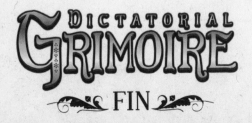

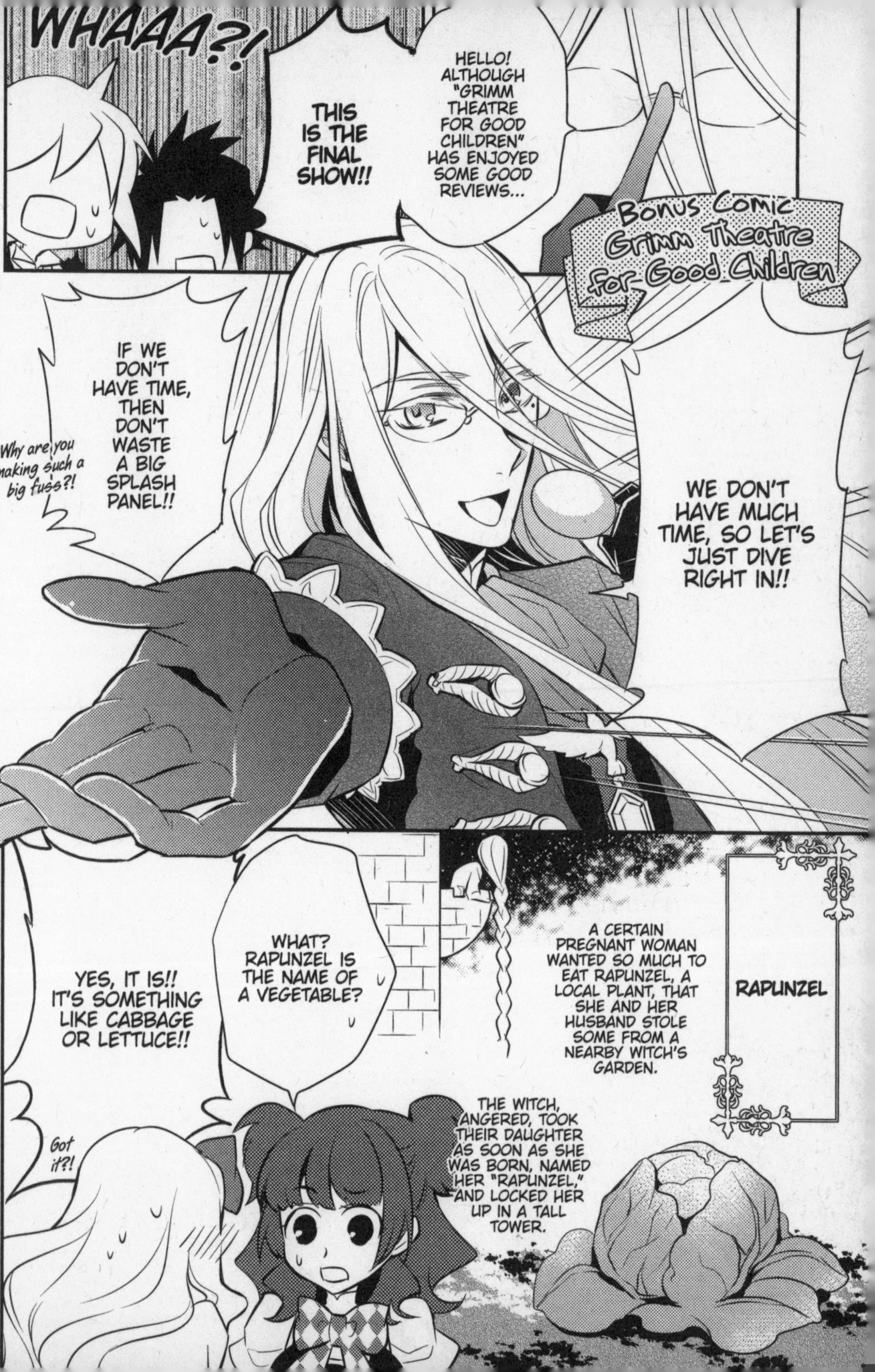
Bonus Comic Grimm Theatre for Good Children
HELLO! ALTHOUGH "GRIMM THEATRE FOR GOOD CHILDREN" HAS ENJOYED SOME GOOD REVIEWS...
THIS IS THE FINAL SHOW!!
WHAAA?!
WE DON'T HAVE MUCH TIME, SO LET'S JUST DIVE RIGHT IN!!
IF WE DON'T HAVE TIME, THEN DON'T WASTE A BIG SPLASH PANEL!!
Why are you making such a big fuss?!
RAPUNZEL
A CERTAIN PREGNANT WOMAN WANTED SO MUCH TO EAT RAPUNZEL, A LOCAL PLANT, THAT SHE AND HER HUSBAND STOLE SOME FROM A NEARBY WITCH'S GARDEN.
THE WITCH, ANGERED, TOOK THEIR DAUGHTER AS SOON AS SHE WAS BORN, NAMED HER "RAPUNZEL," AND LOCKED HER UP IN A TALL TOWER.
WHAT? RAPUNZEL IS THE NAME OF A VEGETABLE?
YES, IT IS!! IT'S SOMETHING LIKE CABBAGE OR LETTUCE!!
Got it?!

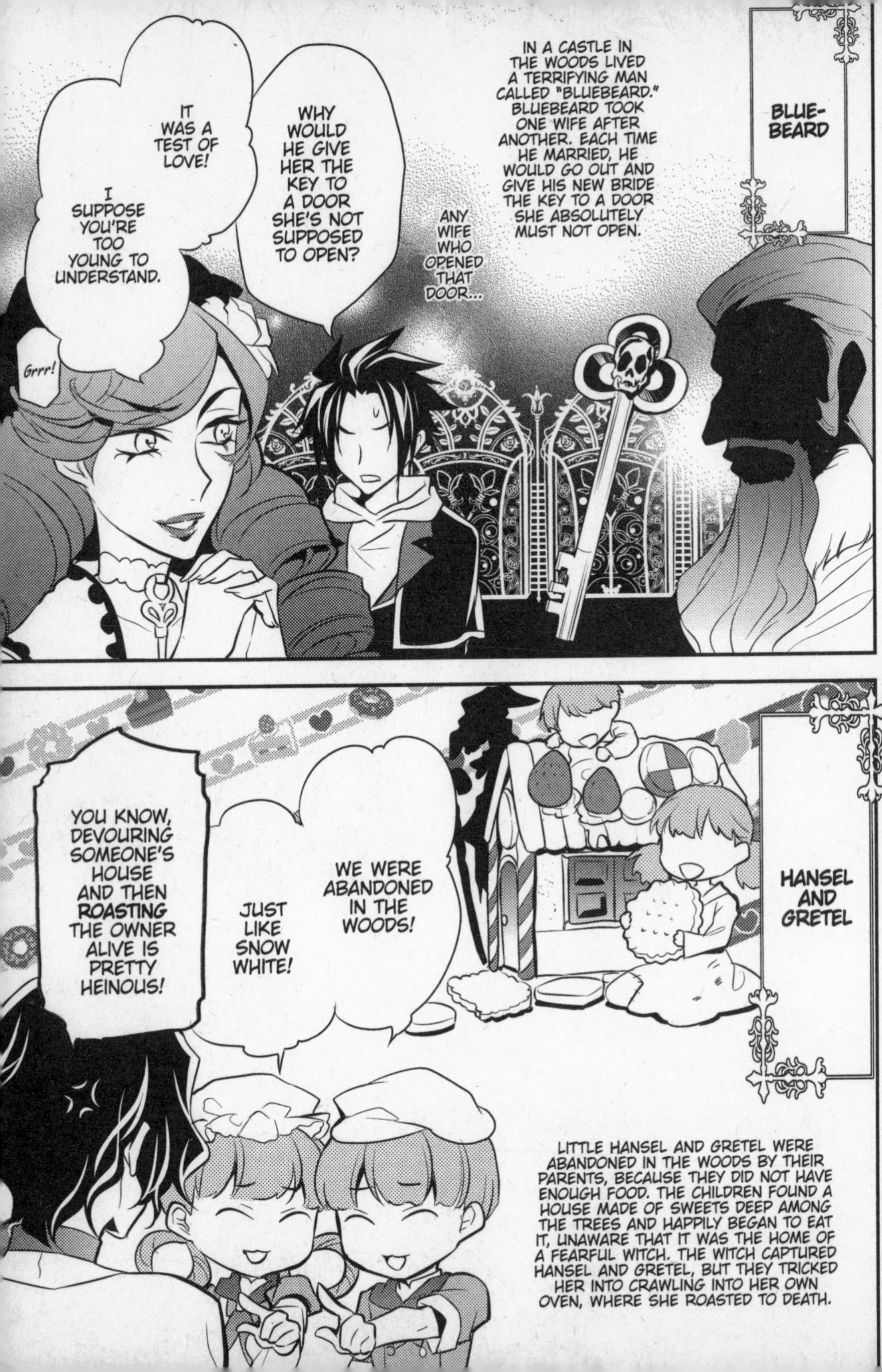
BLUE-BEARD
IN A CASTLE IN THE WOODS LIVED A TERRIFYING MAN CALLED "BLUEBEARD." BLUEBEARD TOOK ONE WIFE AFTER ANOTHER. EACH TIME HE MARRIED, HE WOULD GO OUT AND GIVE HIS NEW BRIDE THE KEY TO A DOOR SHE ABSOLUTELY MUST NOT OPEN.
ANY WIFE WHO OPENED THAT DOOR...
WHY WOULD HE GIVE HER THE KEY TO A DOOR SHE'S NOT SUPPOSED TO OPEN?
IT WAS A TEST OF LOVE!
I SUPPOSE YOU'RE TOO YOUNG TO UNDERSTAND.
Grrr!
HANSEL AND GRETEL
LITTLE HANSEL AND GRETEL WERE ABANDONED IN THE WOODS BY THEIR PARENTS, BECAUSE THEY DID NOT HAVE ENOUGH FOOD. THE CHILDREN FOUND A HOUSE MADE OF SWEETS DEEP AMONG THE TREES AND HAPPILY BEGAN TO EAT IT, UNAWARE THAT IT WAS THE HOME OF A FEARFUL WITCH. THE WITCH CAPTURED HANSEL AND GRETEL, BUT THEY TRICKED HER INTO CRAWLING INTO HER OWN OVEN, WHERE SHE ROASTED TO DEATH.
WE WERE ABANDONED IN THE WOODS!
JUST LIKE SNOW WHITE!
YOU KNOW, DEVOURING SOMEONE'S HOUSE AND THEN ROASTING THE OWNER ALIVE IS PRETTY HEINOUS!

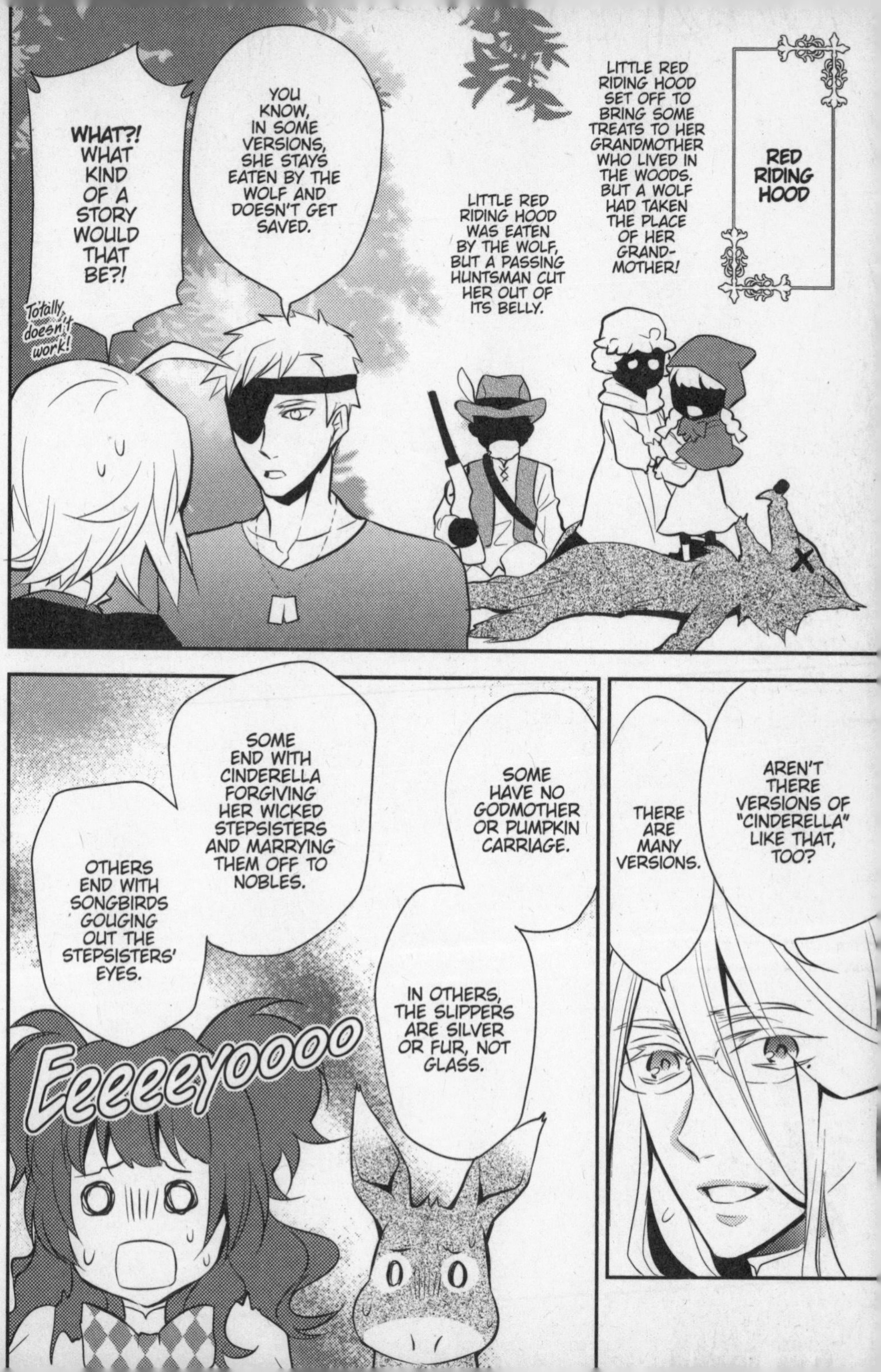
RED RIDING HOOD
LITTLE RED RIDING HOOD SET OFF TO BRING SOME TREATS TO HER GRANDMOTHER WHO LIVED IN THE WOODS. BUT A WOLF HAD TAKEN THE PLACE OF HER GRAND-MOTHER!
LITTLE RED RIDING HOOD WAS EATEN BY THE WOLF, BUT A PASSING HUNTSMAN CUT HER OUT OF ITS BELLY.
YOU KNOW, IN SOME VERSIONS, SHE STAYS EATEN BY THE WOLF AND DOESN'T GET SAVED.
WHAT?! WHAT KIND OF A STORY WOULD THAT BE?!
Totally doesn't work!
AREN'T THERE VERSIONS OF "CINDERELLA" LIKE THAT, TOO?
THERE ARE MANY VERSIONS.
SOME HAVE NO GODMOTHER OR PUMPKIN CARRIAGE.
SOME END WITH CINDERELLA FORGIVING HER WICKED STEPSISTERS AND MARRYING THEM OFF TO NOBLES.
OTHERS END WITH SONGBIRDS GOUGING OUT THE STEPSISTERS' EYES.
IN OTHERS, THE SLIPPERS ARE SILVER OR FUR, NOT GLASS.
Eeeeeyoooo

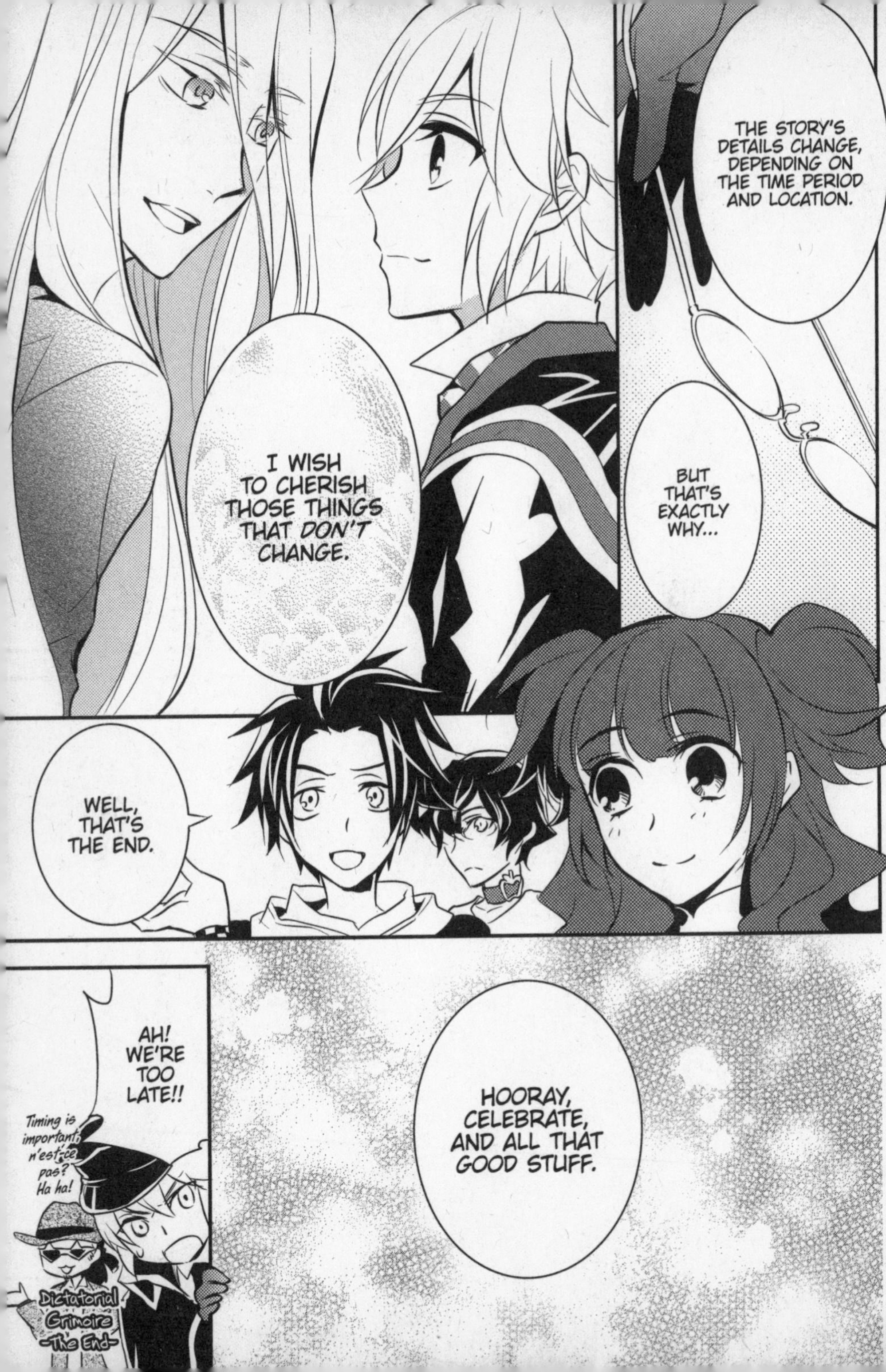
THE STORY'S DETAILS CHANGE, DEPENDING ON THE TIME PERIOD AND LOCATION.
BUT THAT'S EXACTLY WHY...
I WISH TO CHERISH THOSE THINGS THAT *DON'T* CHANGE.
WELL, THAT'S THE END.
HOORAY, CELEBRATE, AND ALL THAT GOOD STUFF.
AH! WE'RE TOO LATE!!
Timing is important, n'est-ce pas? Ha ha!
Dictatorial Grimoire -The End-

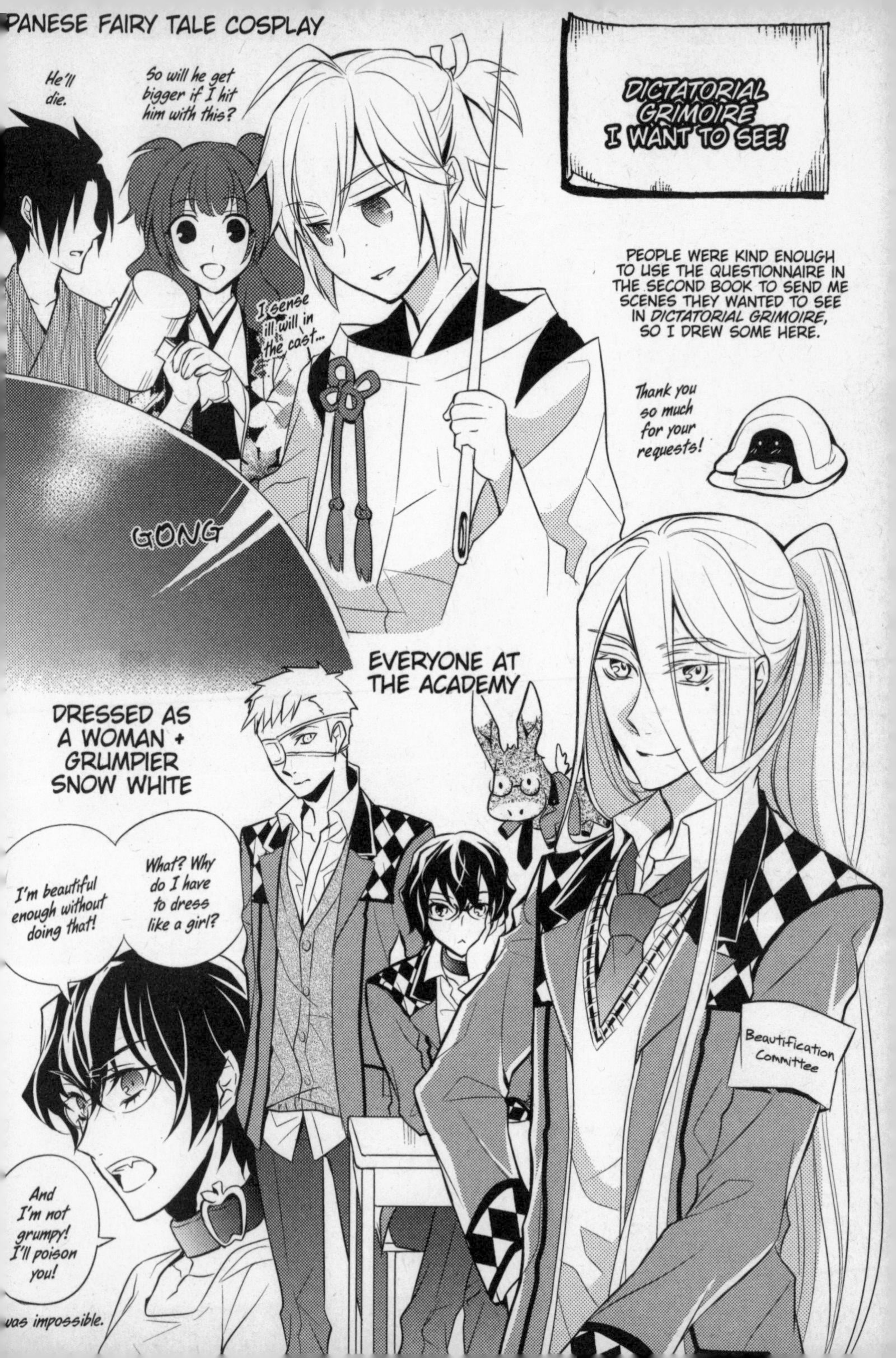
DICTATORIAL GRIMOIRE I WANT TO SEE!
PEOPLE WERE KIND ENOUGH TO USE THE QUESTIONNAIRE IN THE SECOND BOOK TO SEND ME SCENES THEY WANTED TO SEE IN DICTATORIAL GRIMOIRE, SO I DREW SOME HERE.
Thank you so much for your requests!
PANESE FAIRY TALE COSPLAY
So will he get bigger if I hit him with this?
He'll die.
I sense ill will in the cast...
GONG
EVERYONE AT THE ACADEMY
Beautification Committee
DRESSED AS A WOMAN + GRUMPIER SNOW WHITE
What? Why do I have to dress like a girl?
I'm beautiful enough without doing that!
And I'm not grumpy! I'll poison you!
vas impossible.

# CHARACTERS

RAPUNZEL

AGE: ? (LOOKS TO BE 15)
BIRTHDAY: ??
BLOOD TYPE: ??
HEIGHT: 158CM
WEIGHT: NOT TELLING!
LIKES: GRIMM-SAMA!
DISLIKES: HIGH PLACES
HOBBIES: CALISTHENICS
SPECIAL SKILLS: HAIR ARRANGEMENT

RED RIDING HOOD

AGE: ? (LOOKS TO BE 23)
BIRTHDAY: ??
BLOOD TYPE: ??
HEIGHT: 186CM
WEIGHT: 76KG
LIKES: NOTHING IN PARTICULAR
DISLIKES: THE FULL MOON
HOBBIES: GUN COLLECTING
SPECIAL SKILLS: SURVIVAL COOKING

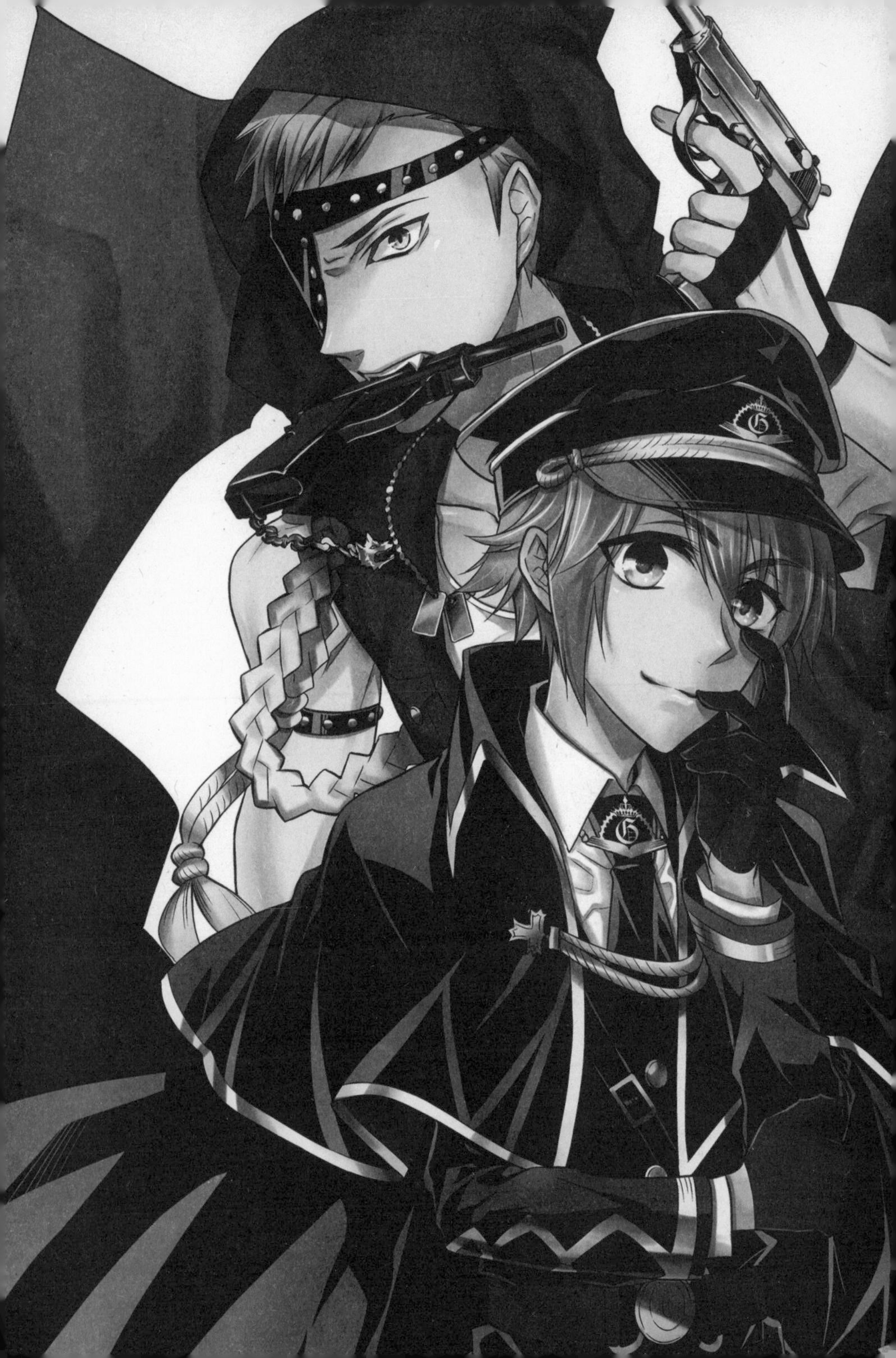

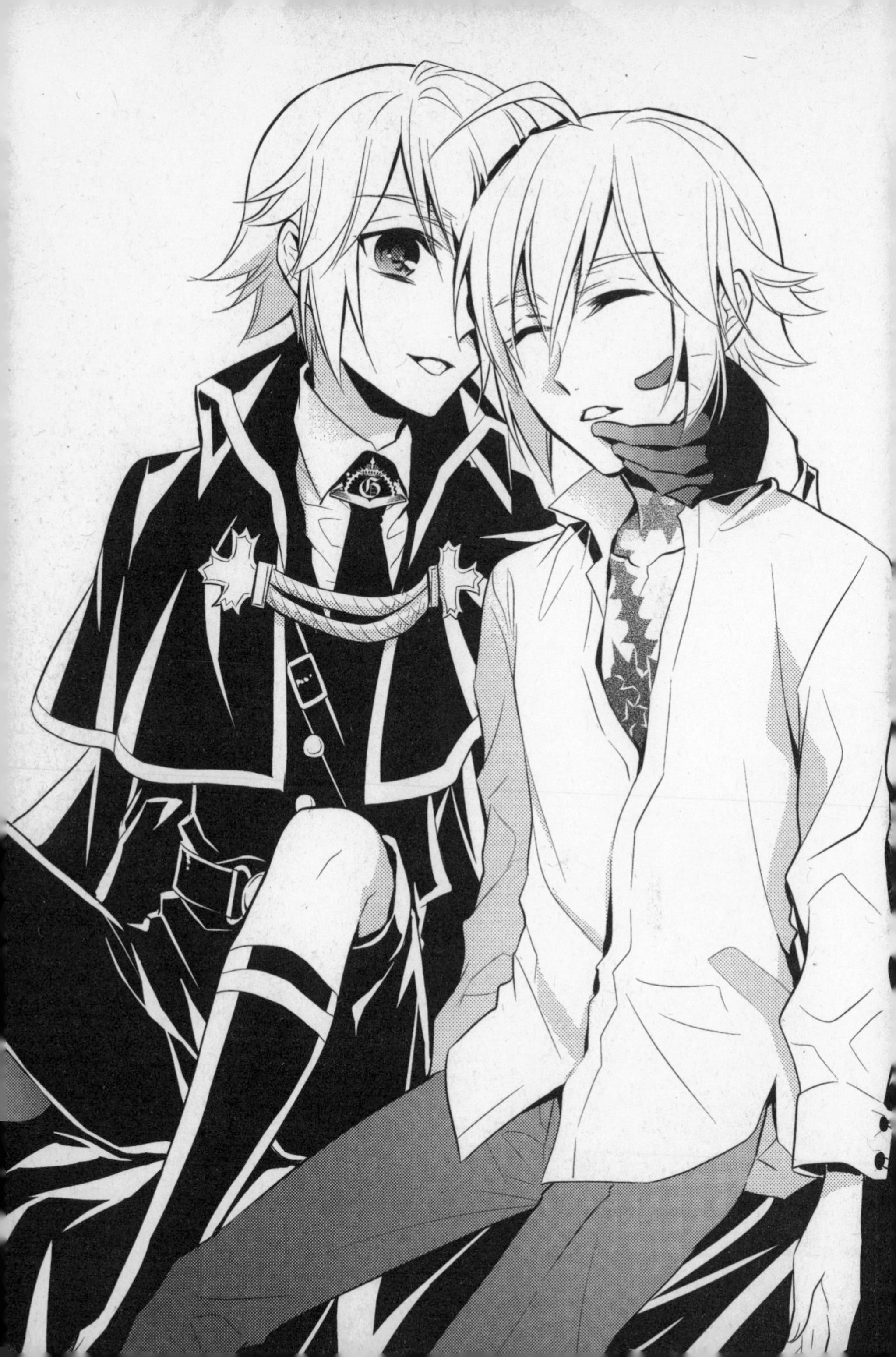

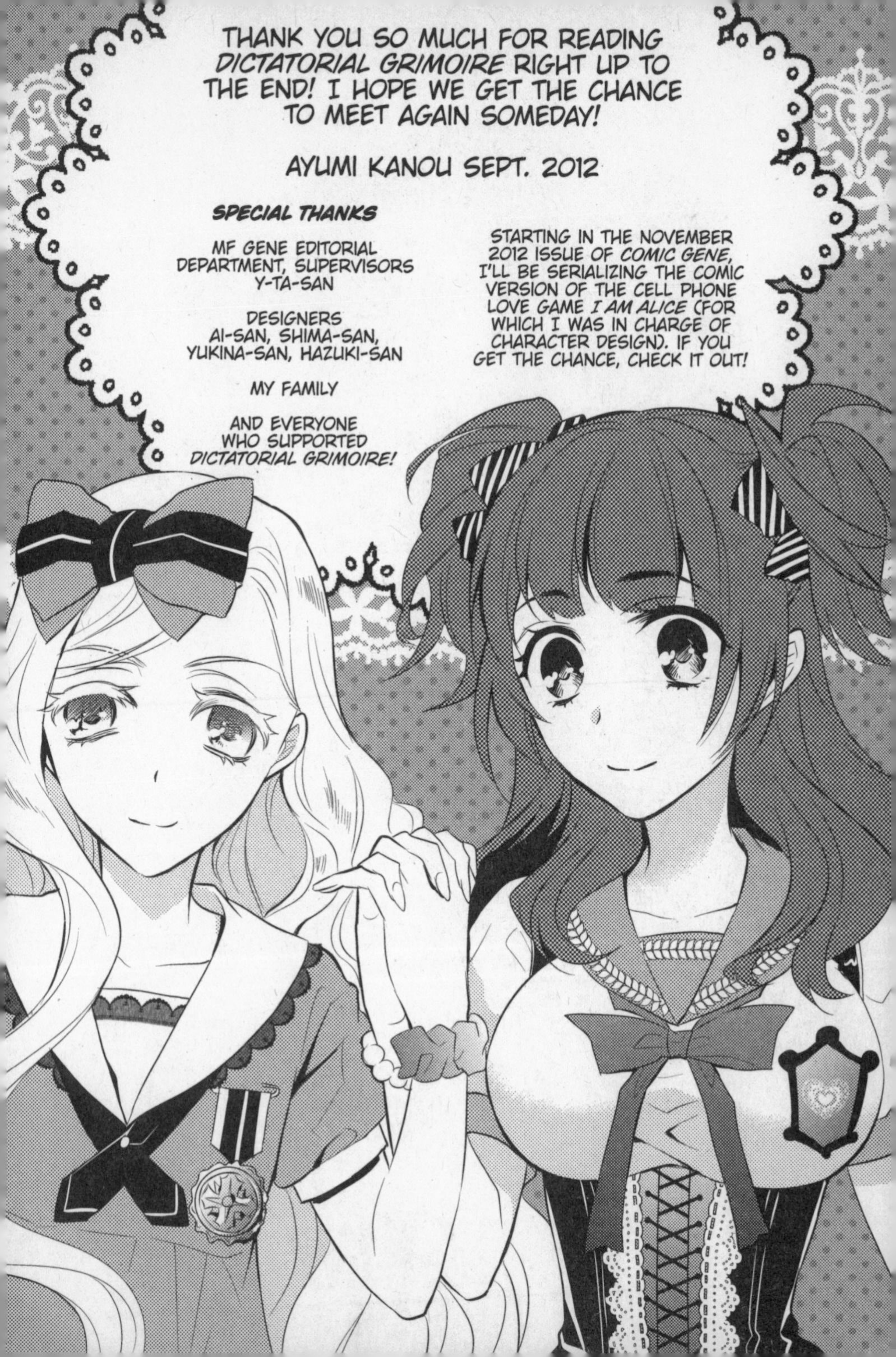
THANK YOU SO MUCH FOR READING *DICTATORIAL GRIMOIRE* RIGHT UP TO THE END! I HOPE WE GET THE CHANCE TO MEET AGAIN SOMEDAY!
AYUMI KANOU SEPT. 2012
***SPECIAL THANKS***
MF GENE EDITORIAL DEPARTMENT, SUPERVISORS Y-TA-SAN
DESIGNERS AI-SAN, SHIMA-SAN, YUKINA-SAN, HAZUKI-SAN
MY FAMILY
AND EVERYONE WHO SUPPORTED *DICTATORIAL GRIMOIRE!*
STARTING IN THE NOVEMBER 2012 ISSUE OF *COMIC GENE*, I'LL BE SERIALIZING THE COMIC VERSION OF THE CELL PHONE LOVE GAME *I AM ALICE* (FOR WHICH I WAS IN CHARGE OF CHARACTER DESIGN). IF YOU GET THE CHANCE, CHECK IT OUT!

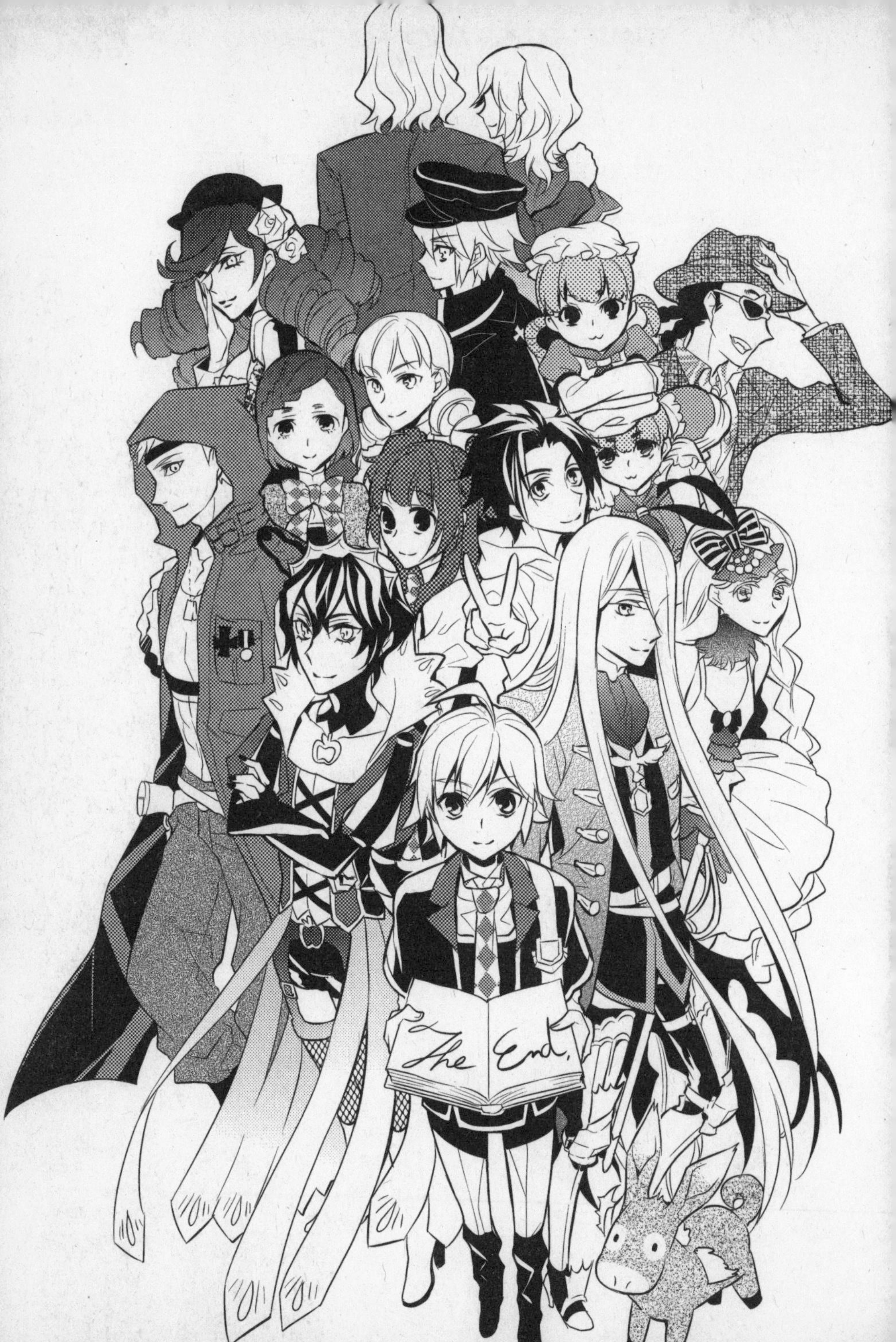
The End.

# DICTATORIAL GRIMOIRE

story and art by **AYUMI KANOU**          **VOLUME 3: RED RIDING HOOD**

TRANSLATION
**Jocelyne Allen**

ADAPTATION
**Shanti Whitesides**

LETTERING
**Jennifer Skarupa**

LOGO DESIGN
**Courtney Williams**

COVER DESIGN
**Nicky Lim**

PROOFREADER
**Janet Houck**

MANAGING EDITOR
**Adam Arnold**

PUBLISHER
**Jason DeAngelis**

DICTATORIAL GRIMOIRE VOL. 3
© Ayumi Kanou 2012
Edited by MEDIA FACTORY.
First published in Japan in 2012 by KADOKAWA CORPORATION, Tokyo.
English translation rights reserved by Seven Seas Entertainment, LLC.
Under the license from KADOKAWA CORPORATION, Tokyo.

Seven Seas books may be purchased in bulk for educational, business, or promotional use. For information on bulk purchases, please contact Macmillan Corporate & Premium Sales Department at 1-800-221-7945 (ext 5442) or write specialmarkets@macmillan.com.

Seven Seas and the Seven Seas logo are trademarks of Seven Seas Entertainment, LLC. All rights reserved.

ISBN: 978-1-937867-95-9

Printed in Canada

First Printing: April 2014

10 9 8 7 6 5 4 3 2 1

**FOLLOW US ONLINE:** *www.gomanga.com*

# READING DIRECTIONS

This book reads from *right to left*, Japanese style. If this is your first time reading manga, you start reading from the top right panel on each page and take it from there. If you get lost, just follow the numbered diagram here. It may seem backwards at first, but you'll get the hang of it! Have fun!!

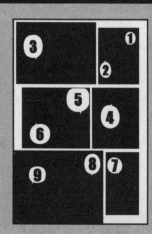